New American Paintings

Catalog of the 1993 New England Open Studios Competition

A Resource for Collectors

THE OPEN STUDIOS PRESS

Needham Heights, Massachusetts

PREFACE

The situation could be worse. After all, it is still easier for an undiscovered artist to cadge some visibility for recent works than for an unknown composer to mount a performance of his new symphony. That must be small comfort to thousands of talented artists who fail to obtain the public exposure their work deserves. I formed The Open Studios Press in 1992 to create a forum for such exposure.

This book is called *New American Paintings* because it contains 216 new American paintings. I considered calling it *The Open Studio* until I realized that the term "open studio" is not as well-known across the country as it is here in New England.

There are almost twenty artists' communities within ten miles of Boston that open their doors for a weekend each year and invite the public in to meet the artists and view their current work. I have visited upwards of a dozen such open studios over the past few years. They are usually crowded, festive events, a far cry from the more dignified if sometimes somber rooms of commercial galleries. Happily for all, open studios tend to be occasions at which collectors, nascent collectors, and latent collectors, buy art.

Some of the work on display at open studios does not necessarily deserve recognition, but much of it does. A few of the artists worthy of wide exposure catch the attention of galleries, but for the most part that attention is intermittent. The late 80s and early 90s have been troubled times for the art world, and they have seen the virtual collapse of the art market. In Boston, for instance, the recession forced many established galleries to close their doors. As a consequence, opportunities for emerging artists have contracted to the point of disappearing.

Occasional competitions and group shows have become the principal outlets for the display of new talent. But success in a competition for inclusion in a small show usually results in exposure to only the small group of hardy art enthusiasts who frequent the small museums, art associations and cooperatives that sponsor such events. For most artists, geography seems to be an enemy of wide public exposure and opportunity, and chance seems to be too good a friend of recognition and success.

To significantly increase the reach of a show, it is necessary to slip the bonds of geography. Slipping those bonds requires moving the artists' work, and the only practicable way to move it is through print. This is the purpose underlying *New American Paintings*. I believe that this publication can act as an open studio for artists across an entire region, whether they work in close proximity to other artists or alone in the woods. Yet anonymity alone does not qualify an artist for publication. Competition to select the best of a region's artists is necessary to do justice to the undiscovered talent "out there."

As soon as the Press was organized in 1992, we divided the country into seven regions and began the Open Studios competitions — close to home. We advertised extensively and mailed our call for artists to thousands across the six New England states. Almost 400 responded, submitting over 5000 slides of their work.

The principal juror, Joseph Thompson, executive director of the exciting new Massachusetts Museum of Contemporary Art project in North Adams, Massachusetts, made an initial selection of 36 artists for inclusion in this New England showing. As the project neared completion, we discovered we could efficiently add pages to our book, so a second jury consisting of a Boston-area collector, an art therapist and a professional illustrator selected 14 additional artists. Finally, the editor and I decided our personal favorites deserved inclusion, and so the final number of artists reached 52.

This first edition is devoted to artists from one small piece of America, albeit a productive one for the arts, New England. Each of six subsequent editions will focus on a different region of the country. They will be published at eight to ten-week intervals, with the Middle Atlantic states and the Southeastern states scheduled for the beginning and end of summer 1993, respectively.

This book represents the launching of a new idea in art publishing, a new opportunity for emerging artists, and a new market for collectors. I would welcome the reactions and comments of all who spend time with the works contained herein. The address and telephone number of the Press may be found on the last page of the book.

H.I. Gliick, Publisher
Needham, Massachusetts

The New American Paintings Series represents a new approach to art publishing and offers a new opportunity for art collecting. This is the first of seven catalogs of the winners' work from seven regional artists' competitions held annually across the country.

There isn't much to read here. Deliberately so! There isn't much to read in most art galleries, either.

*"Paintings exist as facts, in a world of facts, and facts can be perceived and reacted to, but not explained."**

So this is a picture book intended to serve as a gallery for the artists whose work is shown here. Its pages, on behalf of the artists' studios, are continually "open" for browsing by art lovers and collectors.

There may be a few artists whose names you recognize, but it is not the objective of this book to examine the work of people who have been recognized by the art establishment. Rather, its objective is to show you and the art establishment some of the talent yet to be discovered.

With each group of paintings you will find a brief biographical sketch to help you place the artist in time, space and career path. For the purpose of the competition that led to this book and all subsequent competitions and books in the series, "paintings" has been defined as any original, singular, two-dimensional work — excluding photography. While some mixed-media works and monotypes will be found among the 216 works, the vast majority of the paintings are in oil or acrylic.

Collecting each edition of *New American Paintings* over the months and years should enable an art lover to follow the evolution of painting by many of the most talented emerging artists in America — subject, of course, to the vagaries of juries which will change from region to region, edition to edition. It also should enable the collector to discover talent at its source. Addresses and telephone numbers are included for each artist.

You will notice that we have included prices with each artist's spread. Prices are provided for guidance only, and reflect what the artist would ask for a particular work today. The works shown are not necessarily for sale, although most were when the competition began. As you flip through the pages of *New American Paintings*, you will see works ranging from $240 up to $32,000. Only three of our artists have five digit numbers attached to their paintings; the majority of works shown are priced between $1,000 to $2,500. Although we did not, and will never, select or reject work due to its price, the nature of *New American Paintings* should insure that the art shown is always affordably, if not bargain priced.

If you like an artist's work, please contact him or her directly and arrange to visit and view work currently available. If you live too far away to visit an artist in whom you are interested, consider using the mail. As this book is going to press, the publisher is organizing an experimental art purchase escrow service which may be of some assistance.

This service will enable artists to mail low-cost color reproductions and details of works available to interested collectors around the country and then enable collectors to buy with confidence through an independent agency. These services will not command a commission, but will be available for a modest fee. Detailed information should be available directly from the publisher after March 15, 1993.

* *Within Tuscany*, Matthew Spender, Viking Press, 1992.

THE PAINTERS

A native of South Africa, Ilona Anderson came to the United States in the late eighties and currently lives in Brookline, MA. In South Africa, Anderson earned two degrees in teaching, and since coming to the United States, she has earned an MFA from the School of the Museum of Fine Arts, Boston. Over the years, Anderson has curated exhibitions, helped to launch a gallery and lectured at various institutions. She now divides her time between teaching and painting.

Executed primarily in acrylics on canvas, Anderson's large-scale works are painted in a neo-expressionist style with a bold palette. She draws her subject matter from contemporary social and political events – her most recent series focused on the Gulf War – and presents the viewer with taut images laid out in a narrative form.

Anderson has exhibited her work in over two dozen shows since the mid-eighties, including the Carnegie International in Pittsburgh, PA, and two other international invitationals. In 1991 she had her first solo show in the United States at Gallery Eleven, Tufts University.

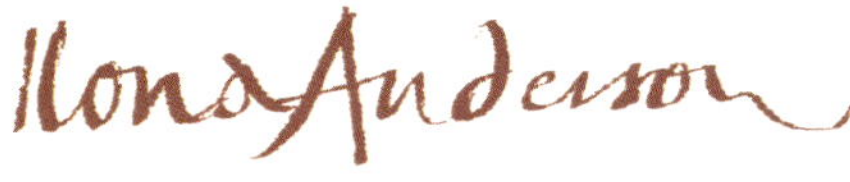

105 Winthrop Road, #3
Brookline, MA 02146
617-734-9502

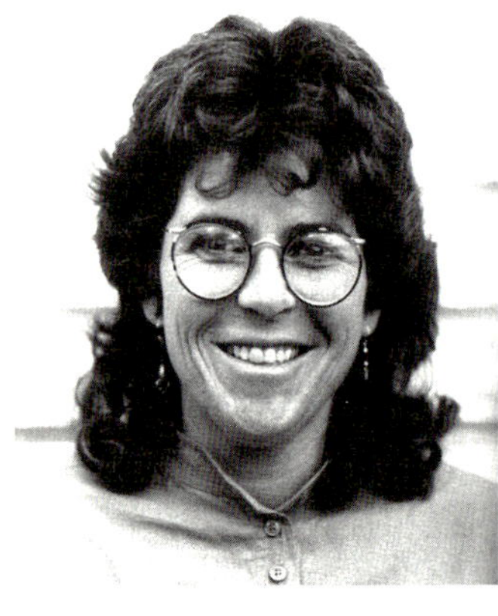

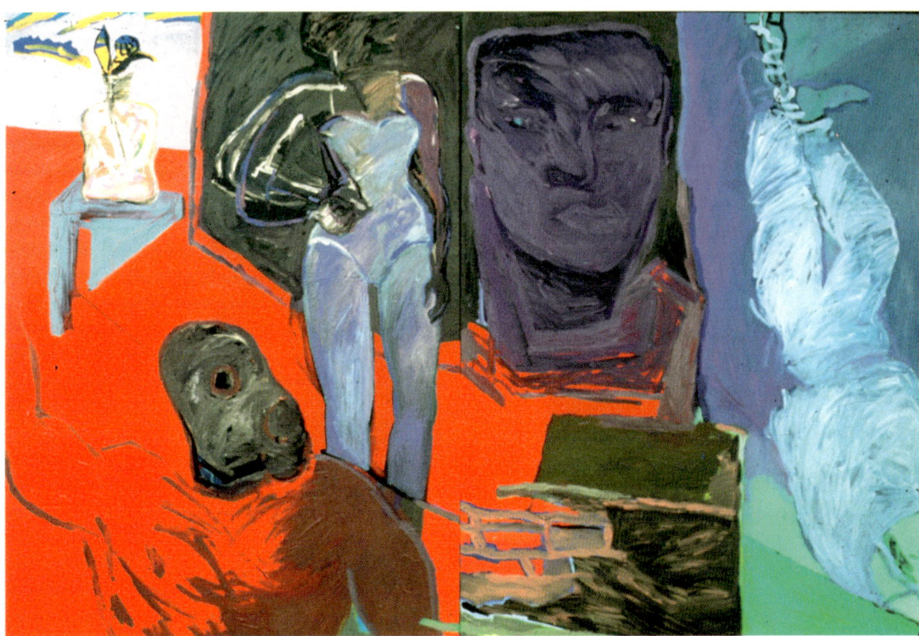

A. New Jersey Turnpike. Acrylic on canvas, 6' x 10' (diptych).

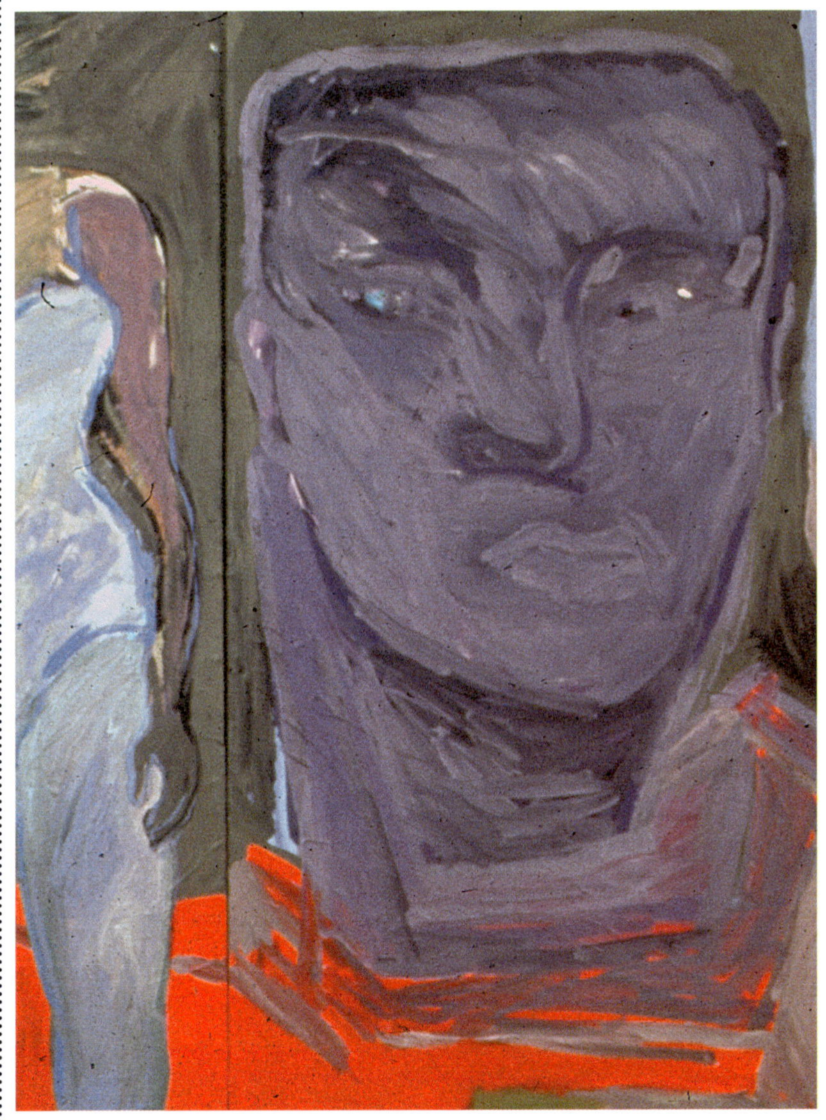

New Jersey Turnpike. Detail.

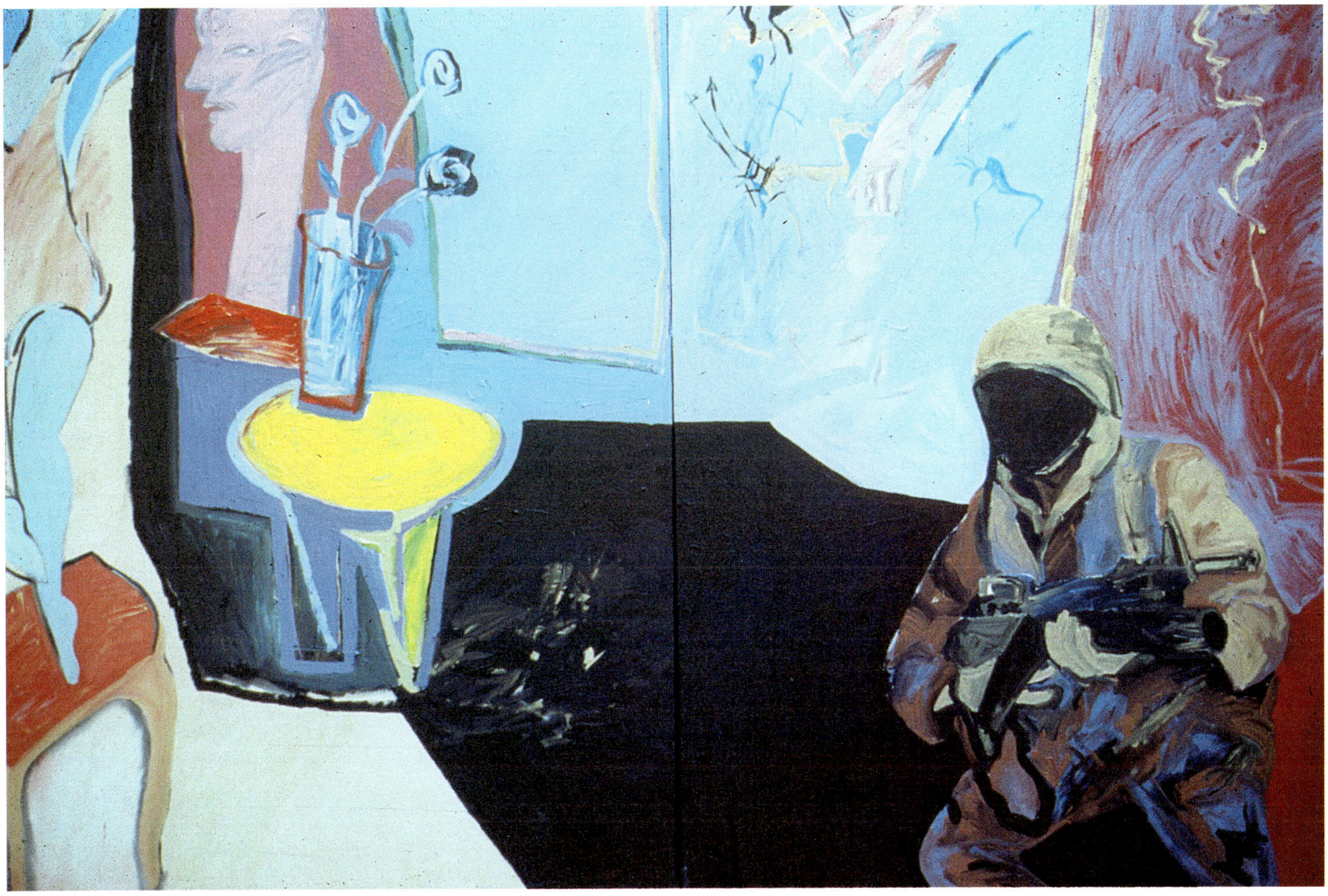

D. **Untitled.** Acrylic on canvas, 6' x 11' (diptych).

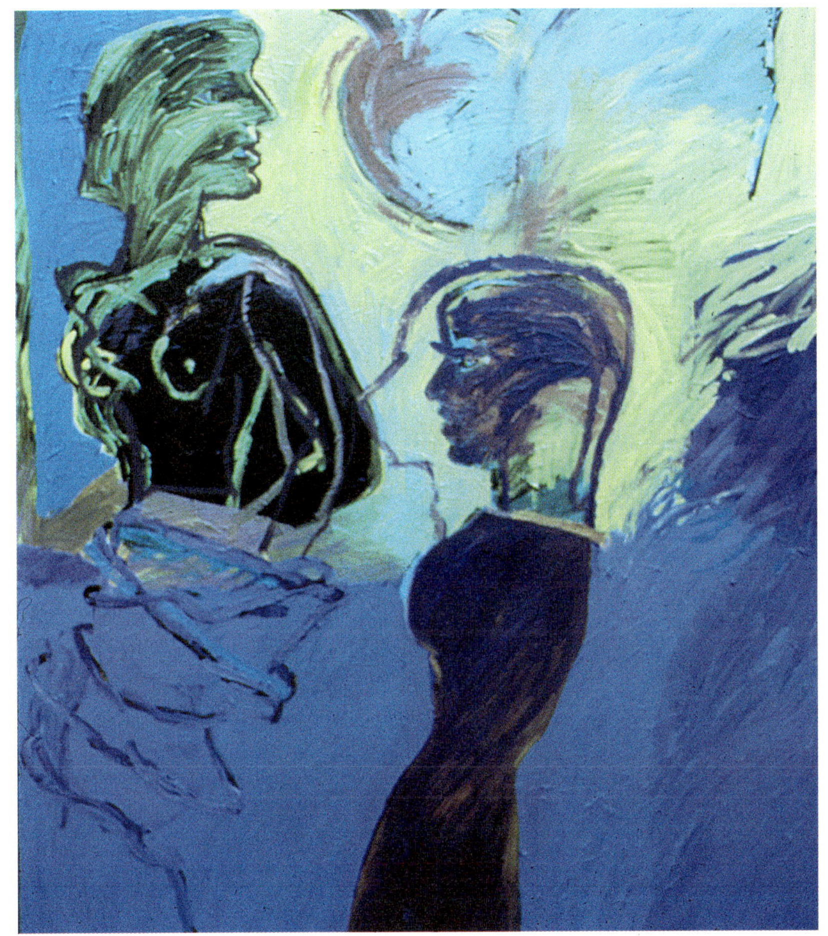

E. Blue Moon.
Acrylic on canvas,
6' x 4'.

PRICE LIST

A ....Contact artist

D ....Contact artist

E ....Contact artist

Laura Anderson is a native of New England. She studied painting at Lassel Junior College for Women, the University of Hartford and the Rhode Island School of Design. Since her education, Anderson has lived in Massachusetts, and devoted her time to painting.

Anderson's geographical background is evident in her painting. Her canvases are bathed in a light that will seem familiar to anyone who has spent time on the New England coast. Working exclusively in acrylics, Anderson has spent the last several years developing a series of paintings that explore the relationship between landscape and man-made structures. These paintings include domestic imagery, such as rockers or Adirondack chairs, juxtaposed with the surrounding landscape.

Anderson's work has been exhibited at solo and group shows throughout New England and New York; most recently at a solo show at Chase Gallery in Boston. Her work has been published in several periodicals, including *American Artist* magazine, which recently awarded her first place in a nationwide competition.

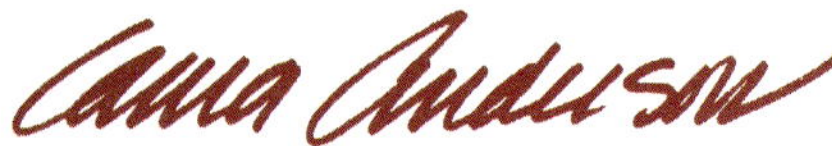

P.O. Box 105
Marion, MA 02738
508-758-9848

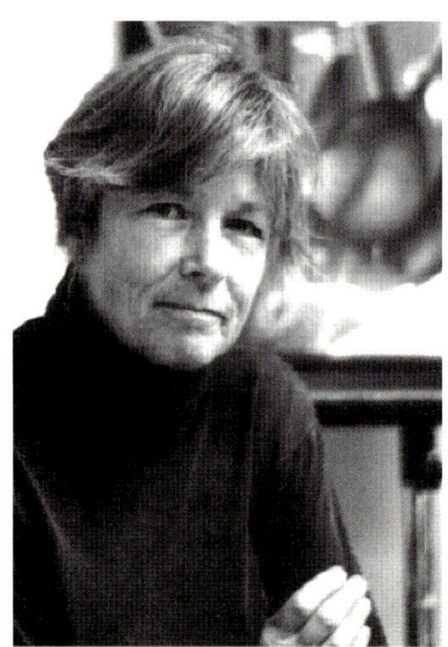

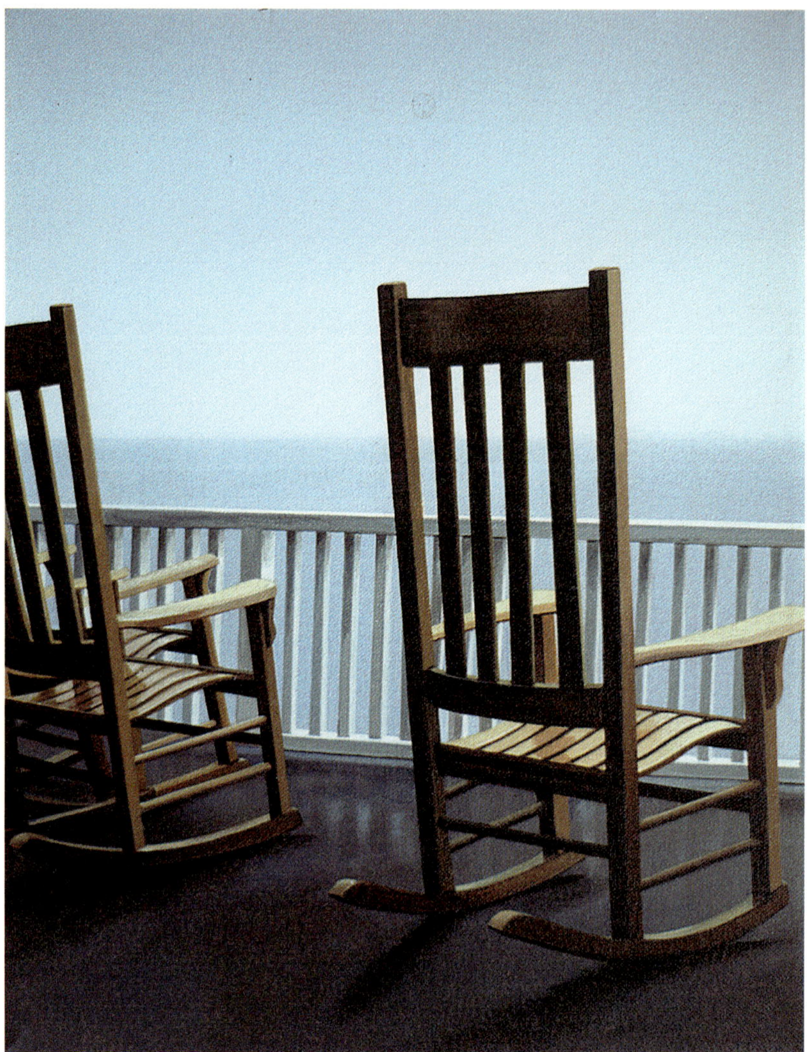

A. Two Rockers. Acrylic on canvas, 14" x 11".

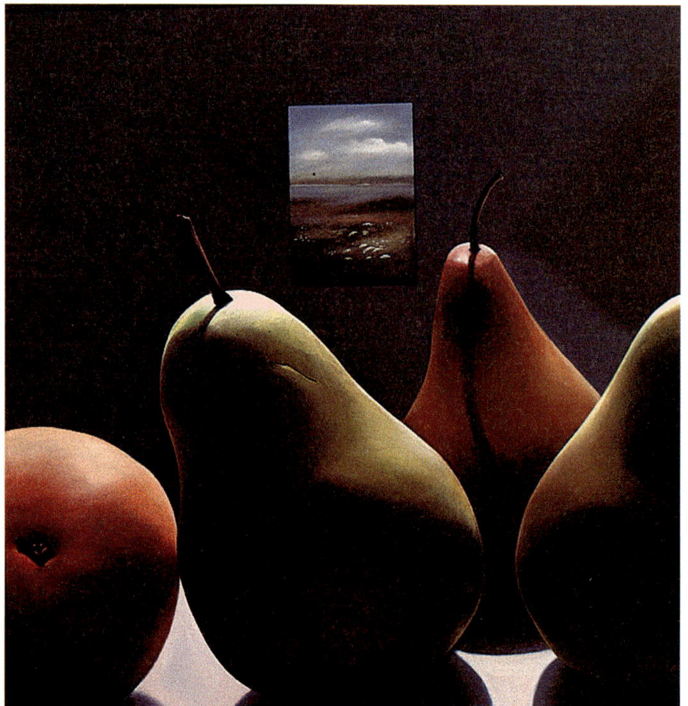

B. Pear Dreams. Acrylic on canvas, 21" x 21".

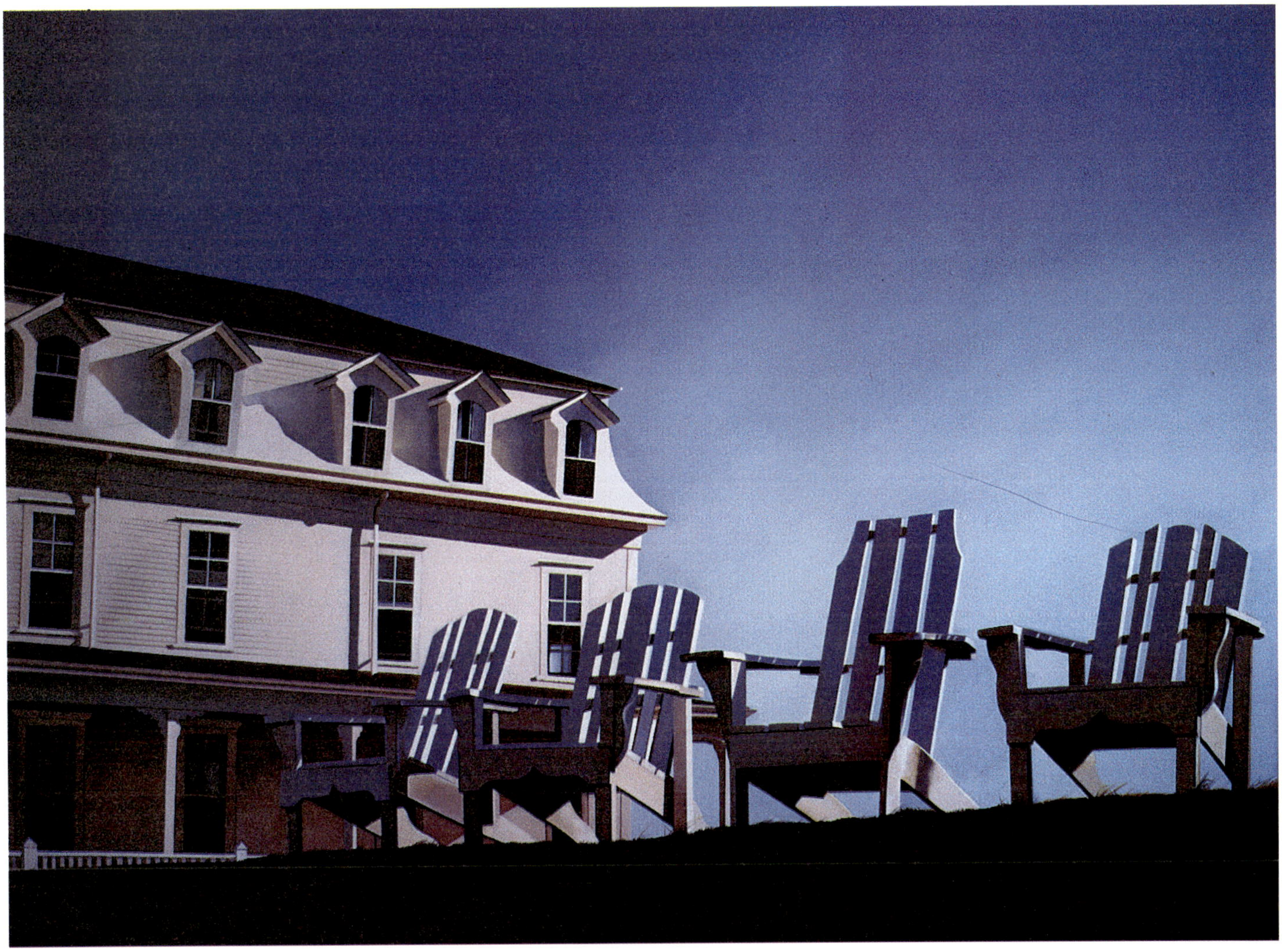

C. **Spring House, August.** Acrylic on canvas, 32" x 44".

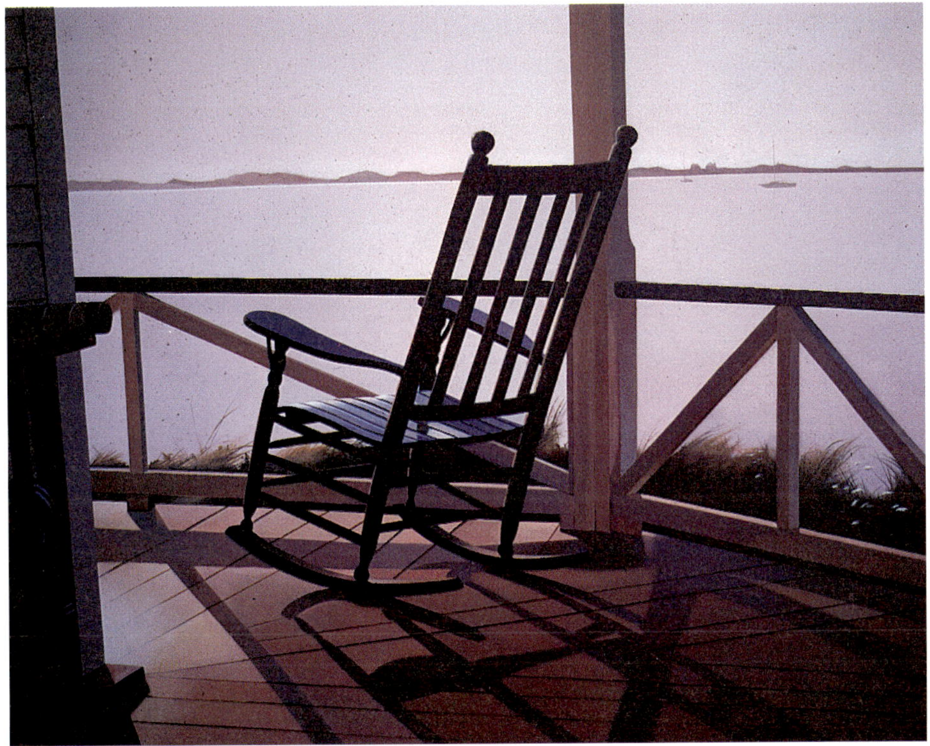

D. Croquet Set. Acrylic on canvas, 24" x 30".

PRICE LIST

A $1,600

B $2,500

C $4,200

D $3,000

Represented by
Chase Gallery
Boston, MA

Anda Barbera recalls attempting to paint her first canvas with oils at the age of ten. During her teen years she experimented with various subject matter and eventually chose to concentrate on landscapes. Barbera received formal training at the Parson's School of Design in New York, from which she graduated in 1983 with a BA in Fine Arts. Since then, Barbera has built careers as a graphic designer and a fine artist. She is currently the art director for Dellwood Publishing Co., Inc., in New York City.

Barbera long ago abandoned oils as a medium and now works with acrylics. She still prefers to paint landscapes and approaches her subject with a style derived from the Impressionist tradition. Her paintings usually include man-made structures – often a house – but her focus is the relationship between the structure and its environment rather than the object itself.

Barbera's work has been exhibited in both solo and group shows. Her awards include First Place in the Richter Art Show, September 1991.

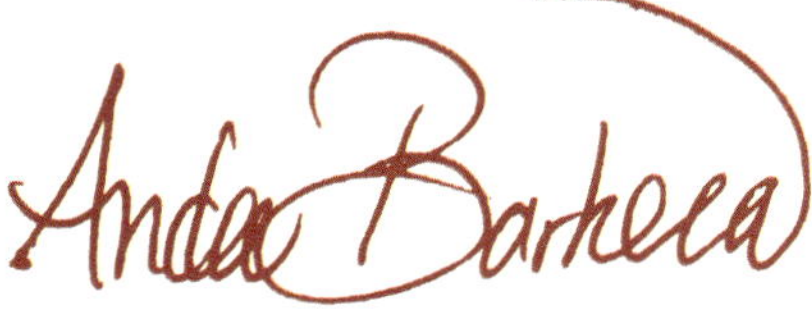

57 Franklin Street
Danbury, CT 06810
203-790-6232

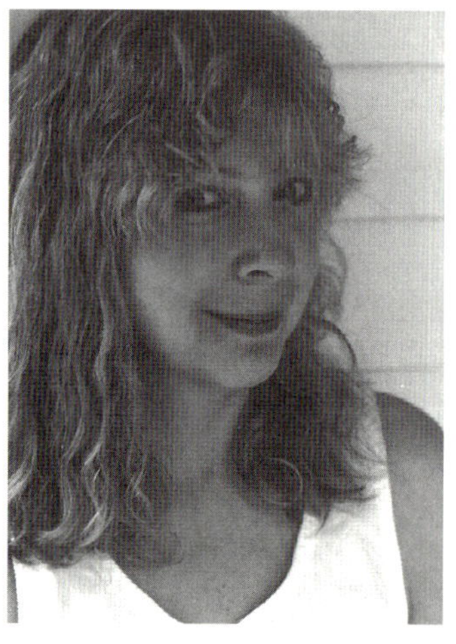

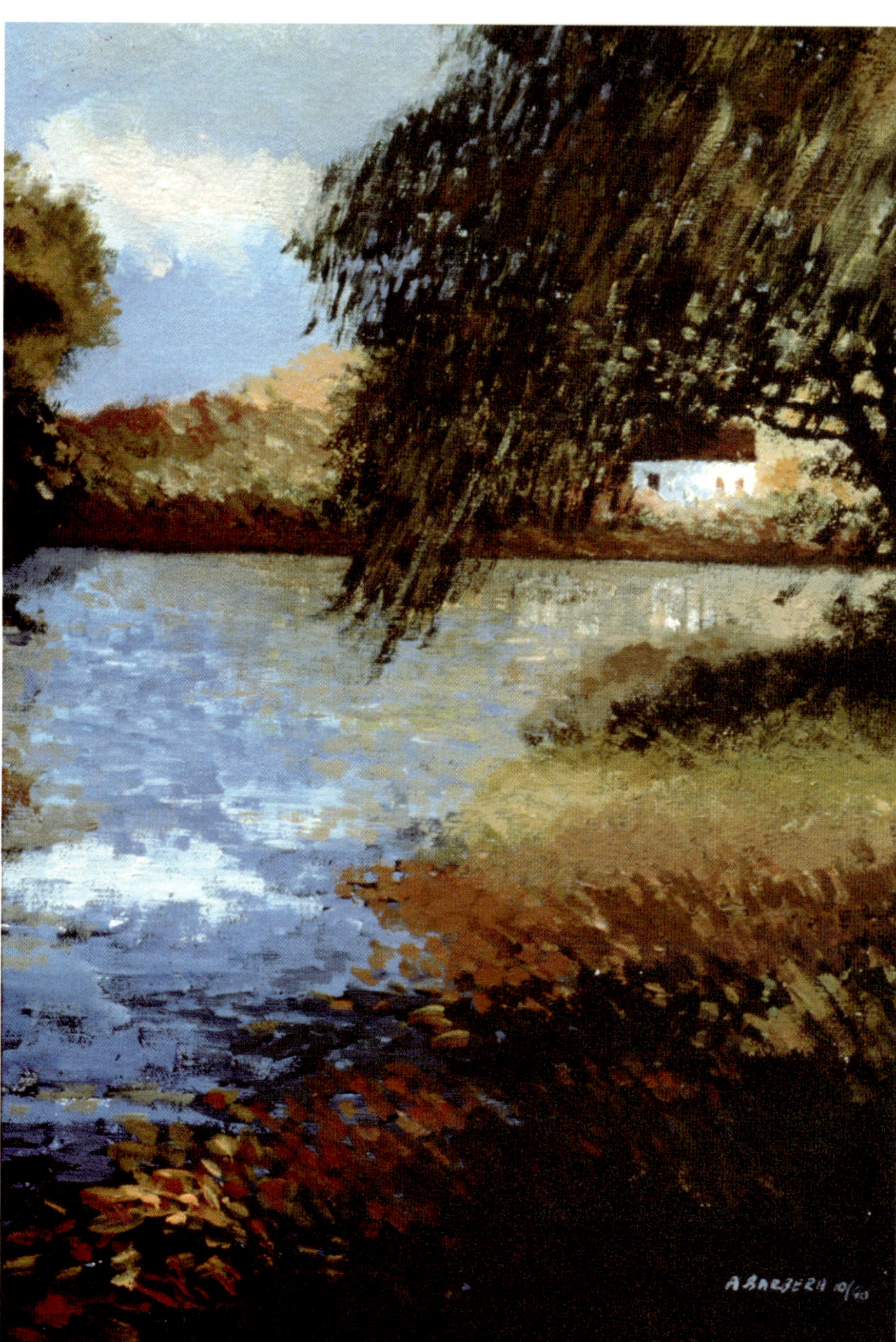

A. Housatonic River in the Fall. Acrylic on canvas, 20" x 16".

PRICE LIST

A $1,000

B $800

C $600

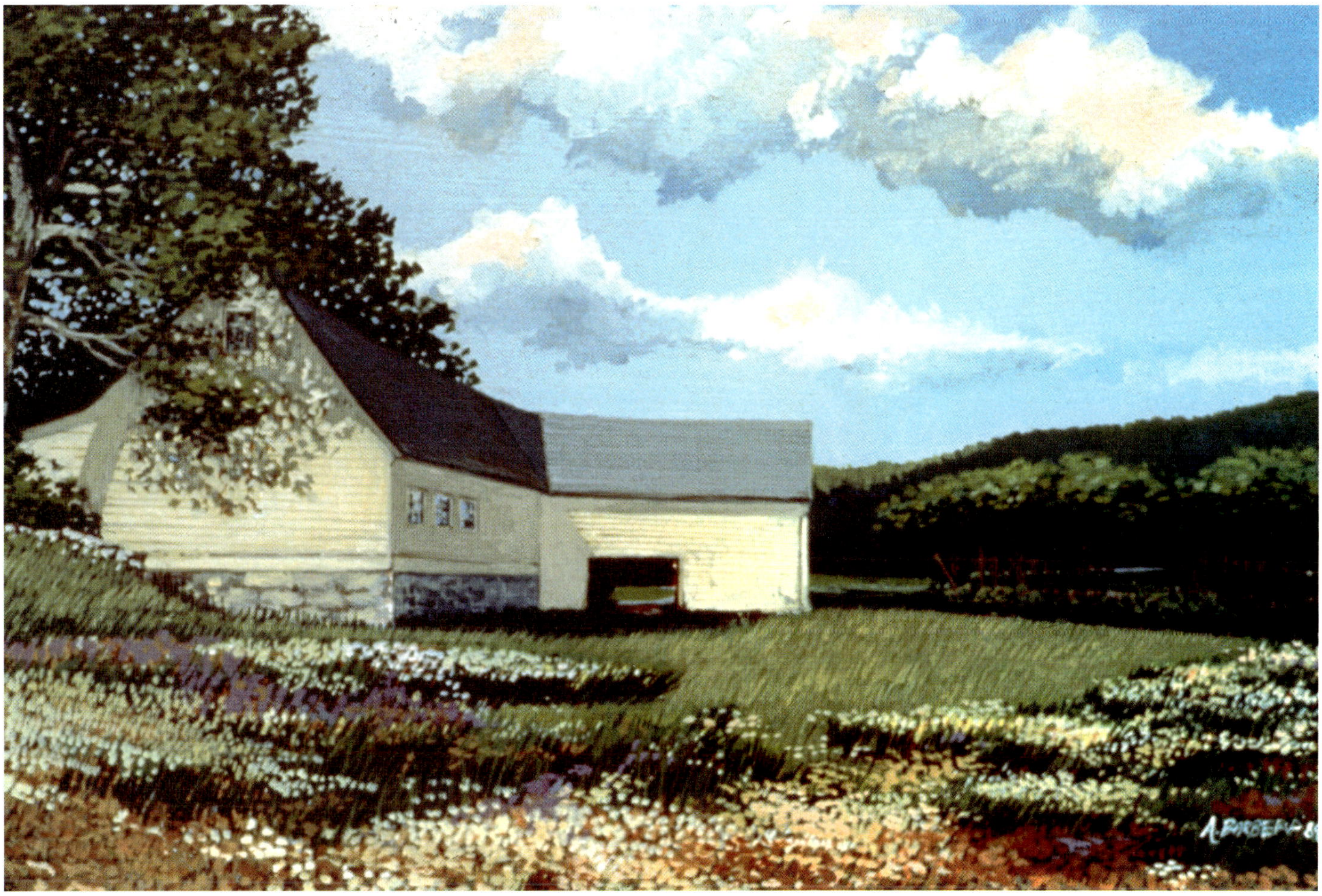

B. Summer Solstice II. Acrylic on canvas, 18" x 36".

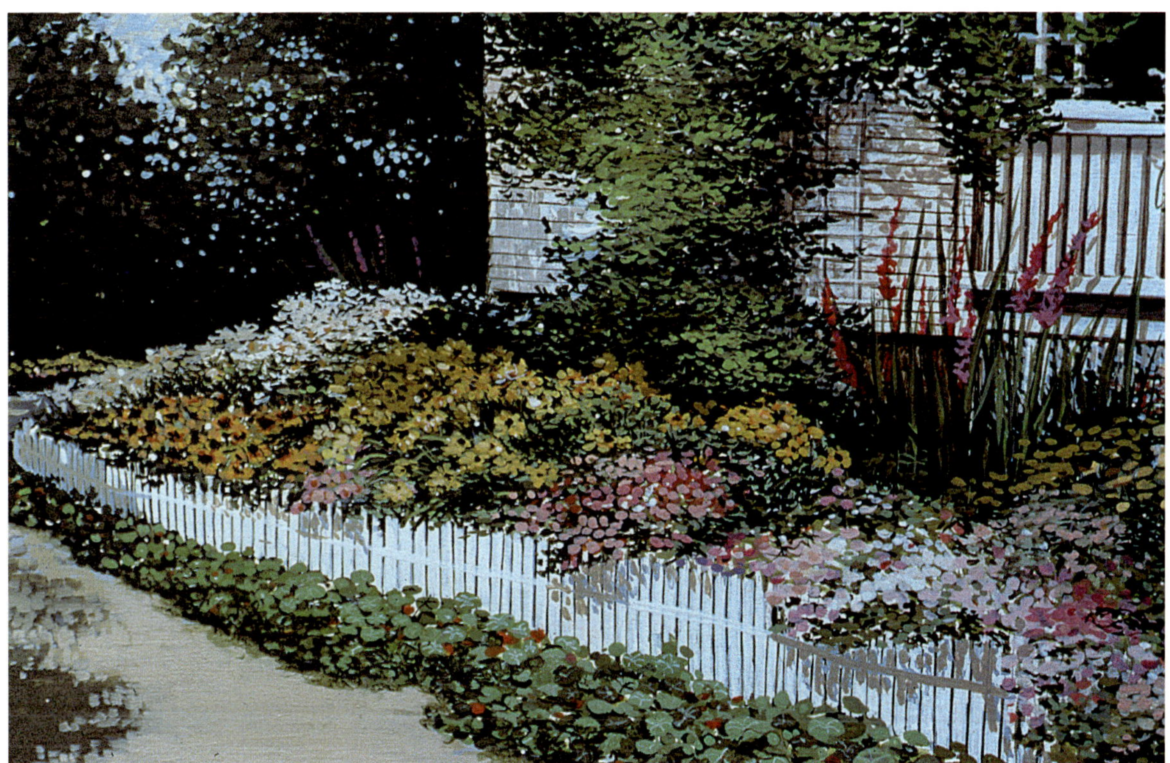

C. My Favorite Garden. Acrylic on canvas, 12" x 24".

June Bisantz-Evans

June Bisantz-Evans, who has lived and worked in Boston, Los Angeles and New York City, now resides in Connecticut with husband, jazz composer, Steve Evans. She studied the fine arts at several institutions, and received her MFA in Painting from the Claremont Graduate School in 1975. Bisantz-Evans has pursued both the visual and performing arts throughout her career. Presently, she divides her time between teaching and painting.

Bisantz-Evans thinks of her paintings as urban landscapes. Her subject matter is simple – a sign or storefront – and chosen to represent that which is uniquely American. Using a photograph as reference and watercolor as a medium, Bisantz-Evans creates photo-realistic images of impressive detail and clarity.

Bisantz-Evans's paintings have been exhibited, among other places, at the Moreau Gallery at Notre Dame University and the Brooklyn Museum. Recently, she was selected to appear in the Connecticut Women Artists' Annual Show at the New Britain Museum and the Silvermine Guild Art Center's annual show of artists in the Northeast.

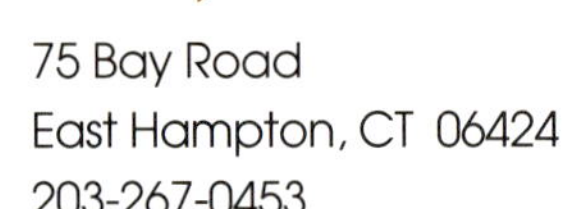

75 Bay Road
East Hampton, CT 06424
203-267-0453

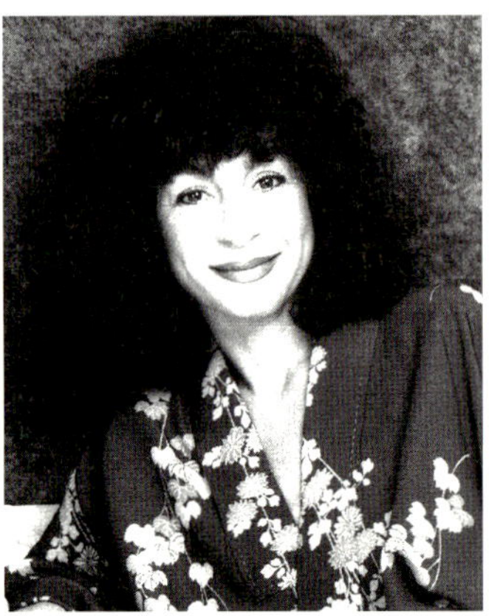

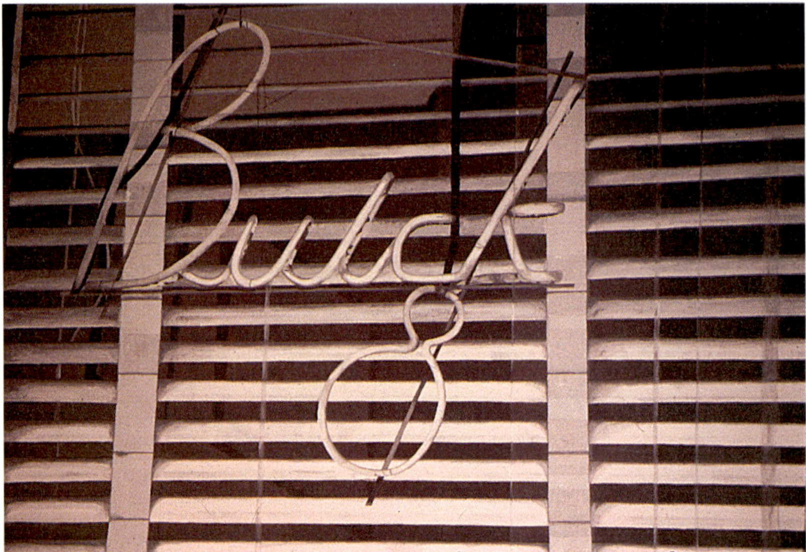

E. Buick 8. Watercolor, 22" x 30".

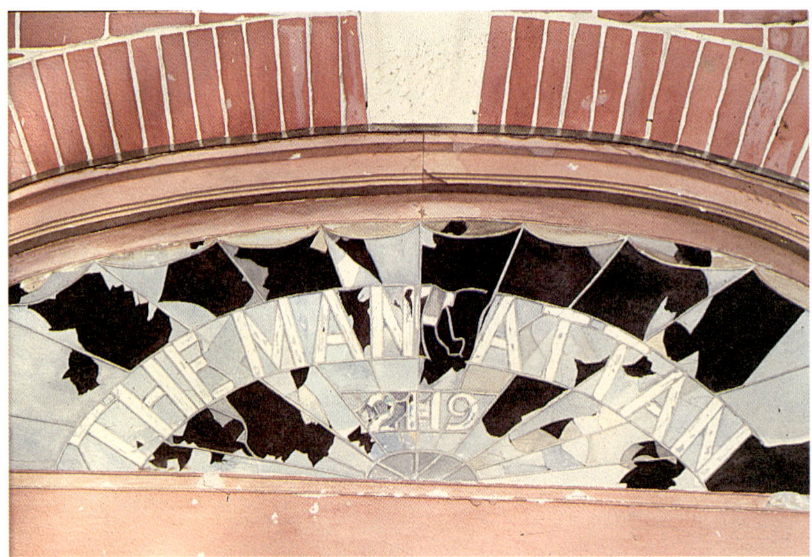

C. Manhattan. Watercolor, 22" x 30".

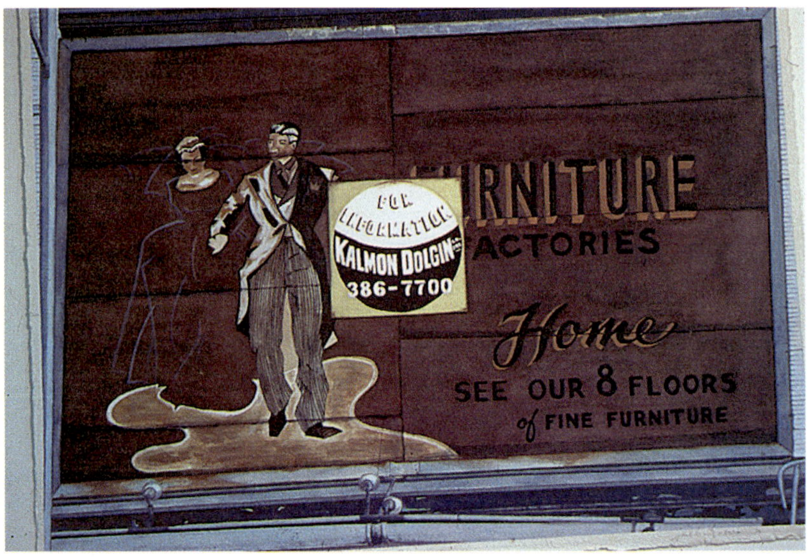

D. Faded Love. Watercolor, 22" x 30".

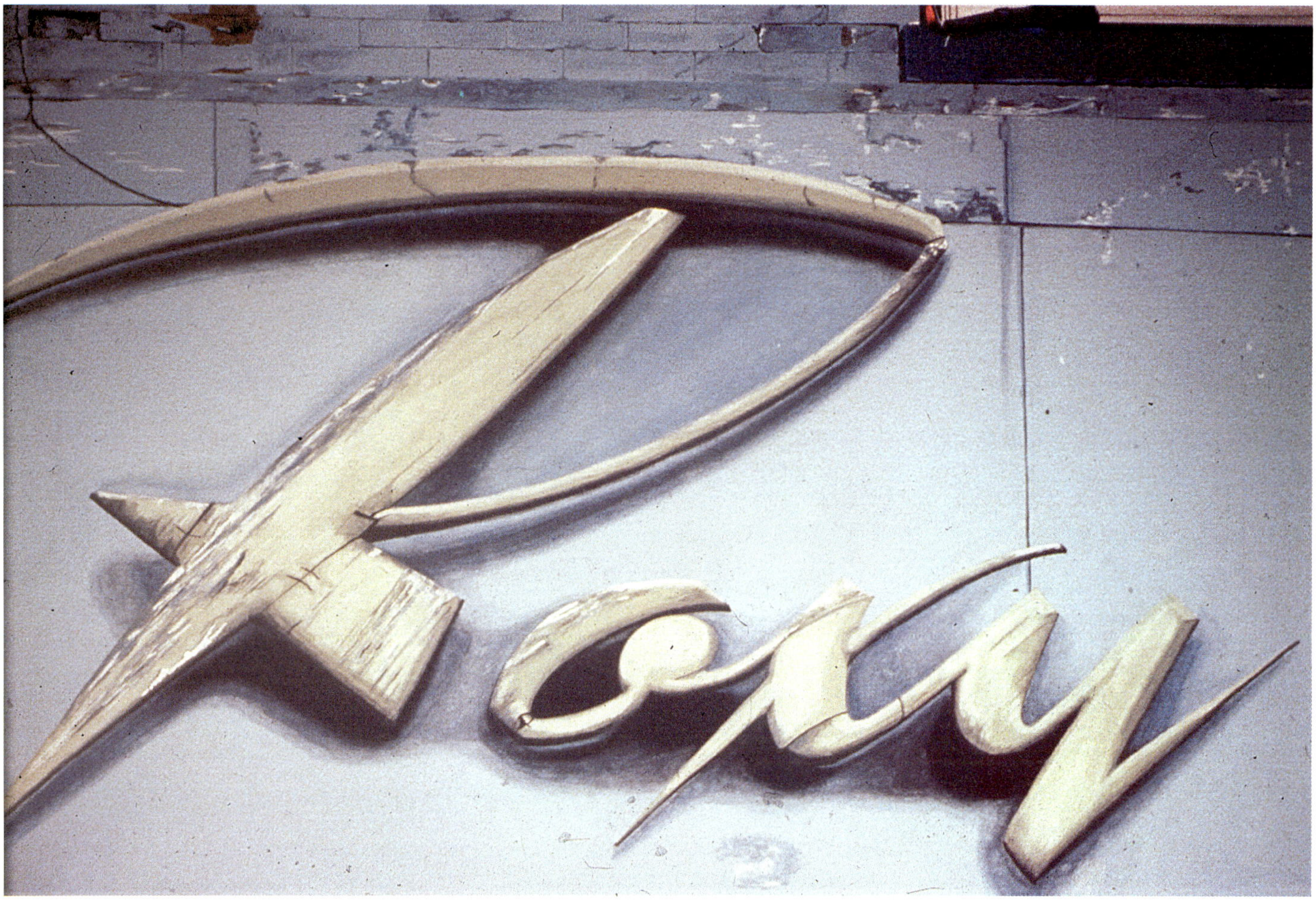

A. Roxy. Watercolor, 22" x 30".

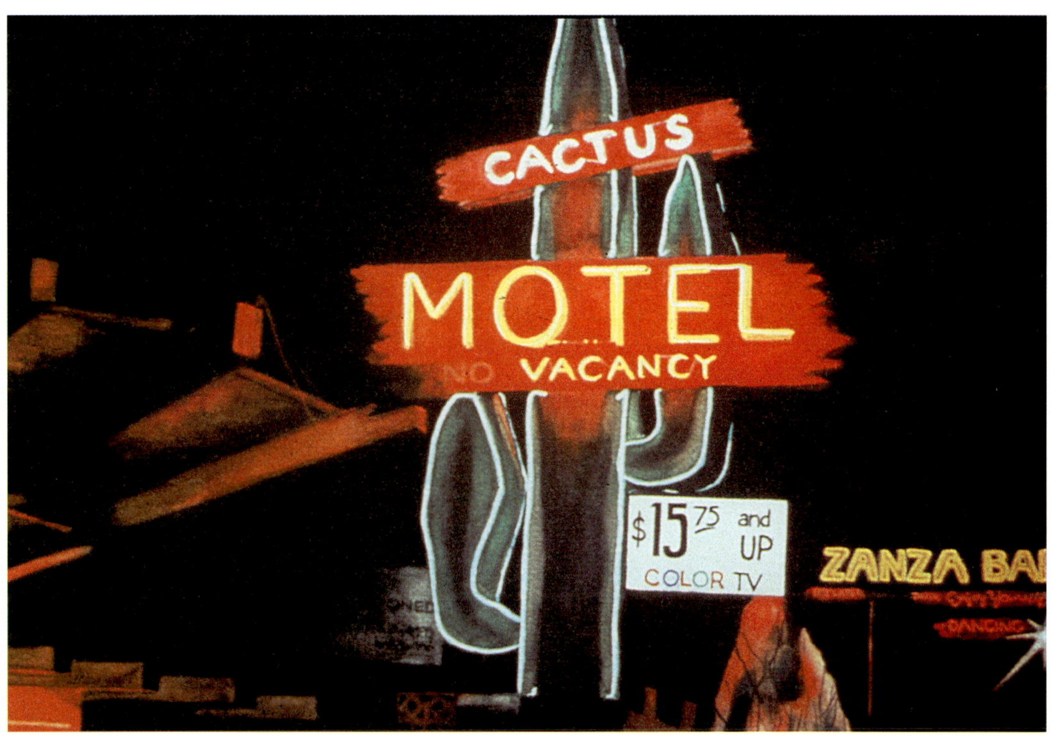

B. Cactus Hotel. Watercolor, 16" x 22".

PRICE LIST

A $1,500
B $1,500
C $1,500
D $1,500
E $500

Alan Bortman is a native of Newton, MA. In 1980 he was chosen as one of only 25 students to attend Syracuse University's Illustration Program. He continued his education at the Massachusetts College of Art in Boston. Since finishing his training, Bortman has worked as an illustrator for Boston area advertising agencies, retail companies, magazines and publishing companies.

Bortman's current focus is more on painting than illustration. His technically polished canvases are executed with oils and influenced by the Pop Art movement. In his most recent work, familiar product designs and typography are juxtaposed with images of everyday life. The paintings encourage the viewer to contemplate the relationships between products and people, and allow Bortman to explore his talents for both commercial and fine art.

Bortman's work has been exhibited at a number of Boston's galleries. He recently had much success at Art Expo 1992 in New York City. His work has been the focus of articles in *Big Beans, The Boston Globe* and *Adweek*.

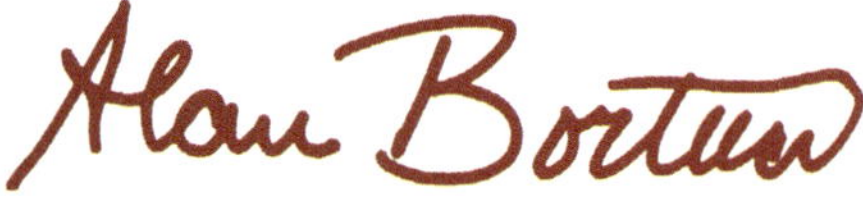

950 Boylston Street, Suite L1-3
Newton Highlands, MA 02161
617-964-5523

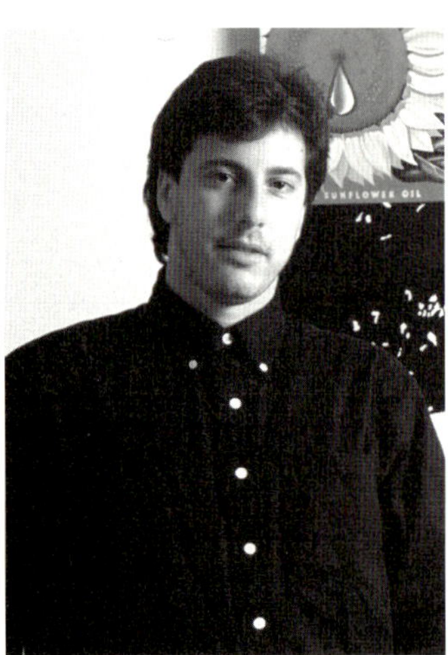

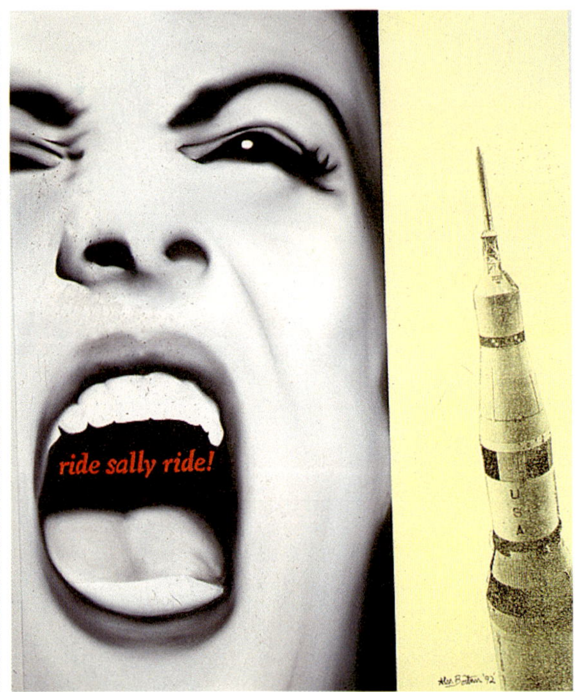

A. Ride Sally Ride. Oil and silkscreen on canvas, 22" x 28".

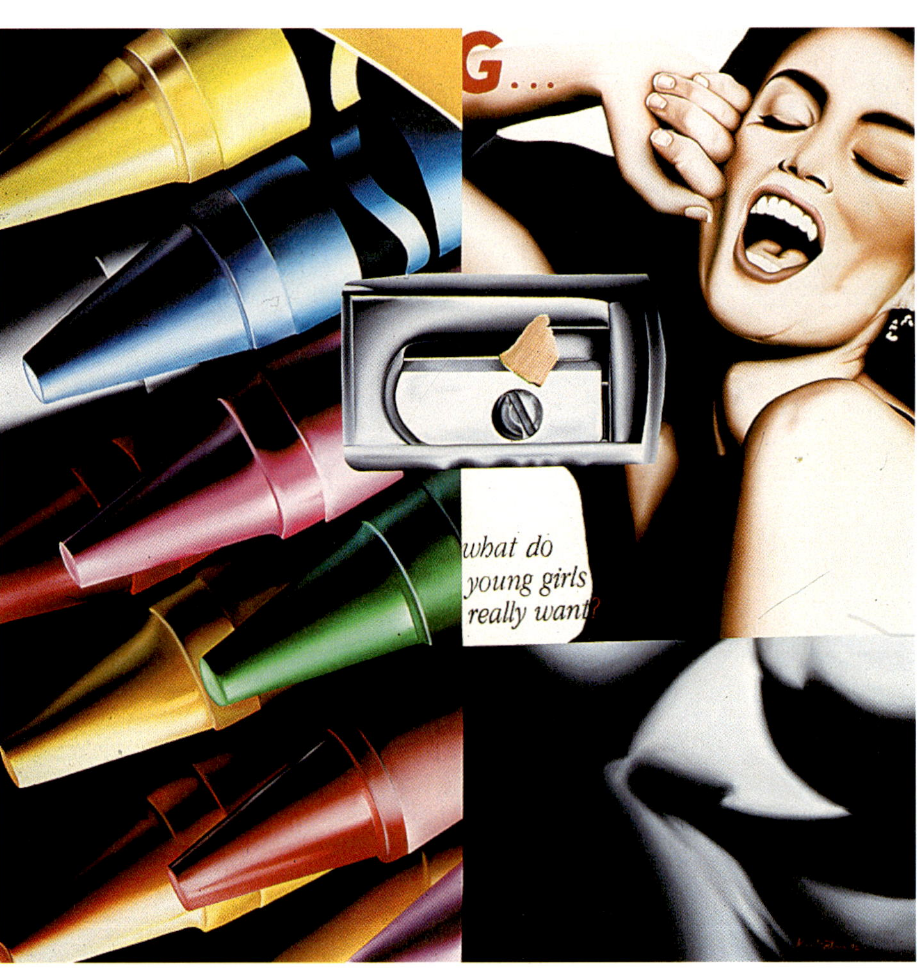

B. Young Girls. Oil on canvas, 64" x 64".

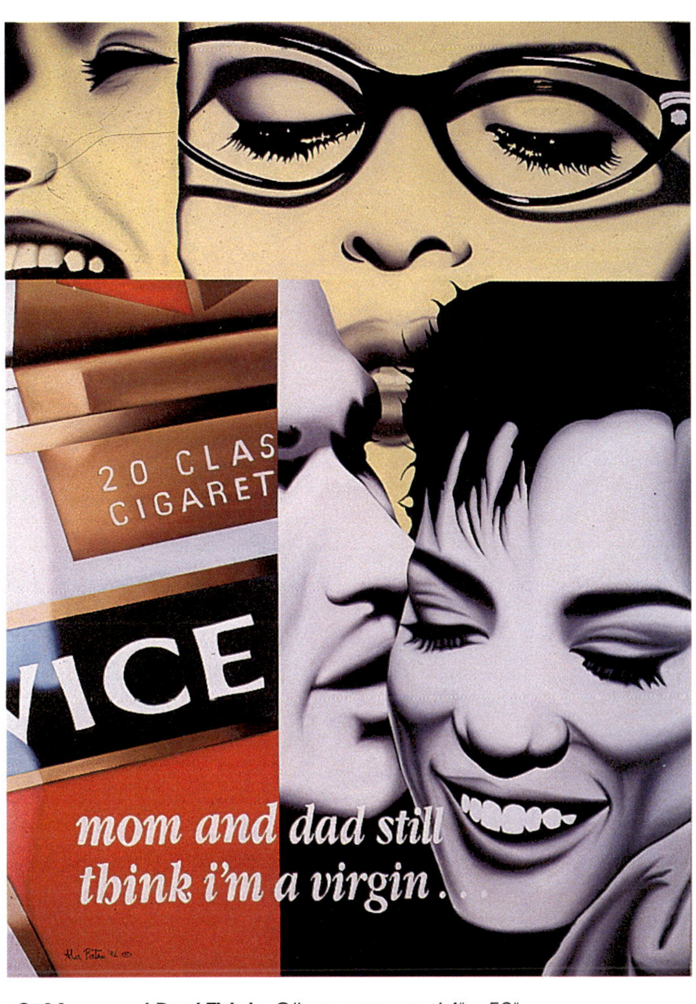

C. Mom and Dad Think. Oil on canvas, 64" x 52".

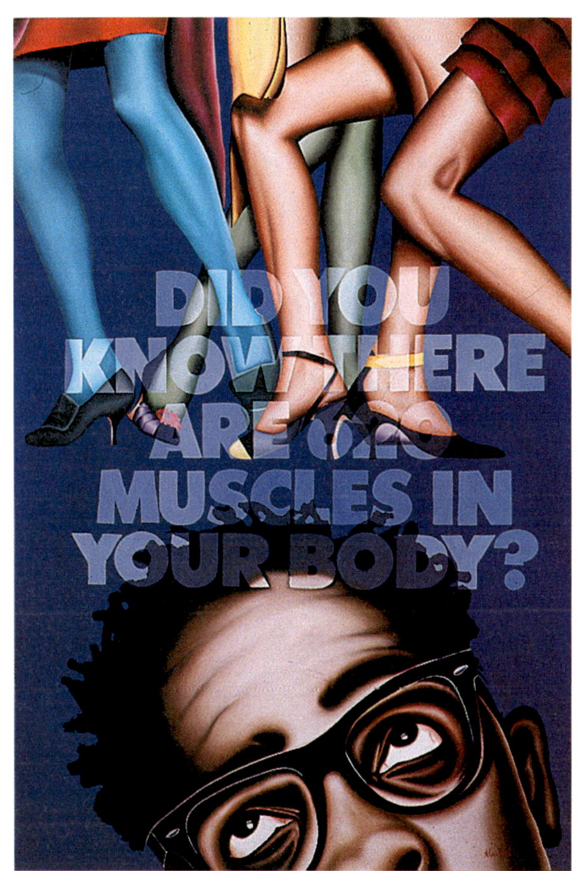

D. 620 Muscles. Oil on canvas, 54" x 42".
Private collection.

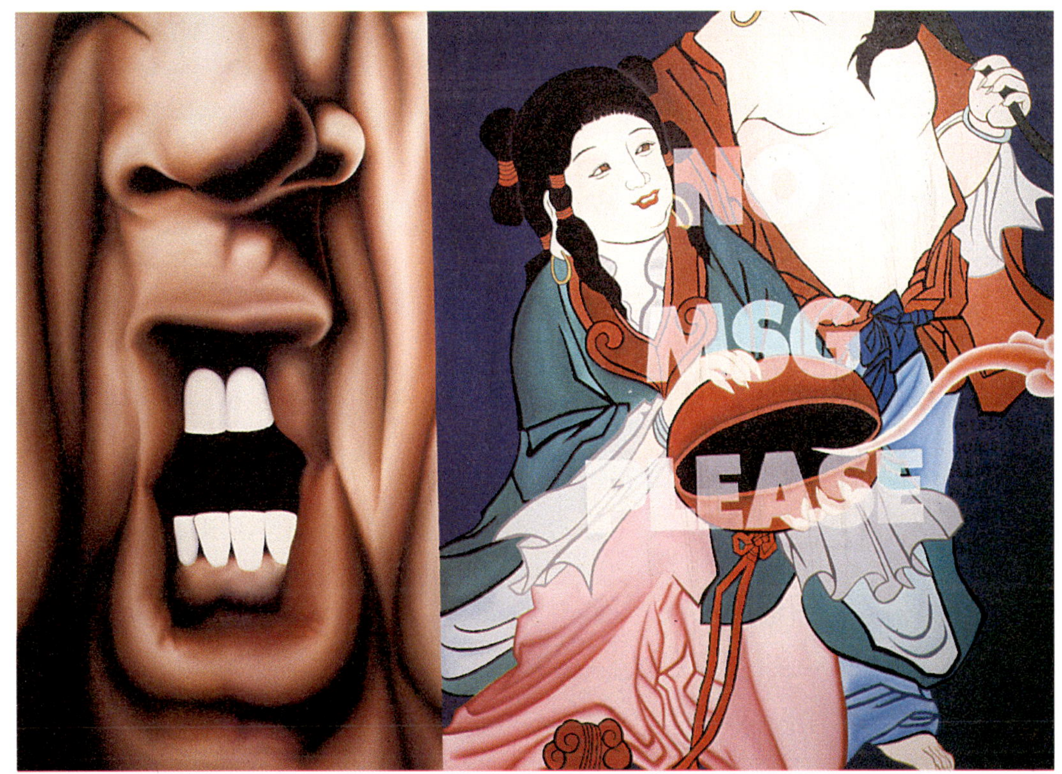

E. No MSG Please. Oil on canvas, 36" x 50".

PRICE LIST

A $1,200
B $5,000
C $4,800
E $3,000

Pat Bräuer

Pat Bräuer started painting while still in high school. She pursued art training at the Creative Arts Workshop, and the Silvermine Guild School of Art, both in Connecticut, and at the Vermont Studio School. Bräuer has also studied oil painting with Fred Sexton, watercolor with Hilda Levy and casein, her present medium, with Madeleine Sharrer.

A board member of the Connecticut Women Artists, Bräuer is active within Connecticut's art community, although she devotes most of her time to painting.

Bräuer draws her subject matter from domestic life and works with a bold palette that ranges from cool Van Gogh blues to fiery Matisse reds. Some of her genre paintings include figures; some are studies of everyday objects such as a chair or window. All demonstrate her keen sense of color interrelationships and effects.

A recipient of the Grumbacher Gold Medallion for Painting, Bräuer has exhibited her paintings in eight solo shows and in juried shows throughout Connecticut and New York. Her work is included in private and public collections in the U.S., Canada and Europe.

Pat Bräuer

200 Livingston Street
New Haven, CT 06511
203-865-8194

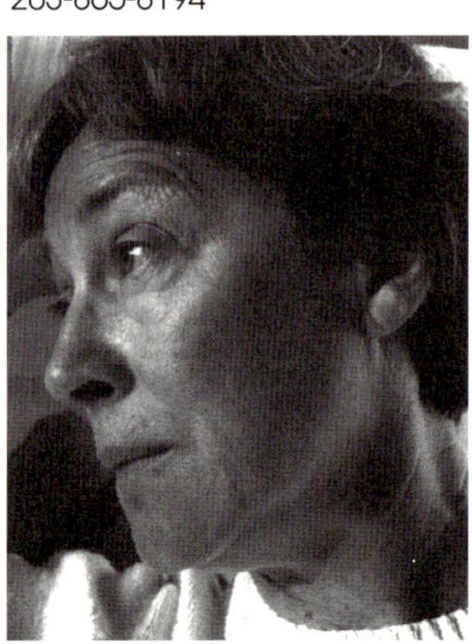

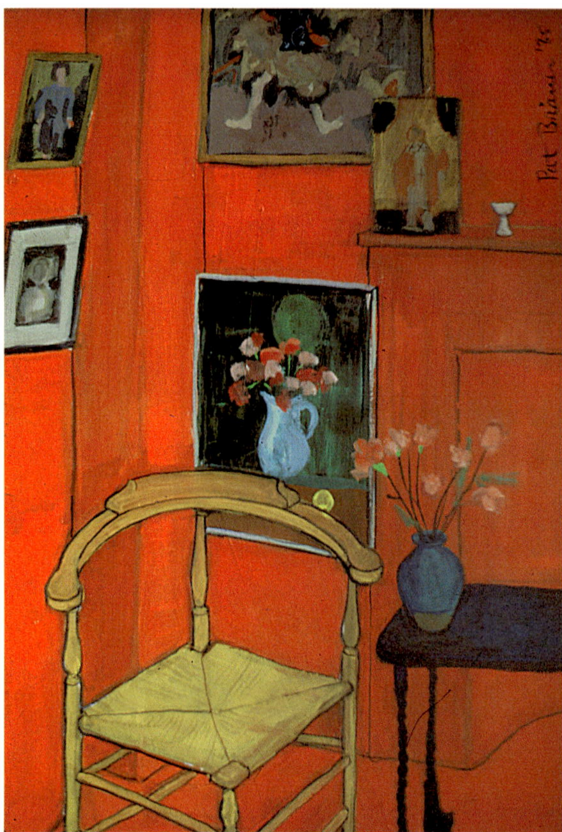

A. Red Room.
Casein, 24" x 16".

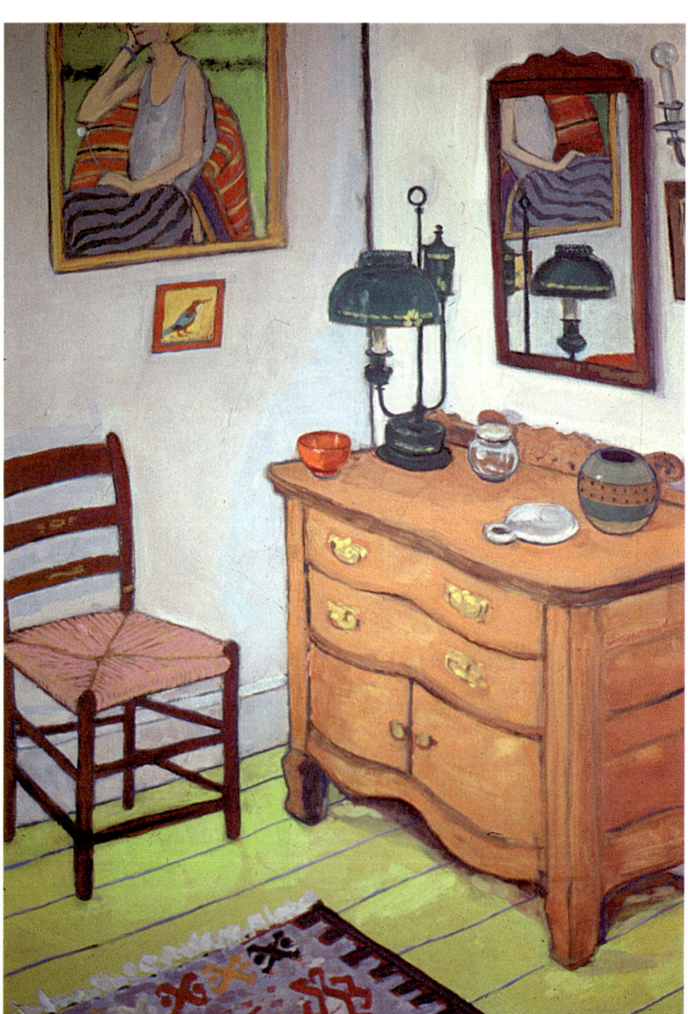

B. Red Chair Left.
Casein, 32" x 24".

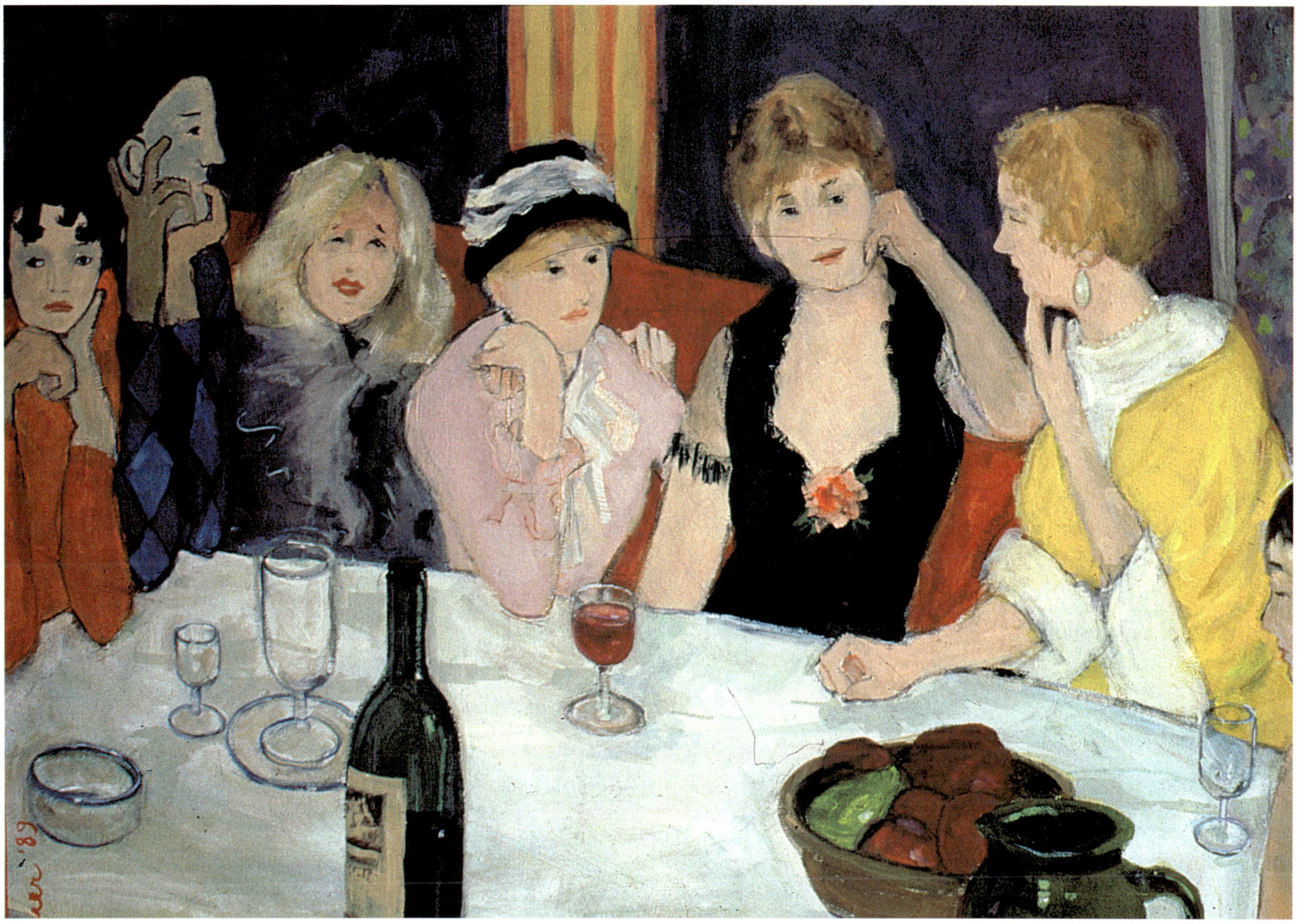

C. **Good Company.** Casein, 28" x 40".

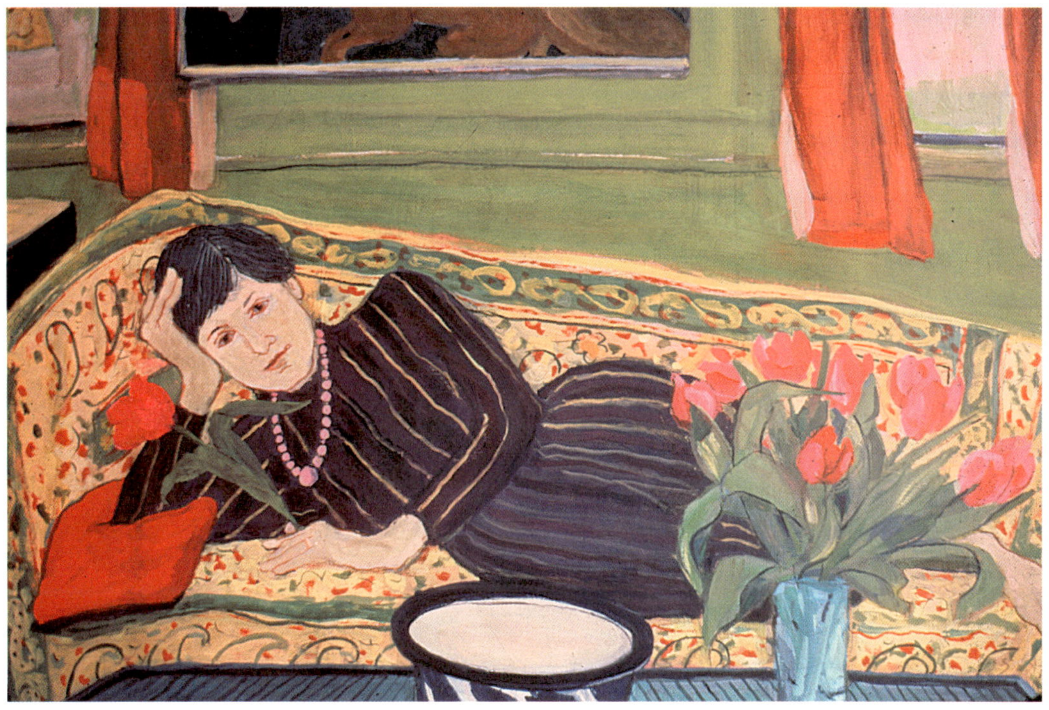

D. Dodie on Sofa. Casein, 24" x 36".

PRICE LIST

A............................$800

B........................$1,800

C........................$1,500

D........................$1,000

Although he is only in his early twenties, Alphonse Camera has already accomplished a great deal. He began his art training at the Yale-affiliated Creative Arts Workshop and the Educational Center for the Arts, both in Connecticut. In 1987, Camera was awarded a scholarship to the Rhode Island School of Design in Providence, RI. He graduated in 1991 with a BFA in Illustration and is now pursuing graduate studies at his alma mater.

In addition to his formal education, Camera has worked as an illustrator and designer, freelancing for Beckett Monthly Sports Publications among numerous other projects.

Camera is an amateur athlete and an avid collector of sport's cards. His love of sports and admiration for professional athletes inspires his paintings. He works with acrylics in combination with collage and various mixed media.

In 1991 and 1989, Camera's paintings were chosen to appear in "Choices," a juried statewide show in Connecticut. Along with continuing his education, he will continue to do commissioned works.

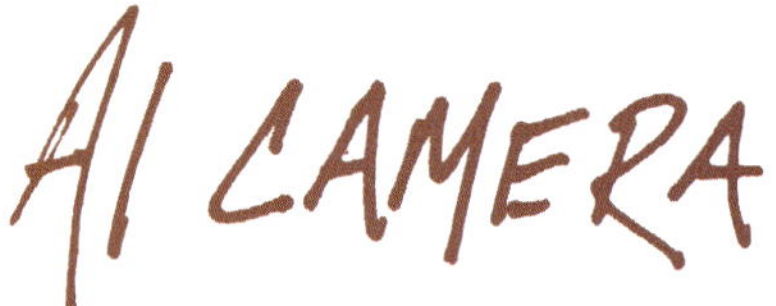

43 Forbes Place
East Haven, CT 06512
203-468-0612

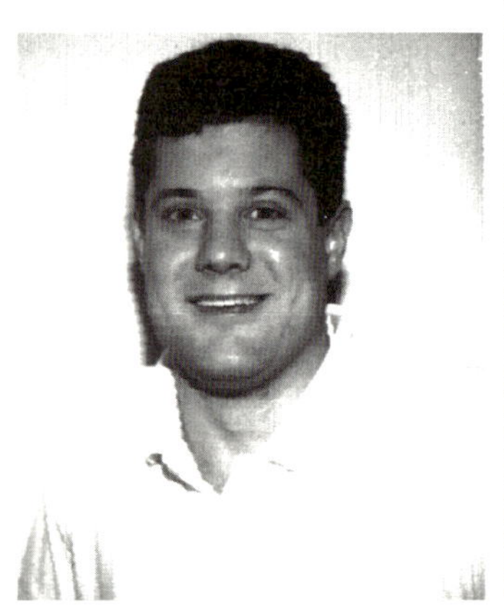

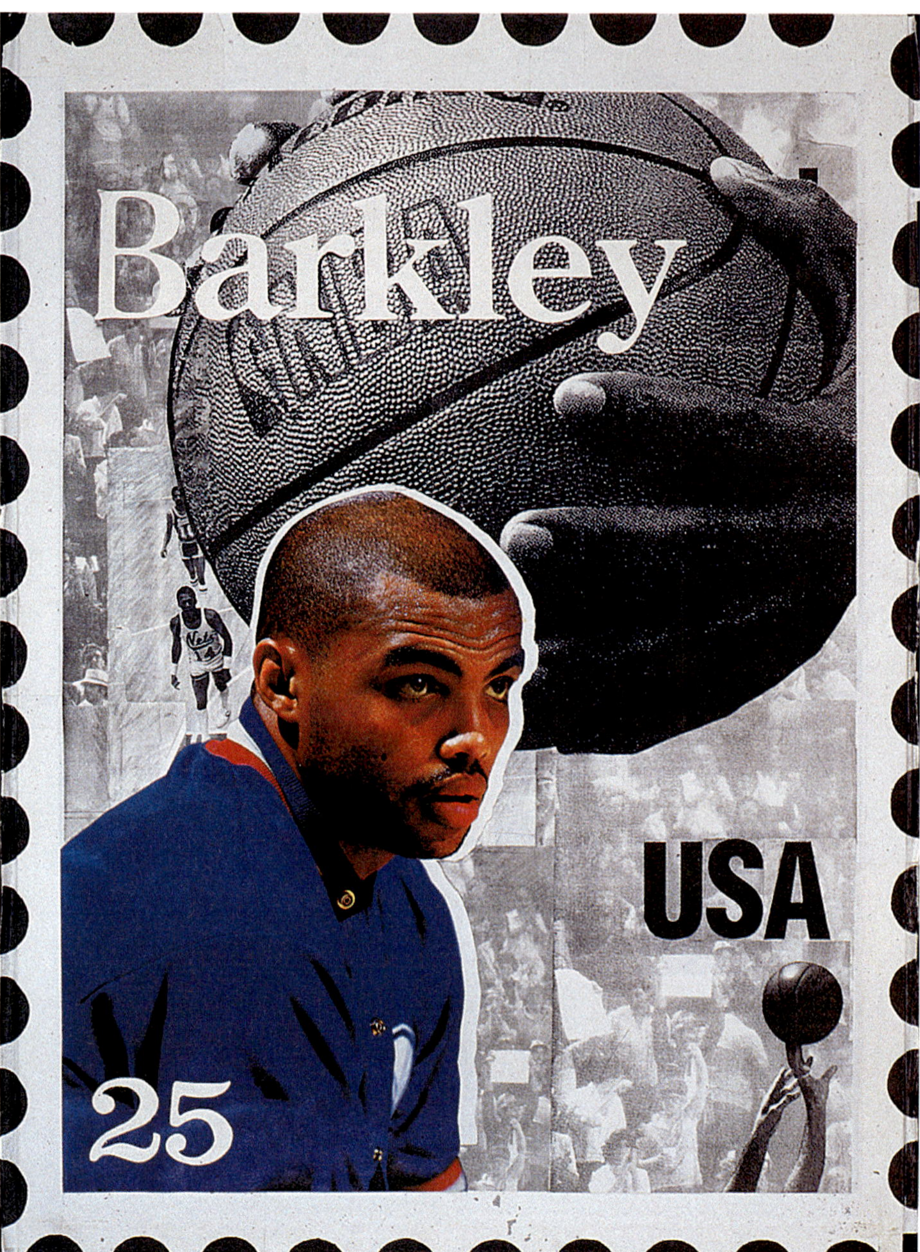

A. Barkley Stamp. Collage/mixed media. 27½" x 20¾".

B. (opposite middle) **Kirby Puckett.** Collage/mixed media, 12" x 36".

C. - F. (opposite top and bottom) **Kirby Puckett.** Details, each 12" x 9".

PRICE LIST

A..........................$825
B.......................$3,900

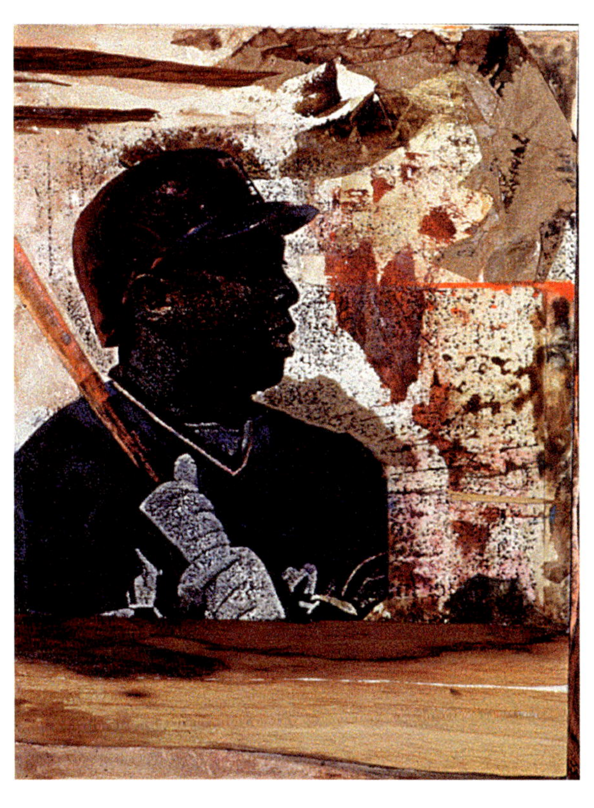

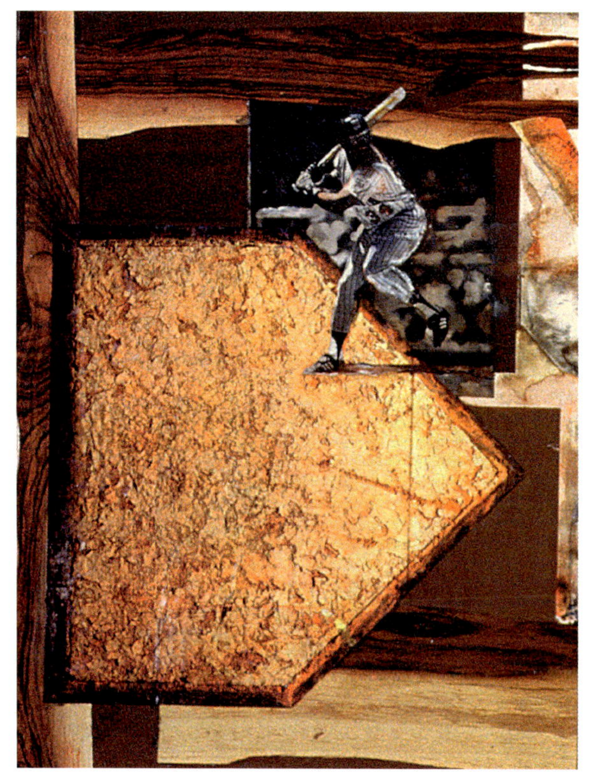

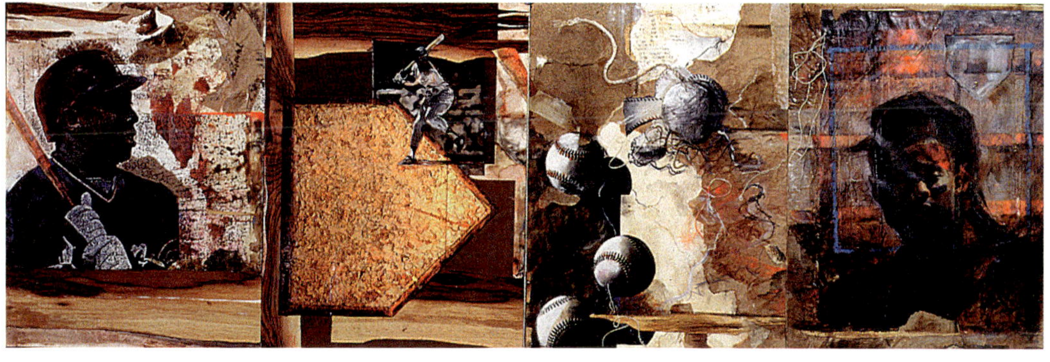

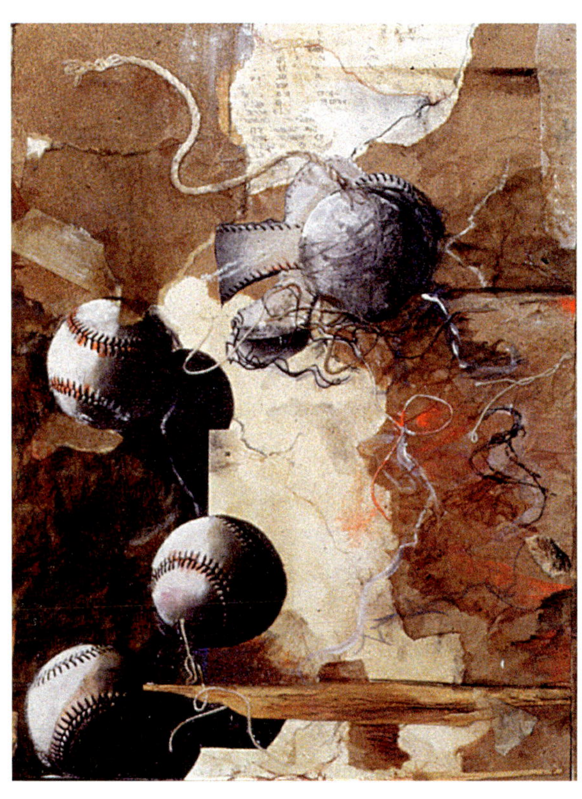

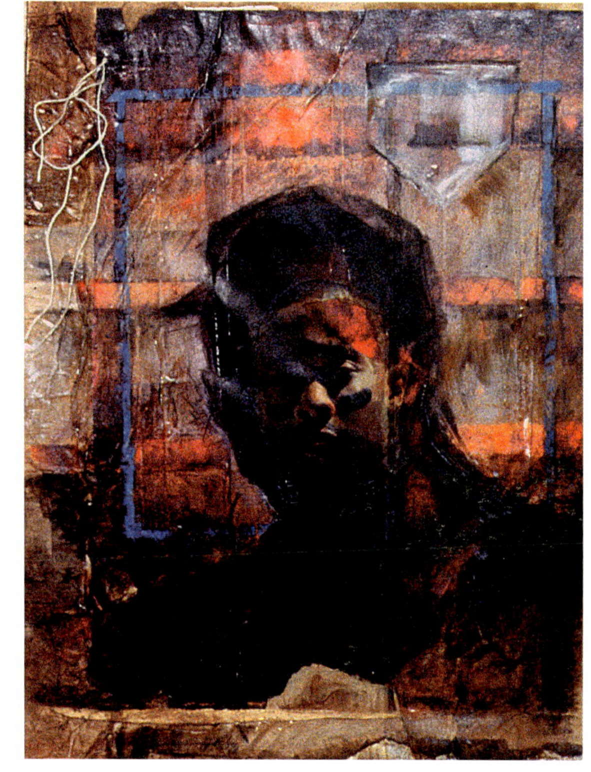

Giovanni John Campopiano

Giovanni John Campopiano was born and raised in Providence, RI, and now lives and works in nearby Cranston, RI. Campopiano graduated from Rhode Island College in 1975 and then took additional art courses at the Rhode Island School of Design.

Campopiano's canvases are large scale and horizontal in structure, a format essential to the work's strong narrative component. Using mixed media with an emphasis on acrylics and collage, he addresses social, political and personal issues, which he researches through self-analysis and empirical observation. Campopiano combines such objects as posters, newspapers and billboards with generic images reproduced by paint and brush.

Campopiano's work has been exhibited in New York City, California, the Midwest and throughout the New England region. In February of 1993, Campopiano will have a solo show at Gallery One in Providence, RI. He was recently made an Artists Fellow of New York City, and was awarded a residency at the Vermont Artists Studio from the New England Foundation for the Arts.

Campopiano

247 Greenwood Street
Cranston, RI 02910
401-277-3588 days
401-461-7733 eves.

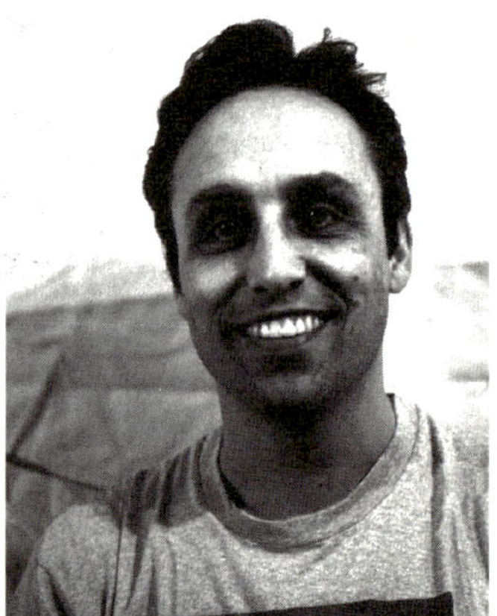

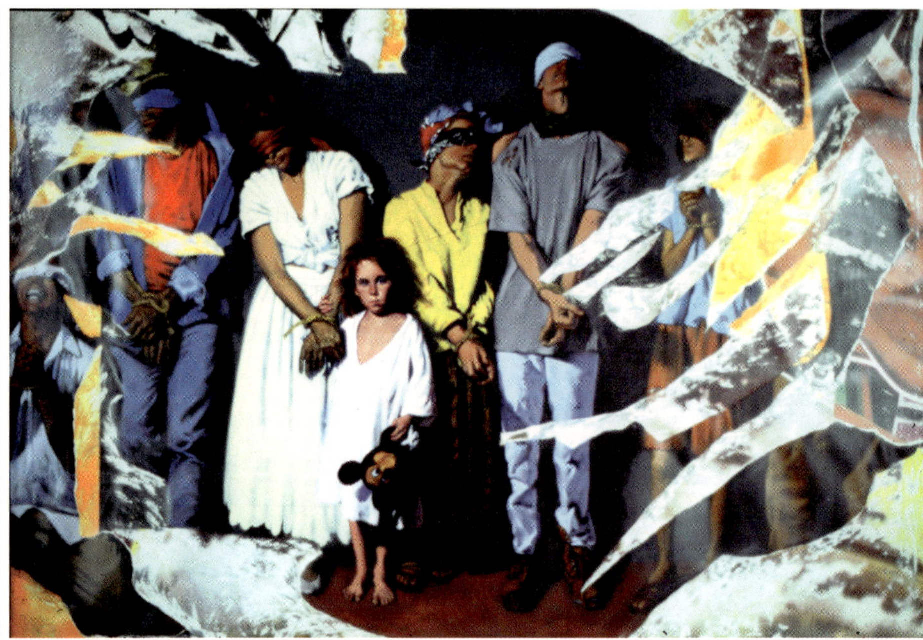

A. Allegory of the Cave. Acrylic and collage, 72" x 96".

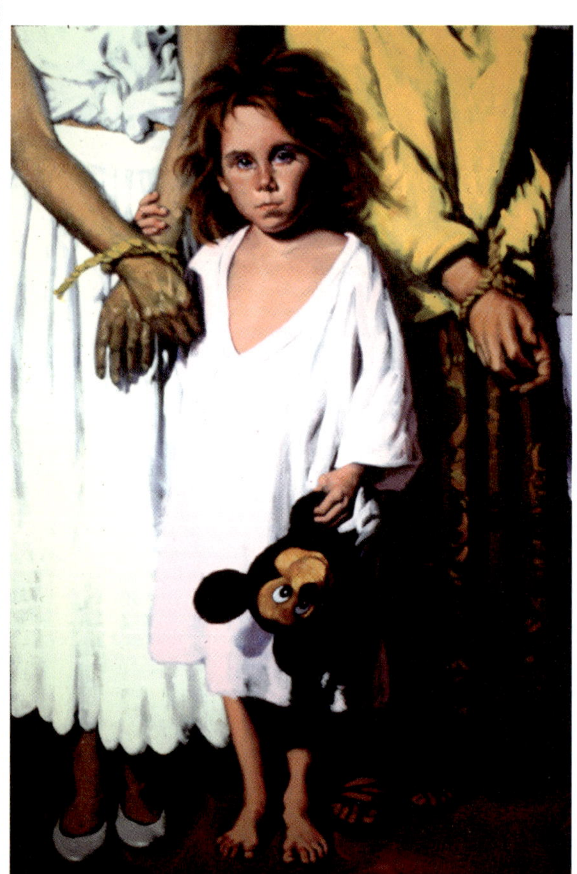

B. Allegory of the Cave. Detail.

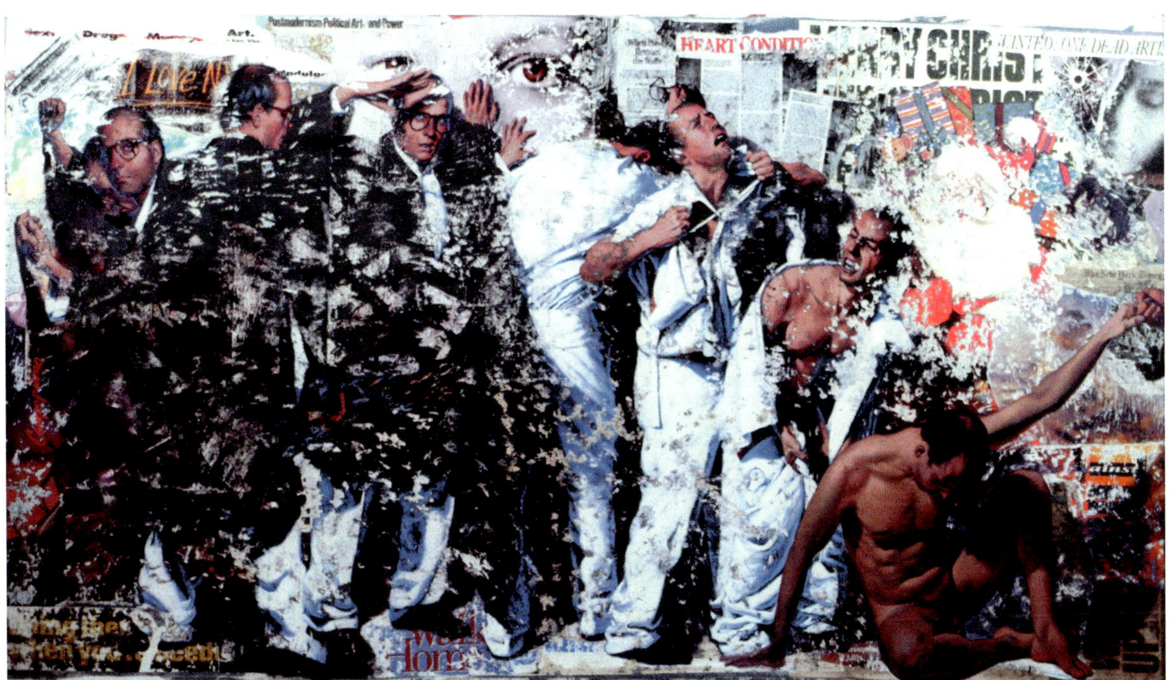

C. . . . and the Epiphany. Acrylic and collage, 72" x 126".

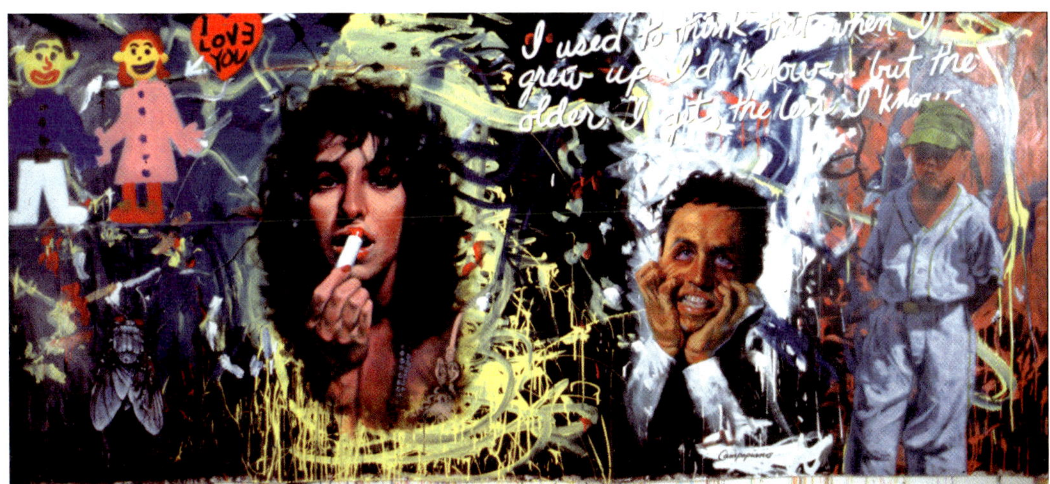

D. Lost Hope, Shattered Dreams. Acrylic and enamel, 53" x 114".

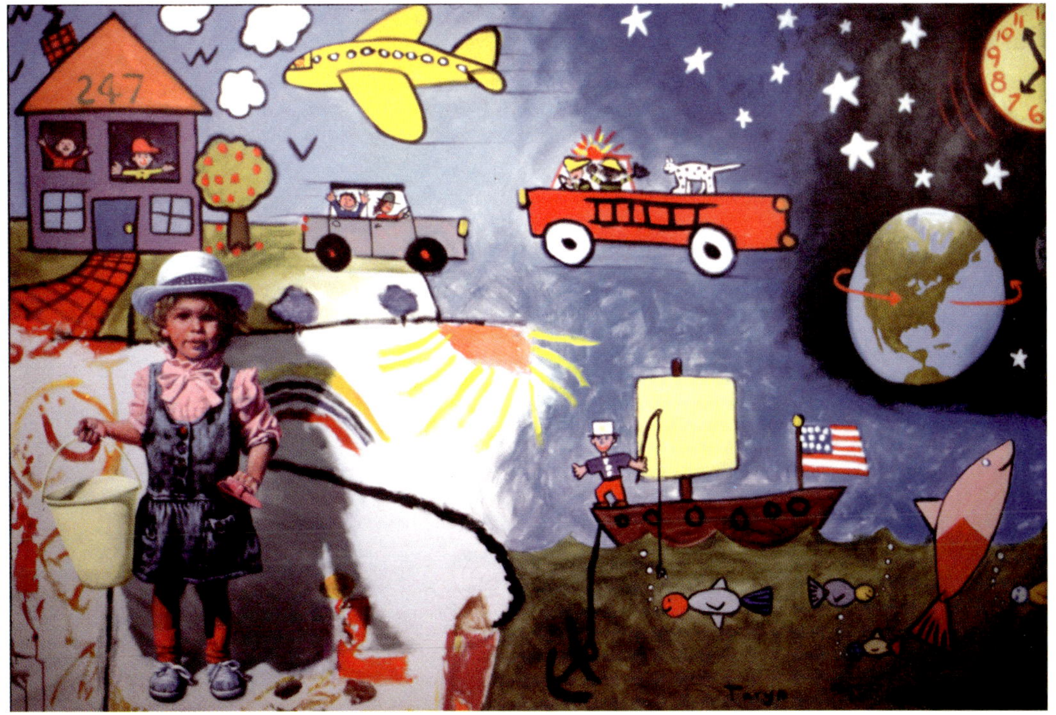

E. (opposite bottom) **Memories #2.** Acrylic on canvas, 72" x 116".

PRICE LIST

A	$3,000
C	$4,000
D	$1,000
E	$2,000

Represented by
Revel Gallery
New York City
Dalton Fine Arts,
Boston, MA

Debra Claffey

Debra Claffey is a painter and printmaker who lives in Jamaica Plain, MA, where she has maintained a studio for over ten years. Claffey received formal art training at Tufts University and the School of the Museum of Fine Arts in Boston. Since her training, Claffey has divided her time between painting and her company, Artist Services, which provides custom framing and graphic design among other sevices.

Claffey's most recent work is a series of local landscapes which are done in a freely brushed expressionist style. She is fascinated with the relationship between abstraction and representation, and her work is a sensitive exploration of this line. Previous work has focused on jazz musicians in performing environments and still life compositions of fruits and flowers.

Claffey has shown extensively in the Boston area, and has executed commissions for both private parties and publications. Her work has been discussed in *Art New England* and other regional publications.

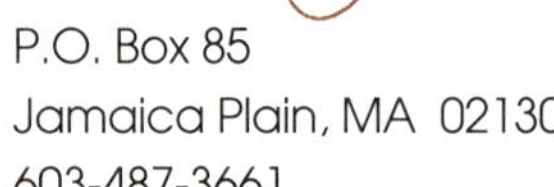

P.O. Box 85
Jamaica Plain, MA 02130
603-487-3661

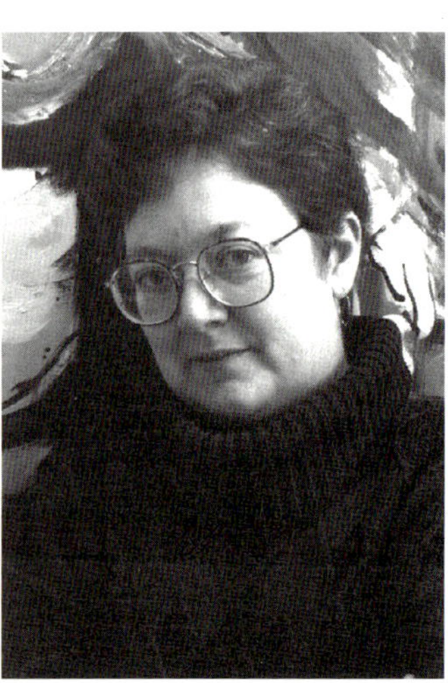

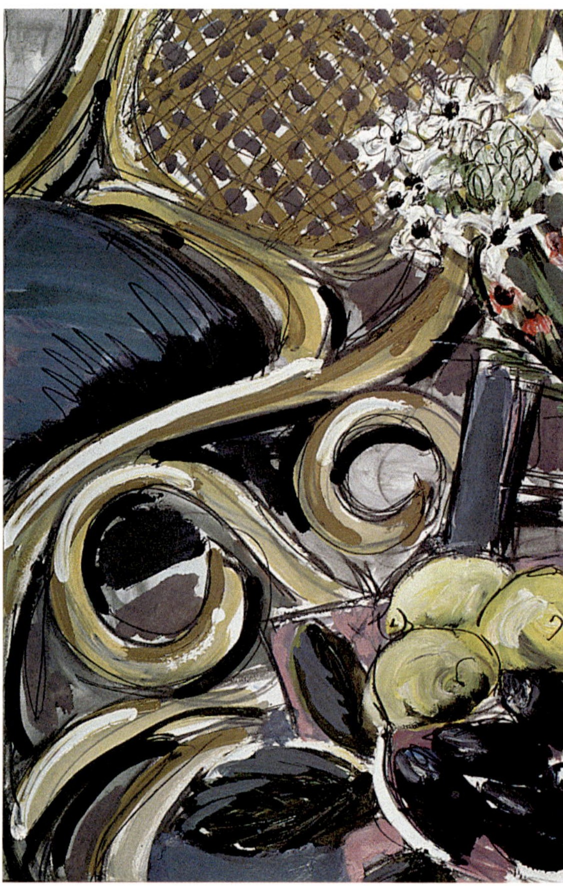

A. Still Life with Rocker, Part 1.
Oil on paper, 22" x 15".

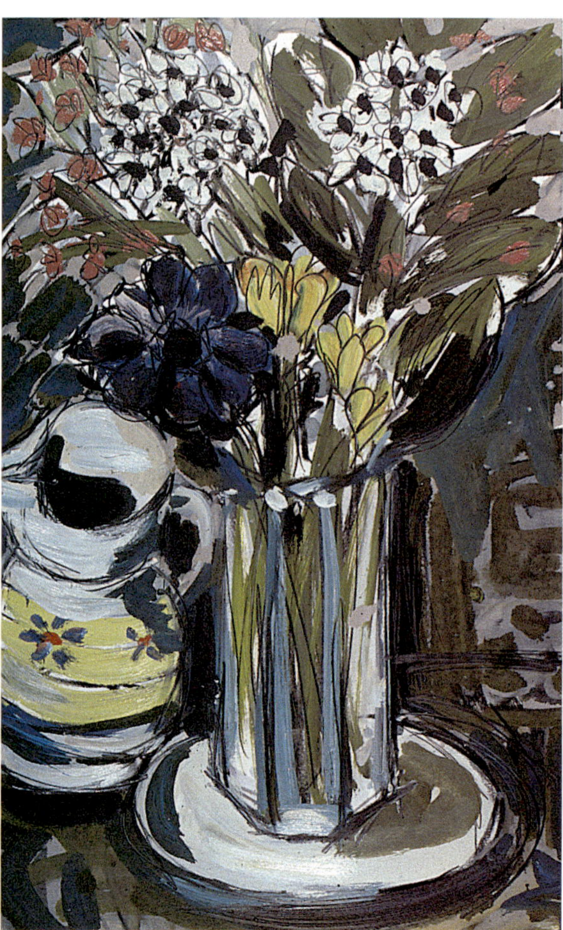

B. Borrowed Pitchers.
Oil on paper, 22" x 15".

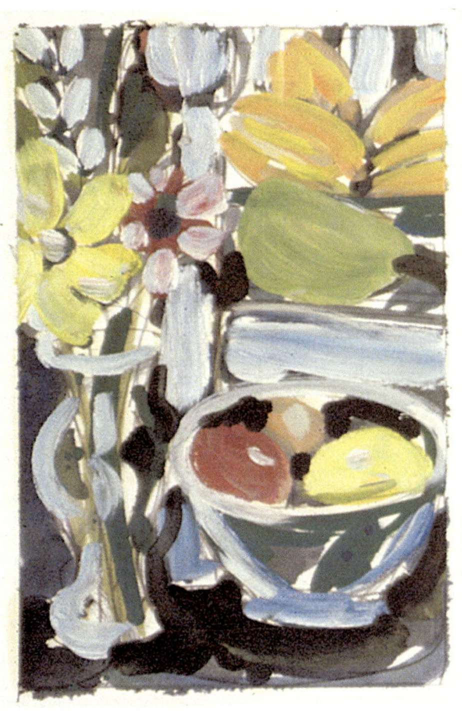
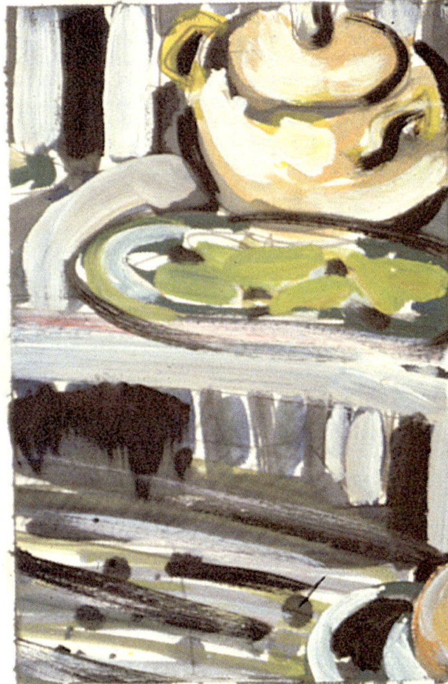
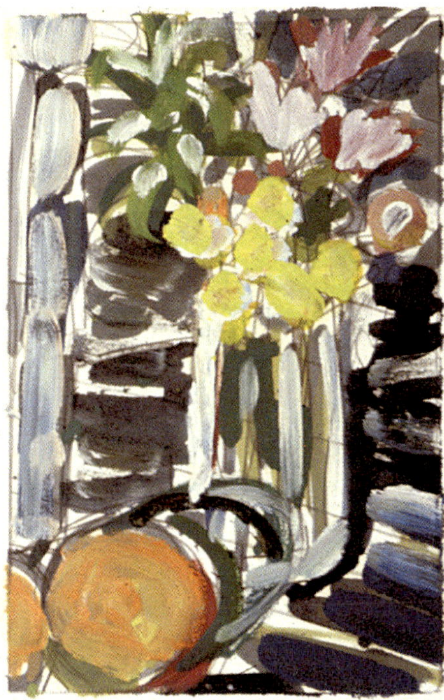

C. Triptych Still Life. Oil on Rives paper, 3 – 10" x 7".

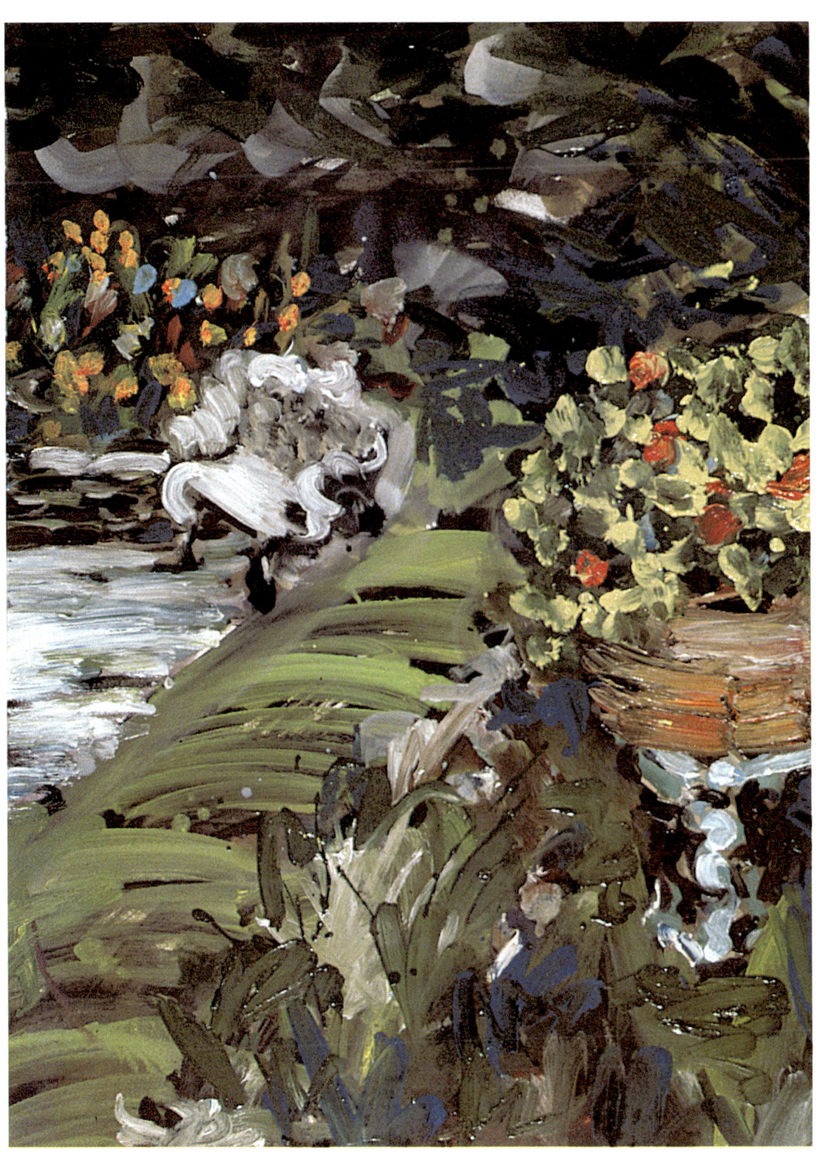

D. Bonnie's Garden II.
Oil on paper, 30" x 22".

PRICE LIST

A..........................$270

B..........................$270

C..........................$520

D..........................$520

Meredith Fife Day

Meredith Fife Day's art training began during childhood with Saturday art classes. When she attended college, Day earned a BA in English before pursuing an education in the fine arts. She subsequently earned an MFA in Painting and Drawing from Louisiana State University and an MFA in Studio Teaching from Boston University.

Over the years, Day has worked in varied capacities in the art world. She currently works for a Boston area publishing firm and also writes and edits for several publications, including *Art New England.*

Day devotes much of her time to painting. Her primary medium is oil on canvas, and her paintings explore the relationship between her internal world and the world around her. With a style that is representational yet conscious of the formal dynamics of abstract painting, Day is able to infuse her still lifes and landscapes with energy and emotion.

Day's paintings have been exhibited at organizations in New England and throughout the United States.

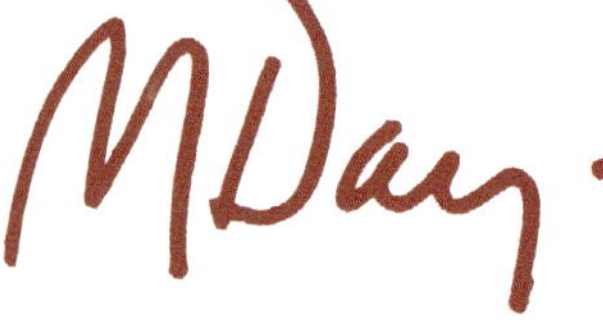

128 Warren Street, #4
Lowell, MA 01852
508-441-9381

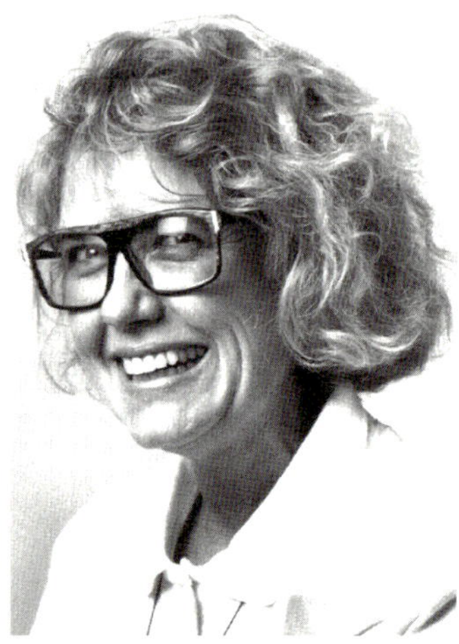

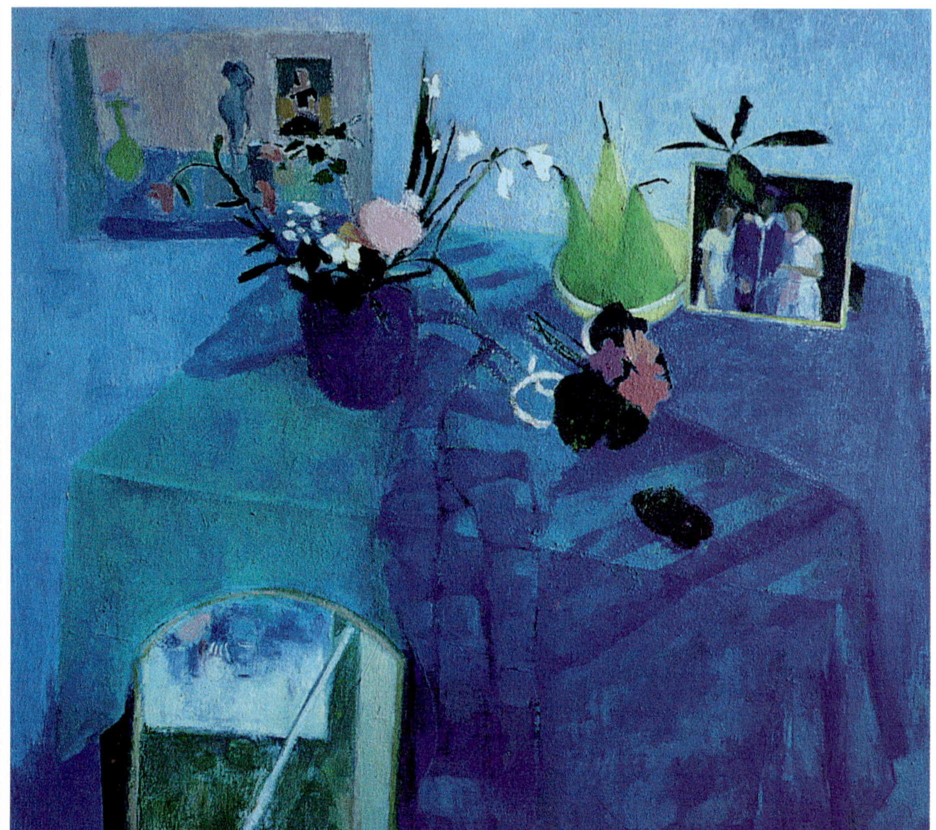

A. Family Portrait. Oil on canvas, 32" x 36".

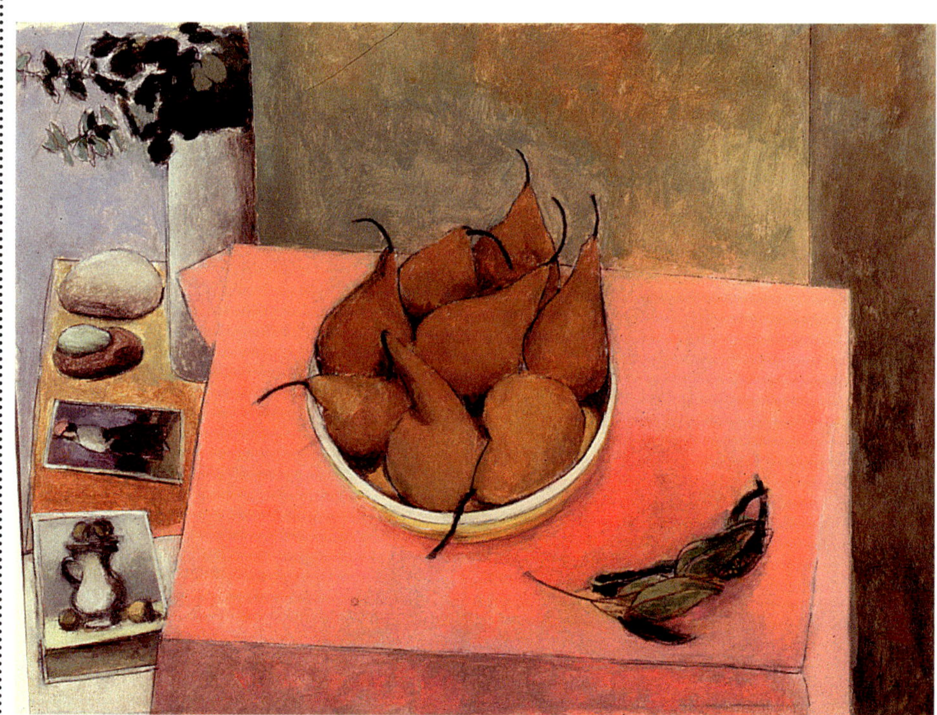

B. Pears. Pencil, acrylic on paper, 21" x 29".

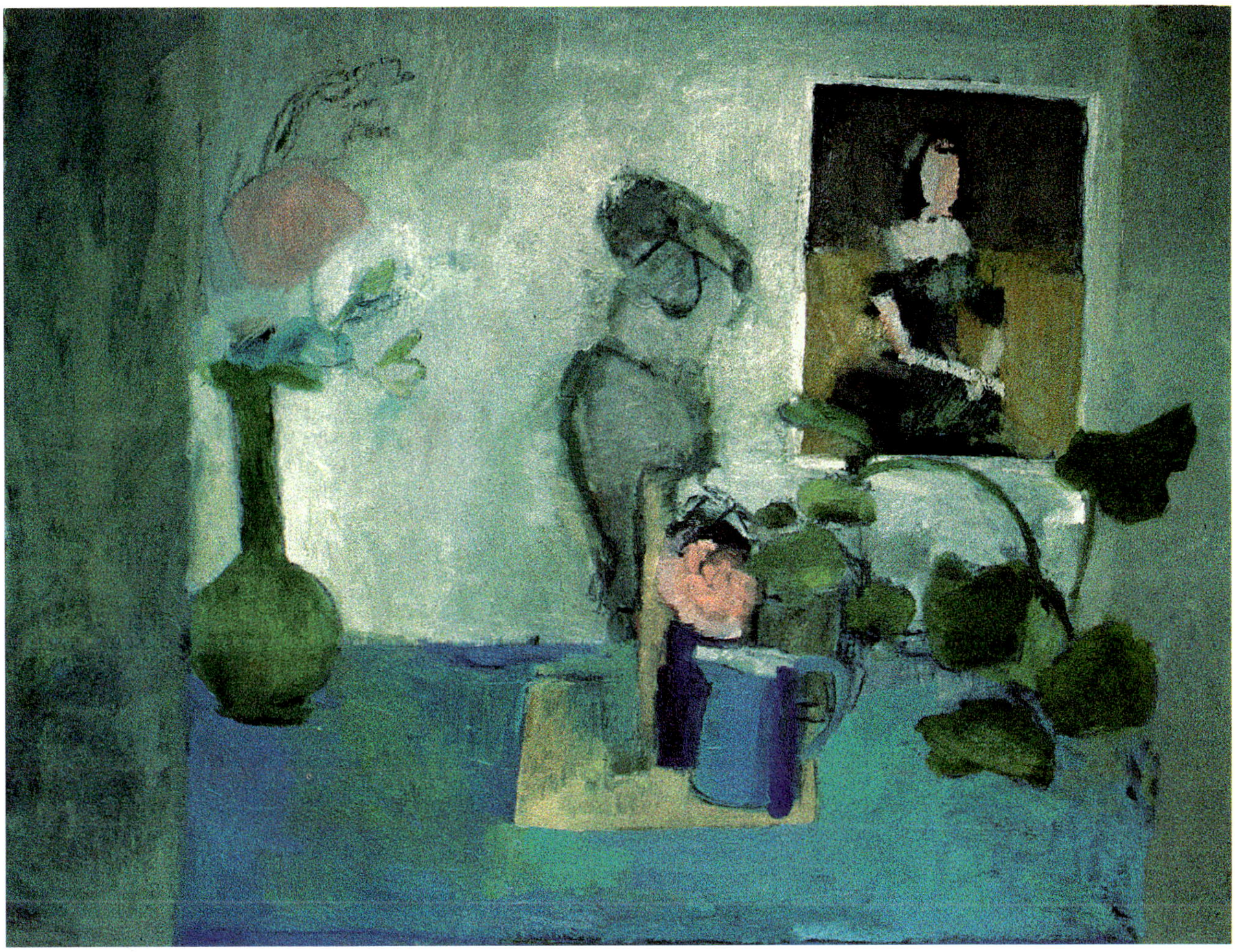

C. Still Life with Goya. Oil on paper, 18" x 26".

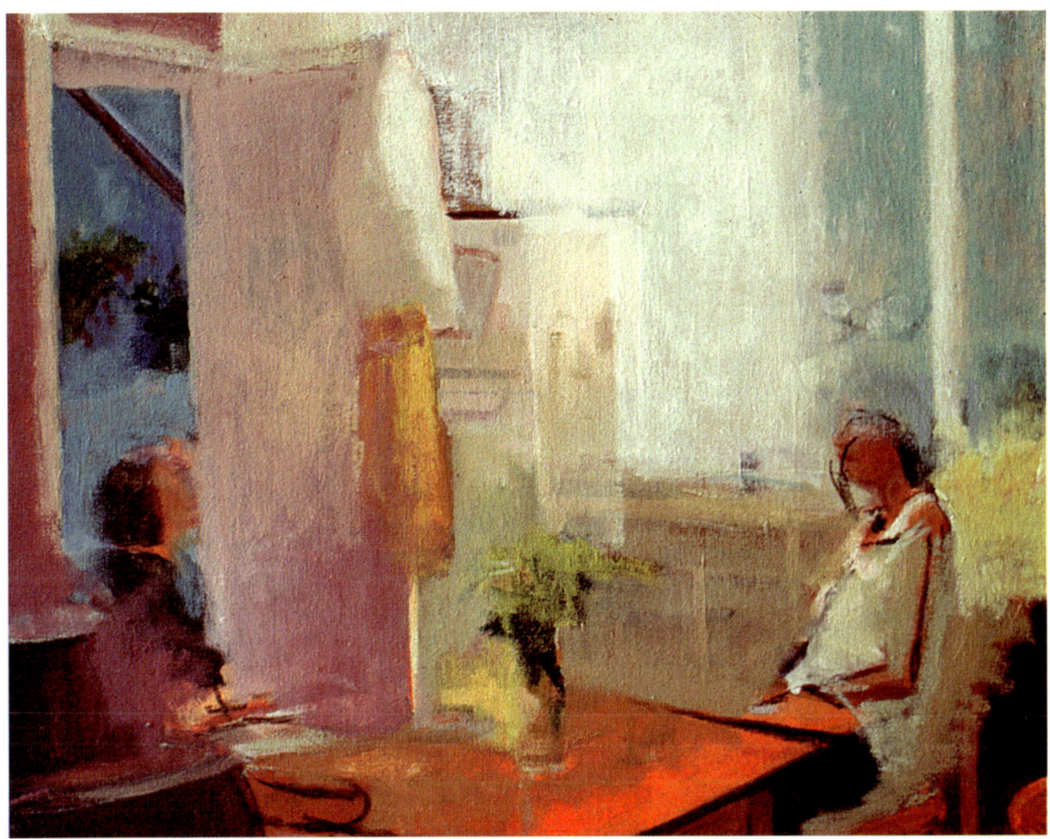

D. Rainy Day Kitchen Talk. Oil on canvas, 16" x 20".

PRICE LIST

A $1,200
B $900
C $900
D..........................$900

Beth Donahue was born in Cambridge, MA, and now maintains a studio a short distance away in Dover. She attended Regis College in Weston, MA, and the School of the Museum of Fine Arts, Boston. Donahue has taught printmaking, lectures on art in the Boston area and writes for her town newspaper, the *Dover Reporter*.

Donahue's paintings merge aspects of Eastern and Western culture. Her strongly personal works are inspired by nature, memory and the images that emerge from accidental events. As an abstract painter concerned with surface effects, Donahue explores experimental techniques with paint, ink, gold leaf and collage to achieve density in her mixed media pieces.

Since 1990, Donahue has exhibited in over 30 national and international shows. Invitationals for 1992 included exhibits at the Chapelle de la Sorbonne, Paris, the Musee de la Commanderie D'Unet, Bordeaux, and a solo exhibition in New York City. Among her many awards is the prestigious Copley Master Award from the Copley Society in Boston.

beth donahue

49 Walpole Street
Dover, MA 02030
508-785-1415

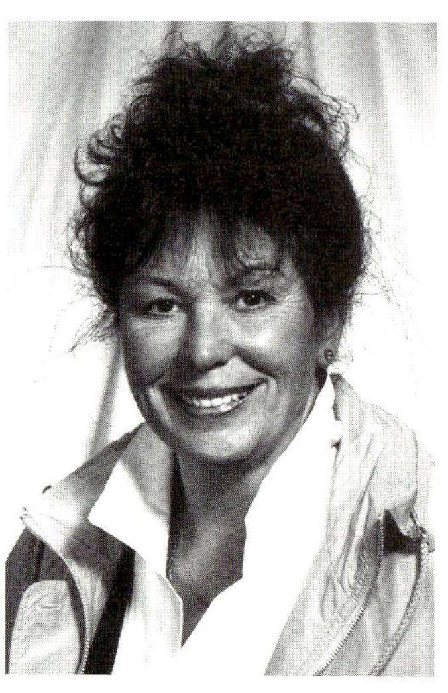

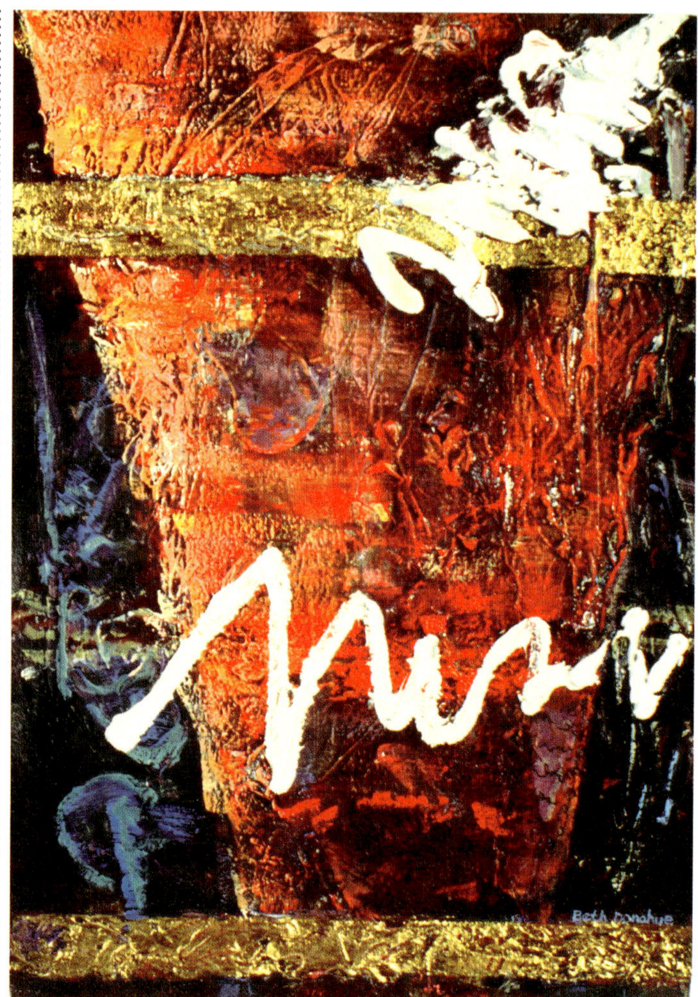

A. Zen Series #20. Mixed media on handmade paper, 42½" x 32½".

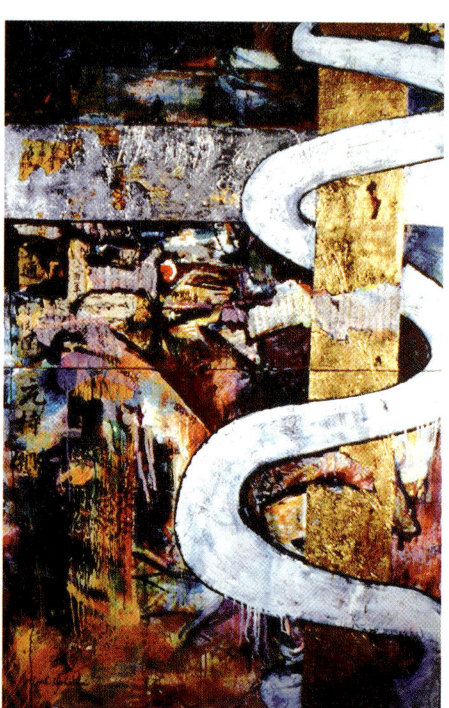

B. Zen Series #15. Mixed media on linen, 72" x 48" (diptych).

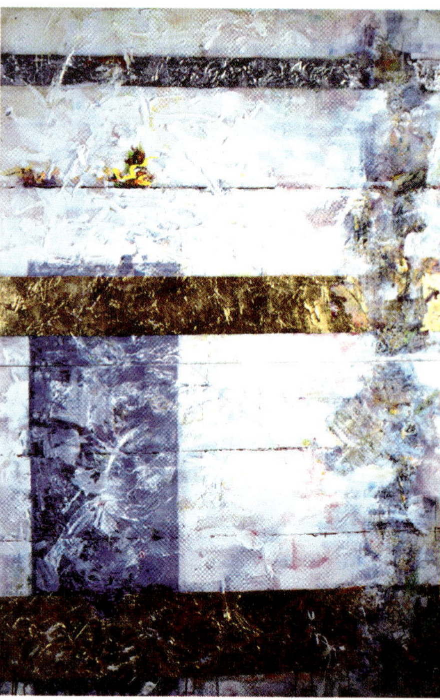

C. Zen Series #18. Mixed media on linen, 72" x 48" (diptych).

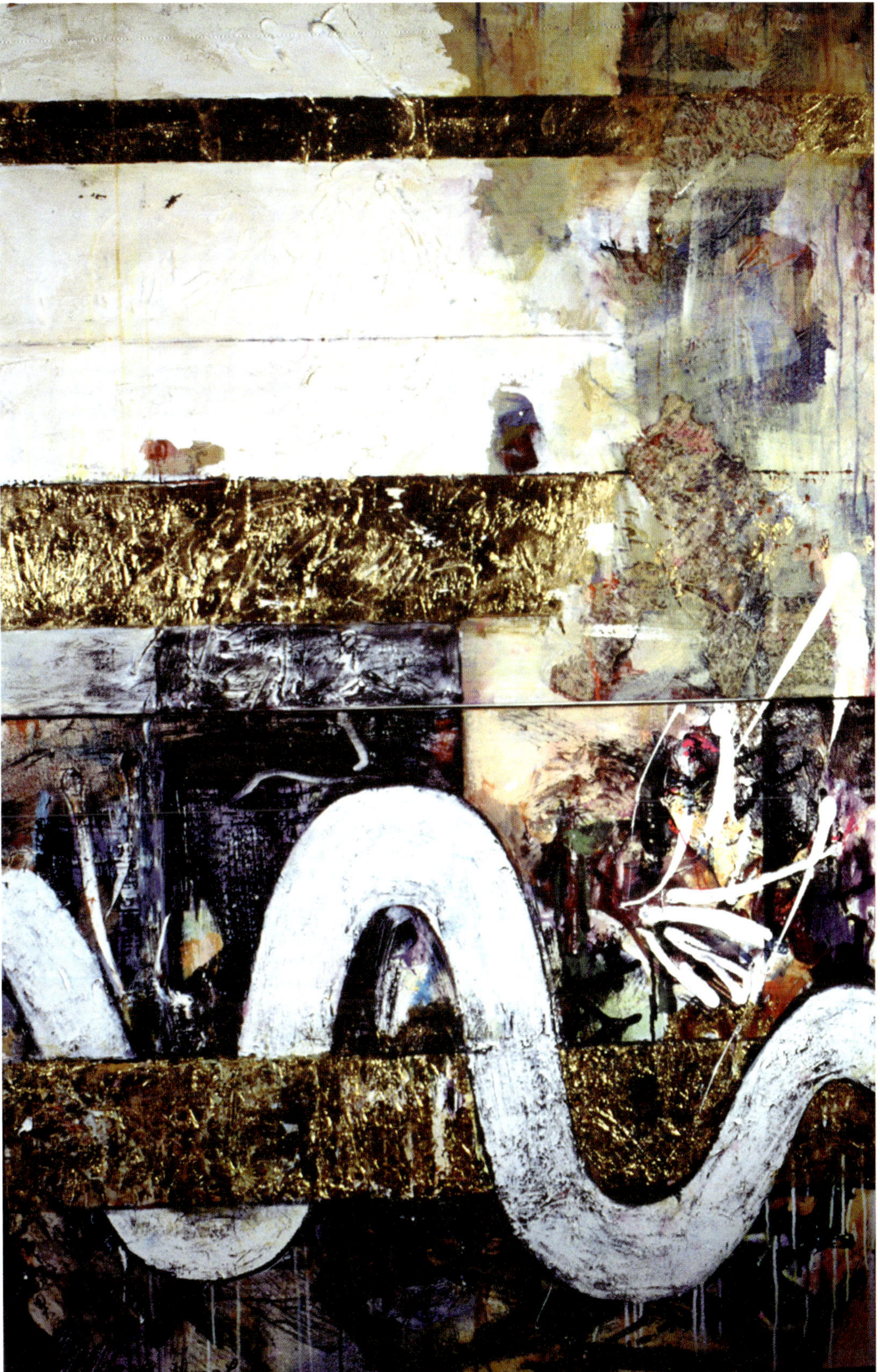

D. Zen Series #17. Mixed media on linen, 72" x 48" (diptych). Award: First Prize, Copley Society, Boston, MA.

PRICE LIST

A $2,500

B $4,000

C $5,000

D $7,000

Randy Eckard was born in 1949 and raised in Hickory, NC. He now spends May to November of each year in Vermont and the winter months in Florida. With his migratory lifestyle, Eckard has drawn inspiration from the contrasts between Florida winters and New England summers. He is fascinated by the ever-changing patterns of light on the landscape.

In 1973, Randy graduated from the Ringling School of Art in Sarasota, FL, with a degree in Commercial Design/Advertising. He has since done everything from sign painting to pottery.

Eckard works with watercolor in a photorealistic style. He uses landscapes and building façades as subject matter. Close attention to detail, texture and color are integral to his realistic vision, and light plays an essential role in his paintings. The subtle or dramatic interplay of light and shadow becomes the subject of the painting, more than the objects the light reveals.

Randy has received over 100 awards in juried watercolor shows throughout New England and the Southeast.

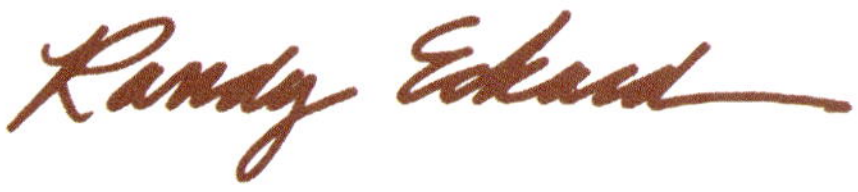

RD 1, Box 4690
Wolcott, VT 05680

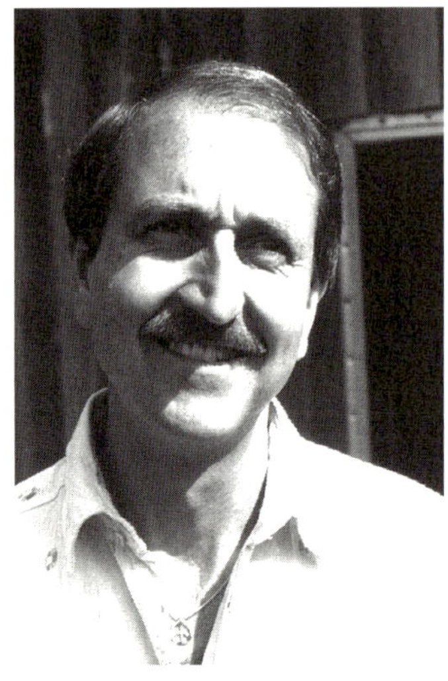

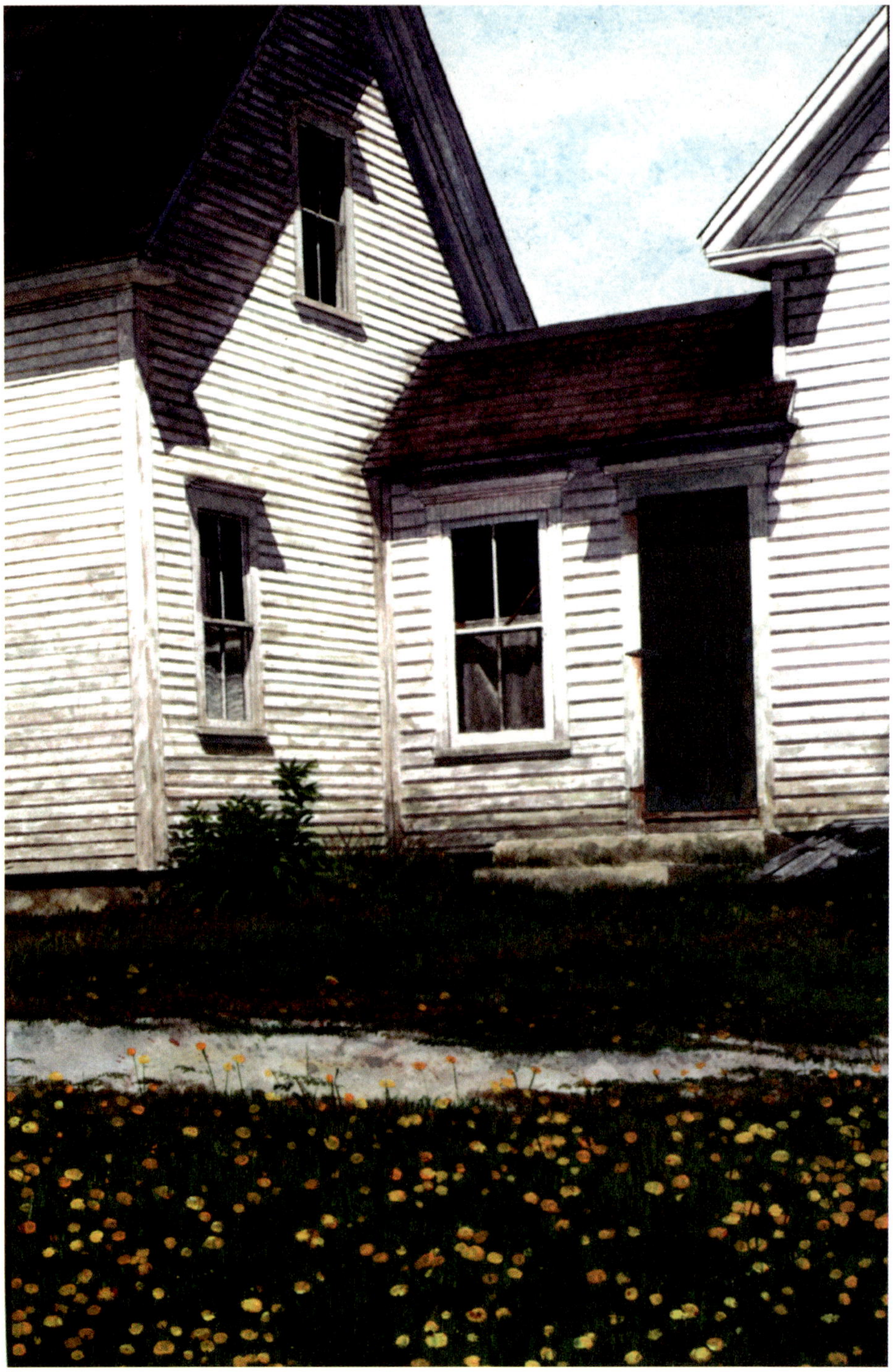

A. A Bit of Maine. Watercolor, 12" x 8".

PRICE LIST

A..........................$450
B......................$2,400
C......................$1,800
D......................$2,000

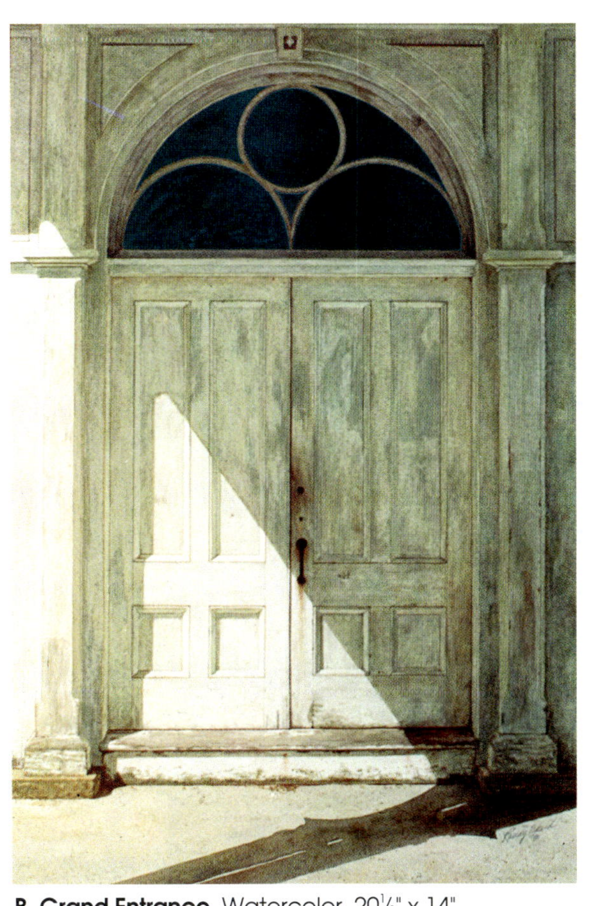

B. Grand Entrance. Watercolor, 20½" x 14".

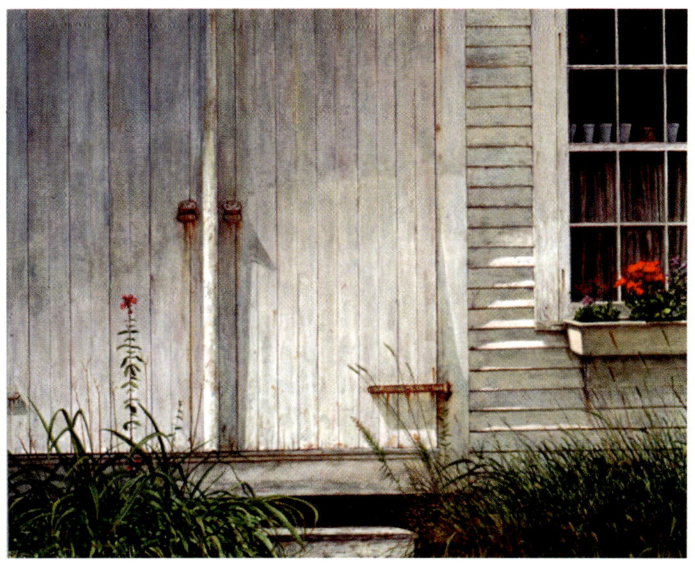

C. New England Style. Watercolor, 14" x 20½".

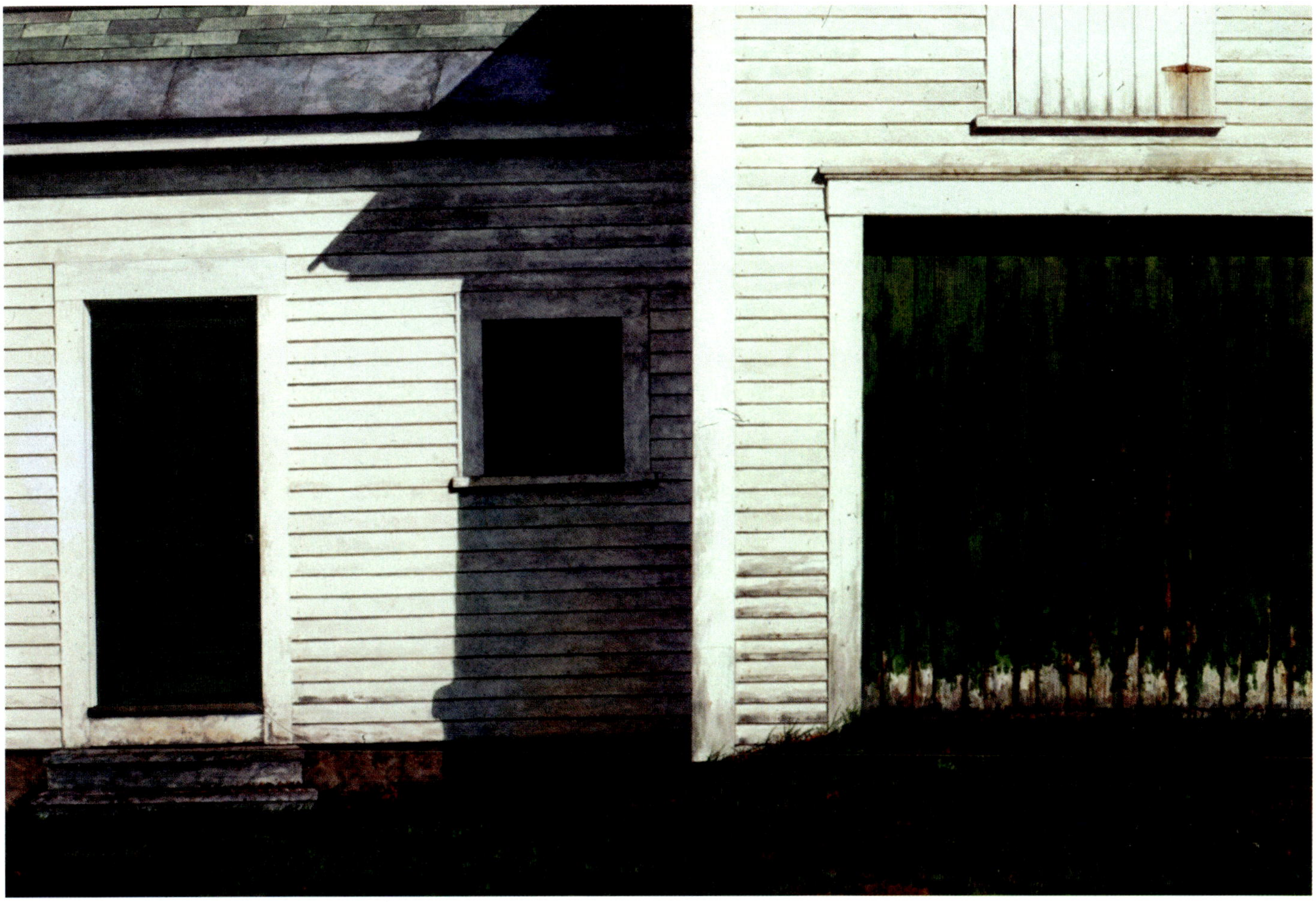

D. Along Route 2. Watercolor, 14" x 20½".

James Flora was born in Bellefontaine, OH, when Woodrow Wilson was president. He studied for two years at Urbana University before transferring to the Art Academy of Cincinnati for a further five years of training. Flora and his bride then moved to Connecticut, where they presently live.

After taking a cruise around the world in 1980, Flora began to focus on his present subject matter, the great ocean liners of the past. Flora works mainly with acrylics, the medium he finds to be his best tool for rendering the exacting detail of his ships. While he portrays the ships themselves with painstaking accuracy, Flora lets his imagination dictate the setting. The decks are busy with activity and crowded with people he would like to have accompany him on a cruise. You may find Groucho Marx, Charlie Chaplin and a myriad of other recognizable figures.

Flora began to exhibit his work in 1982. He has shown throughout Connecticut and more recently has had exhibits in New York and New Jersey.

James Flora

7 St. James Place
Rowayton, CT 06853
203-866-4766

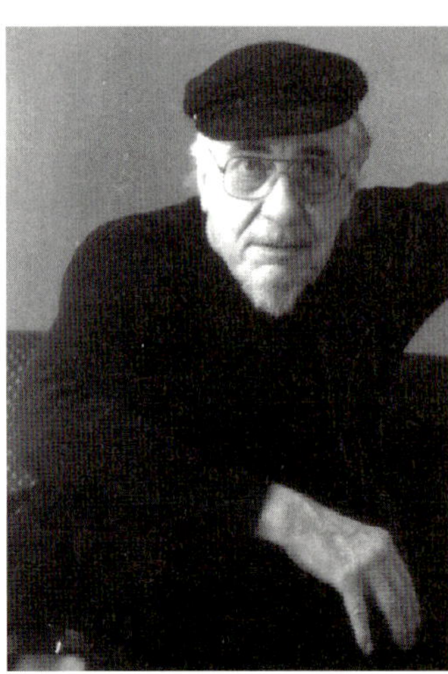

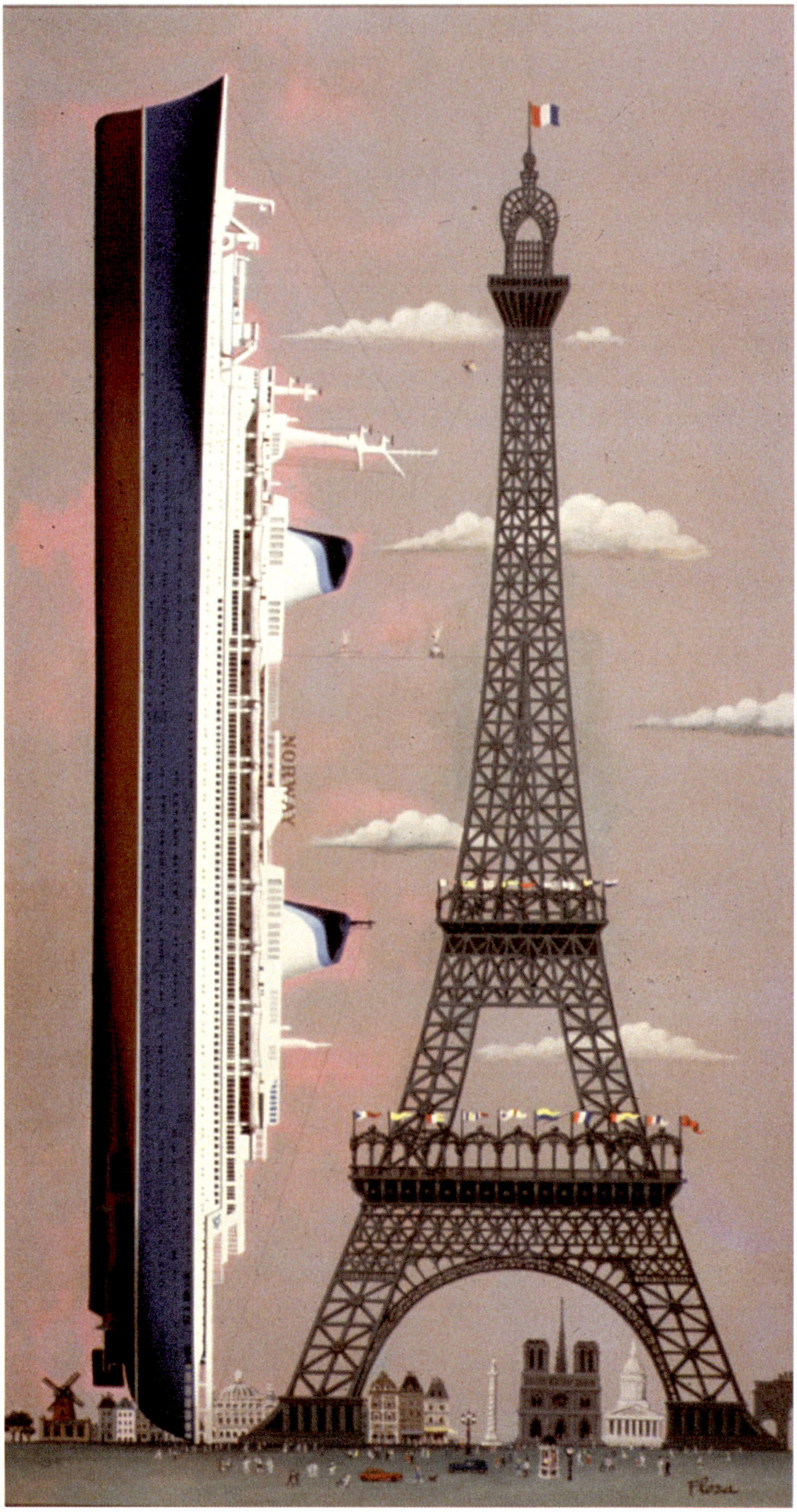

A. *The Norway* and the Eiffel Tower. Acrylic on canvas, 36" x 18".

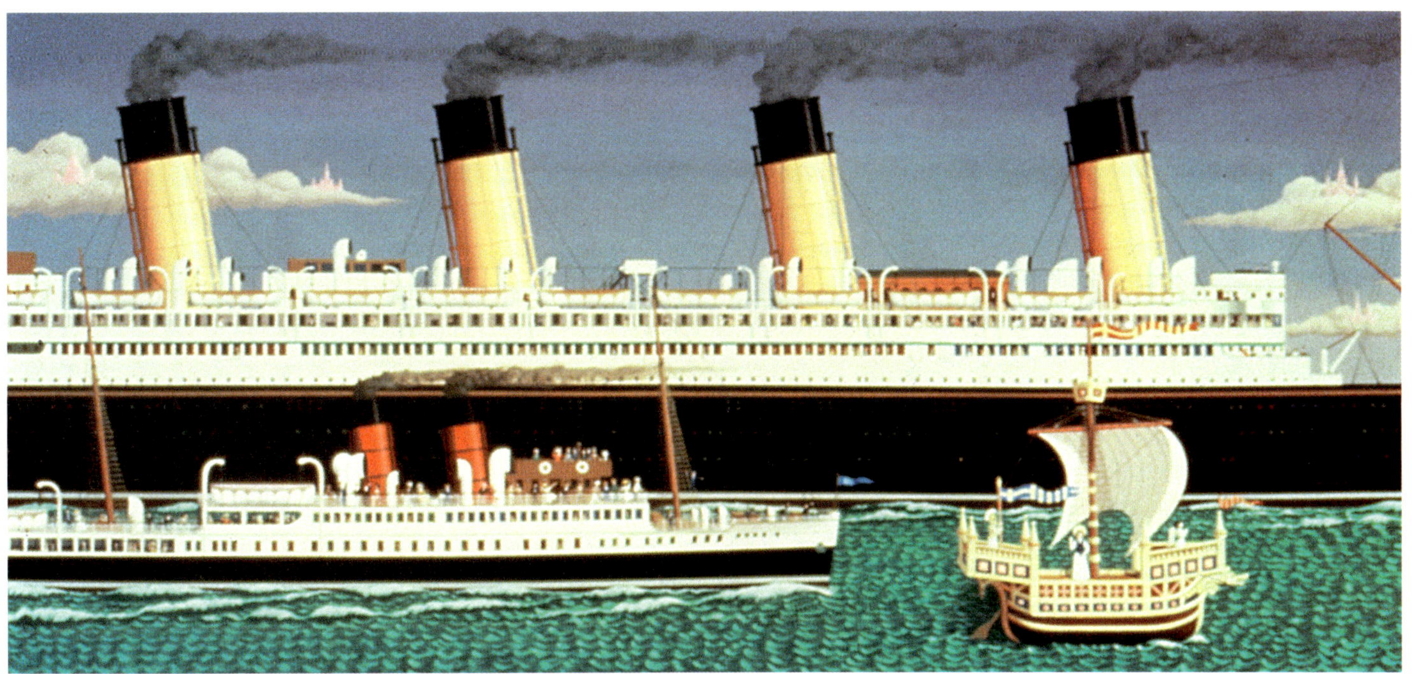

B. *St. Ursula* on the Clyde. Acrylic on canvas, 20" x 48".

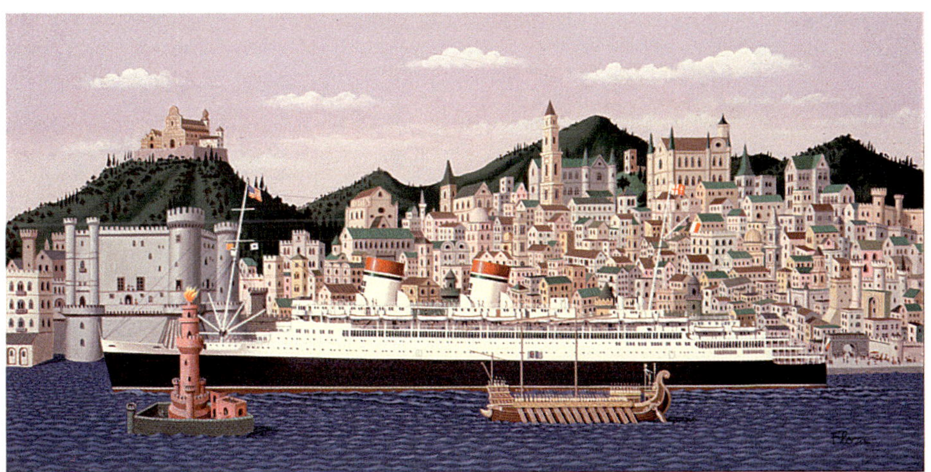

C. The *Conte di Savoie* in Naples Harbor. Acrylic on canvas, 18" x 36".

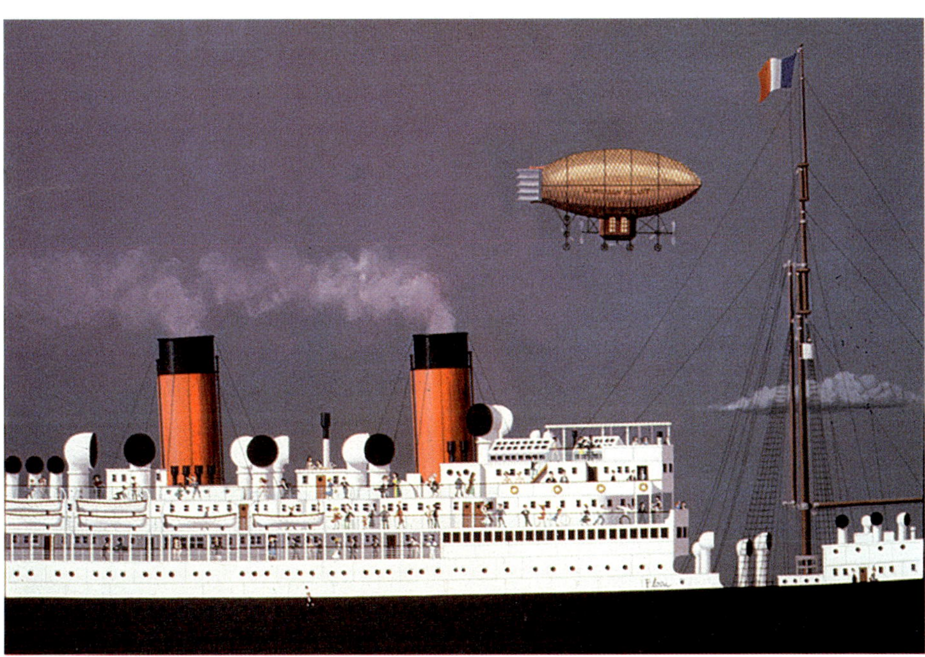

D. *L'Espagne*. Acrylic on canvas, 24" x 36".

PRICE LIST

A $2,500
B $3,000
C $2,500
D $2,500

Chawky Frenn is a young Lebanese artist who lives and works in Boston, MA. He received his BFA from the Massachusetts College of Art in Boston and his MFA from the Tyler School of Art at Temple University in Philadelphia; he spent the second year of graduate studies at Temple Abroad in Rome. Frenn currently devotes his time to painting and teaching.

Frenn executes his oil on canvas paintings with virtuoso technique. It was during his stay in Rome that he found the subject matter that has engaged him since: old, broken dolls' heads heaped in a storefront. These dolls became metaphors for helpless children, the weak, the poor and the manipulated. Frenn's work is an active meditation on man's struggles with good and evil, mortality and eternity, illusion and truth, spirit and flesh...

Frenn's work has been exhibited nationally, and has received positive critical attention, including reviews in *The Boston Globe* and *Art New England*. His work is included in the collection of Mr. Luis A. Ferre, founder of the Museo de Arte de Ponce, PR.

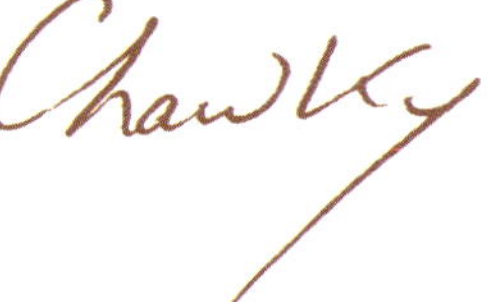

79 Waltham Street
Boston, MA 02118
617-423-6904

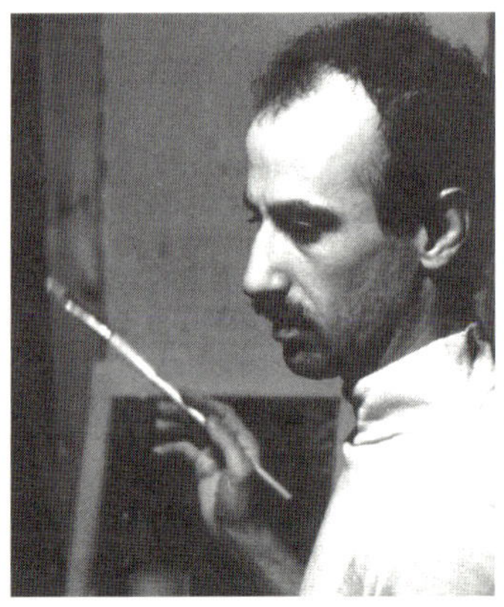

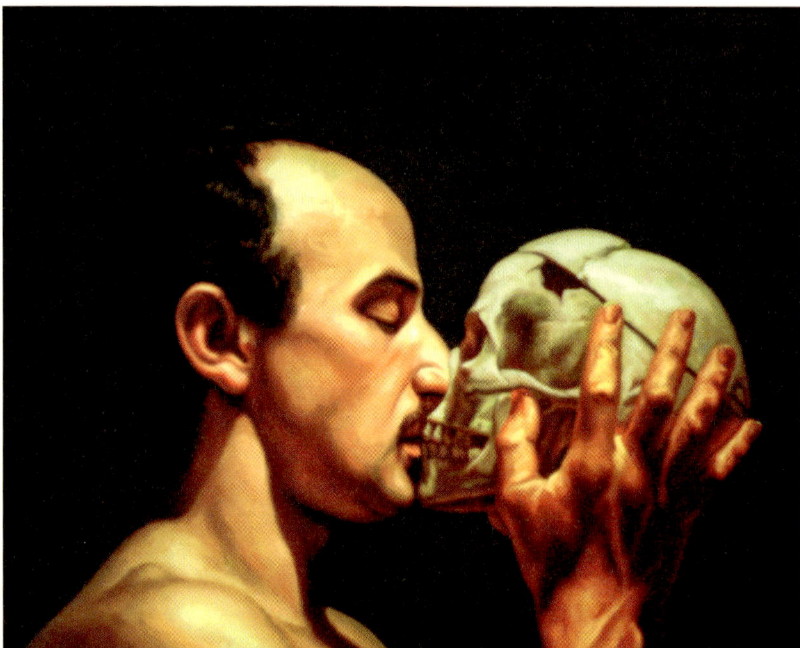

A. The Kiss. Oil on canvas, 48" x 60".

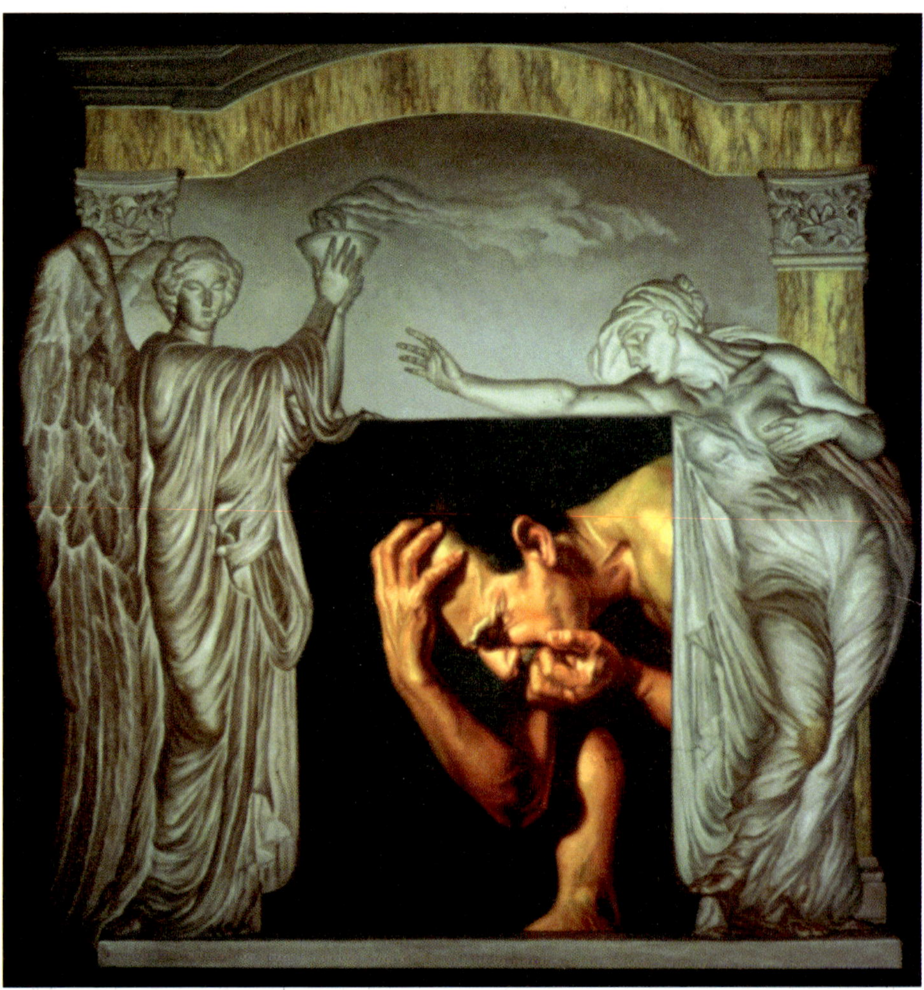

B. Between Spirit and Flesh. Oil on canvas, 84" x 92".

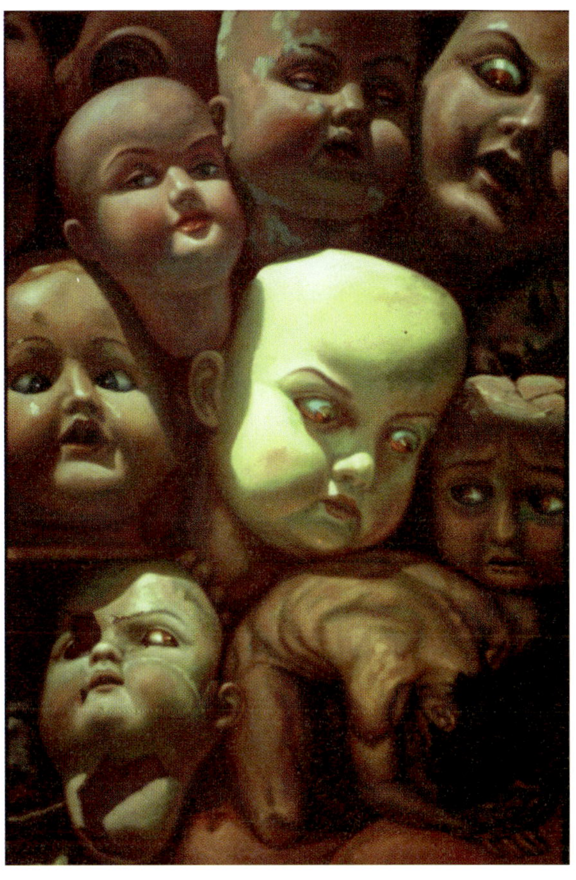

C. The Sleep of Reason Produces Monsters.
Oil on canvas, 72" x 48".

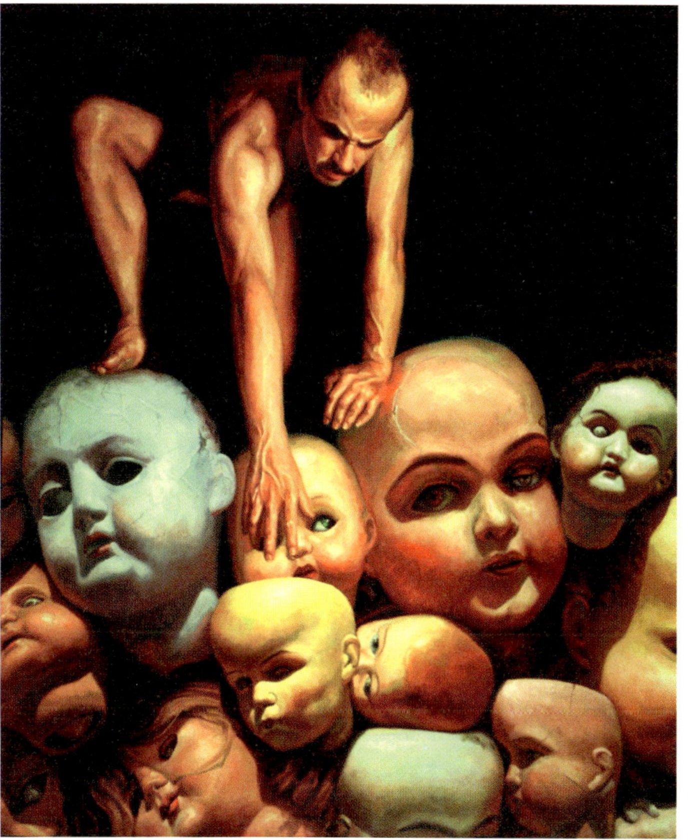

D. Ton Silence M'appelle. Oil on canvas, 72" x 48".

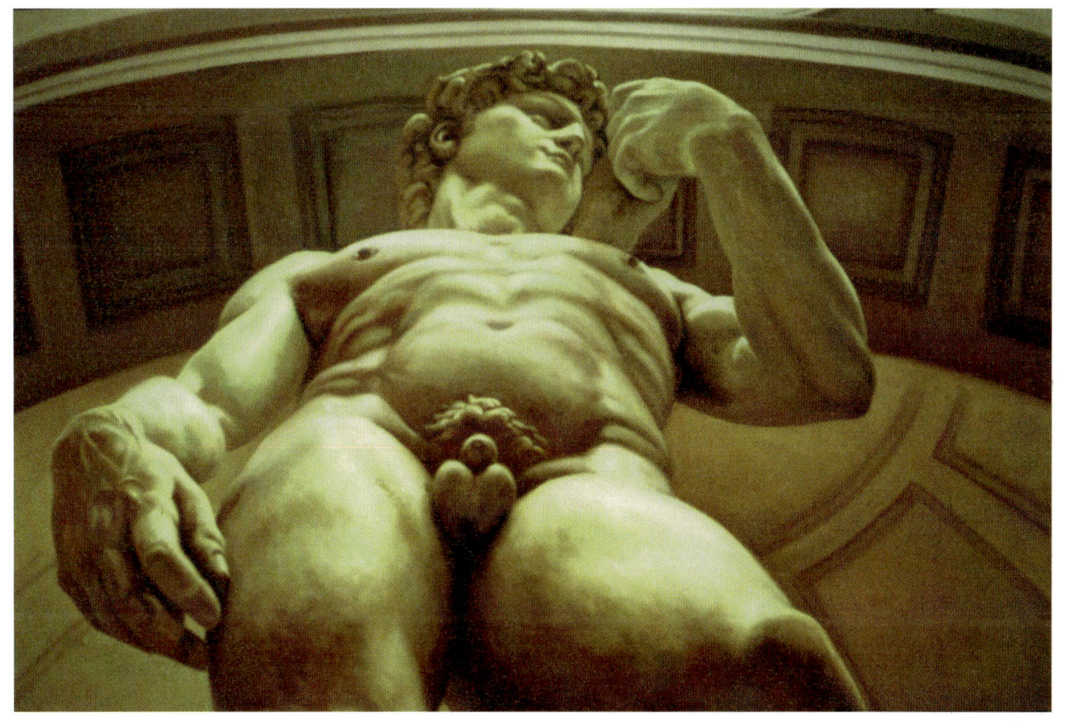

E. Pornography is in the Eye of the Beholder. Oil on canvas, 48" x 72".

PRICE LIST

A $9,000
B $10,500
C $6,500
D $6,500
E $6,500

Represented by
The Lowe Gallery
Atlanta, GA, and
Santa Monica, CA
Goforth-Rittenhouse Galleries
Philadelphia, PA

Tighe Hanson

Tighe Hanson was born in Iowa and lived in various locations throughout his childhood. He received formal art training at the University of Iowa, from which he graduated in 1979 with a BFA. Since 1980, Hanson has lived and worked in the Boston area. He currently maintains a studio in Somerville, MA.

Hanson usually paints in acrylics on canvas, working and reworking his images to achieve a kind of dialogue between the various elements. His paintings mix figurative, landscape, still life and abstract elements; the images are from life, photographs and imagination. It is his hope that ultimately there can be a dialogue between the painting and the viewer.

During the past four years, Hanson has had three solo shows, including a 1991 show at the Blue Mountain Gallery in New York City. His work has been exhibited in group and juried shows in the Boston area, as well as in Connecticut and New York. Among his awards is the Grumbacher Award for Best in Show from the annual "New England Juried Exhibition" sponsored by the South Shore Art Center, Cohasset, MA.

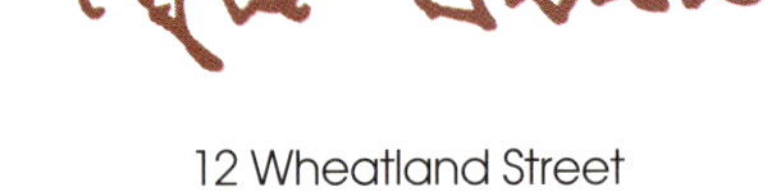

12 Wheatland Street
Somerville, MA 02145
617-625-8596

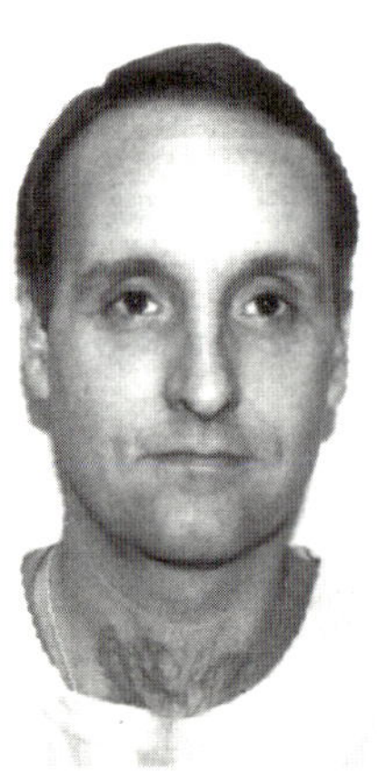

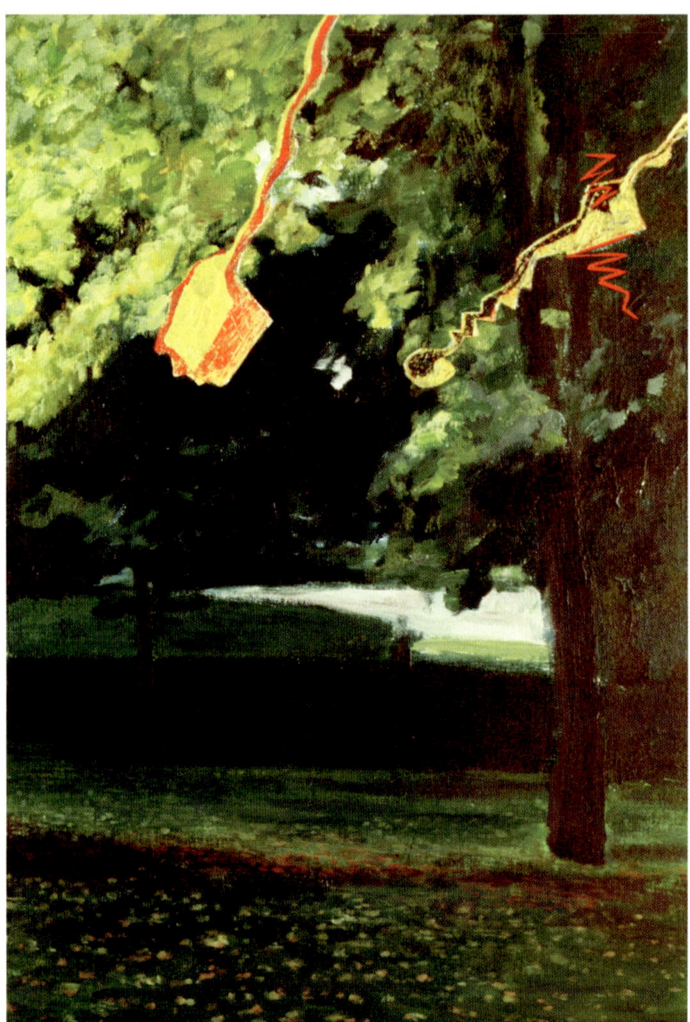

A. Swoop-Swoop. Acrylic on canvas, 26" x 18".

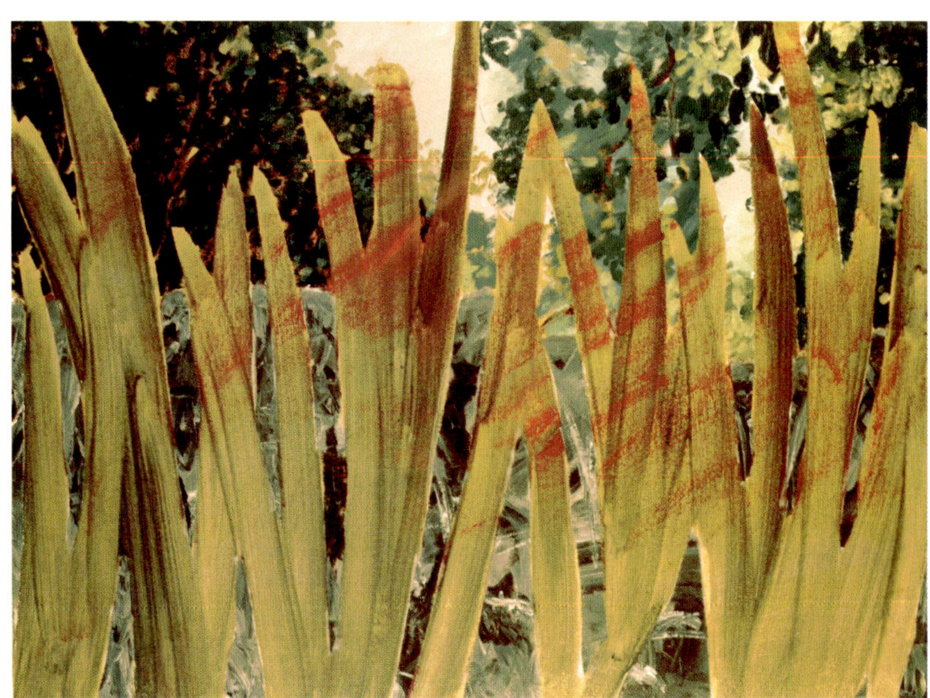

B. Big Grass. Acrylic on canvas, 26" x 36".

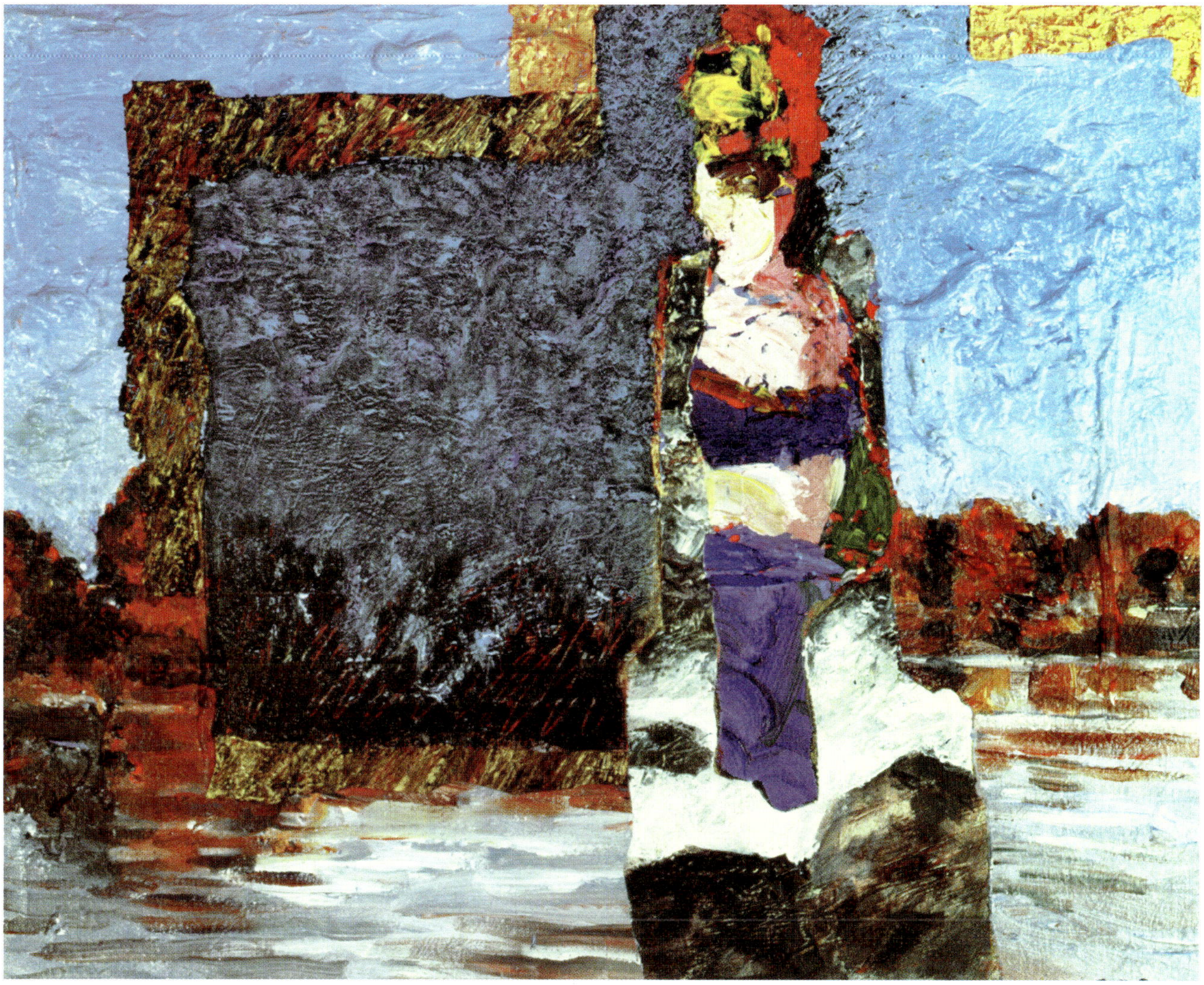

C. (above) **Autumn Goddess.**
Acrylic on canvas, 16" x 20".

PRICE LIST

A $1,100

B $1,100

C $750

D $600

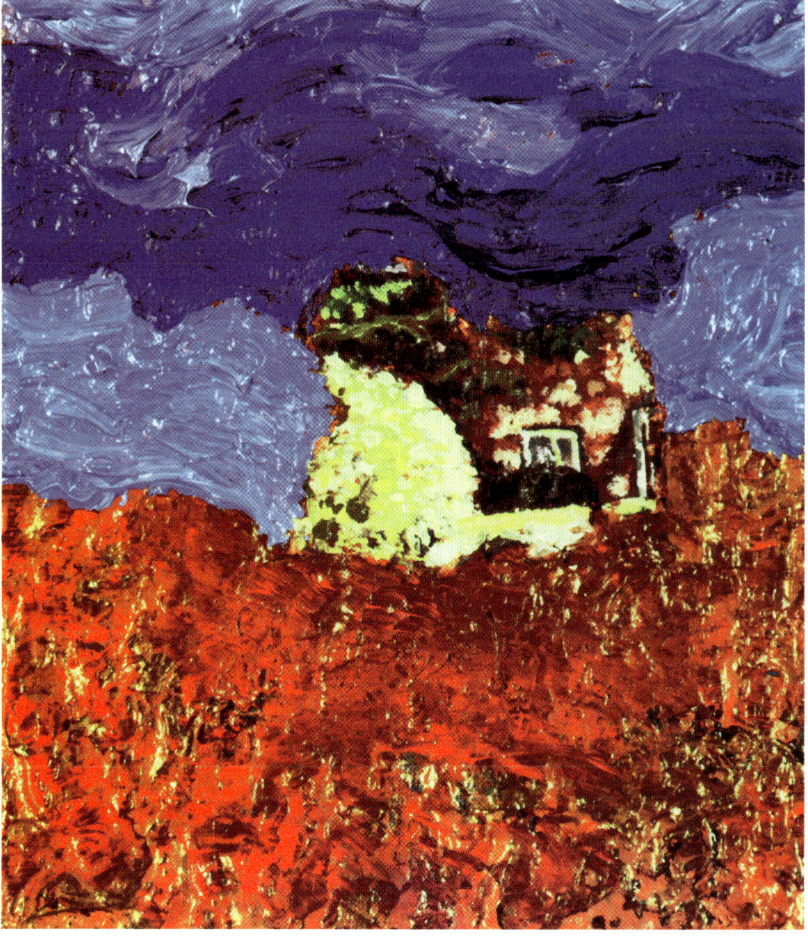

D. (left) **The Meadow.**
Acrylic on canvas, 9" x 8".

Timothy Harney

Timothy Harney is a Massachusetts native. He was born in Beverly, where he still lives, in 1955. His studio is a short distance away in Marblehead. Harney attended the University of Massachusetts, Amherst, receiving his BFA in 1983 and an MFA in Painting in 1985. He currently teaches painting and drawing at the University of New Hampshire and the DeCordova Museum School in Lincoln, MA.

Harney works in oil, acrylic, charcoal, mixed media collage and anything else in between. His paintings vary in size from the large-scale to miniatures. People are Harney's primary subject, and his portraits are intensely personal. He endows them with an expressive character that he develops through his use of color.

Since 1980, Harney has had 16 solo shows, his most recent one at the Cliff Michel Gallery in Seattle, WA. Group exhibitions have included shows at the Museum of Fine Arts in Boston and in New York at the American Academy and Institute of Arts and Letters.

T Harney

22 Broadway
Beverly, MA 01915
508-922-5685

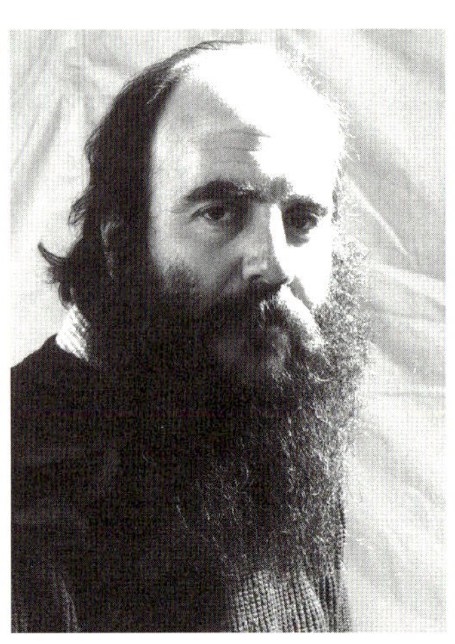

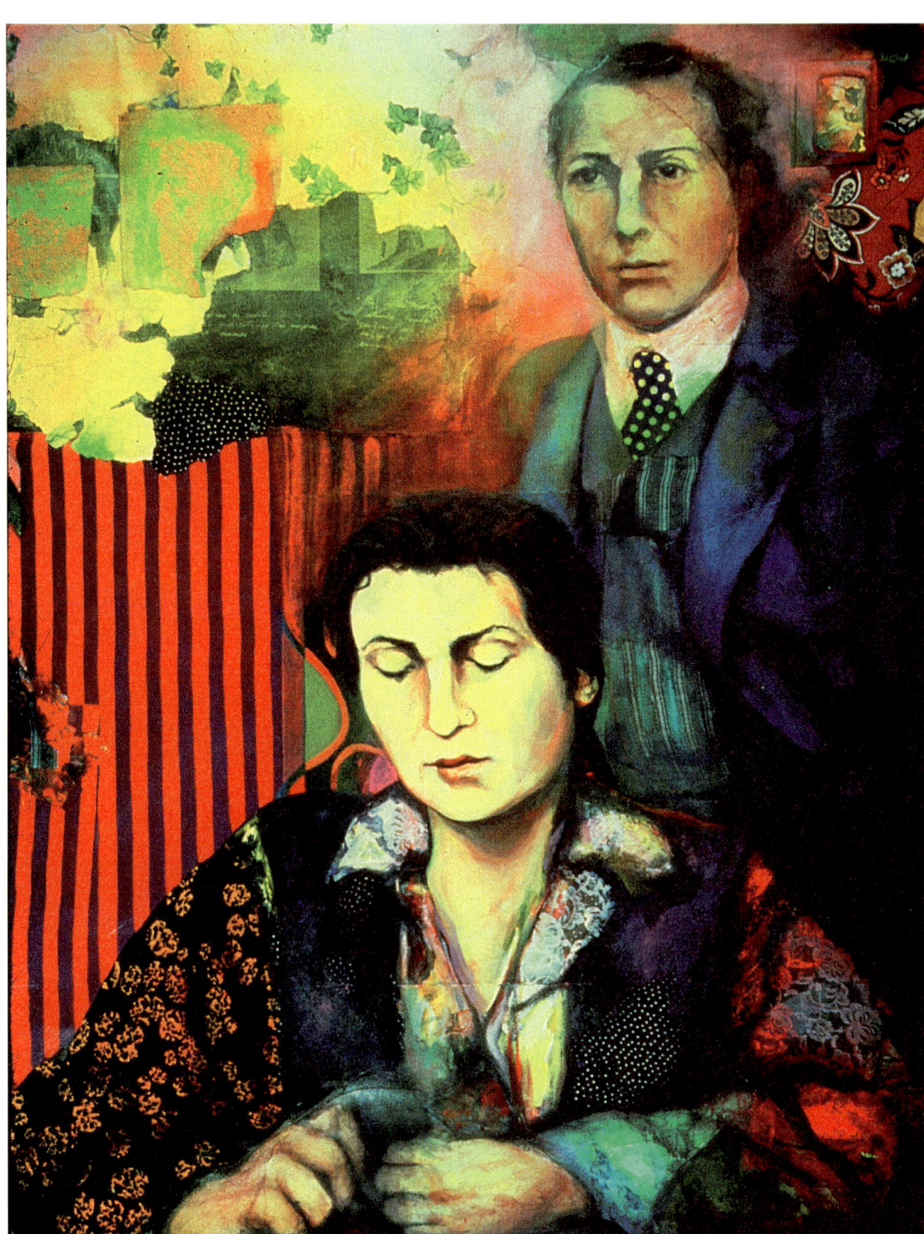

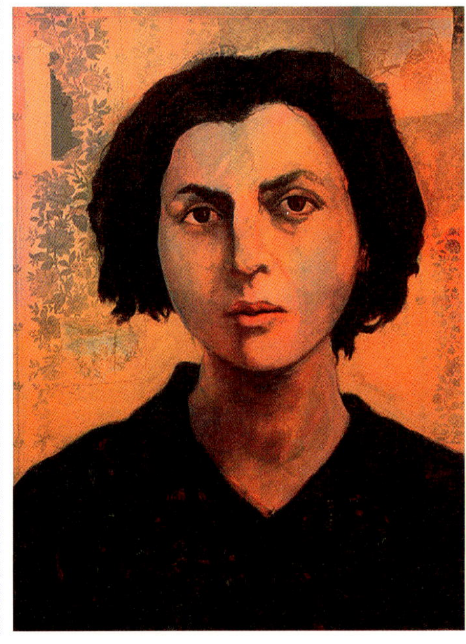

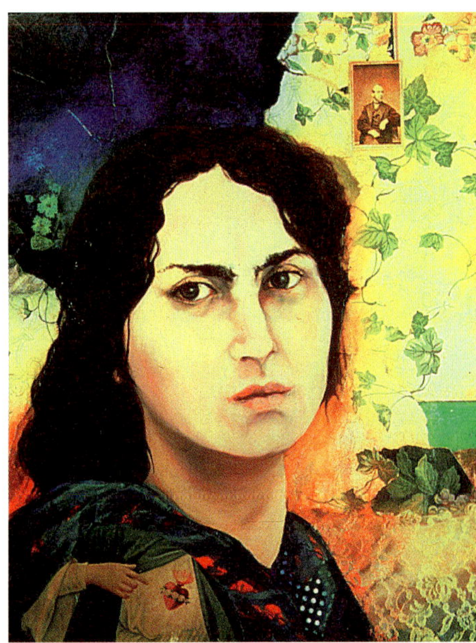

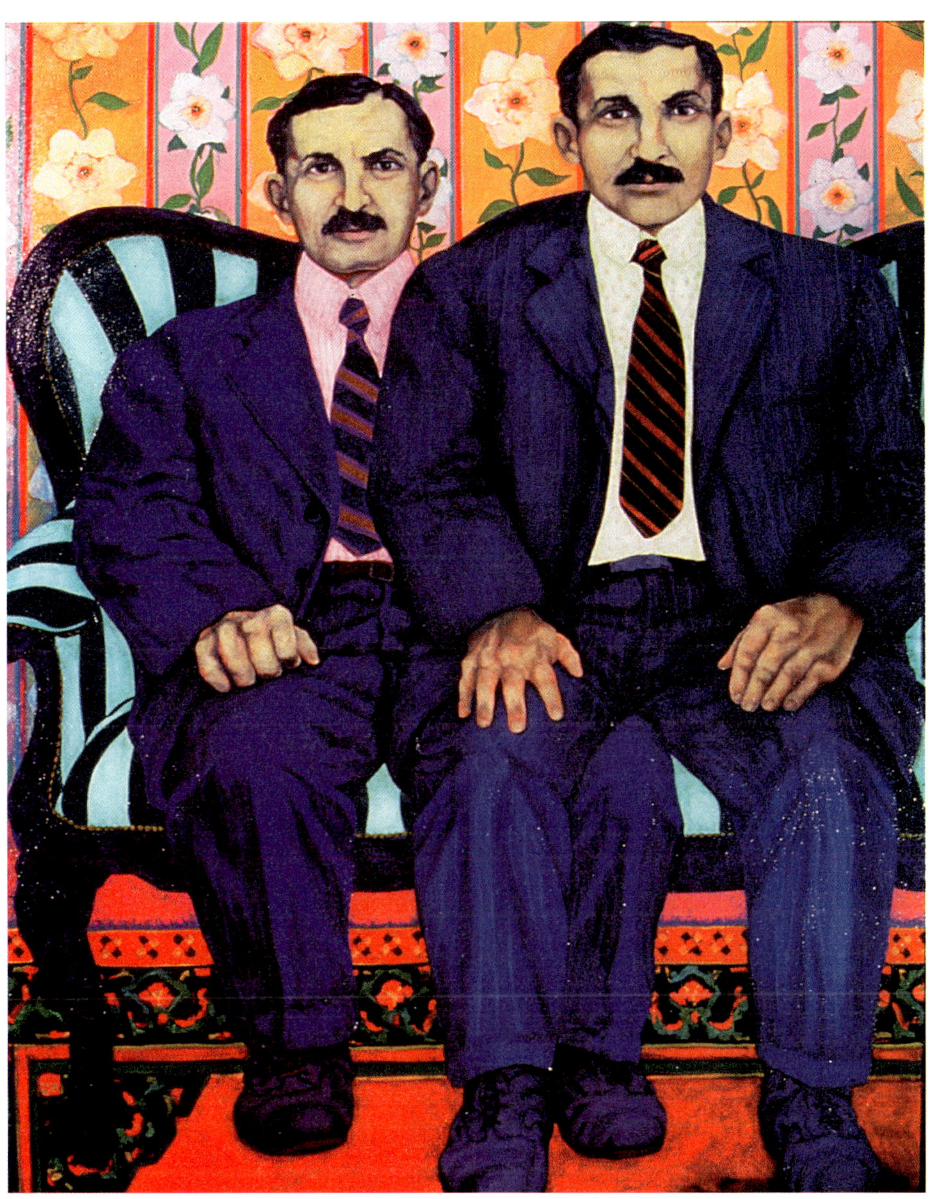

PRICE LIST

A $5,000
B $2,000
C $1,400
D $7,000
E $1,800
F $1,800

Represented by
Clark Gallery
Lincoln, MA

A. (opposite top)
The Reading, Pelham and Paris.
Acrylic and mixed media collage/paper, 56¾" x 45".

B. (opposite bottom left)
The Painter of Tbilisi.
Acrylic and mixed media collage/paper, 40" x 30".

C. (opposite bottom right)
Homage to Rossetti and My Brother Bob.
Oil, acrylic and mixed media collage/paper, 28½" x 22½".

D. (above)
The Armenian Brothers.
Oil on canvas, 74" x 61".

E. (bottom right inside)
Three Friends.
Acrylic and mixed media collage/paper, 33" x 20½".

F. (bottom right outside)
The Imperfect Vow.
Acrylic and mixed media collage/paper, 44" x 30".

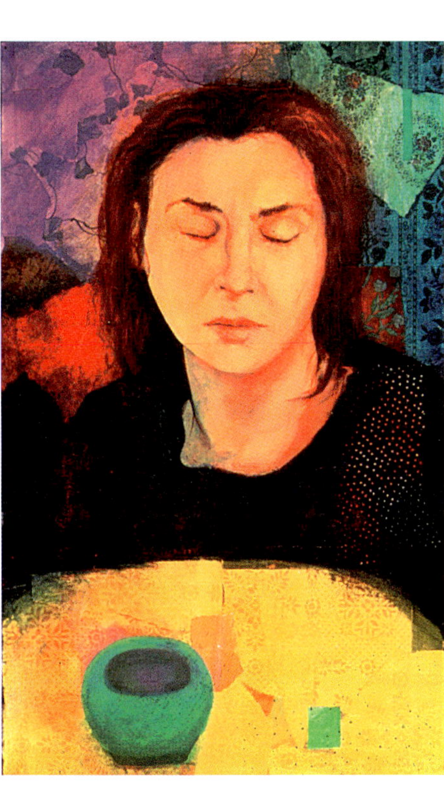

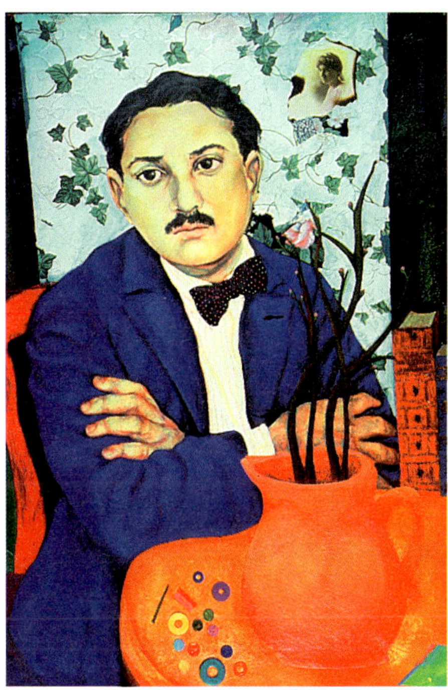

Suzanne **Hodes**

Suzanne Hodes grew up in New York City and finds inspiration in the energy and dynamism of city life. MA. She studied at Radcliffe College and Brandeis University in Massachusetts, and received an MFA from Columbia University in 1962. Hodes now maintains a studio in Waltham, MA.

Hodes works in a variety of media, including oil, pastel and monotype. She imbues her paintings with a strong presence by means of her ability to convey light and atmosphere and her feeling for color and structure. The city, landscapes and expressive portraiture provide themes from which she draws her subject matter.

Hodes has exhibited in over 75 group and one-person shows in New England, New York and the San Francisco area, including shows at the Straus Gallery and Rockefeller University in New York City, the Newport Art Museum in Rhode Island and a current show organized by the Ashuah-Irving Gallery at Beacon Construction in Boston. Collectors of her work include the Fogg Art Museum, the DeCordova Museum and Houghton Mifflin Company.

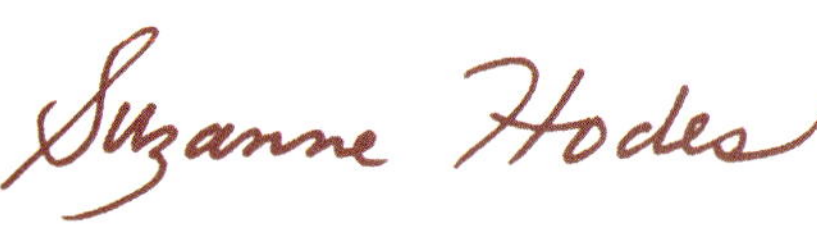

Artists West Studios
144 Moody Street
Waltham, MA 02154
617-894-4124

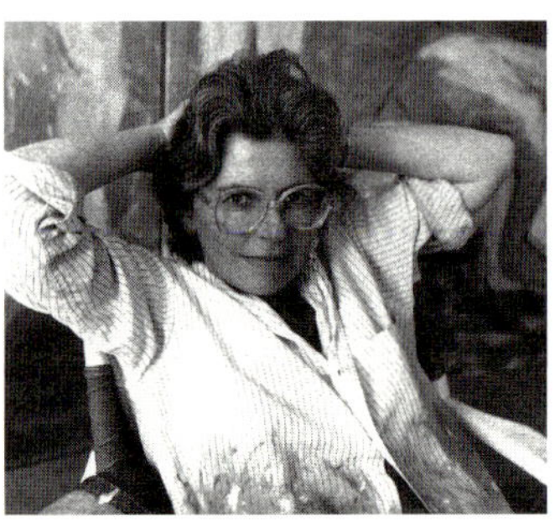

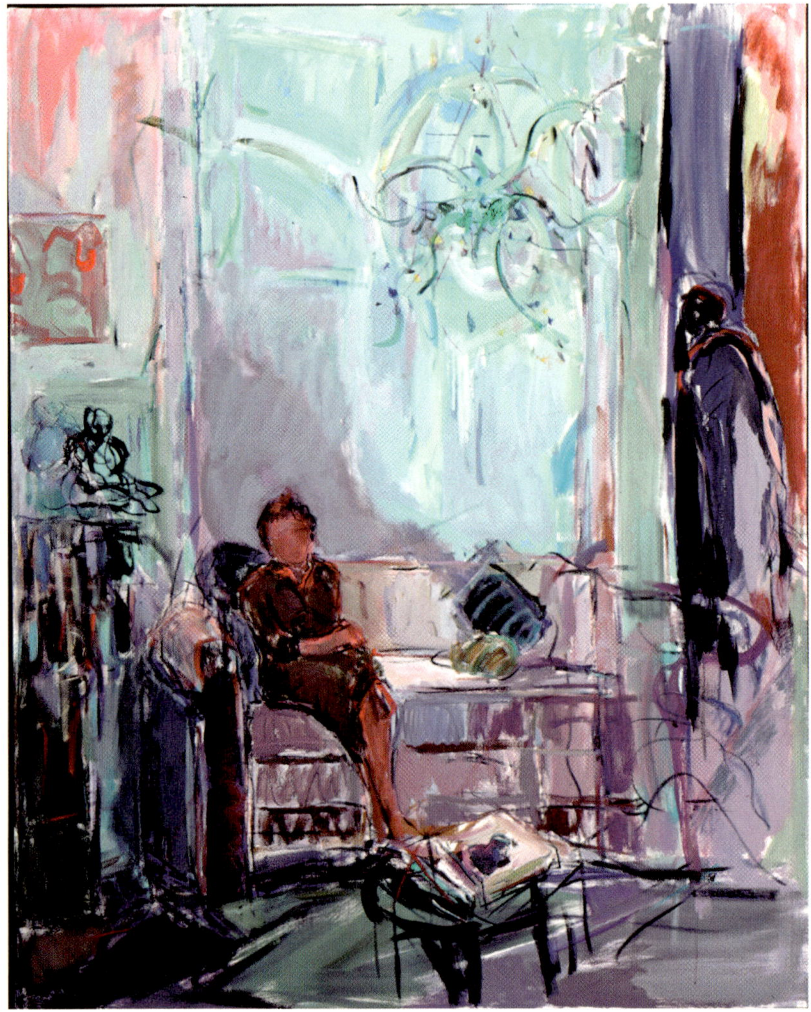

A. Interior with Figures. Oil on canvas, 54" x 44".

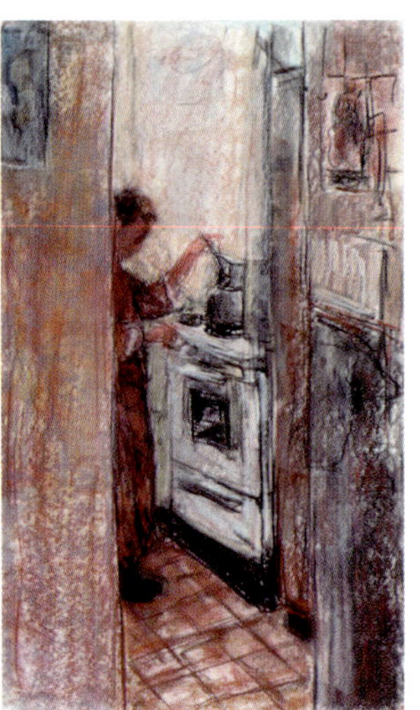

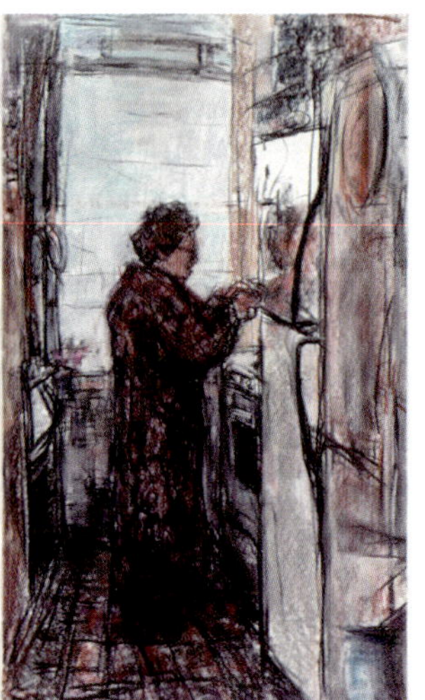

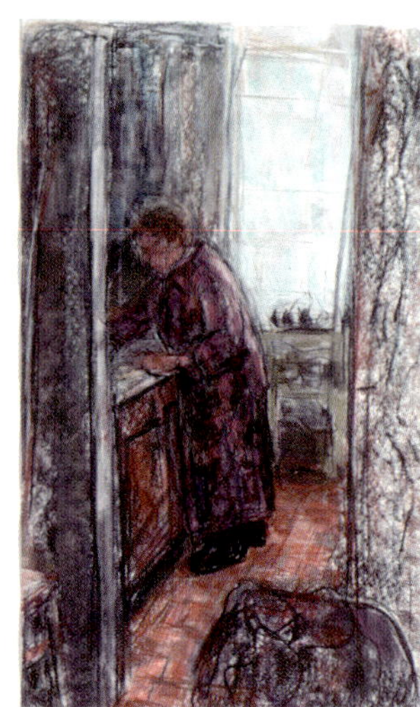

B. My Mother Three Times. Oil on canvas, 50" x 92".

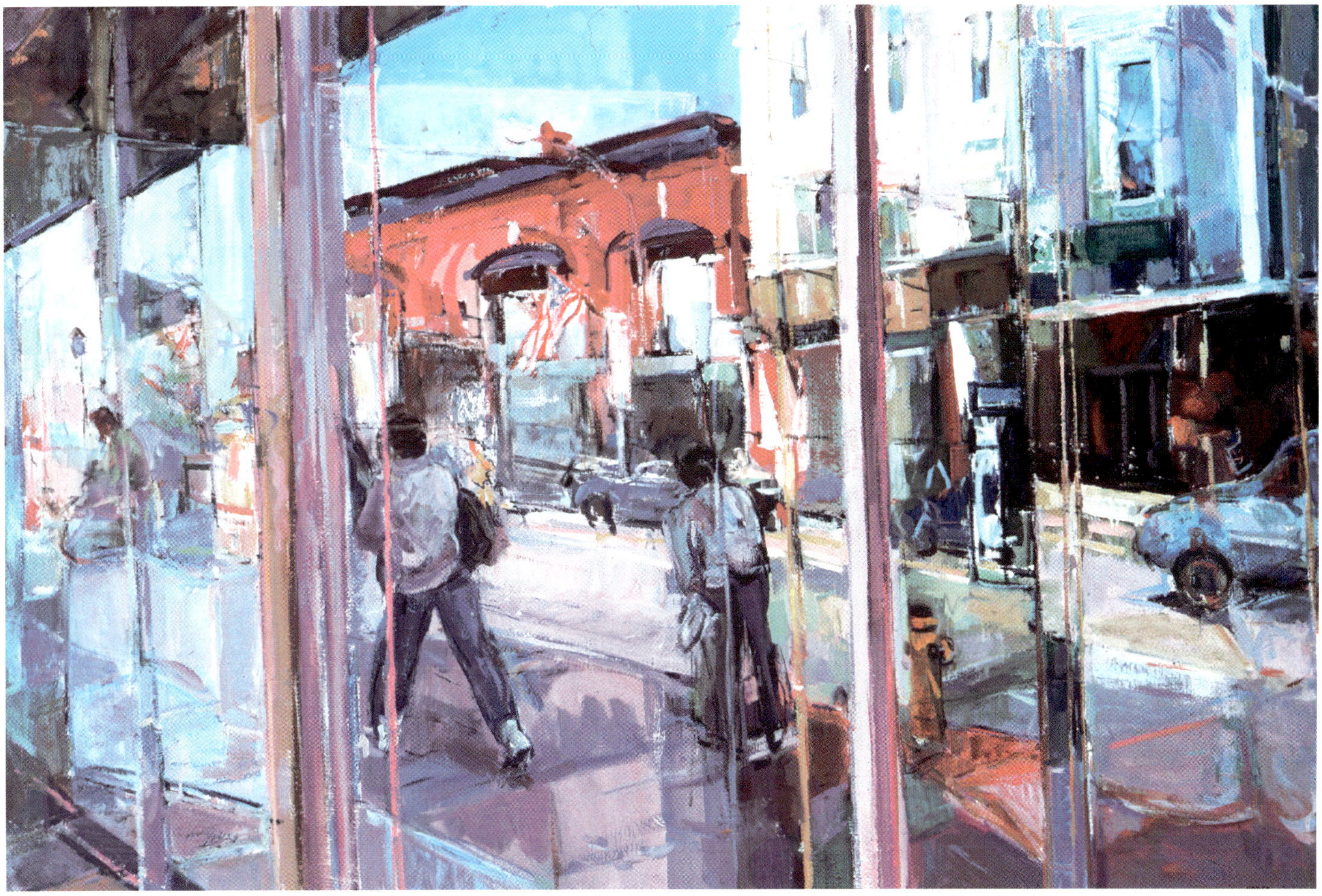

C. Memorial Day Reflections. Oil on canvas, 40" x 60".

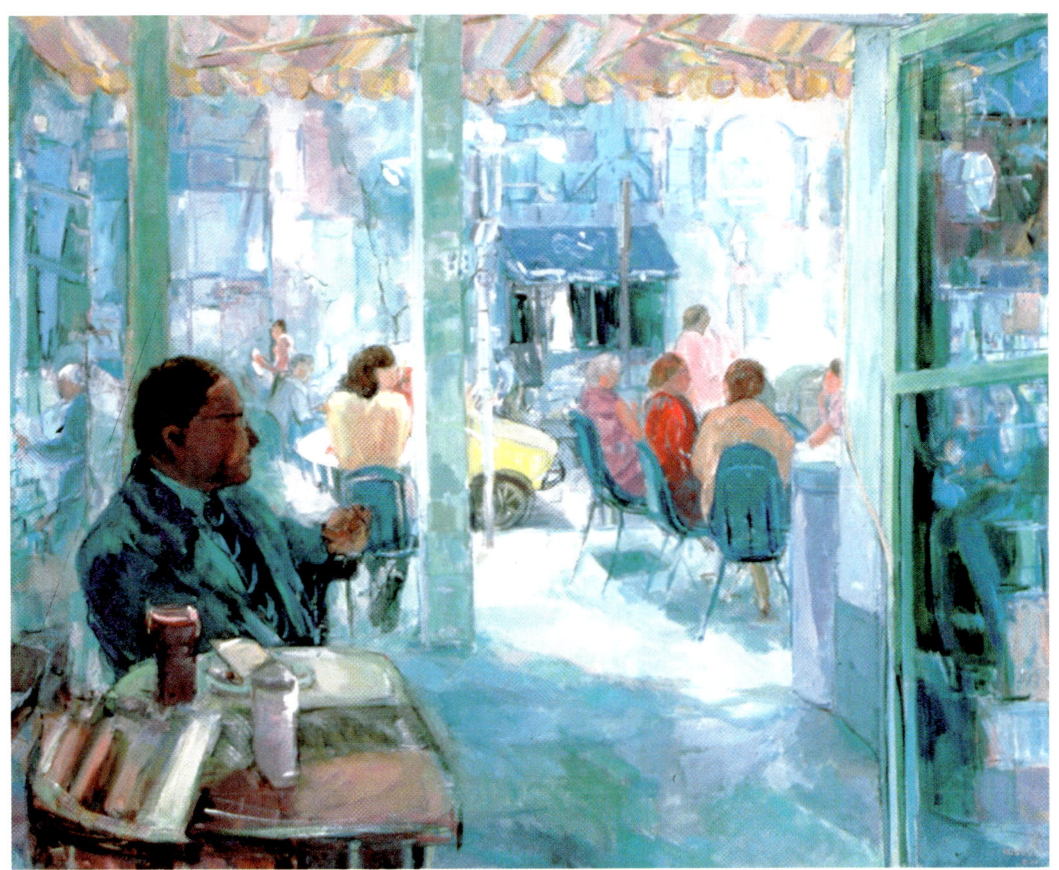

D. Newbury St. Cafe. Oil on canvas, 48" x 60". Courtesy of the Golda Meir House.

PRICE LIST

A $4,800

B $5,600

C $5,000

D $5,600

Represented by
Boston Corporate Art
Boston, MA,
Tofias Gallery
Waltham, MA

Christine Hopkins

Christine Hopkins was raised in Rhode Island and now lives and works in Brookline, MA. She received formal training at Boston University, earning a BFA in 1980. Other training has included course work at the New England School of Photography in 1977. She is now a full-time artist.

Hopkins is an abstract painter who works large scale. Stylistically, her work derives from that of Mark Rothko and other color-field painters. Her pieces aim to transcend the flat surface of the canvas, and Hopkins employs thin layers of acrylic to build texture and form. This technique sustains the luminosity of the pigments and creates a myriad of subtle tones and color gradations on the canvas.

In the past nine years, Hopkins' paintings have been included in over two dozen exhibitions. Recently, her work was a part of "Distinct Voices" at the Federal Reserve Bank Gallery and "New Art '92" at Kingston Gallery, both in Boston. Her painting has been discussed in numerous published reviews, including articles in *The Boston Globe* and *The Boston Phoenix*.

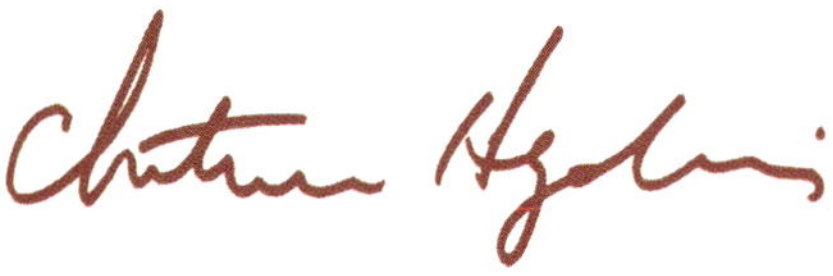

72 St. Paul Street, #3
Brookline, MA 02146
617-730-9432

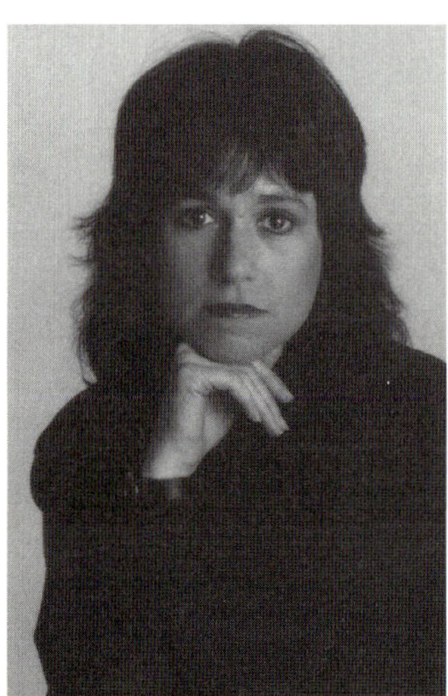

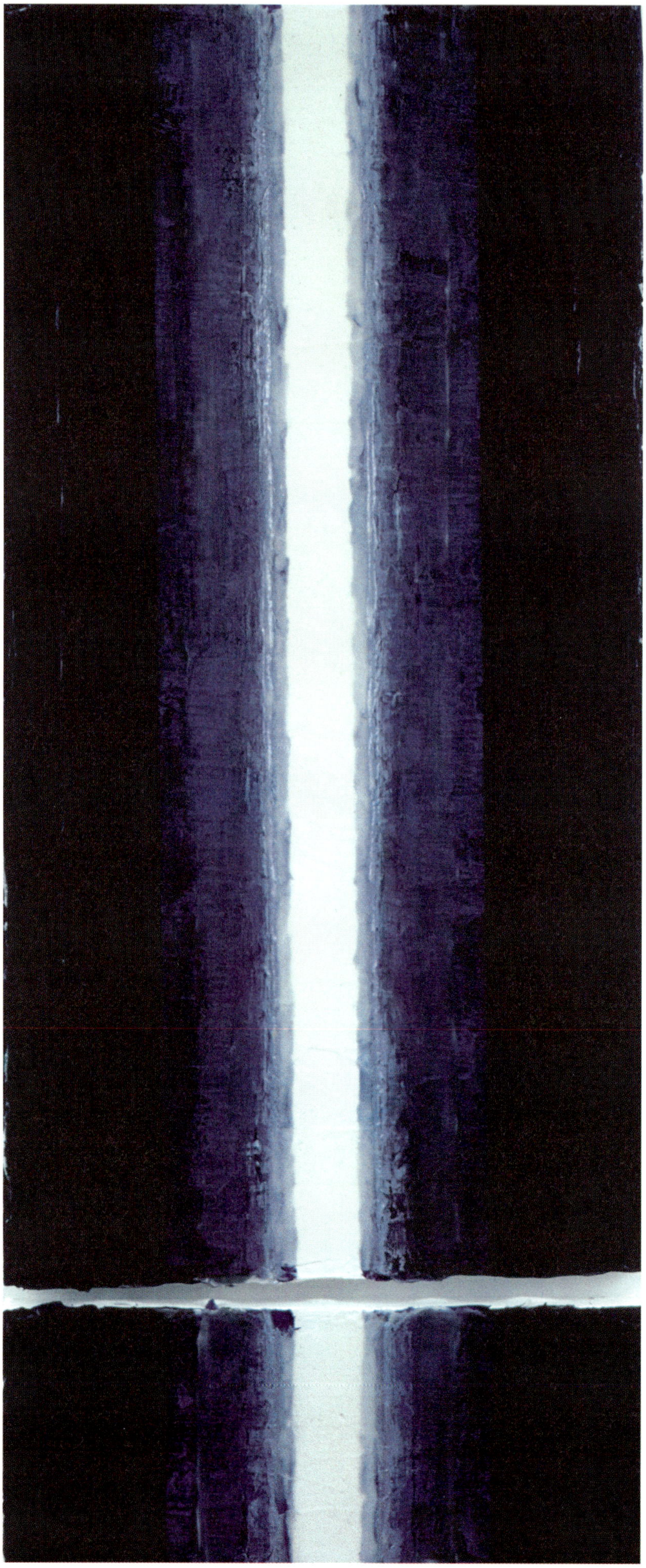

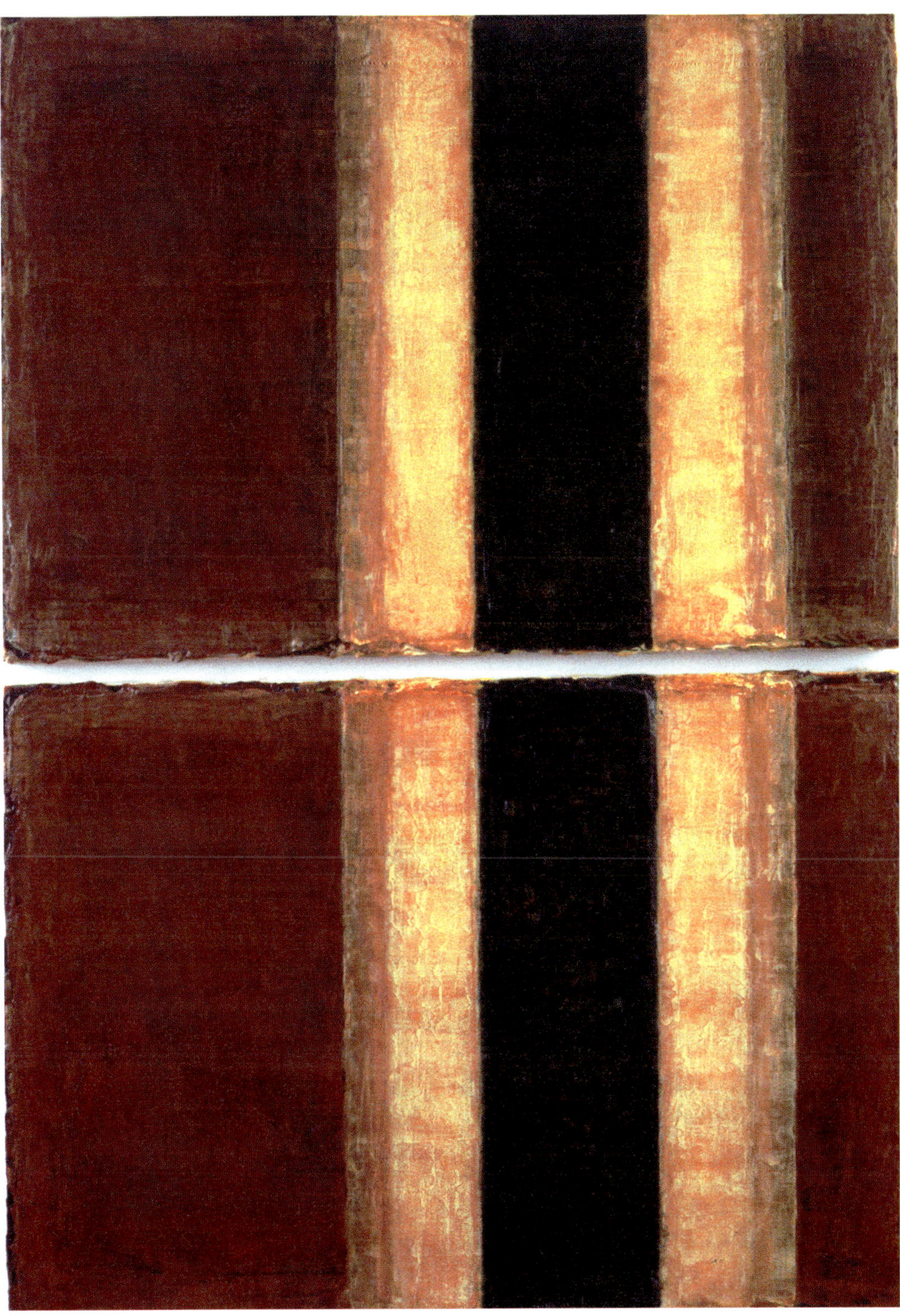

B. Terrazo from El Pazzo. Acrylic on canvas, 56" x 40" (diptych).

A. (opposite) **The Line of Least Resistance.**
Acrylic on canvas, 46" x 20" (diptych).

PRICE LIST

A $2,500

B $3,500

Sarah Hutt

Sarah Hutt has lived in New England for over two decades. She presently resides in Boston where she maintains a studio and independently offers community service aimed at fostering a bond between Boston's art community and the public. Hutt attended the School of the Museum of Fine Arts in Boston.

Hutt works with mixed media, blending the processes of monoprinting, drawing and writing into a form of storytelling. Impressions and images from daily living are combined with written statements of feelings into a universal language/image. She uses words as visual elements within the whole, rather than as descriptive tools

In the past four years, Hutt has exhibited in over 20 group and solo shows in the Boston area. Recently, her work was the focus of a one-woman show at Gallery 28 at the New England School of Art and Design in Boston. Her paintings are in several public and private collections, including that of the DeCordova Museum and the Boston Public Library's Print and Drawing Department. Hutt's awards include a Pollock Krasner Foudation Grant.

Sarah Hutt

1140 Washington Street
Boston, MA 02118
617-482-4722

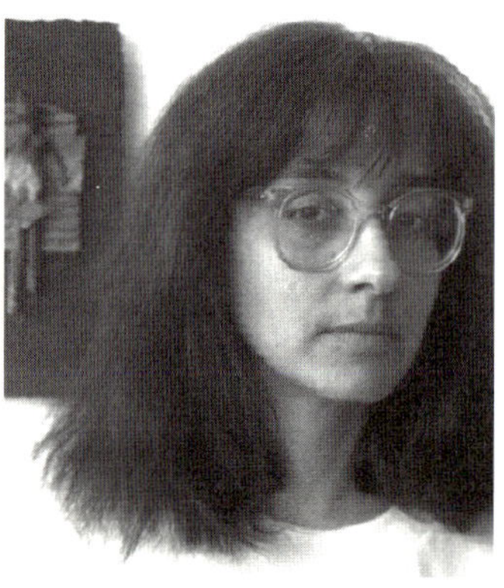

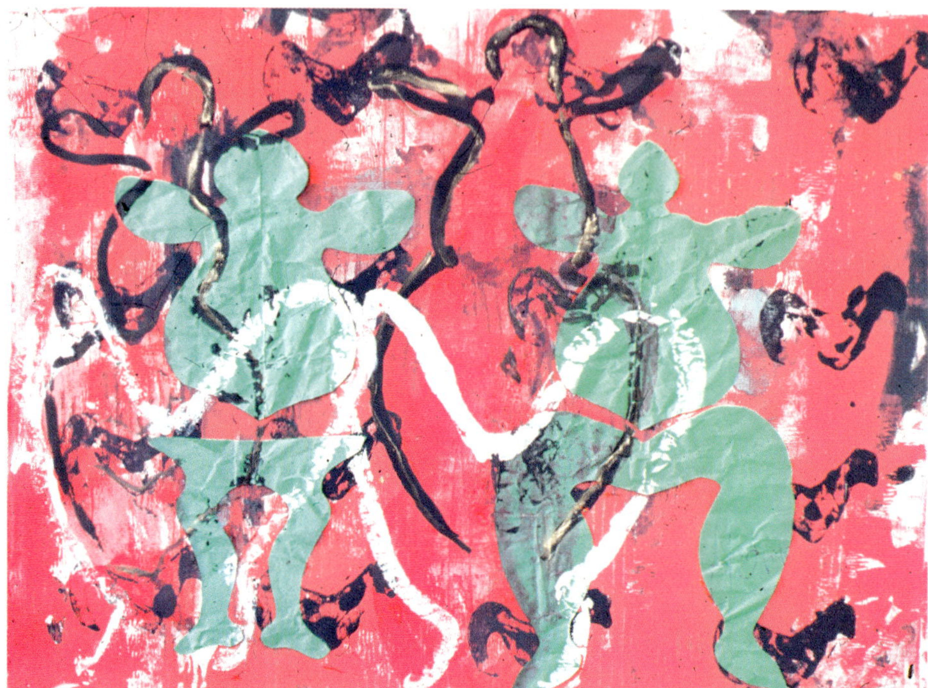

A. Personal Council. Pigment, paint and chalk on paper, 22" x 30".

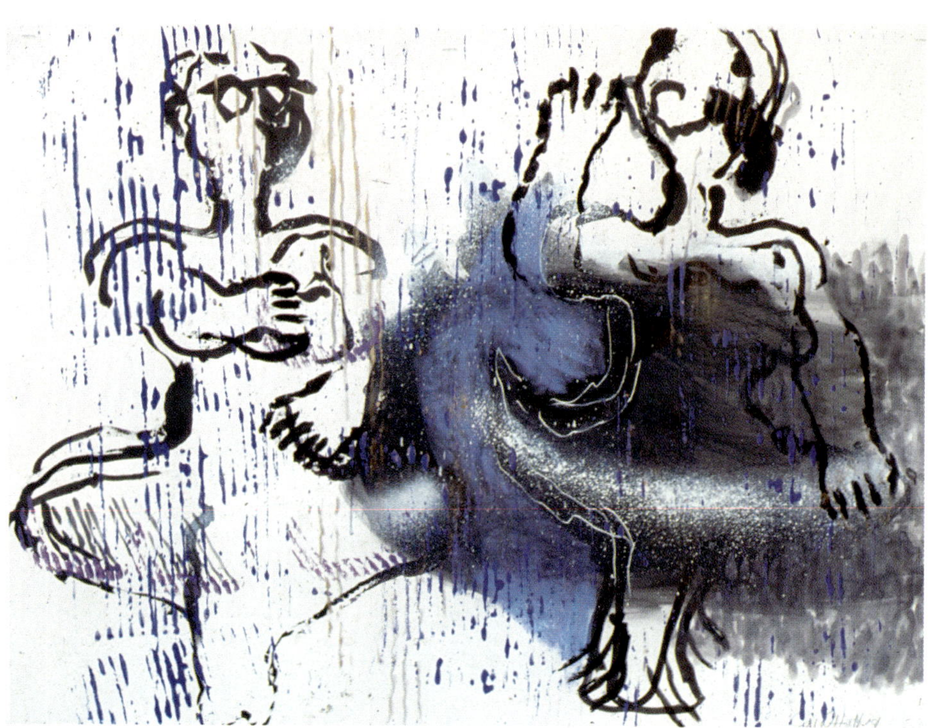

B. Dancers. Pigment, paint and chalk on paper, 22" x 30".

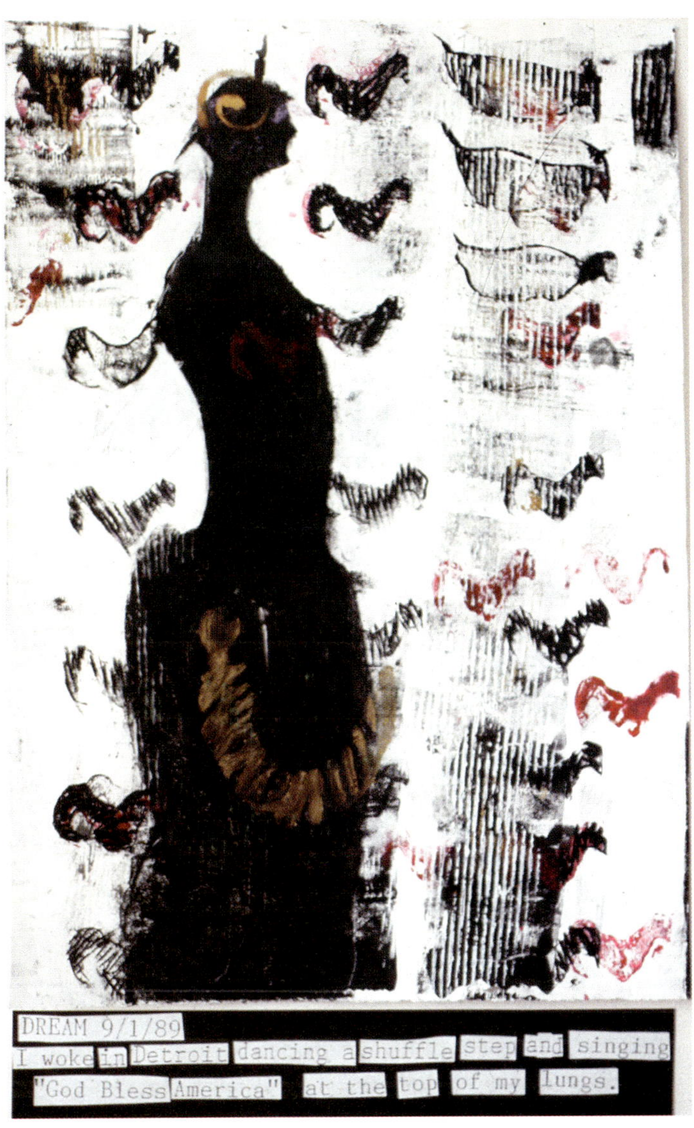

C. Dream 9/1/89. Pigment, paint and collage on paper, 42" x 53".

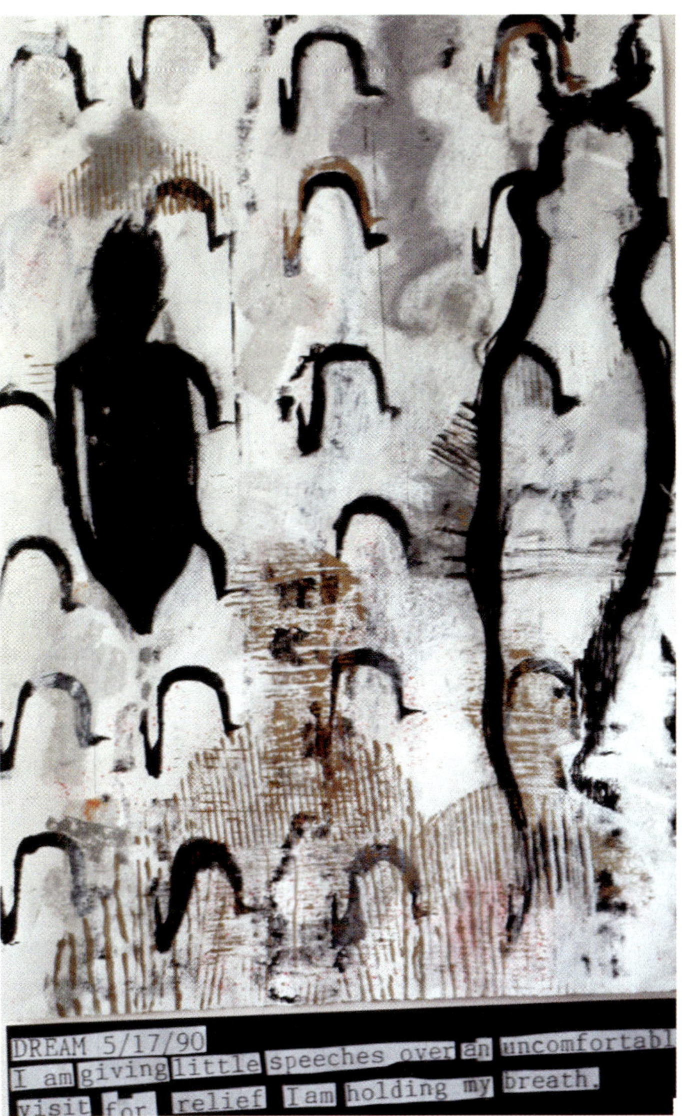

D. Dream 5/19/90. Pigment, paint and collage on paper, 42" x 53".

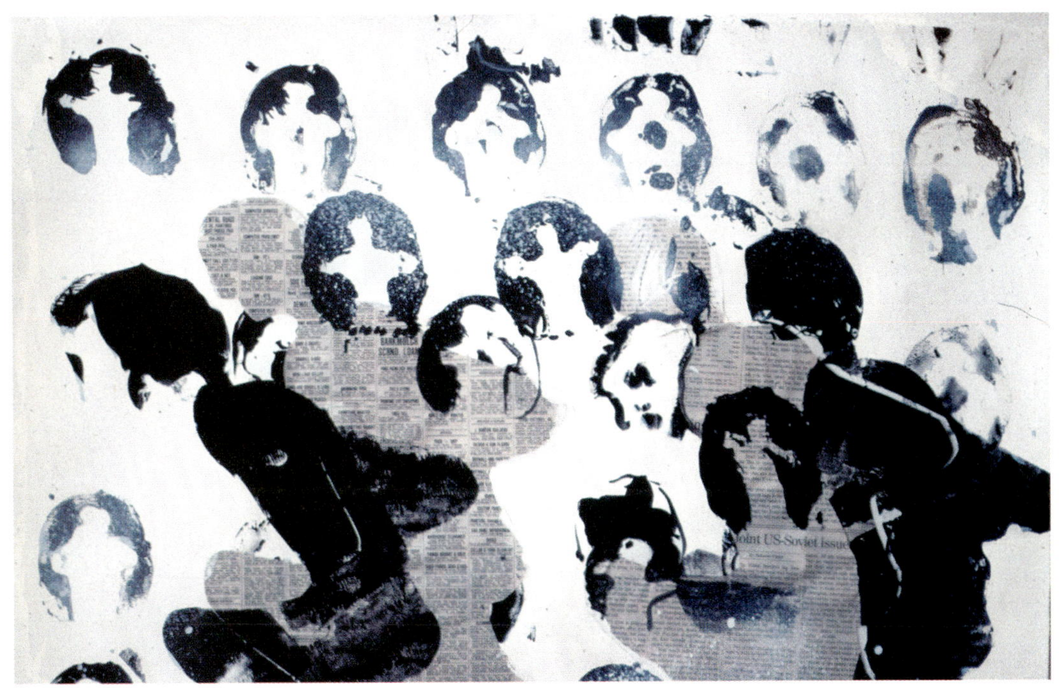

E. Reoccurring Dream. Chalk, paint and collage on paper, 22" x 32".

PRICE LIST

A..........................$500
B..........................$500
C......................$1,500
D......................$1,500
E..........................$500

Paul Inglis

Born in Quincy, MA, in 1963, Paul Inglis recalls being interested in the fine arts at a young age. He attended the Massachusetts College of Art, where studies under George Nick and Paul Celli influenced his development as a painter. Upon graduating, Inglis traveled across America for five months, painting directly from nature and training his eyes to see color and tone.

Inglis executes his work in oils on canvas. His subject matter is drawn largely from Boston's urban landscape, and his intimate paintings are created from direct observation — usually in one sitting. By working swiftly and spontaneously — as is evident by his lively brushstroke — Inglis captures a specific moment. His sense of lighting and atmosphere give his scenes an immediate, tactile presence.

Since traveling across the United States, Inglis has exhibited his work frequently. In 1992, he had a one-man show at the St. Botolph Club in Boston, and his work was included in the Virdian Gallery's fourth national juried exhibition in New York City. Inglis has received numerous awards for his paintings.

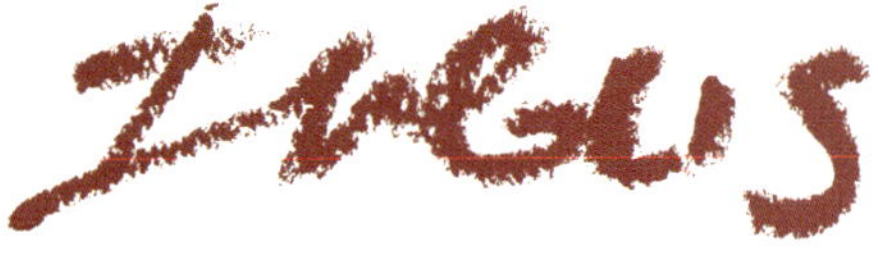

63 Endicott St., Studio #508
Boston, MA 02113
617-720-5730

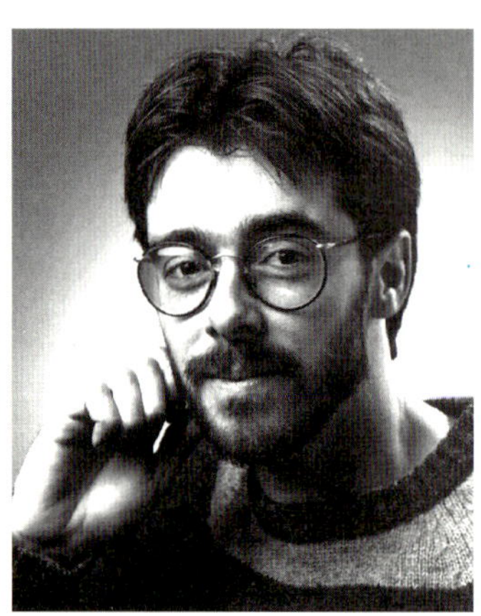

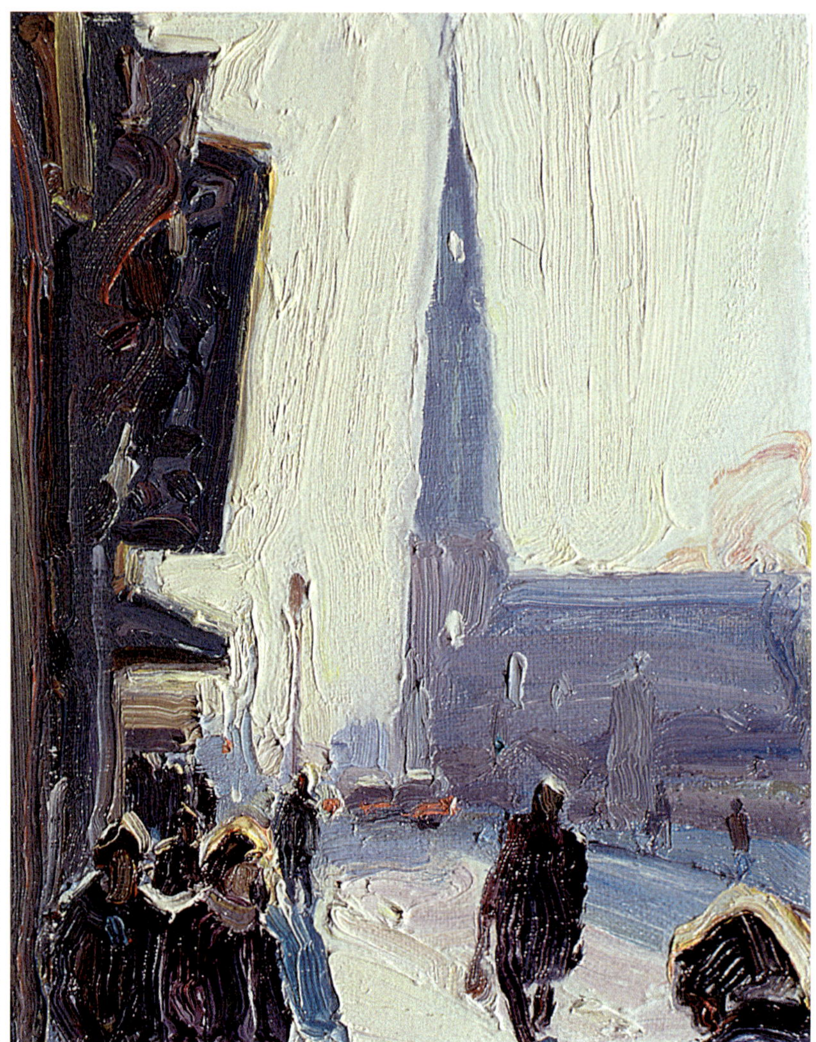

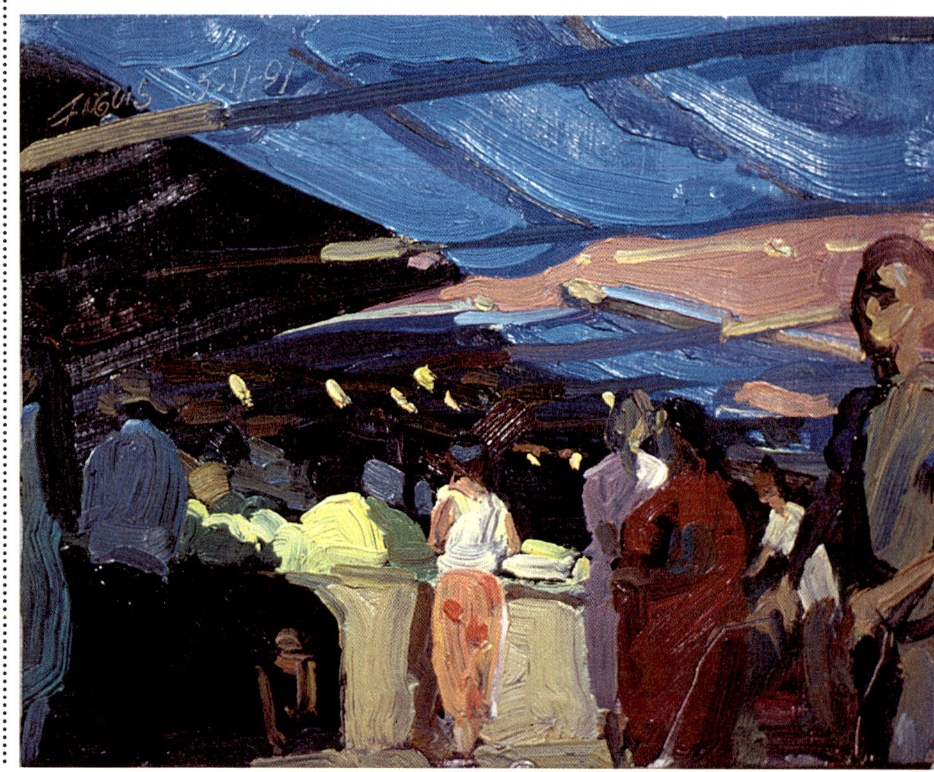

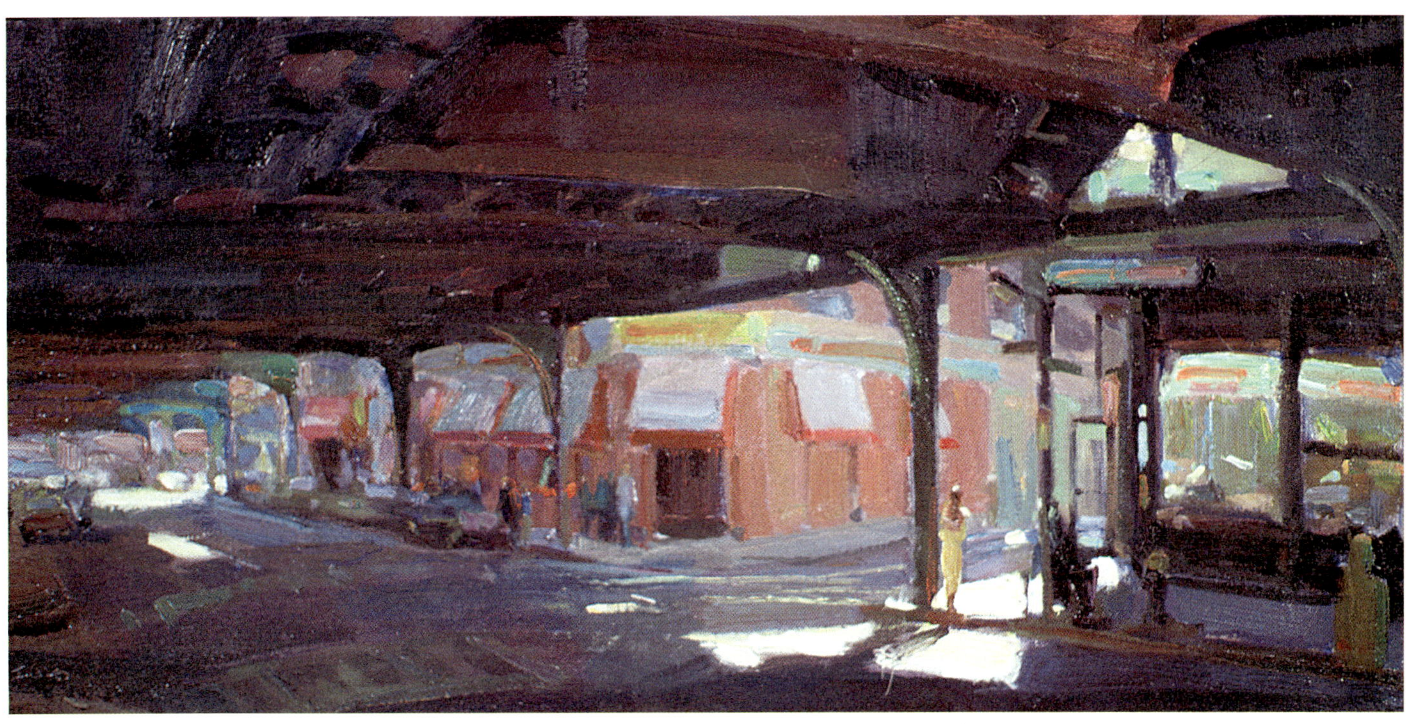

A. (opposite top) **4 O'Clock.** Oil on canvas. 10" x 8".

B. (opposite bottom) **Haymarket Sq.** Oil on canvas. 8" x 10".

C. (above) **Untitled**. Oil on canvas. 16" x 32".

D. (right middle) **Polcaris**. Oil on canvas. 9" x 12"

E. (right bottom) **Frog Pond**. Oil on canvas. 9" x 12"

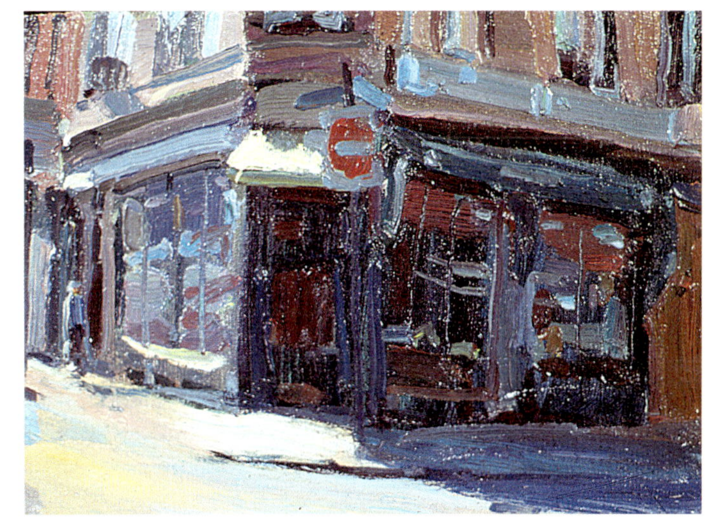

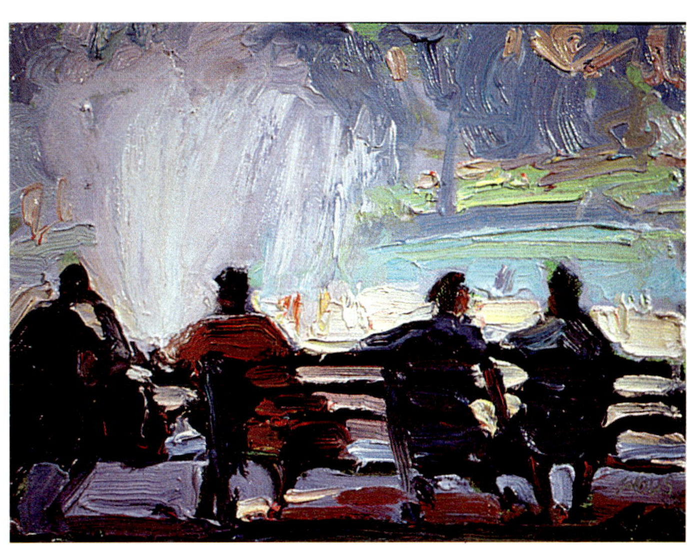

PRICE LIST

A..........................$500

B..........................$500

C......................$1,200

D..........................$500

E..........................$500

Chet Jones

Born in Boston, MA, Chet Jones now lives in Sharon, MA, where in 1987 he renovated a small 19th-century hammer factory to serve as his studio and home. Despite strong roots in Massachusetts, Jones has travelled extensively, spending time in Mexico, Italy and the British Isles.

Jones studied the fine arts at Boston College, graduating with departmental honors. He received a scholarship to the Skowhegan School of Painting and Sculpture, and also did graduate work in Florence, Italy. He now divides his time between painting and freelance illustration work for various publications, including *Offshore* magazine.

Landscapes have long been Jones' preferred subject. He works primarily in oil on canvas, and his paintings are concerned with traditional romanticism and naturalistic perceptions. A specially equipped road studio allows Jones to work close to his subject matter. At his home studio, he reworks and refines the imagery in order to increase its subjectivity. His personal, figurative images are notable for the light that pervades them.

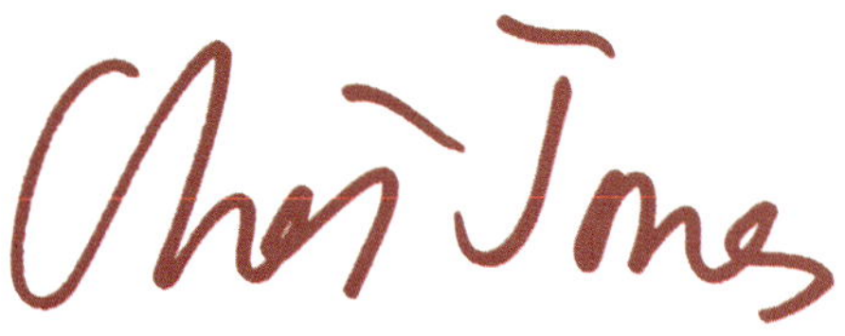

135 Ames Street
Sharon, MA 02067
617-784-7650

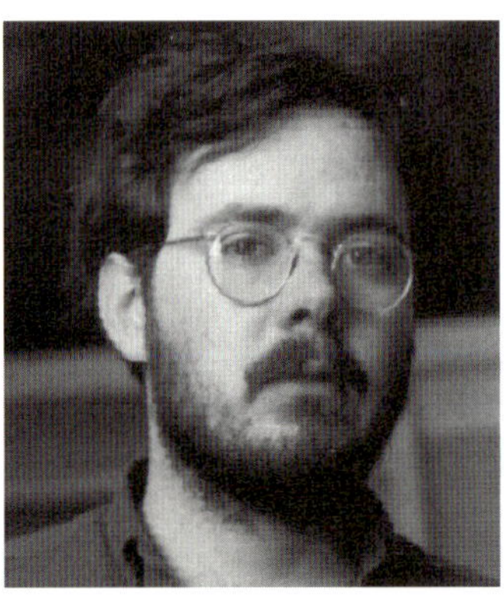

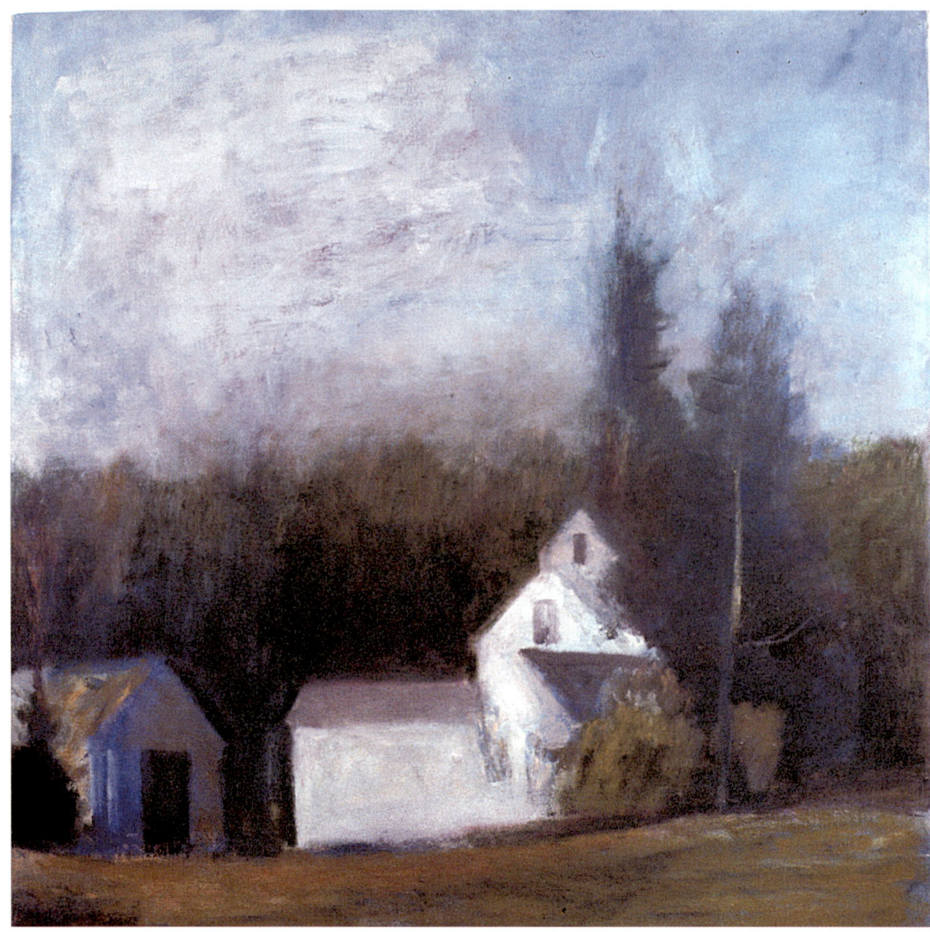

A. Two Trees. Oil on canvas, 22" x 26".

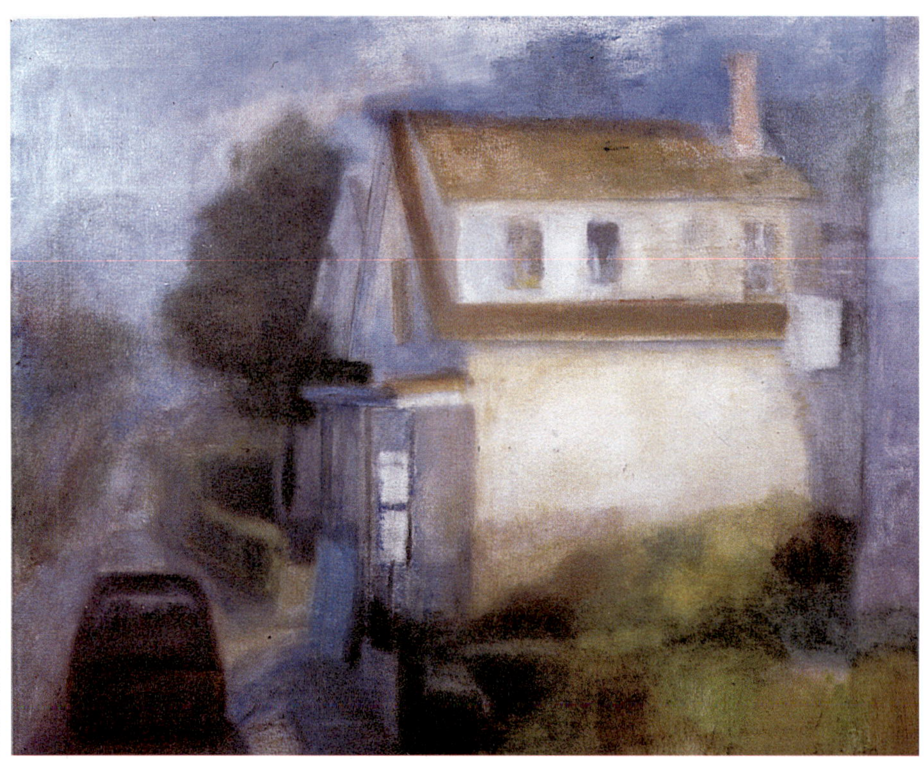

B. House, Bradford Street. Oil on canvas, 22" x 26".

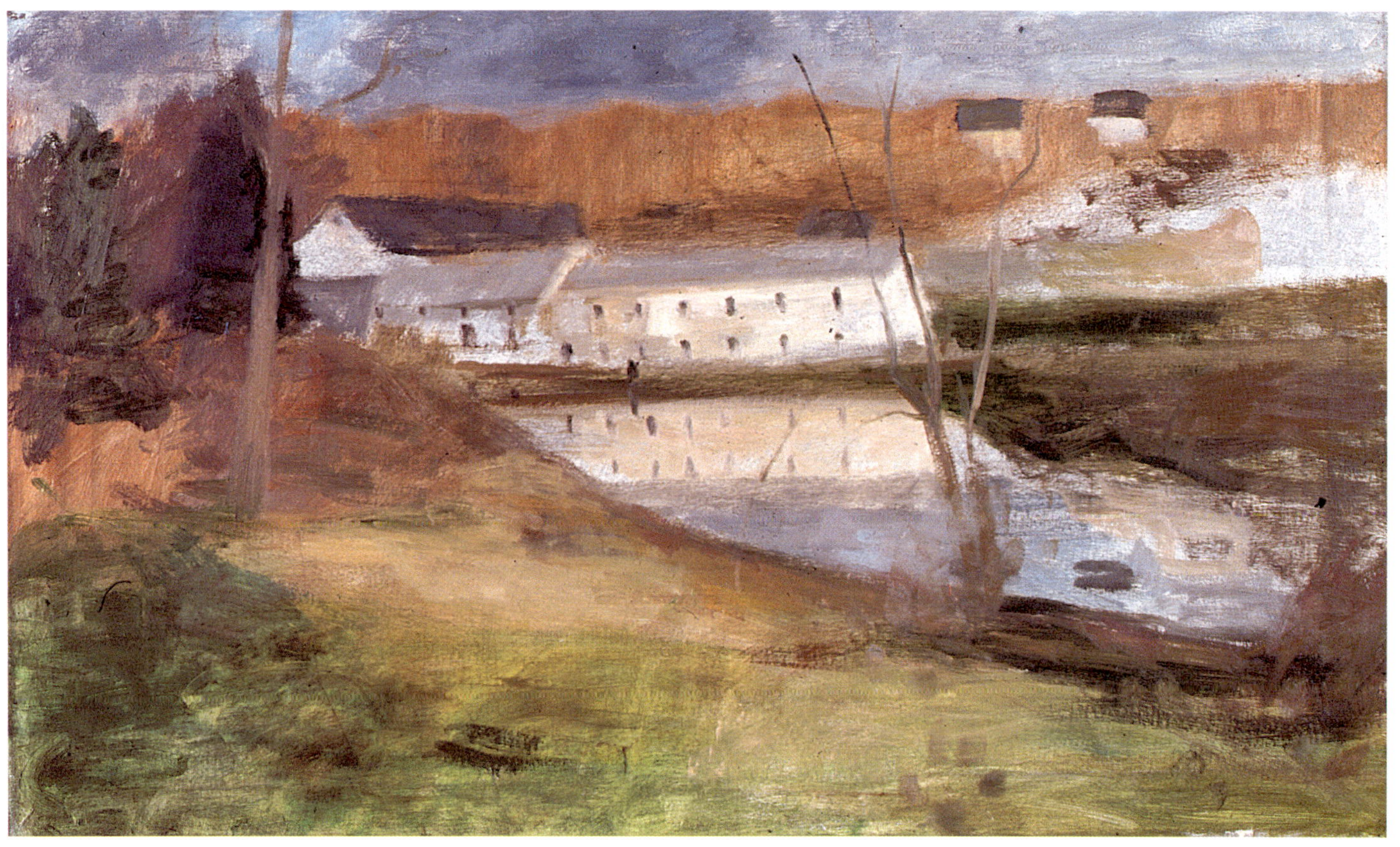

C. Mills Falls, Newton. Oil on canvas, 18" x 26".

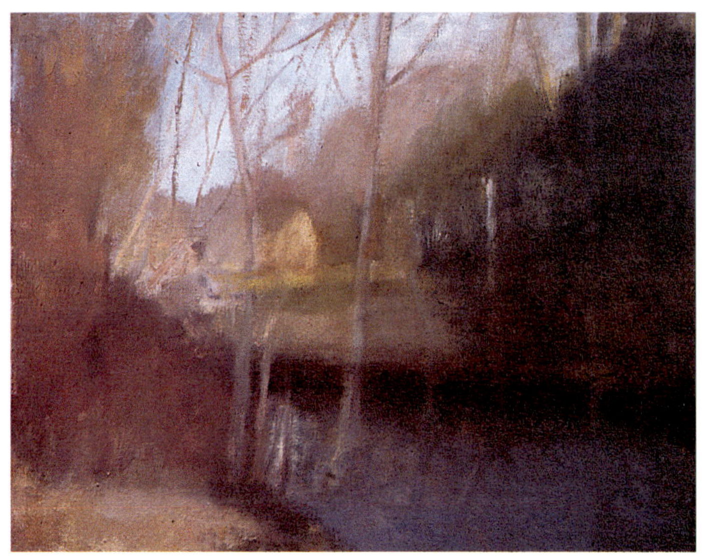

D. Charles River II. Oil on canvas, 18" x 22".

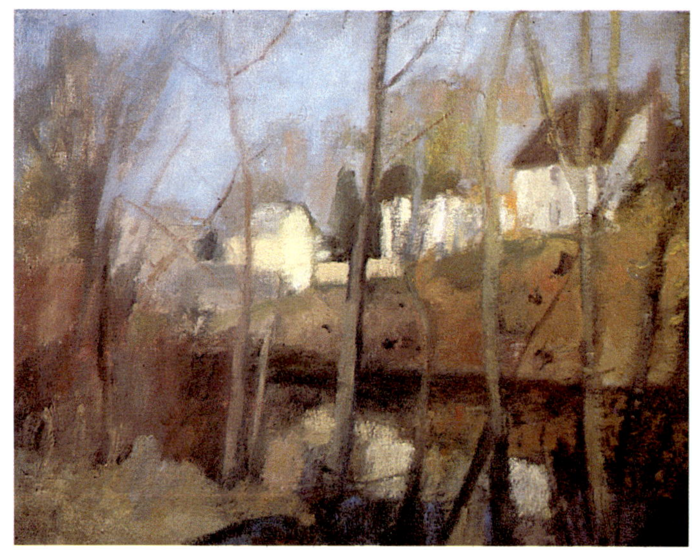

E. Charles River. Oil on canvas, 18" x 22".

PRICE LIST

A $1,100

B $1,100

C $1,250

D $850

E $850

Laurie Kaplowitz

Laurie Kaplowitz has been a full-time artist since 1975, when she completed graduate work at American University. Although much of her time is devoted to painting, Kaplowitz also teaches art classes at the University of Massachusetts, Dartmouth. She currently maintains a studio just west of Boston at ARTISTSPACE in Wellesley.

Kaplowitz executed her latest series of large canvases in acrylics. The paintings represent her exploration of the human experience. Kaplowitz employs various images and forms – some cryptic, some clear – to serve as metaphors for her feelings; they act as the building blocks of the world she creates on canvas. The human form is her central concern, and it is always firmly anchored in her work.

Kaplowitz has exhibited her paintings in New York City, Washington DC, and throughout New England. Her most recent solo show was in September 1992 at the Ashuah-Irving Gallery in Boston. She has received several grants, including an Artists Foundation grant from the Massachusetts Council on the Arts.

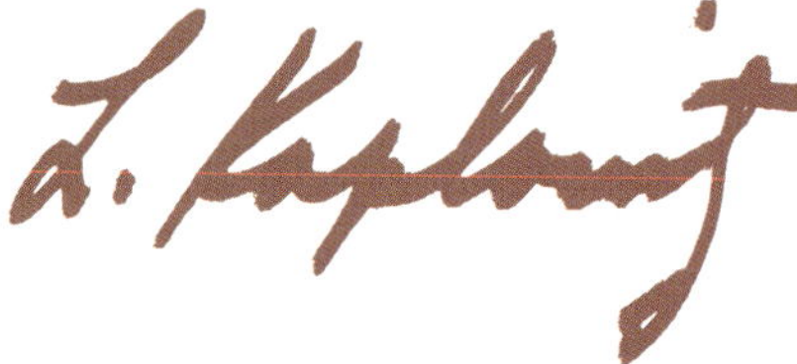

39 Colbert Road East
Newton, MA 02165
617-482-3343

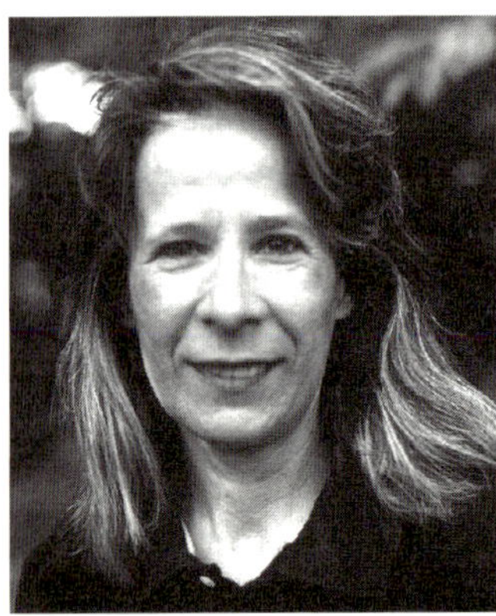

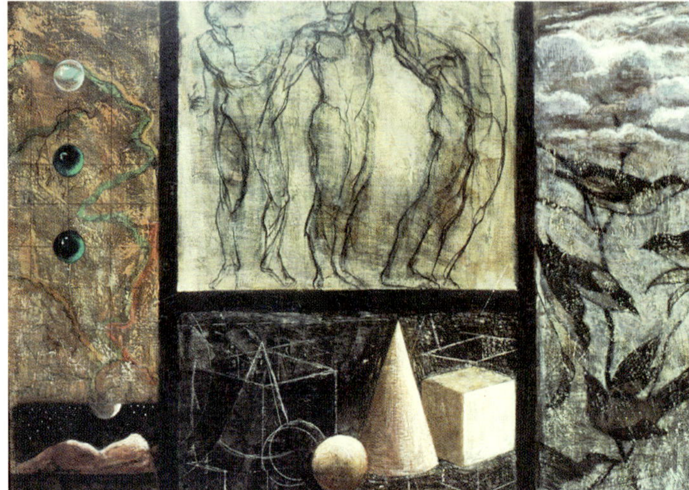

A. Age of Reason: Dream Cycle. Acrylic on canvas, 38" x 50".

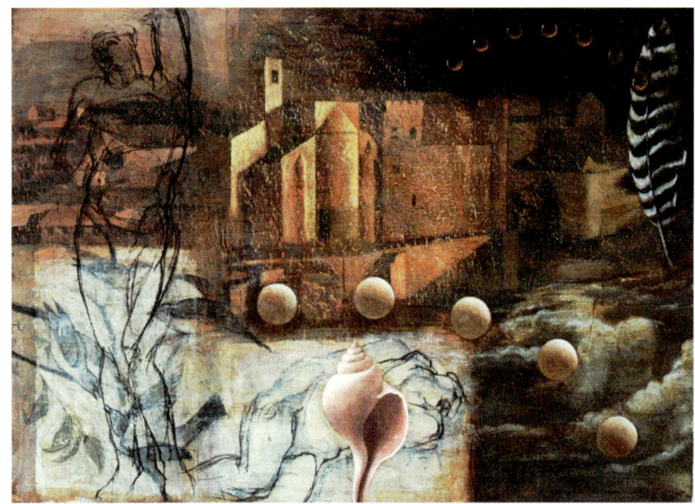

B. Age of Reason: Migration II. Acrylic on canvas, 38" x 50".

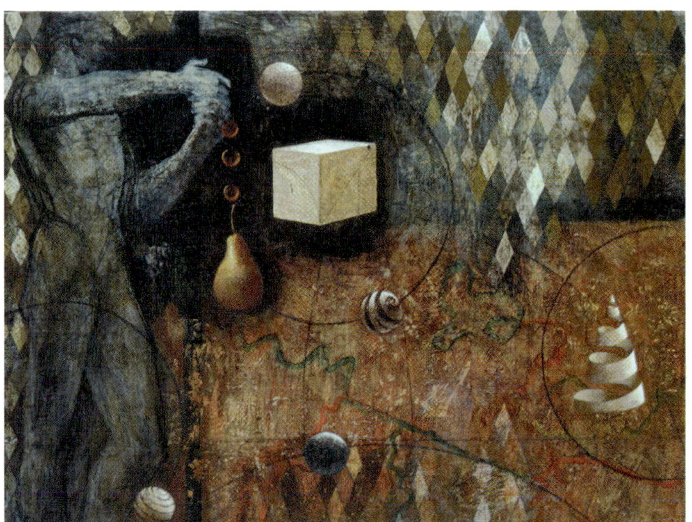

C. Age of Reason: Form and Function. Acrylic on canvas, 38" x 50".

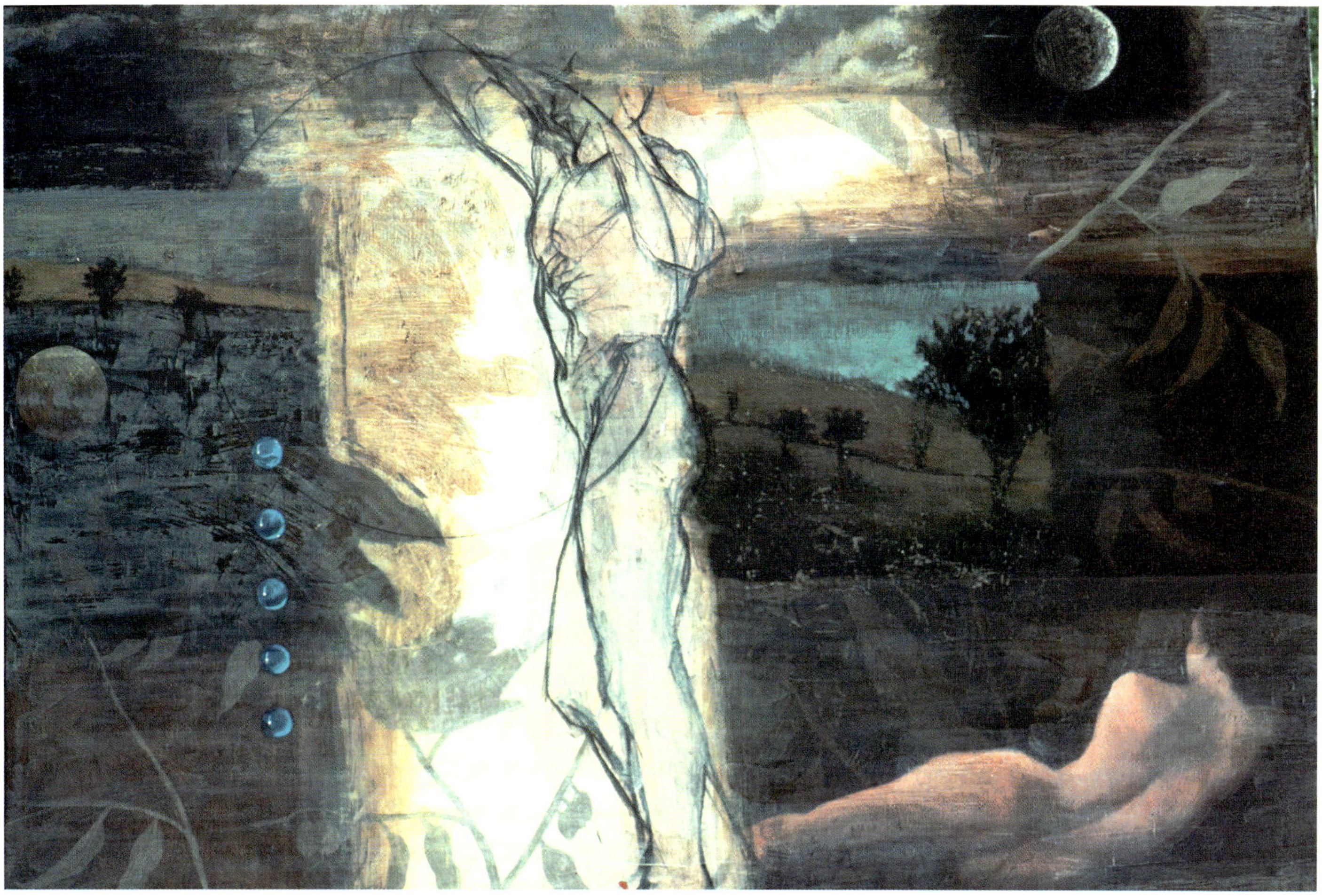

D. Age of Reason: Dream of Love. Acrylic on Canvas, 38" x 50".

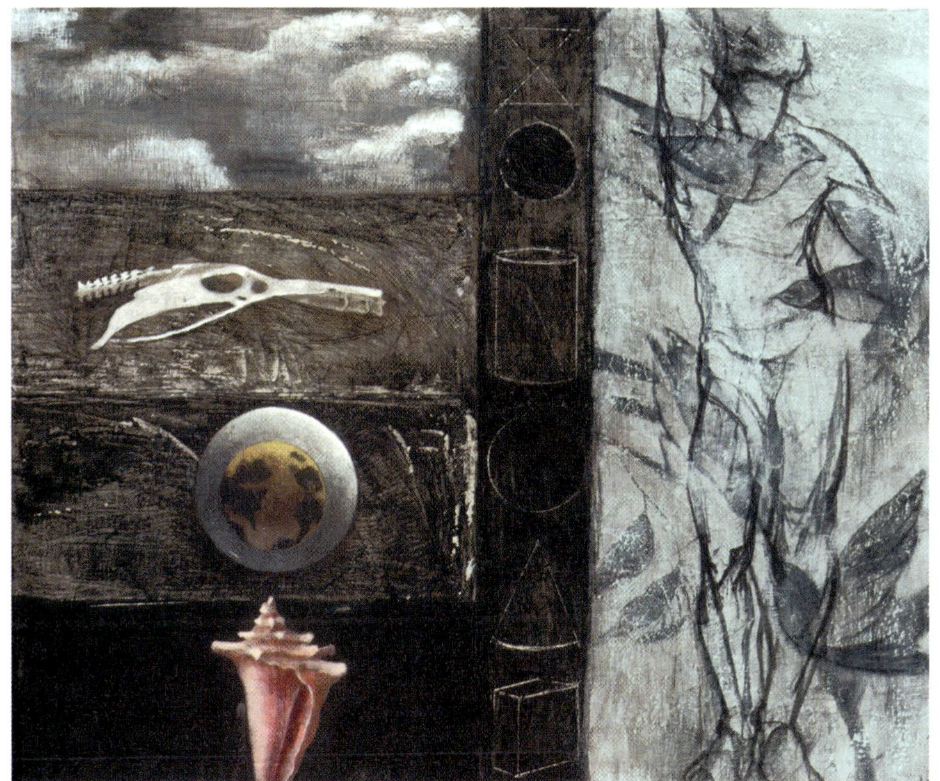

E. Age of Reason: Ascent. Acrylic on canvas, 30" x 36".

PRICE LIST

A $4,500

B $4,500

C $4,500

D $5,000

E $4,000

Represented by
Ashuah-Irving Gallery
Boston, MA

Gregory **Kitterle**

Born in Beverly, MA, Gregory Kitterle has spent his entire life in the Boston area. Although artistic endeavours were not encouraged during his teen years, he opted to attend the Monserrat College of Art, where he completed two years of course work and has since taught. Kitterle presently maintains a studio in Boston's South End.

Kitterle creates in two formats, large canvases and smaller works on paper. He draws his subject matter from folk tales and mythology, but is more concerned with the reality behind the stories. Partly universal and partly personal, Kitterle's paintings can be thought of as mirrors. This intention is echoed by the reflective quality of the work, which is executed in an oil/shellac medium.

Notable shows in recent years include his participation in the Currier Gallery's 1989 biannual of emerging New England talent, and his 1992 solo show at Gallery Per Tutti in Boston. Gallery Per Tutti is a haven for emerging New England artists, and under the direction of owner Geddy Moody, offers an affordable alternative to the traditional gallery scene.

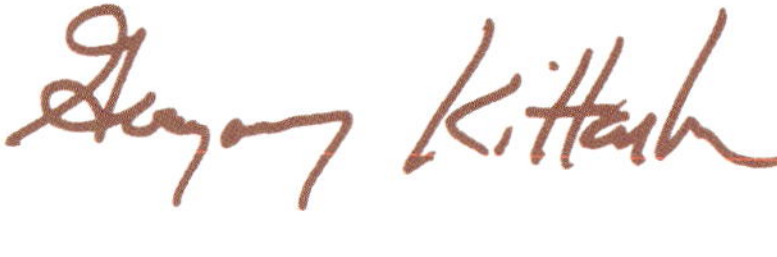

59 Wareham Street
Boston, MA 02118
617-542-5781

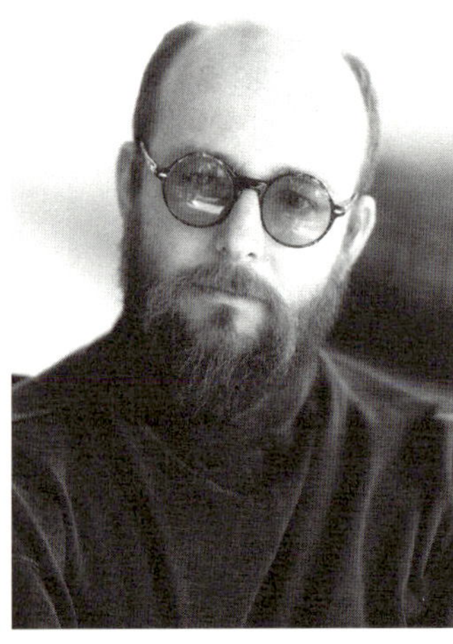

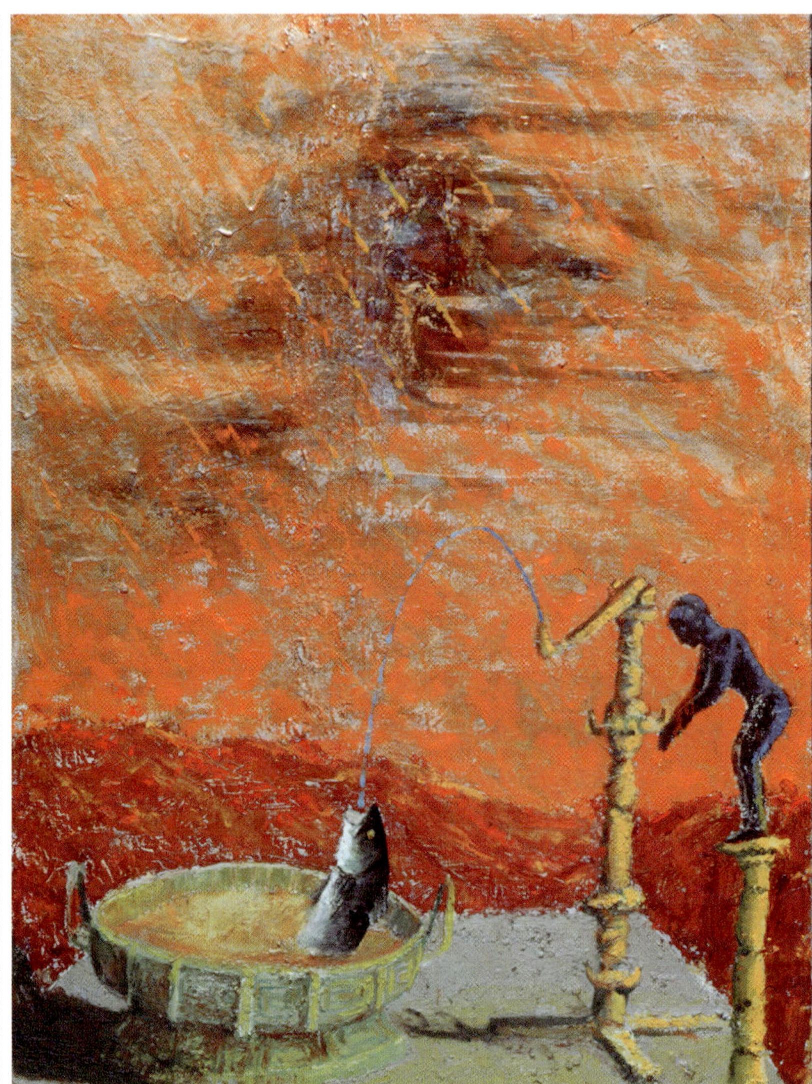

A. Thirsty Fish. Oil on canvas, 48" x 36".

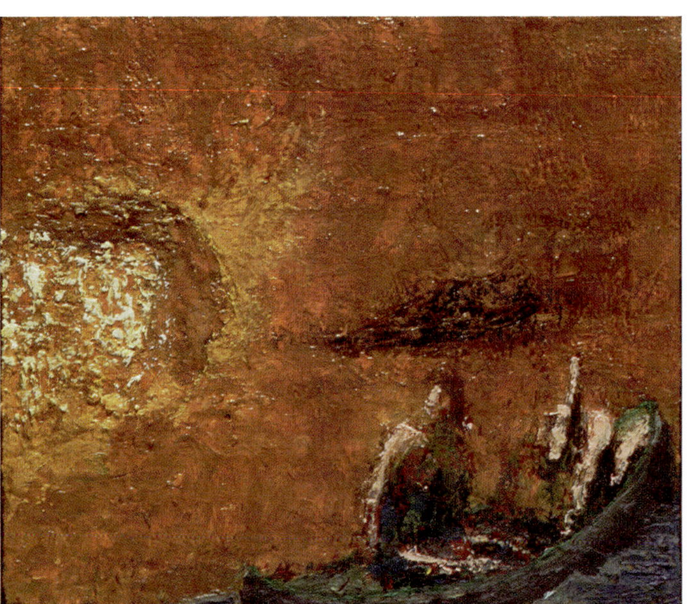

B. Cure. Oil/shellac on paper, 14" x 16" x 3¾".

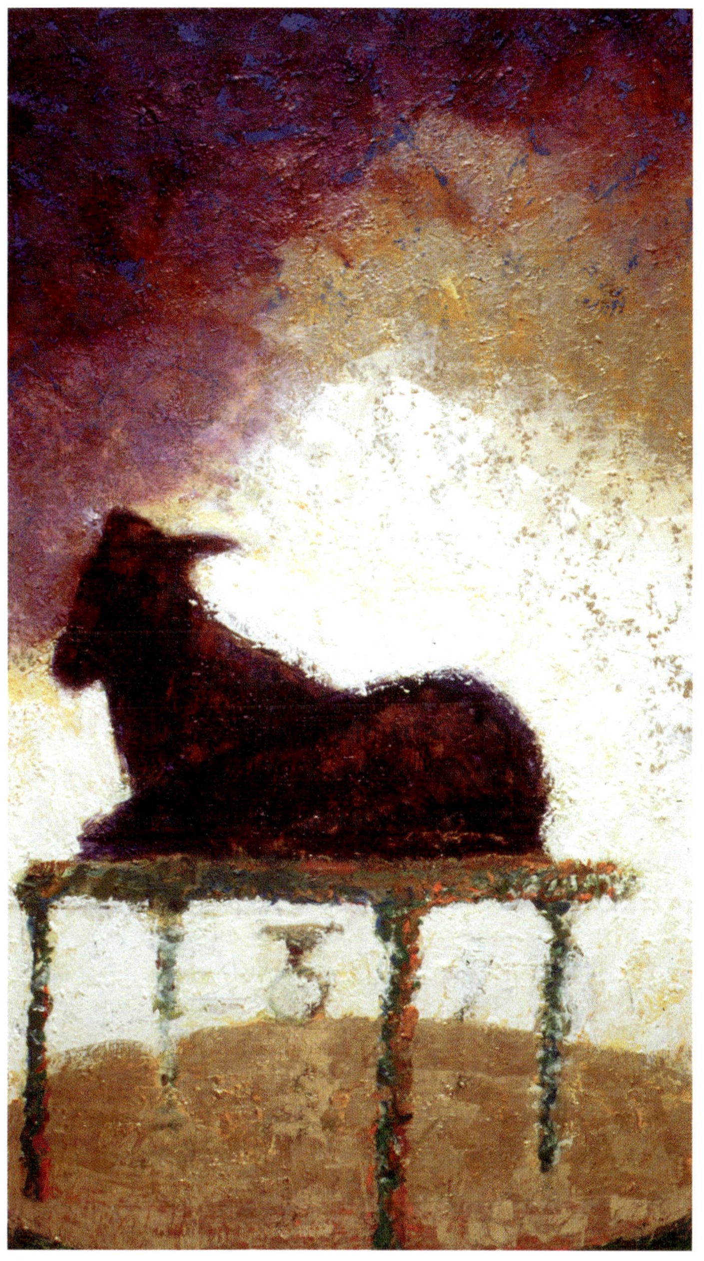

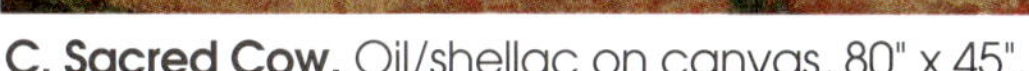

C. Sacred Cow. Oil/shellac on canvas, 80" x 45".

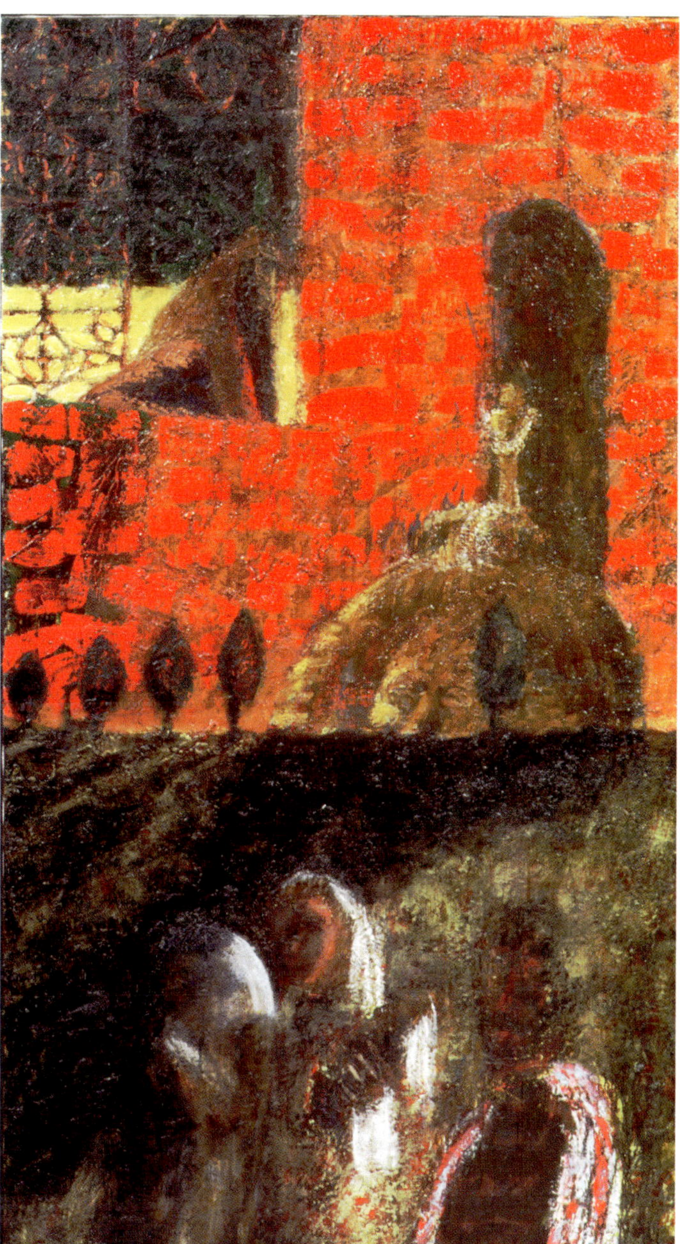

D. Allegory. Oil/shellac on canvas, 80" x 45".

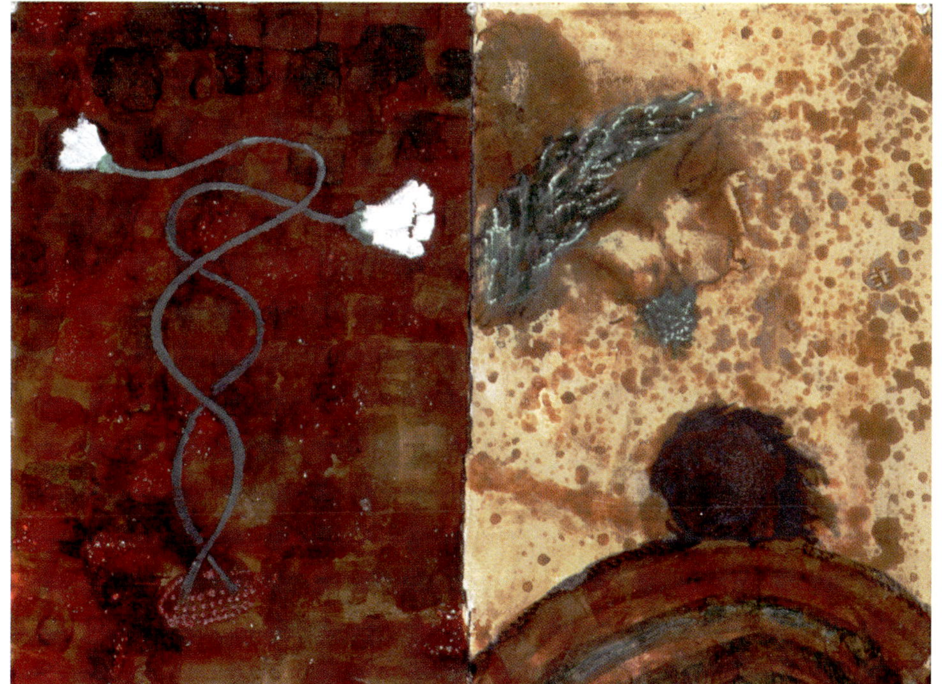

E. Allegory
Oil/shellac on paper, 22" x 30".

PRICE LIST

A $1,500
B $800
C $2,000
D $3,500
E $900

Represented by
Gallery Per Tutti
Boston, MA

Beth Ladd

Beth Ladd was born in Vermont and came to the Boston area in 1963. She now maintains a studio just west of Boston at ARTIST-SPACE in Wellesley. Ladd studied traditional painting and sculpture techniques at Cornell University and the School of the Museum of Fine Arts, Boston.

Ladd works in oils at present, creating large canvases which are mounted on stretchers of more than usual thickness. This permits her heavily impasted surface imagery to extend around the sides of the canvas.

Ladd's paintings address psychological themes portrayed by free-floating figures that populate a pristine and primal environment. Ladd paints in a forceful, expressionistic style. The brushstokes are bold, the paint is succulent, and the colors are vivid. Although they celebrate the environment, the paintings also reflect the poignancy and incongruity of contemporary human experienece.

Recent exhibitions of Ladd's oil paintings include solo shows at the Bromfield Gallery in Boston and the Pindar Gallery in SoHo, New York City. Her work has also been shown at various group shows in and around Boston.

Beth Ladd

11 Washburn Avenue
Wellesley, MA 02181
617-237-7858

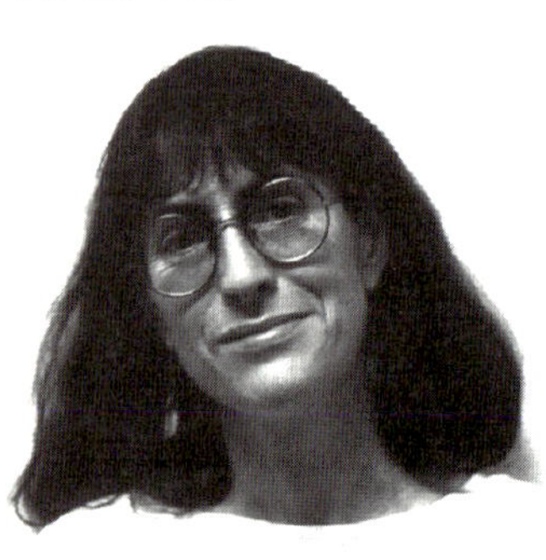

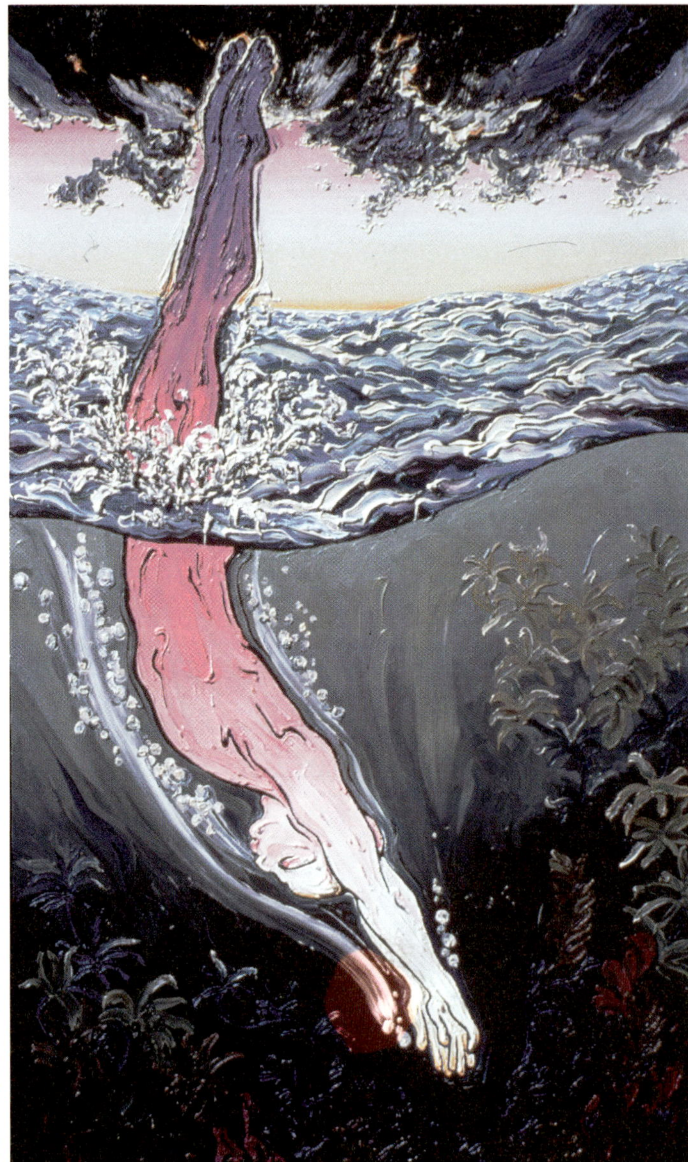

A. Stolen Sunrise.
Oil on canvas,
84" x 48".

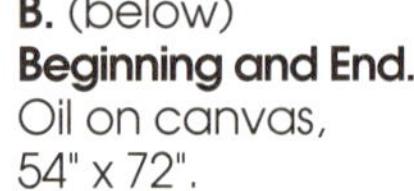

B. (below)
Beginning and End.
Oil on canvas,
54" x 72".

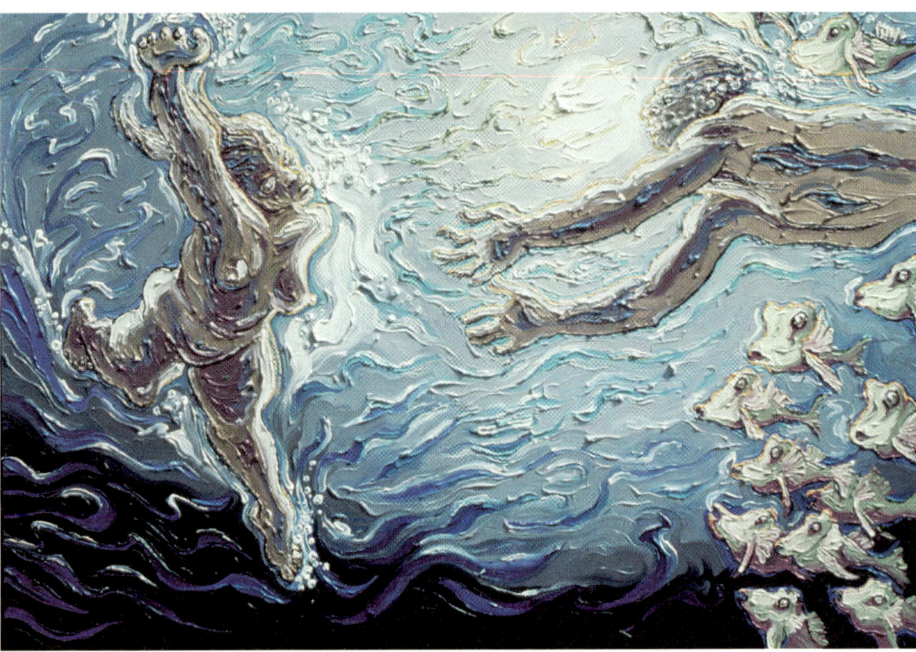

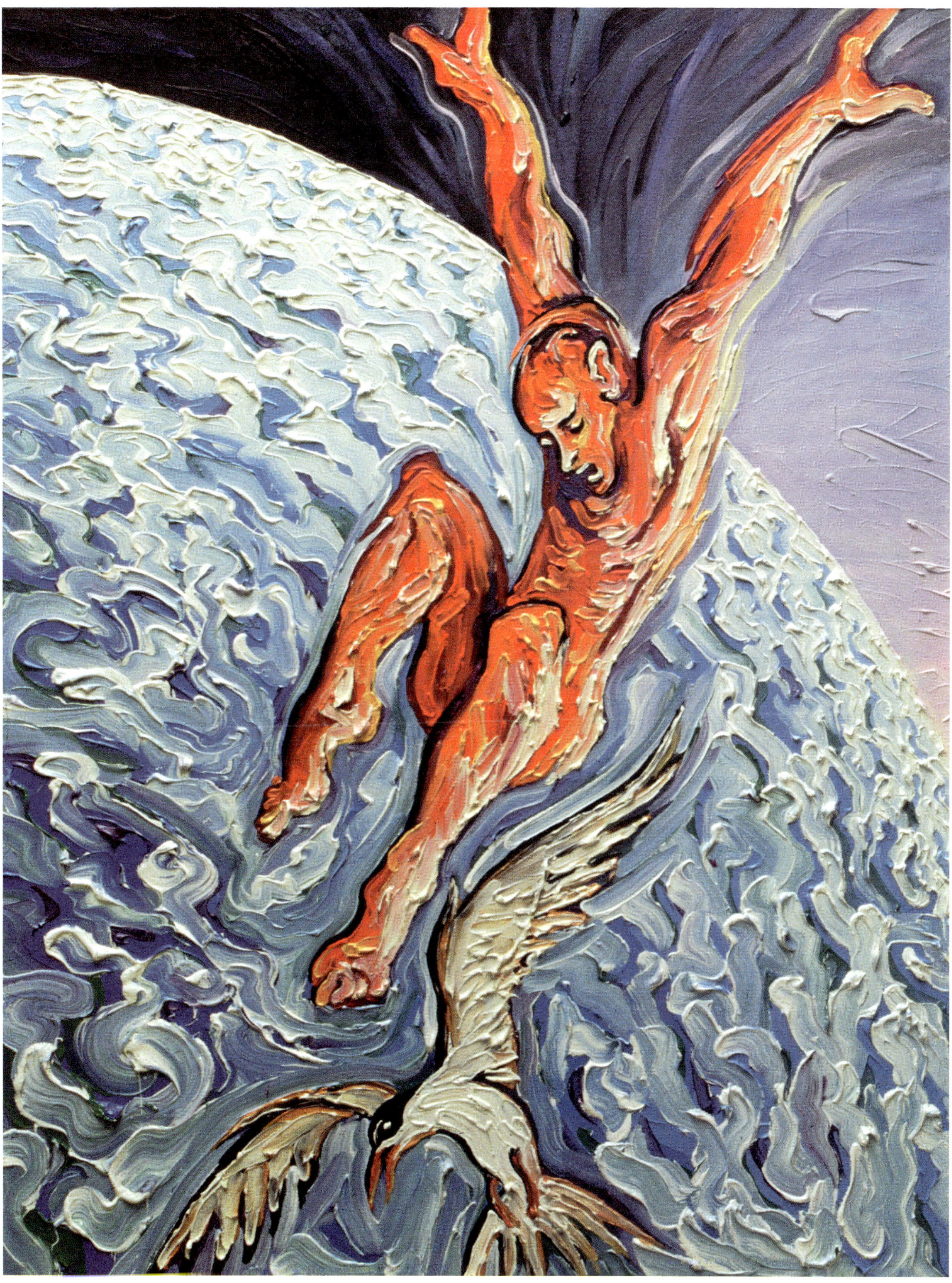

C. Free Fall. Oil on canvas, 44" x 34".

PRICE LIST

A $2,600

B $2,200

C $1,100

Christina Lanzl

Christina Lanzl was born in Los Angeles and raised in rural Bavaria, Germany. She has lived in Boston since 1987. Lanzl received her BA at Stuttgart University and completed her MA at Boston University. She has studied painting at the Massachusetts College of Art and the School of the Museum of Fine Arts in Boston. Currently the director of the Bromfield Gallery in Boston, Lanzl is also active in various organizations within Boston's art community.

Lanzl's style is conscious of the German Expressionist movement. Her experience of two distinct cultures has given Lanzl a keen interest in the subject of identity. Since moving to America, the concept of multiculturalism has become a central concern. Artistically, her German heritage can be seen in her expressive use of color and her interest in emotional content.

Lanzl has shown her work throughout the northeastern U.S., including a solo show at the Boston Architectural Center, and in Germany. In 1991 she won the Award for Innovation and Vision from *Artist* magazine.

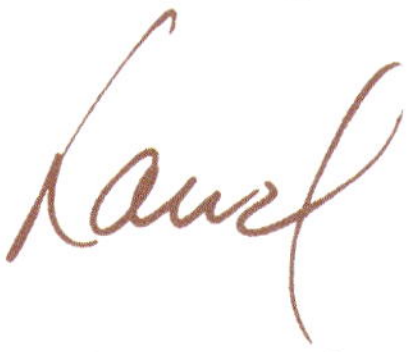

94 Wyman Street
Boston, MA 02130
617-524-6992

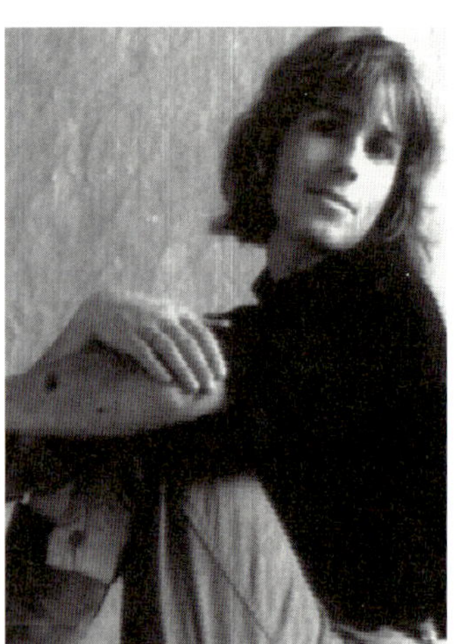

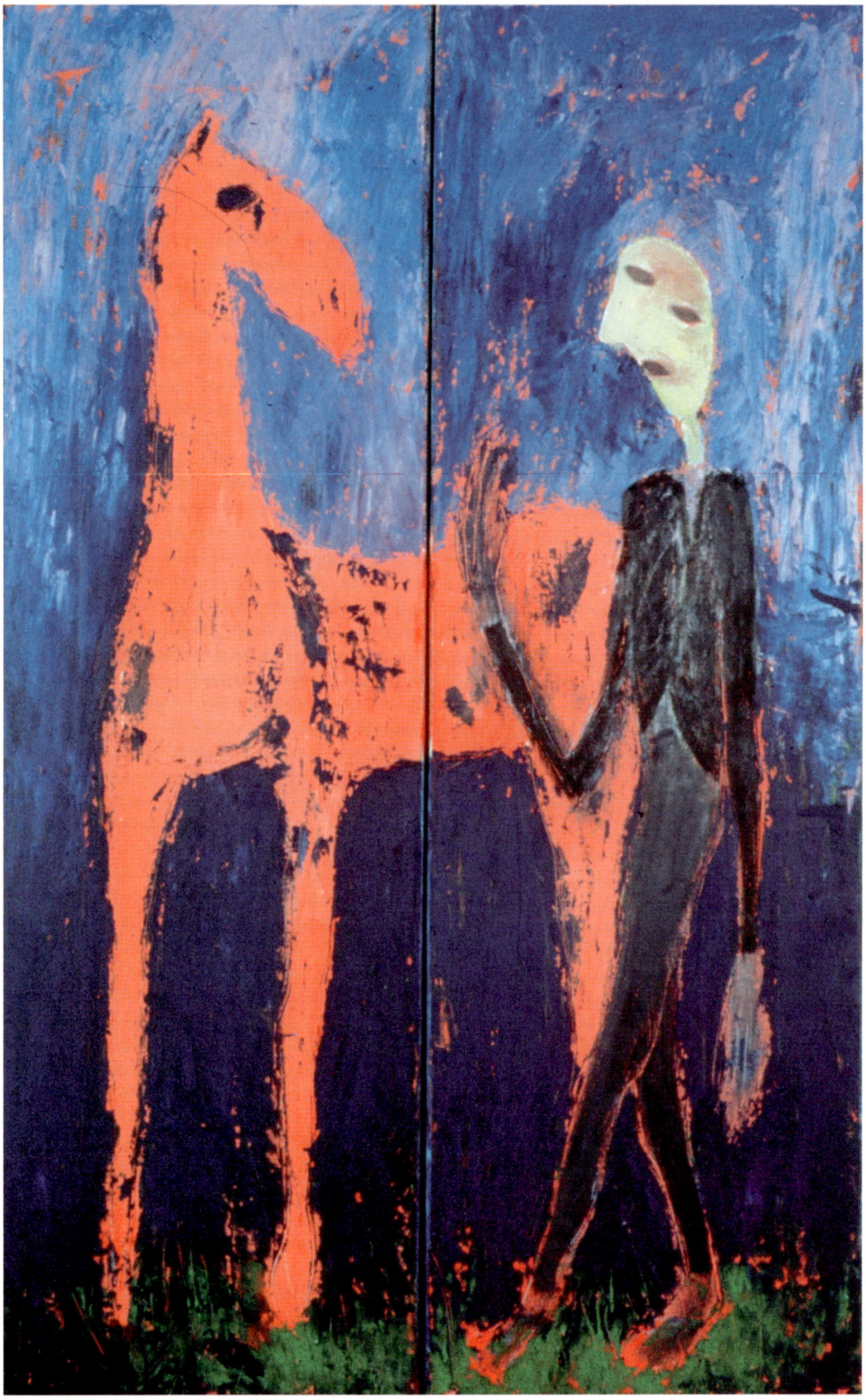

A. My Red Horse. Putty, wax, oil on canvas, 57" x 18".

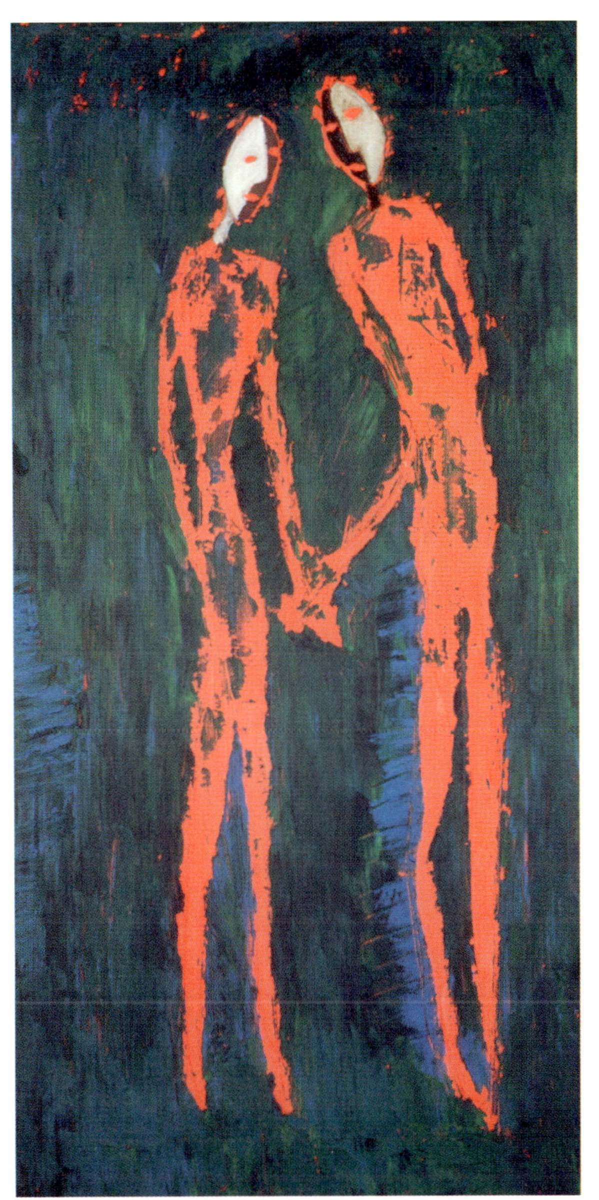

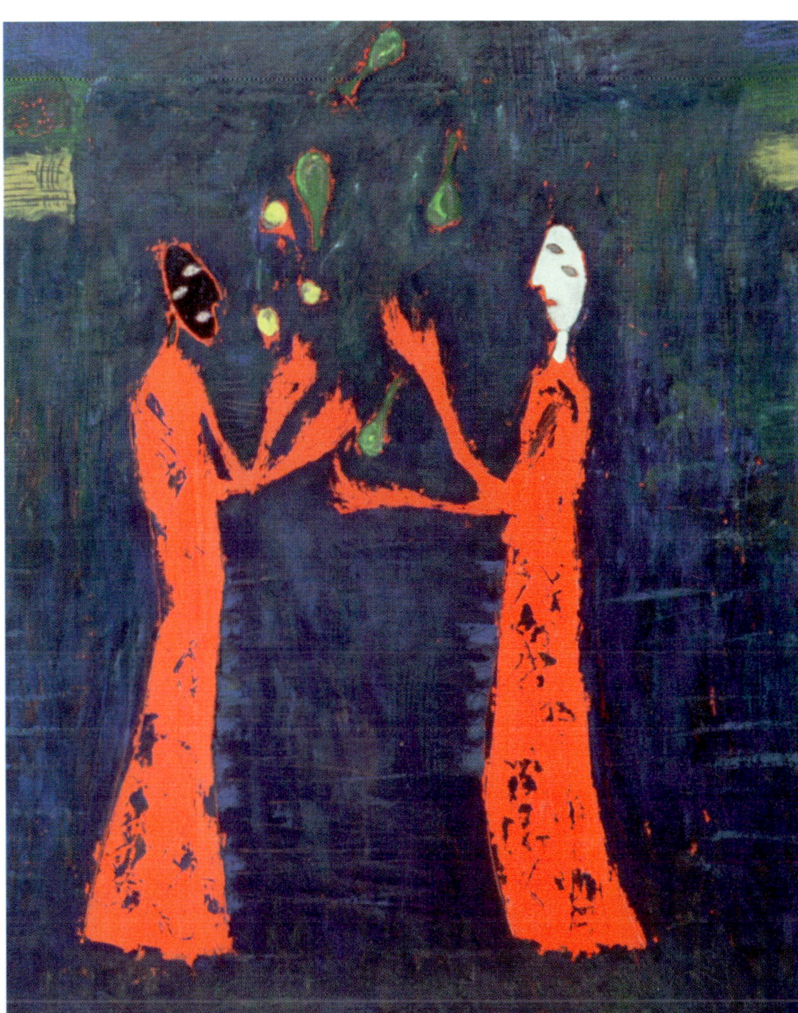

C. Jugglers. Putty, wax, oil on canvas, 42" x 35".

B. (left)
Romance.
Putty, wax, oil on canvas, 50" x 26".

PRICE LIST

A..........................$900

B..........................$700

C..........................$500

D..........................$350

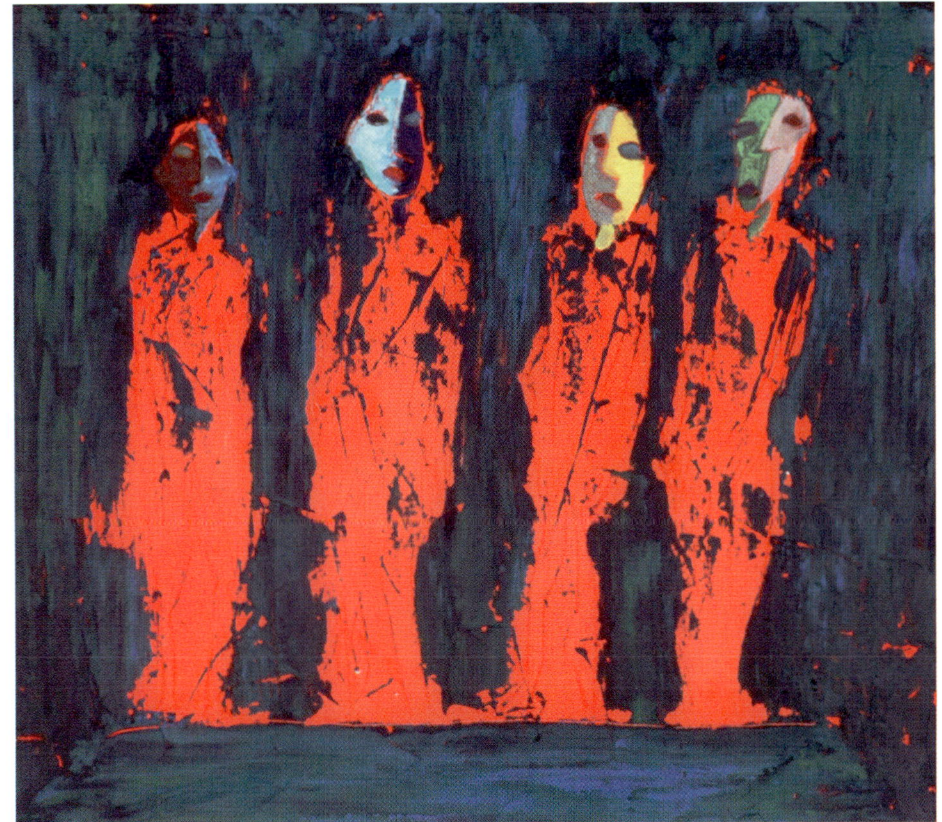

D. The Beauty Contest.
Putty, wax, oil on canvas, 24" x 27".

Gayle LeRoy

Born in St. Louis, MO, in 1942, Gayle LeRoy received her art training at Pasadena City College, the Chouinard Art Institute, and Otis Parsons, Los Angeles. Since moving to Connecticut in 1990, LeRoy has taught both privately and at the Ridgefield Guild of Artists.

Working in oils on very large canvases, LeRoy creates objective imags that deal with subjects ranging from landscapes and interiors, to the figure in genre scenes, to portraits. Her paintings are executed in a painterly and expressionistic style, a direction LeRoy intends to explore further in future works.

In the past three years, LeRoy's paintings have been exhibited in close to 20 shows. She has exhibited in group shows in California, as well as at the Childs Gallery in New York City and the Discovery Museum juried exhibition in Bridgeport, CT. Her work can be found in collections throughout the United States, from Tuscon to New York.

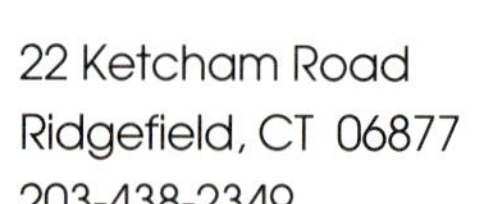

22 Ketcham Road
Ridgefield, CT 06877
203-438-2349

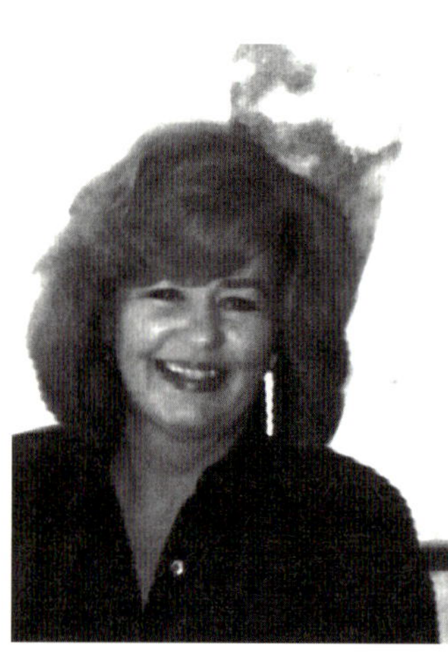

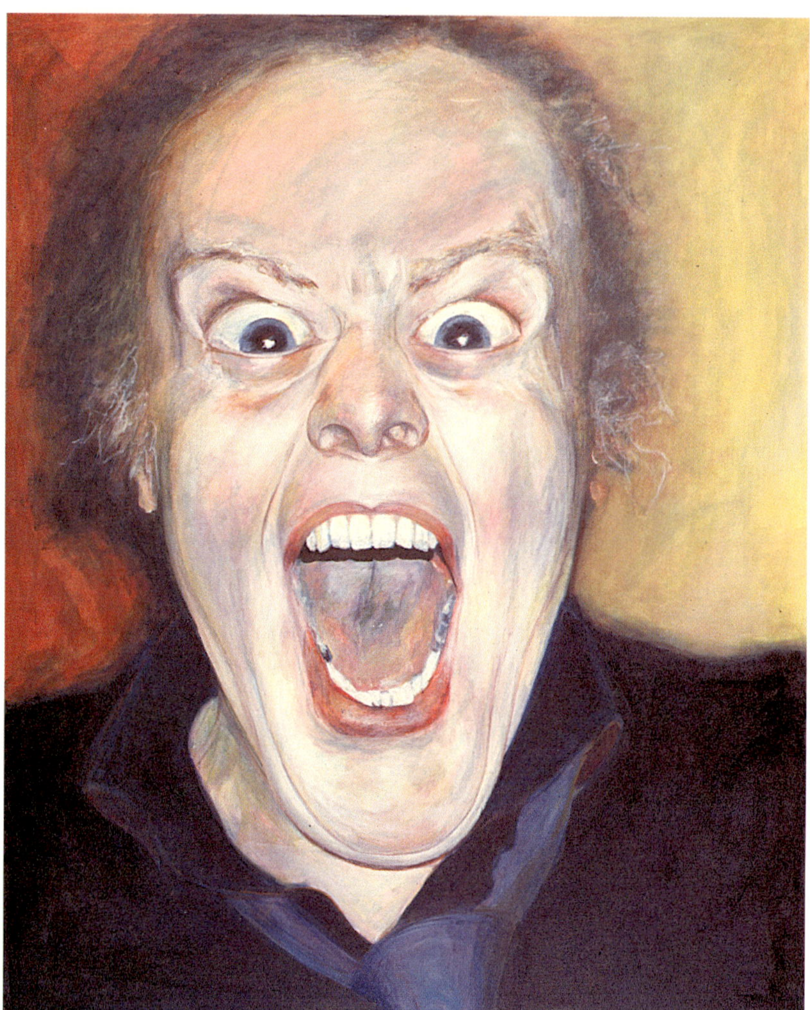

A. Mawx. Oil on canvas, 66" x 54".

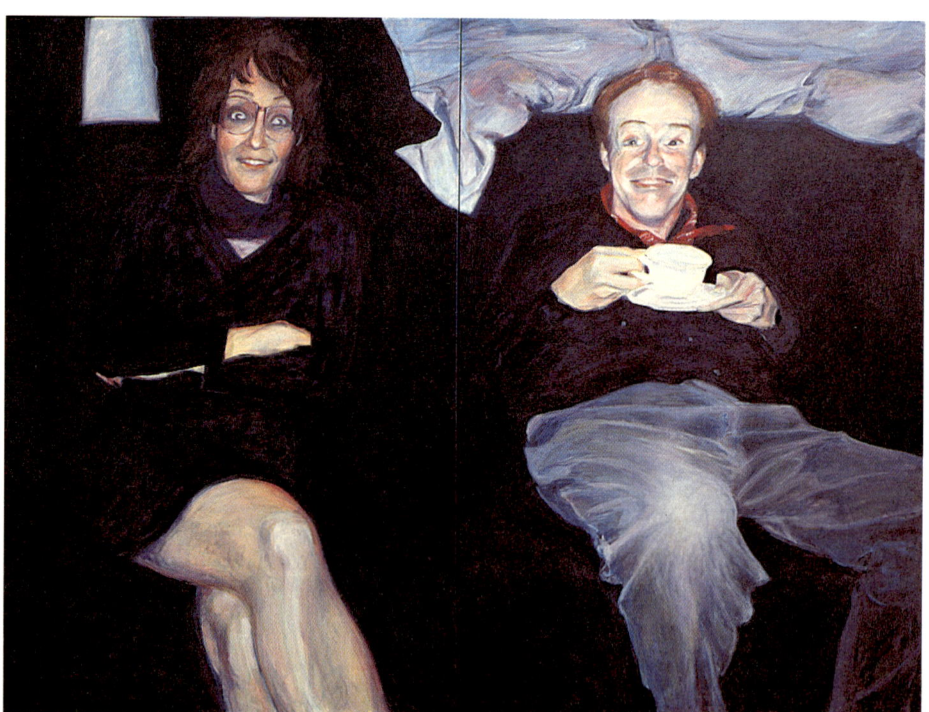

B. I Love Your Coffee. Oil on canvas, 62" x 84" (diptych).

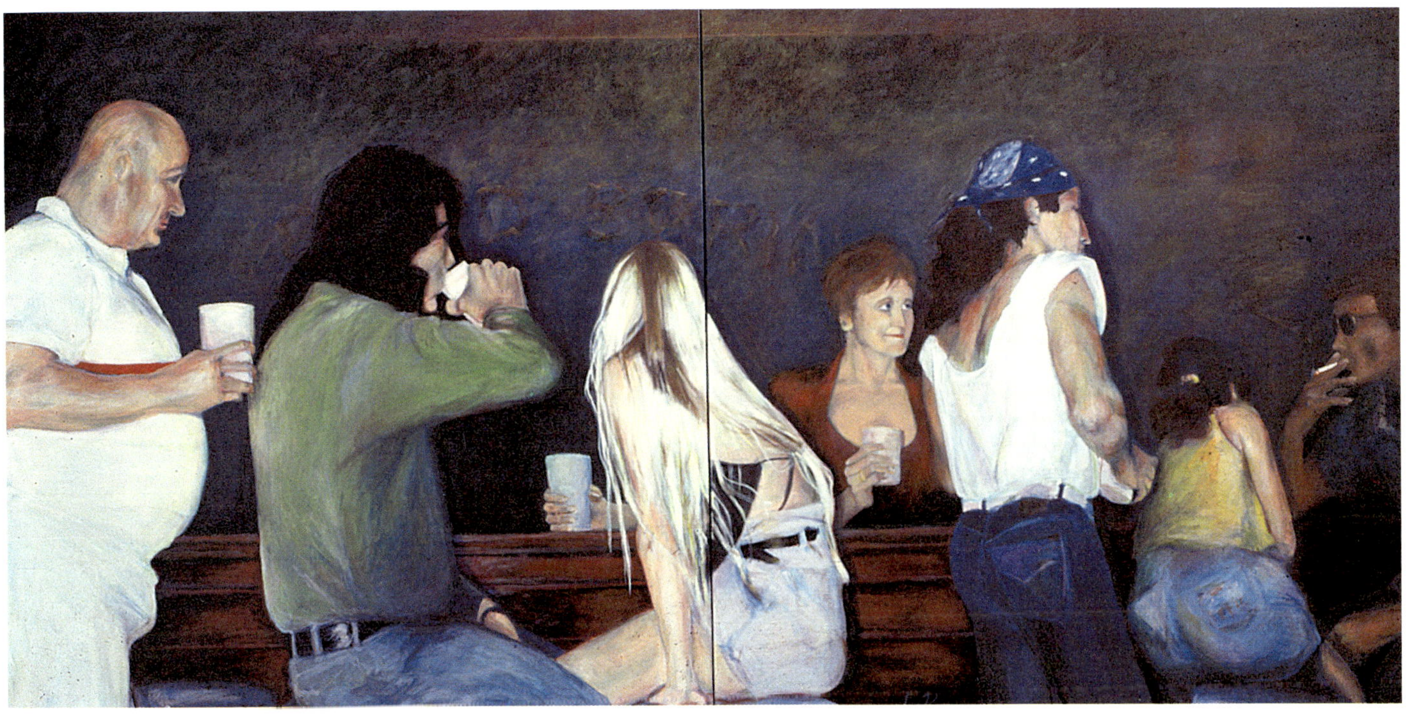

C. Another Day in Paradise. Oil on canvas, 48" x 96" (diptych).

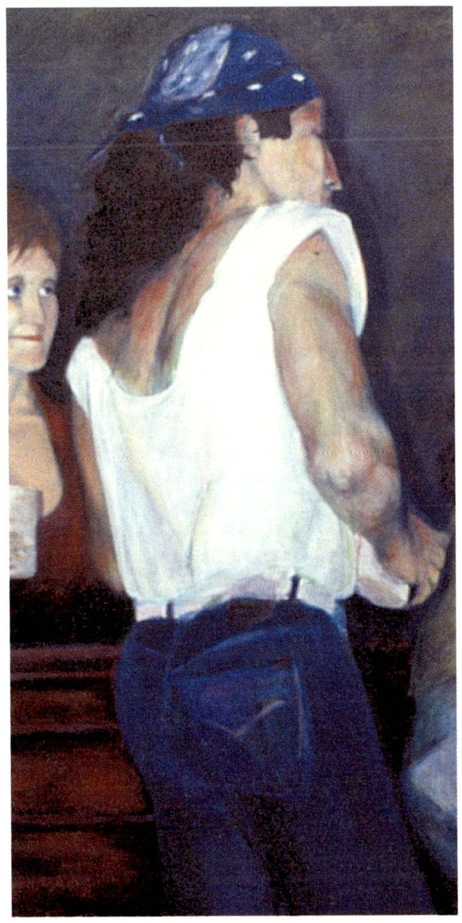

D. Another Day in Paradise. Detail.

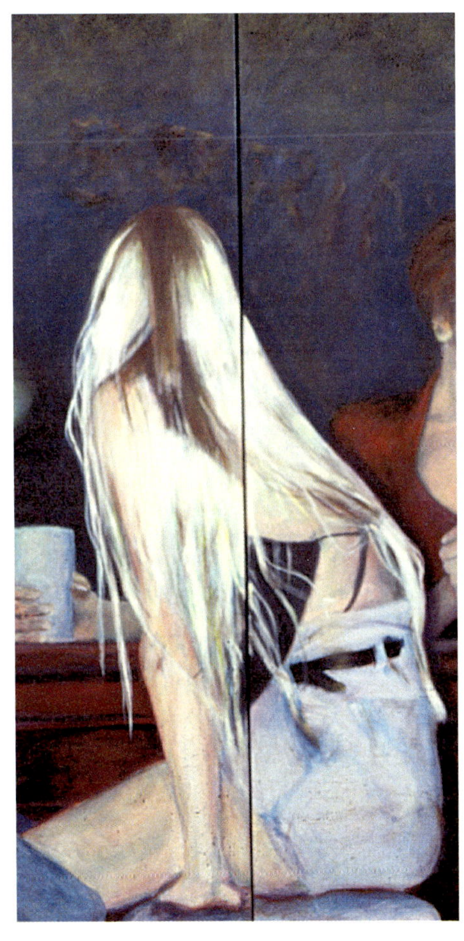

E. Another Day in Paradise. Detail.

PRICE LIST

A $8,000

B $8,500

C $11,000

It was after graduating from the University of Connecticut that Edward Markiewicz first began to seriously explore realism. Portraiture was initially his preferred subject matter, and he won First Prize for a self-portrait in the Connecticut Academy of Fine Arts annual competition. While he still paints an occasional portrait, Markiewicz has turned more often to still lifes, which he executes with bravura technique, in a photorealistic style.

Markiewicz's paintings offer an uncompromising view of reality. The subjects he depicts are the everyday objects that we take for granted. They are painted as they exist: fruit with bruises, people with blemishes. Through this unsentimental use of detail, Markiewicz pays homage to the beauty all around us.

Markiewicz has exhibited his work in over three dozen shows since 1986. In 1992, he exhibited at Douglas Gallery in Stamford, CT, Gallery East in East Hampton, NY, and most recently at James Jeffrey Gallery in Danbury, CT.

Edward Markiewicz

152 Roger Street
Hartford, CT 06106
203-956-1820

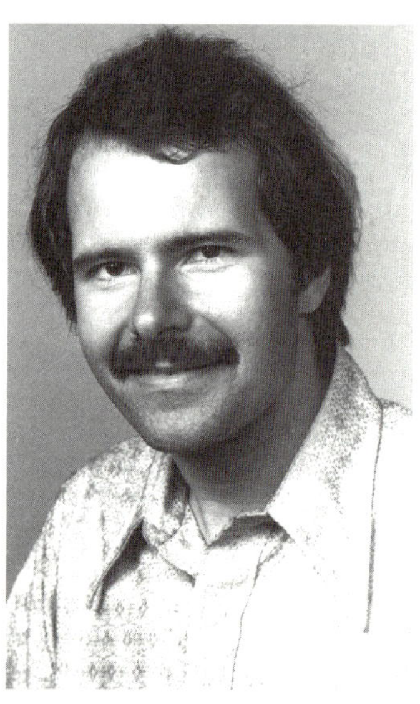

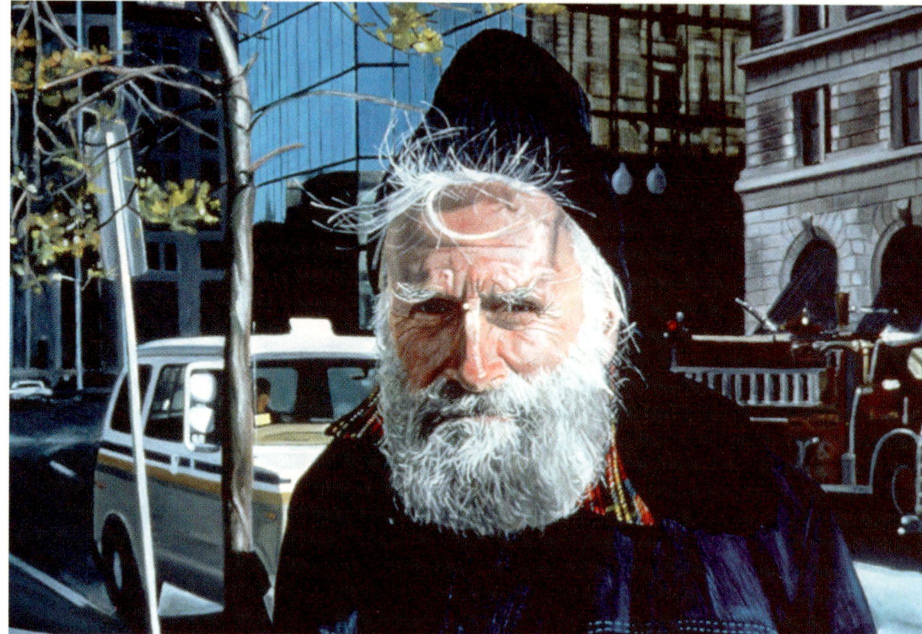

A. The Bostonian. Oil on canvas, 18" x 24".

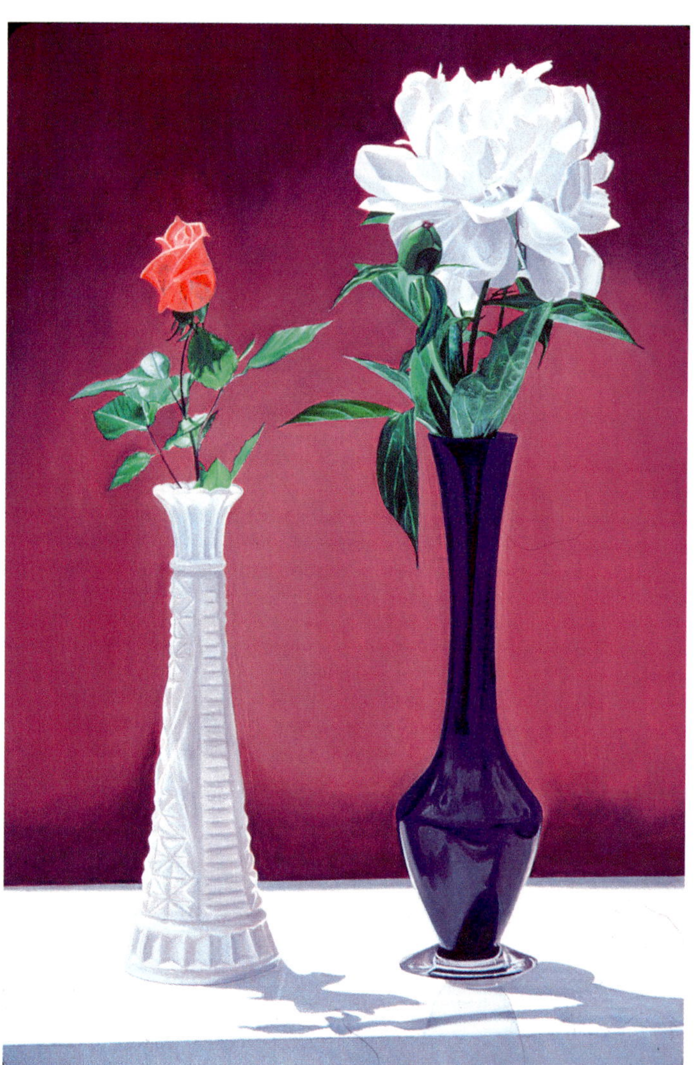

B. Double Flower Study. Oil on canvas, 36" x 36".

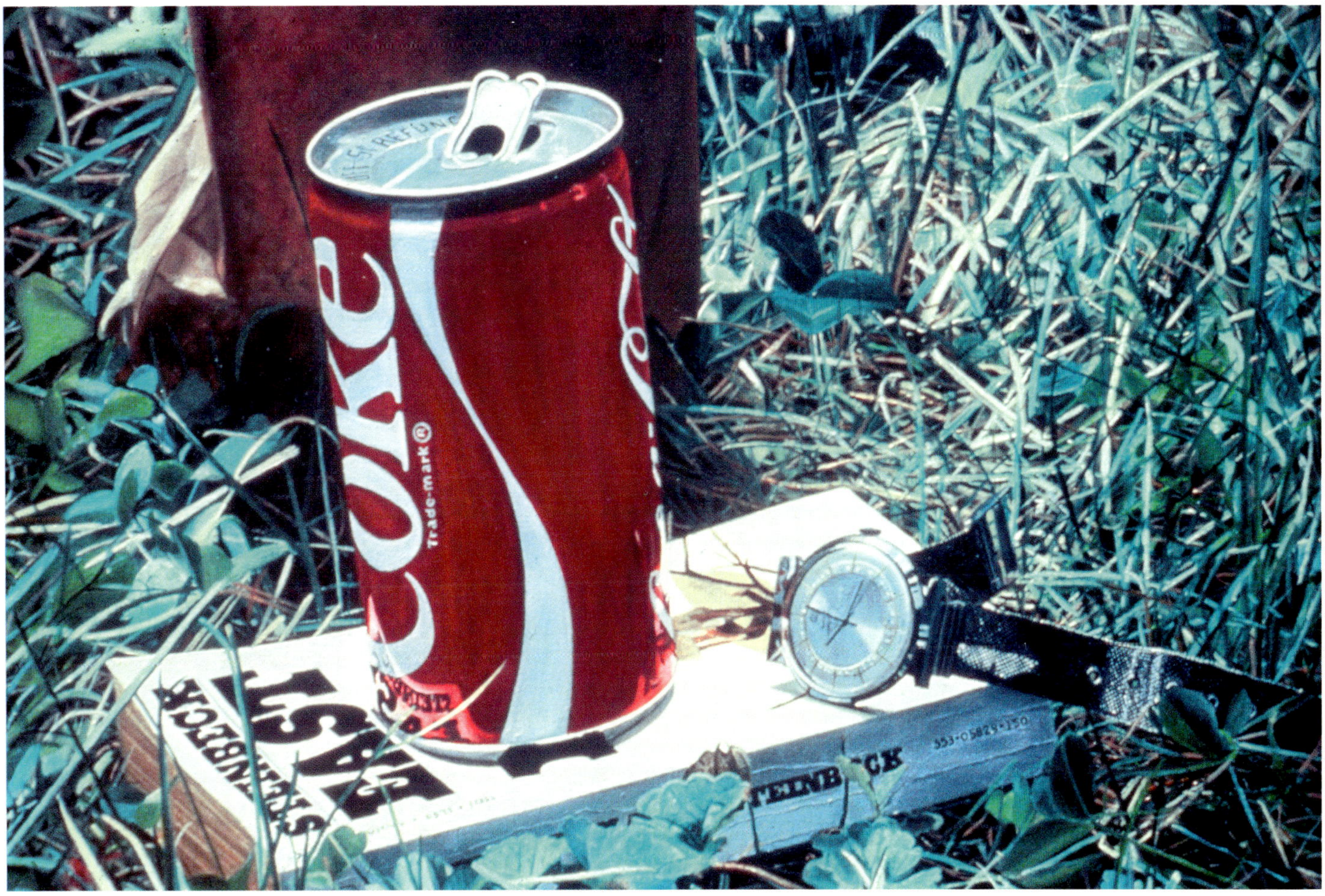

C. Stop Time I. Oil on canvas, 30" x 40".

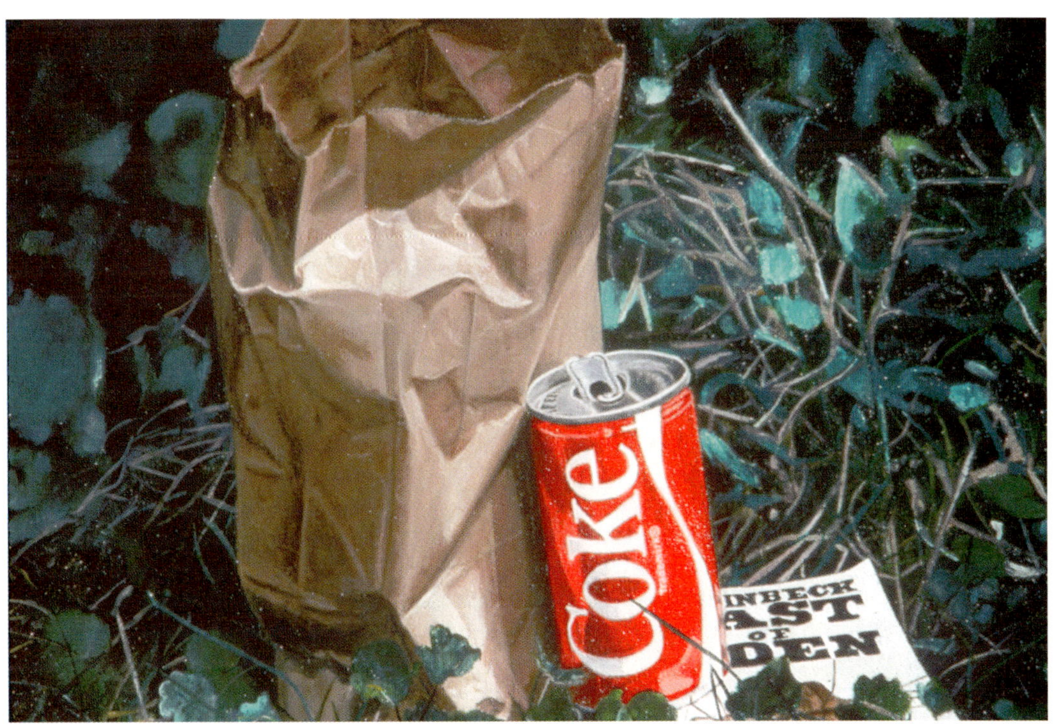

D. Late Afternoon. Oil on canvas, 16" x 20".

PRICE LIST

A $1,200

B $1,500

C $2,400

D $1,200

Represented by
Gallery East
East Hampton, NY

Marjorie Moore was born in Akron, OH, and attended Syracuse University where she received a BFA in 1966. After two years with the Peace Corps in Iran, she settled in Boston, MA. Moore has lived and worked in Brunswick, ME, since 1977.

Moore executes her paintings primarily in oils on linen and canvas. Her artistic focus is on human/animal relationships and issues of anthropomorphism. Many of the works explore childhood images of our culture and mesh autobiographical elements with topical issues. Her view of the world is simultaneously serious and humorous – cultural critique mixed with a loving irony toward subject matter.

Since 1980, Moore's work has been exhibited throughout New England in over a dozen solo shows and close to three dozen group shows, including a 1990 solo exhibition entitled "Perspectives" at the Portland Museum of Art. Her awards include a regional fellowship from the New England Foundation for the Arts in 1992, and her work has been reviewed by regional and national publications.

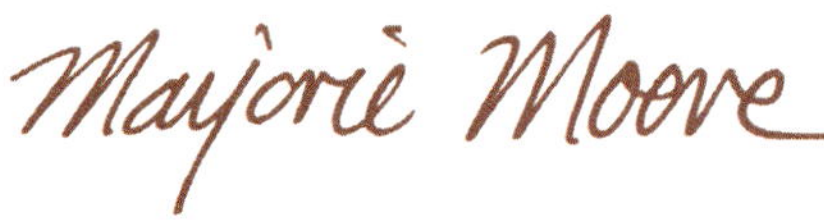

37 School Street
Brunswick, ME 04011
207-729-8661

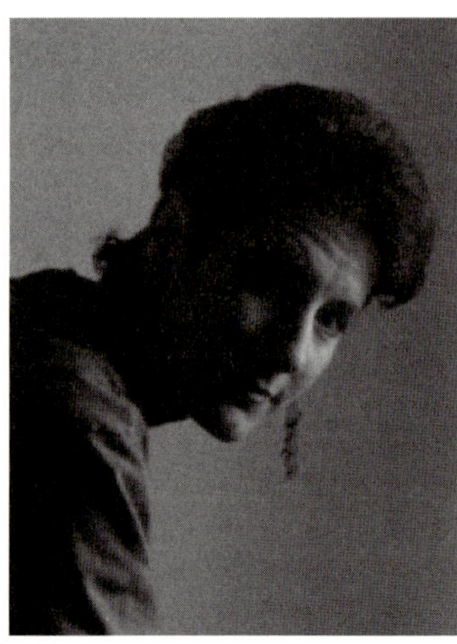

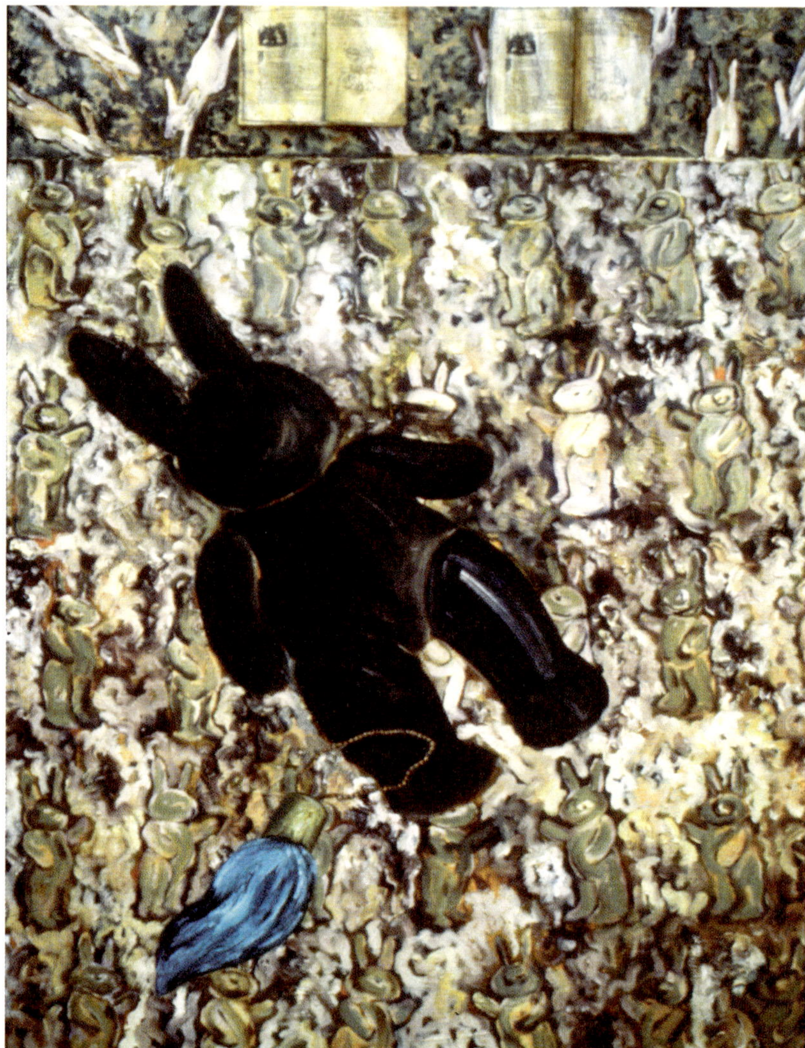

A. Double Luck Bunny. Oil on canvas/collaged books, 60" x 48".

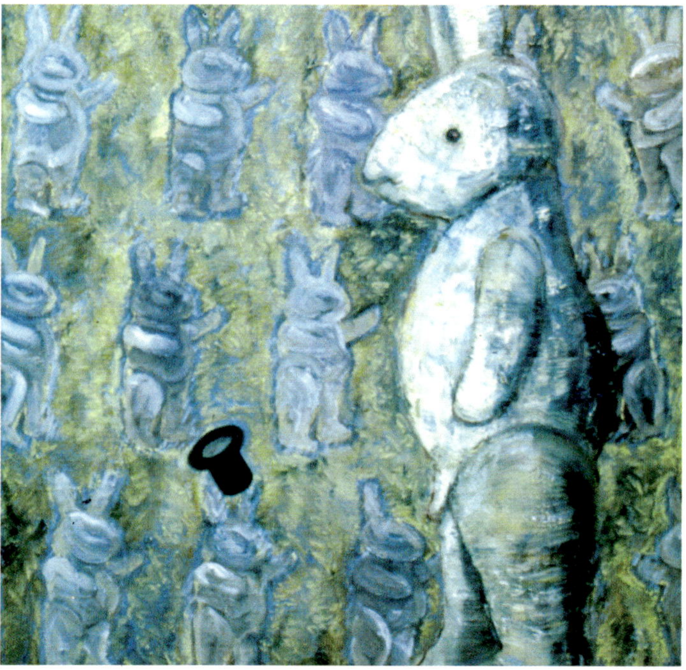

B. Is the Magic Gone? Oil on linen, 30" x 30".

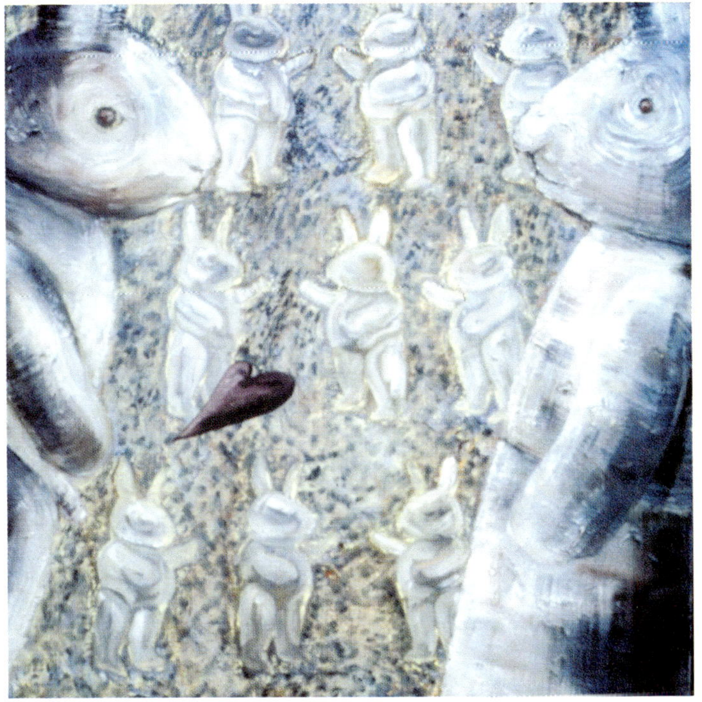

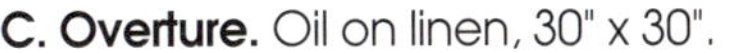

C. Overture. Oil on linen, 30" x 30".

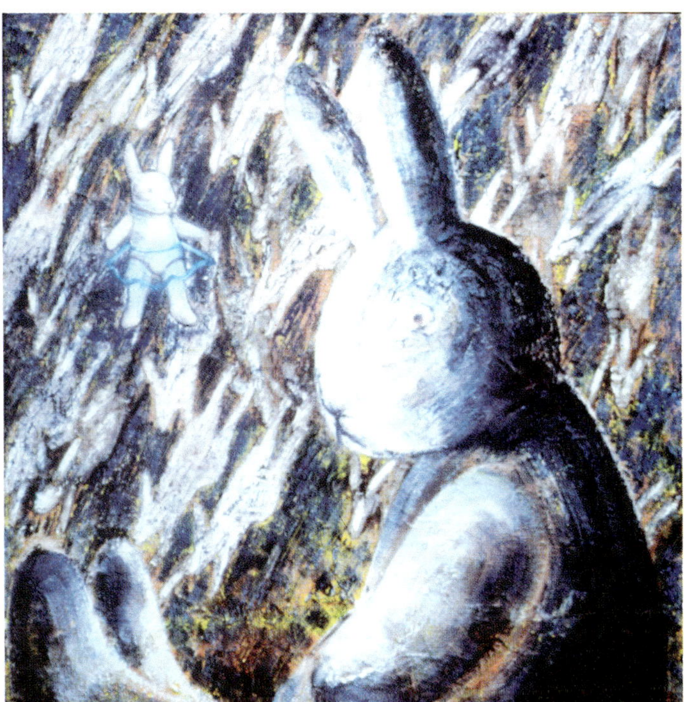

D. After the Storm. Oil on linen, 30" x 30".

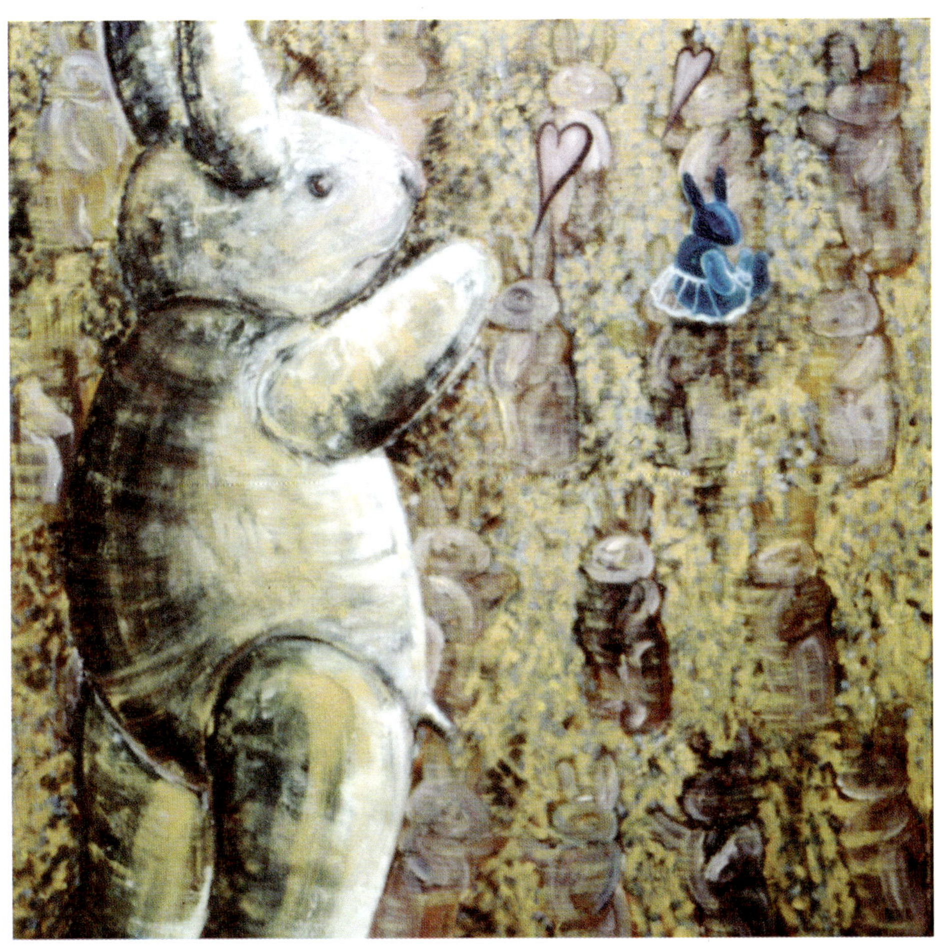

E. Encounter. Oil on canvas, 36" x 36".

PRICE LIST

A $3,500

B $1,800

C $1,800

D $1,800

E $2,200

Represented by
Howard Yezerski Gallery
Boston, MA

Robert Noreika

Robert Noreika is a native of Connecticut and now maintains a studio and gallery at the Farmington Valley Arts Center in Avon. Since graduating from Paier College of Art in Hamden, CT, Noreika has worked as a freelance graphic designer and illustrator. His illustrations have been commissioned by *Game and Fish, Outdoor Canada* and *Yankee Magazine,* among others. When he is not painting, Noreika teaches at the Farmington Valley Arts Center and is often a guest lecturer at art leagues throughout Connecticut.

Noreika's art is driven by a love of nature and a passion for the creative process itself. He employs the watercolor medium to focus on his favorite subject, the natural outdoors – scenes that depict wildlife and game fishing are his specialty. Noreika's command of his medium invites the viewer into intimate outdoor scenes and lets them sit by a babbling brook or walk through sun-bathed woods.

Noreika's work is represented in many public and private collections in Europe and the United States.

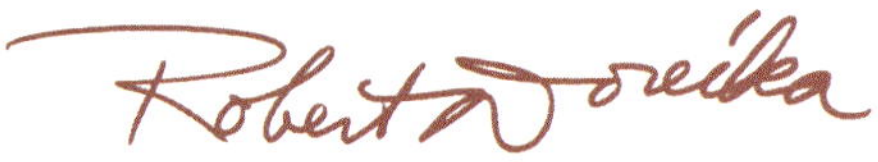

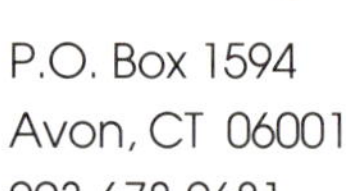

P.O. Box 1594
Avon, CT 06001
203-678-0681

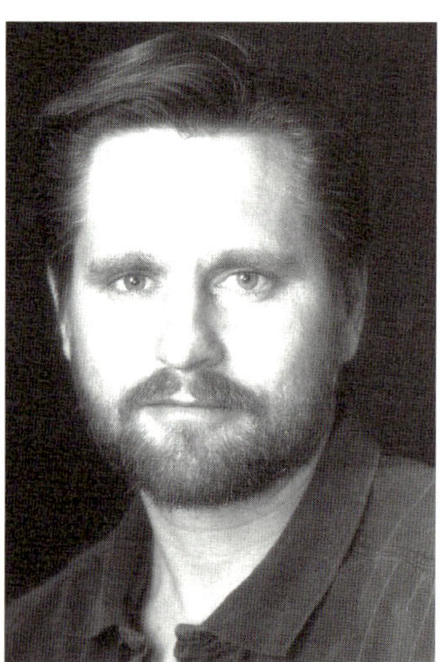

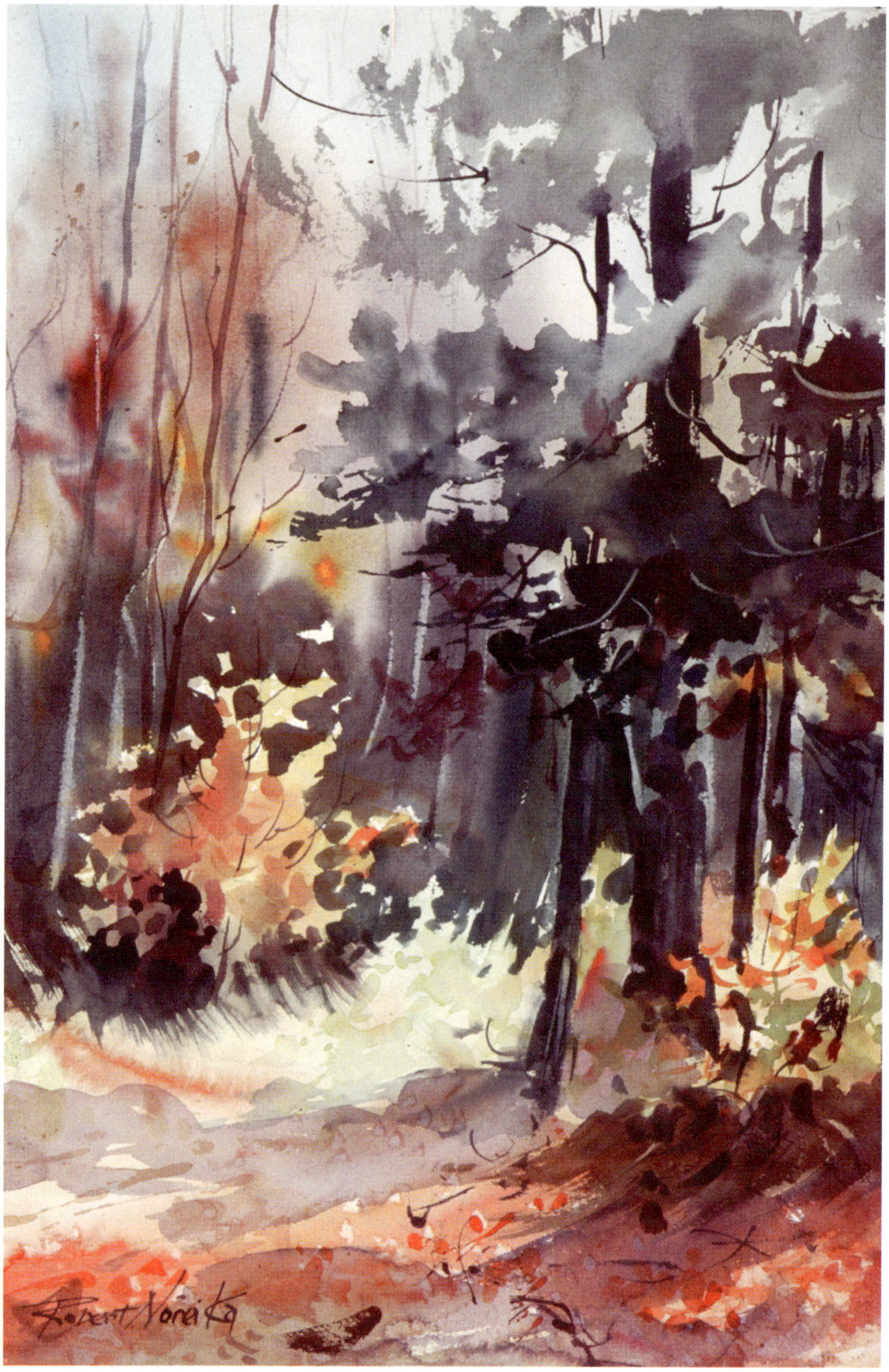

A. Foliage Light. Watercolor, 22" x 15".

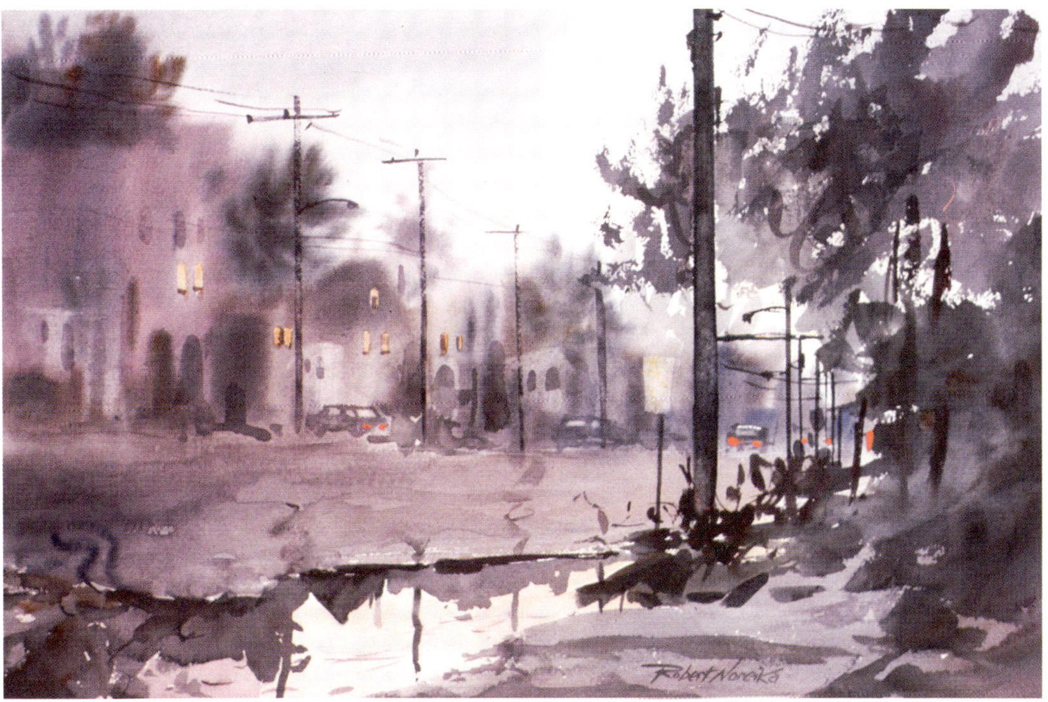

B. After the Rain. Watercolor, 22" x 30".

PRICE LIST

A..........................$650

B.......................$1,400

C $650

D..........................$650

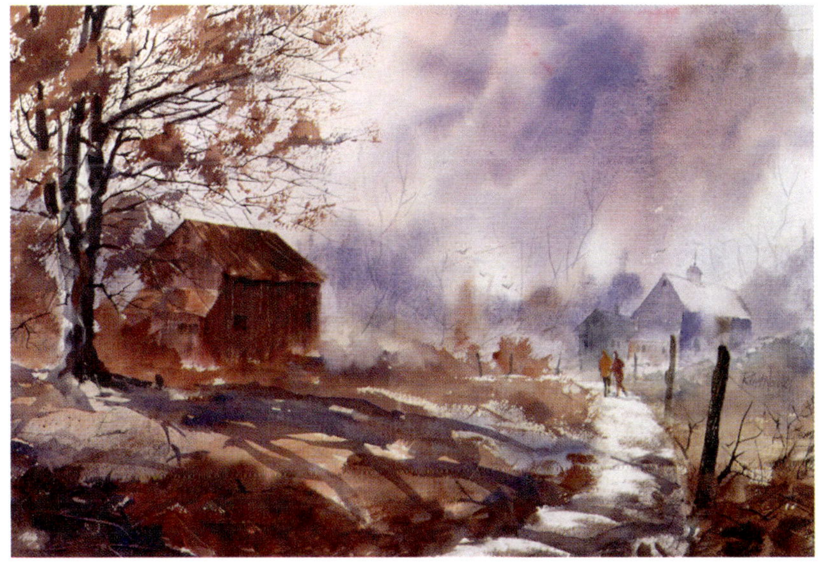

C. Mohegan Path.
Watercolor, 15" x 22".

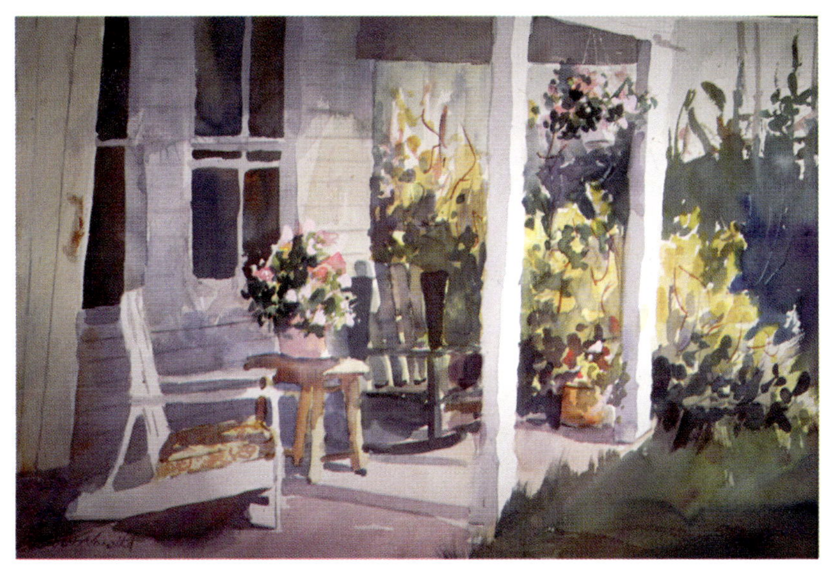

D. Stonington Porch.
Watercolor, 15" x 22".

T J **Norris**

TJ Norris is a Boston based multi-media artist. Born in 1965, he started making "art" at age 10. During the 1980s he studied at the Massachusetts College of Art and the Nova Scotia College of Art & Design in Canada.

Along with creating his own work, Norris is active in the Boston area arts community as a freelance contemporary art curator and published poet. He wears another hat as Visual Arts Program Coordinator for Very Special Arts, an international nonprofit arts organization that designs visual and performing arts programs for integrated audiences and artists, with and without disabilities.

Collage and assemblage are the media that Norris uses to fuse found objects, images and text into works that explore sexual, emotional and social issues. Recently he completed two full-scale, room-sized installations incorporating audio loops, video and specialized lighting. This work earned Norris a grant from the Massachusetts Cultural Council in 1991.

His works have been exhibited in Boston, New York City, Baltimore, Halifax, Nova Scotia, and New Hampshire and are included in many private and public collections across the country.

292 Shawmut Avenue
Boston, MA 02118
617-451-8029

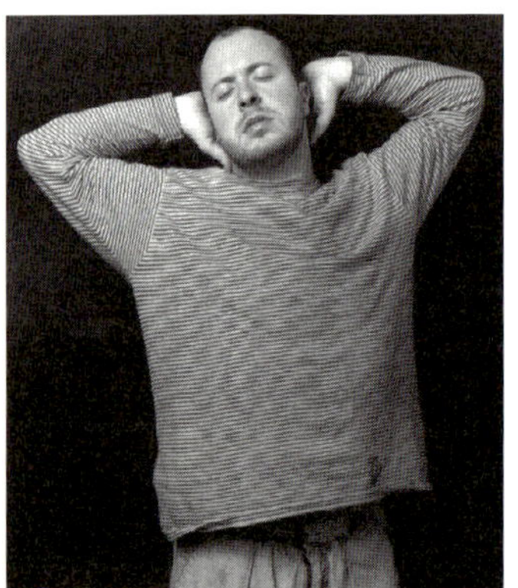

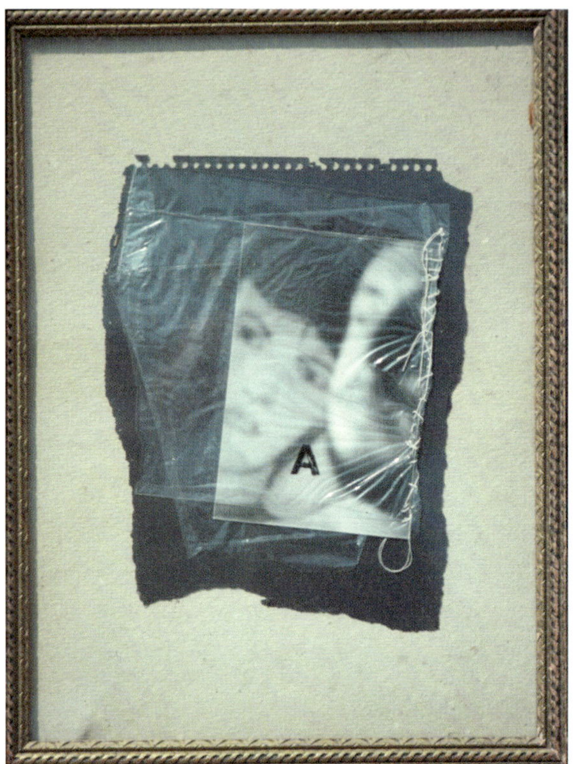

A. Exhibit A. Silver print/mixed media, 12¾" x 9¾".

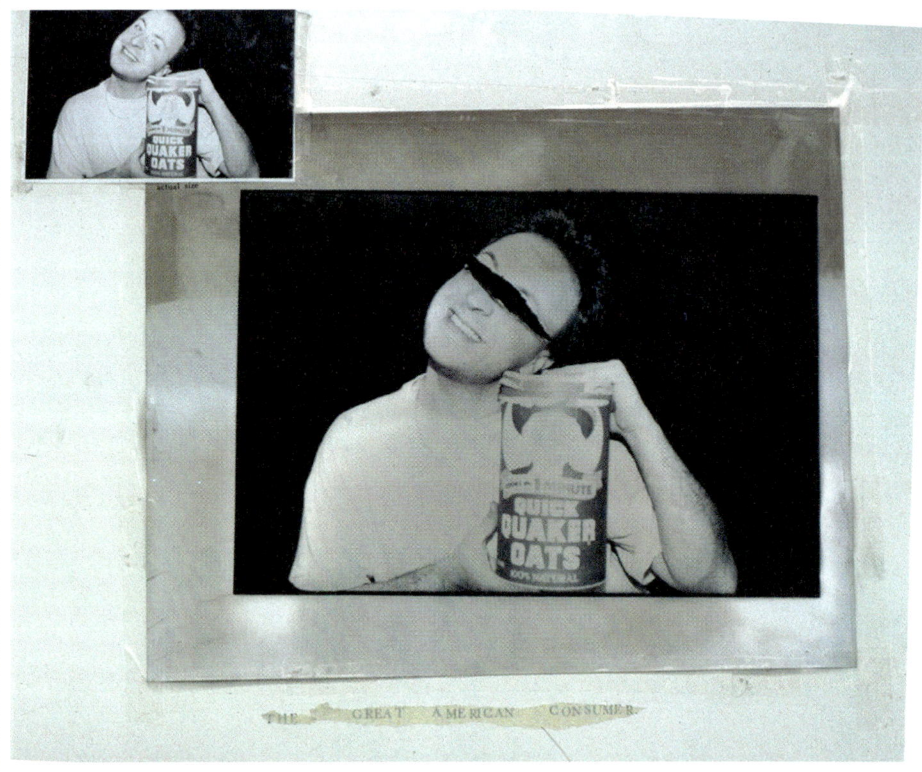

B. Actual Size. Silver prints/mixed media, 16" x 20".

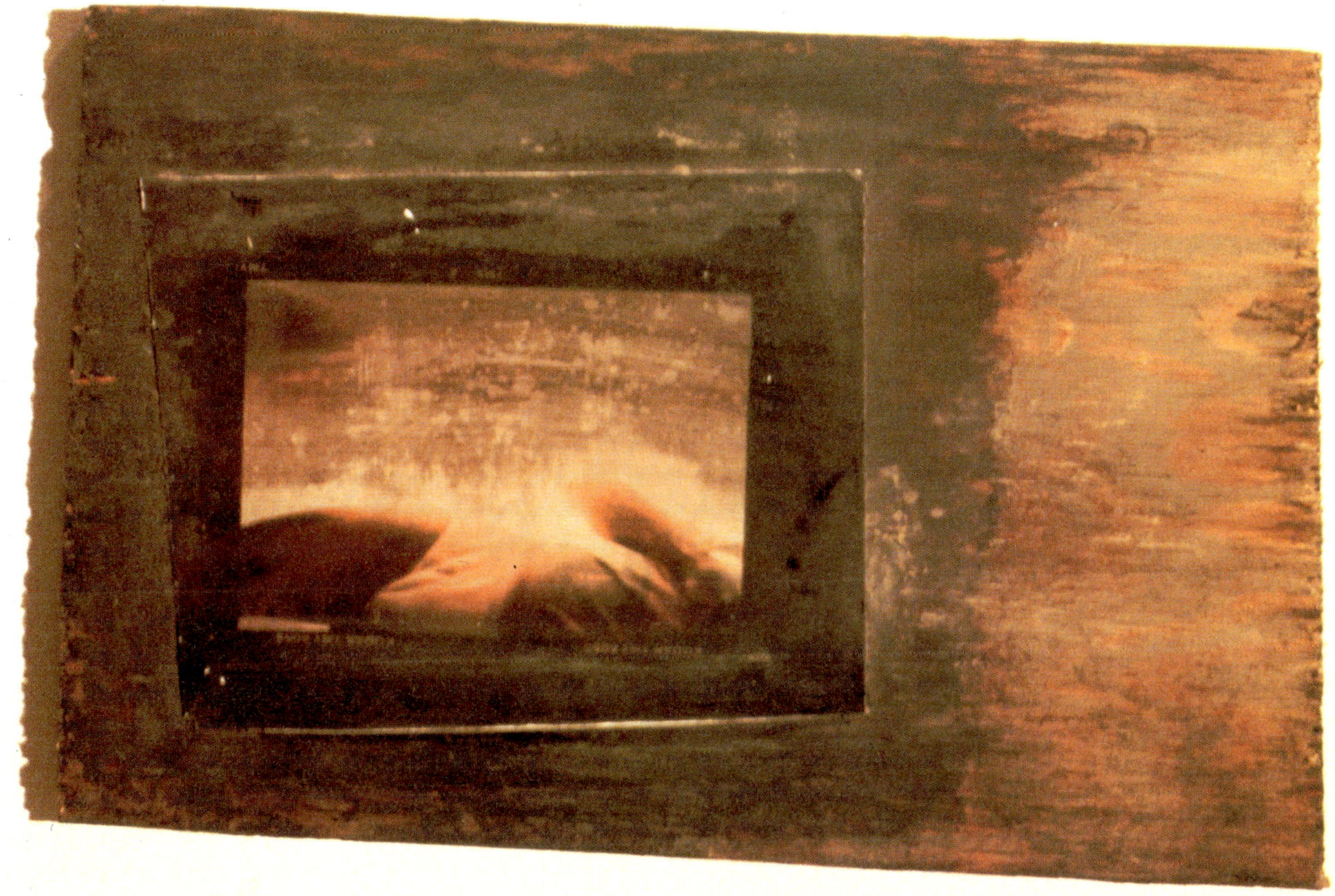

C. **Silent Obsession.** Silver print/mixed media on wood, 8" x 5".

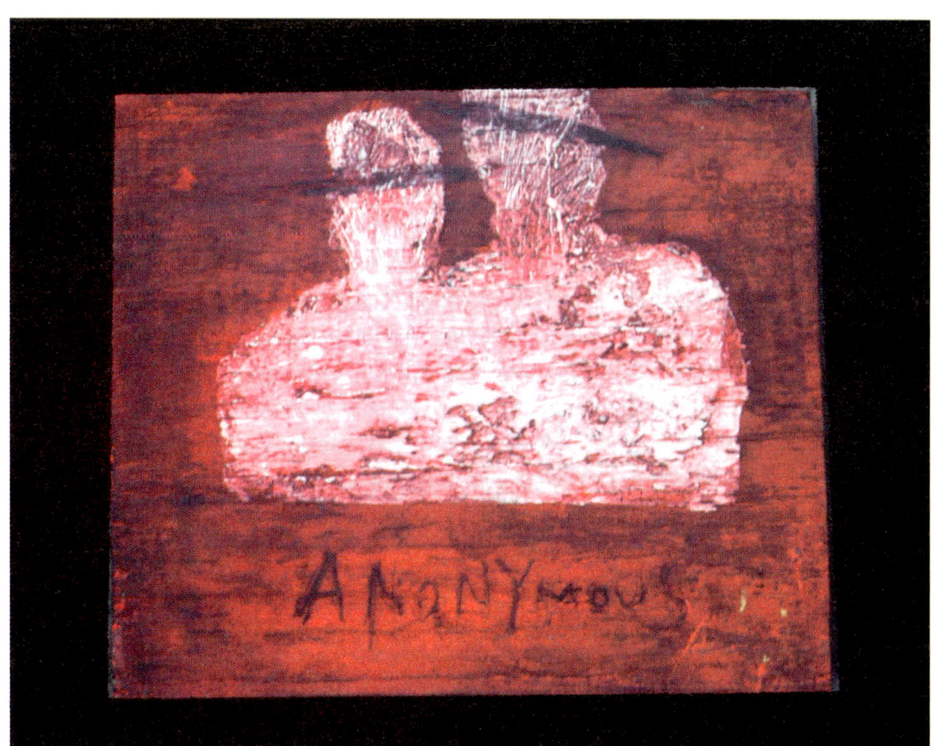

D. Anonymous One. Oil pastel, india ink and gouache on wood, 4" x 3½". Collection of the artist.

PRICE LIST

A..........................$900

B.......................$1,200

C.........................$600

D..........................$800

Nick Paciorek was born and raised in Chicago, IL. He came to New England five years ago, and now lives and works in Providence, RI. Paciorek received formal training at the Maryland Institute College of Art, graduating in 1985 with a BFA. He also attended the Art Institute of Chicago and the American Academy of Art.

Paciorek's oil paintings are a celebration of color and light in the Fauve tradition. Using bold strokes and an uninhibited palette, he puts on canvas what is often ordinary to the eye and transforms it into an extraordinary experience of movement and energy. Paciorek chooses such subjects as cityscapes in the early morning light, or the frenetic activities of workmen on a construction site. The viewer is invited to explore these worlds through his unique and vivid interpretation.

Since 1986, Paciorek has exhibited his work in an annual solo show – a two-person show in 1990 – at the Foxhall Gallery in Washington, DC. His paintings have also been shown in Chicago, Philadelphia and other cities across the United States.

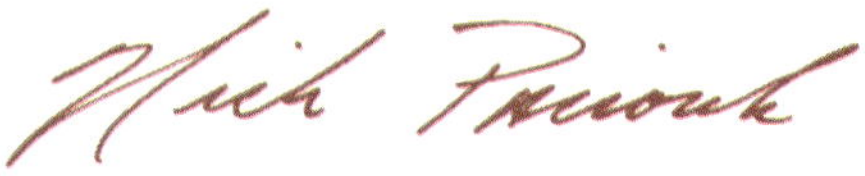

Nick Paciorek
63 Blaisdell Avenue
Pawtucket, RI 02860
401-728-1729

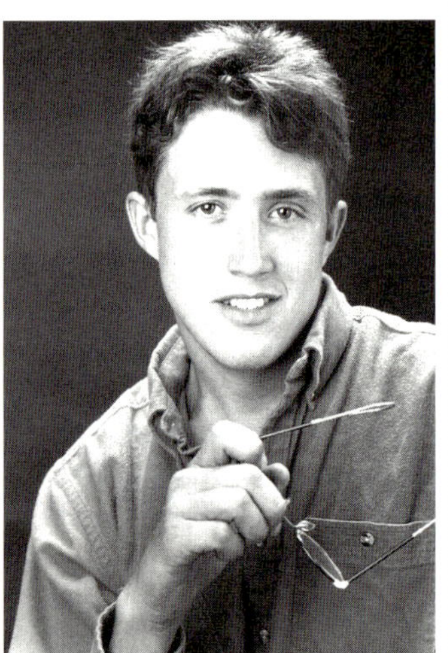

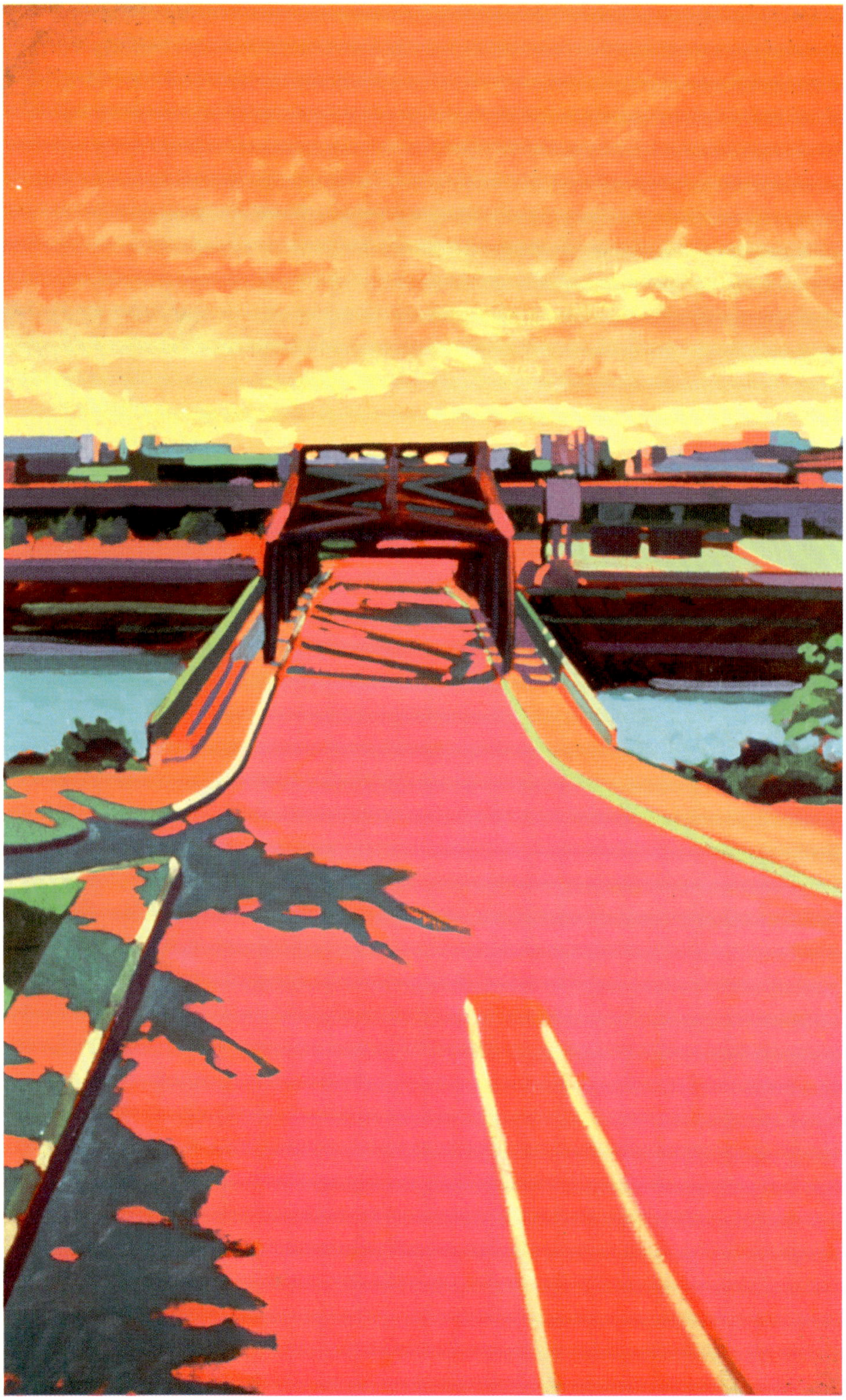

A. Point Crossing. Oil on paper, 57" x 35". Courtesy of Po Gallery.

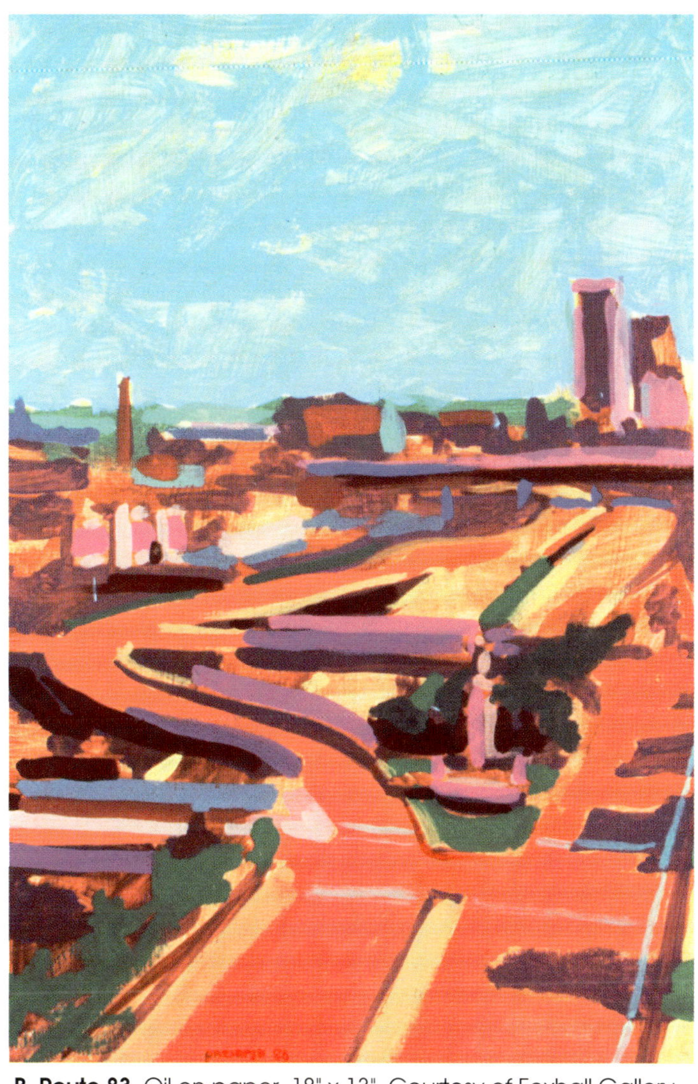

B. Route 83. Oil on paper. 18" x 13". Courtesy of Foxhall Gallery.

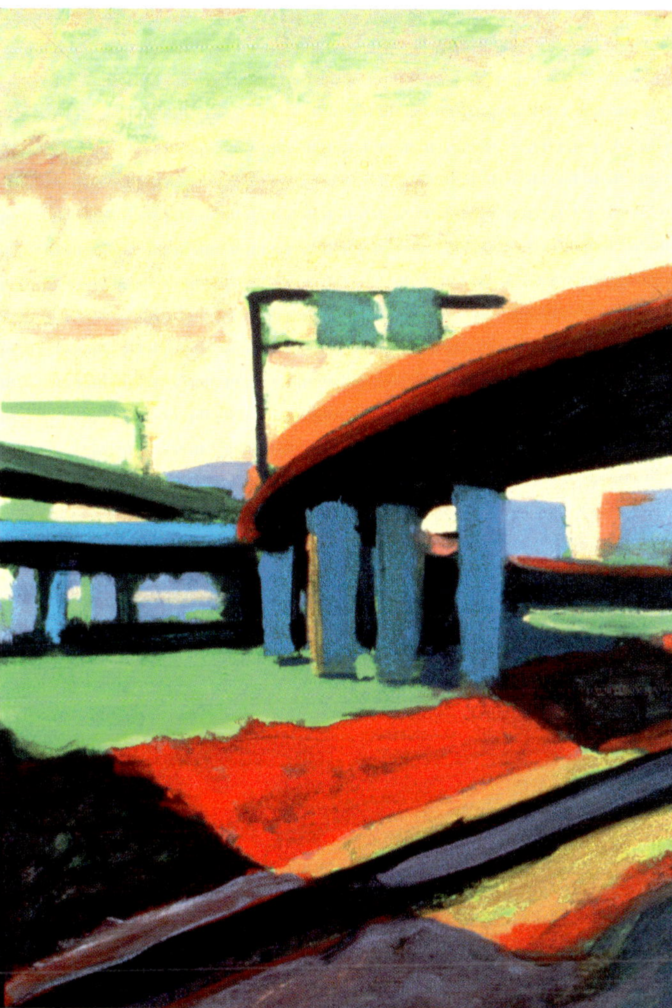

C. Baltimore Encounter. Oil on paper, 21" x 14". Courtesy of Po Gallery.

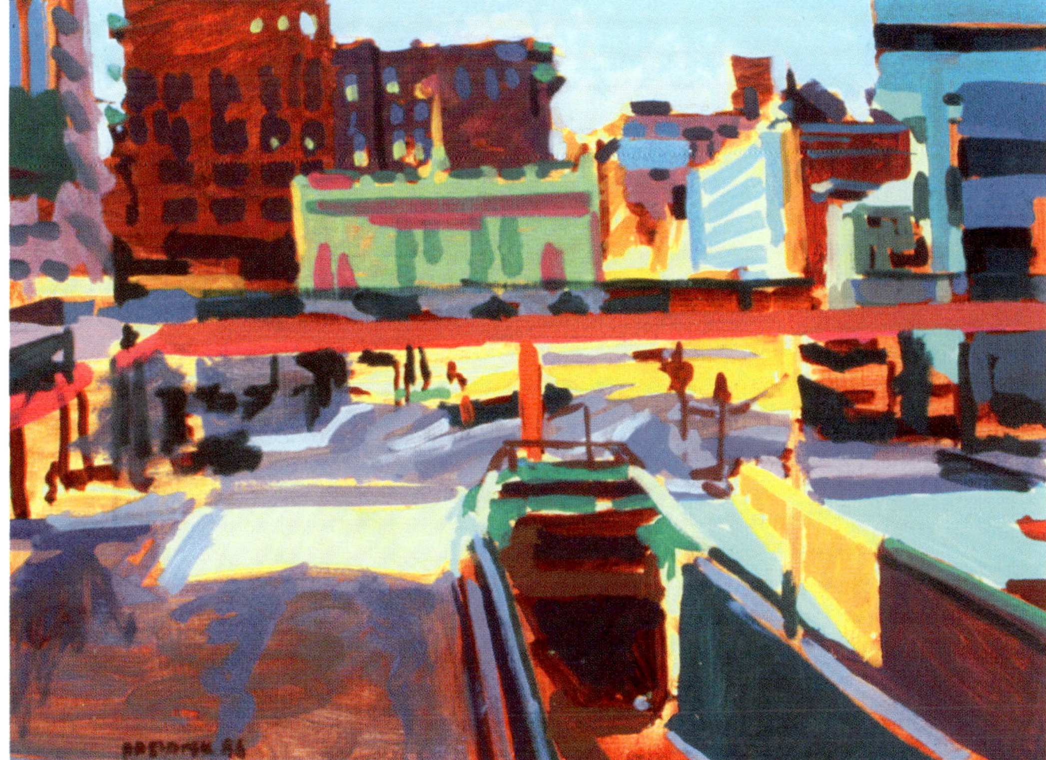

D. Crossway. Oil on paper, 17" x 23". Courtesy of Foxhall Gallery.

PRICE LIST

A $1,500

B $700

C $700

D......................$650

Represented by
Po Gallery
Providence, RI
Foxhall Gallery
Washington, DC

Brenda Phillips attributes her decision to become an artist to the creative environment of a small secondary school she attended in Florida. She received formal art training at Mount Holyoke College in South Hadley, MA, graduating in 1978 with a BA. Although Phillips focused on sculpture for three years, studies under Marion Miller revealed her true calling to be painting. Before moving to New Hampshire, where she now lives and works, Phillips spent time in California and New York City.

Phillips creates both large and small works. She draws on the same subject matter for both, but the media differ. Her large works are oil paintings executed on primed paper or canvas; the smaller works are mixed media. Phillips begins developing her works without a preconceived idea of the final painting. The images are drawn from her personal mythology, and the themes evolve as she paints.

In the past three years, Phillips' paintings have been the focus of five solo shows, and they have been included in several group exhibitions, most recently at the Gerard Gallery of the Winsor House in Winsor, VT.

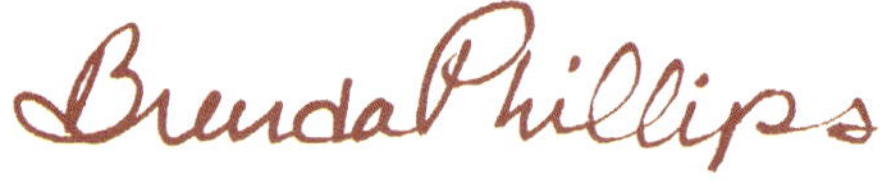

RFD 2, Box 59, River Rd.
West Lebanon, NH 03784
603-675-2757

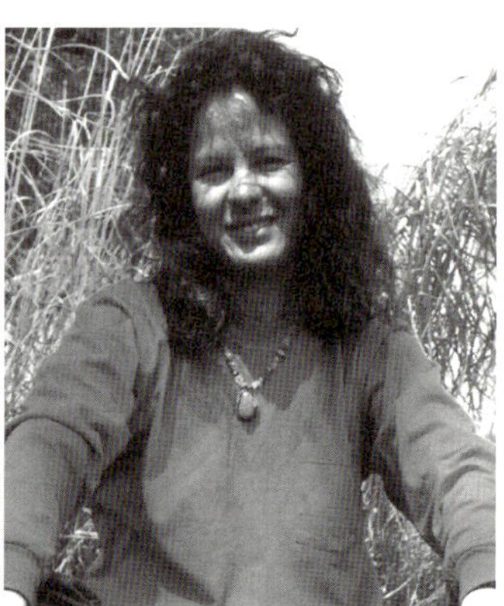

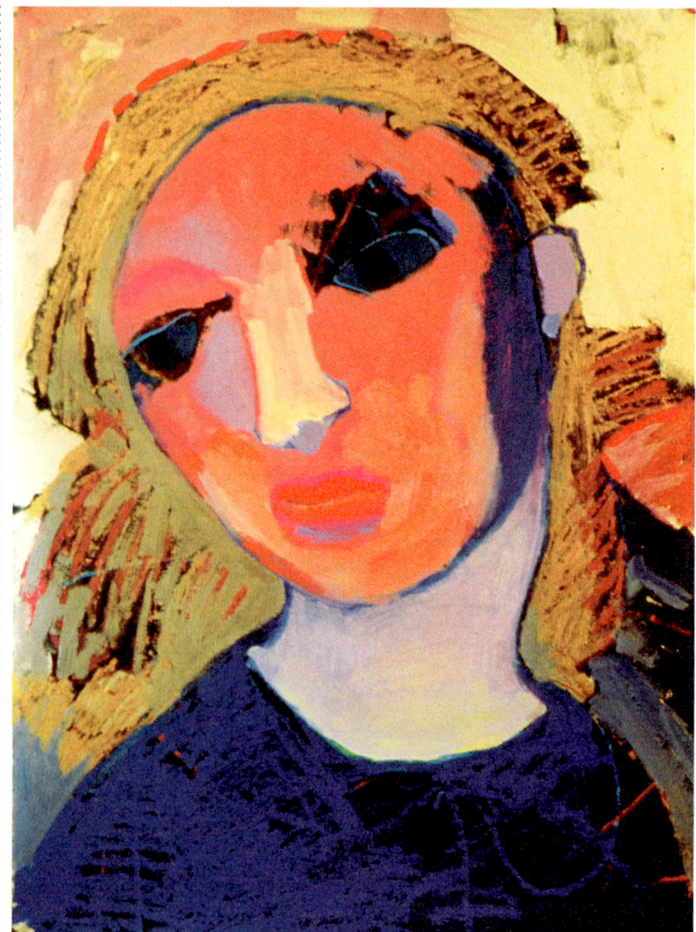

A. Mona Lisa. Oil on paper, 28" x 21".

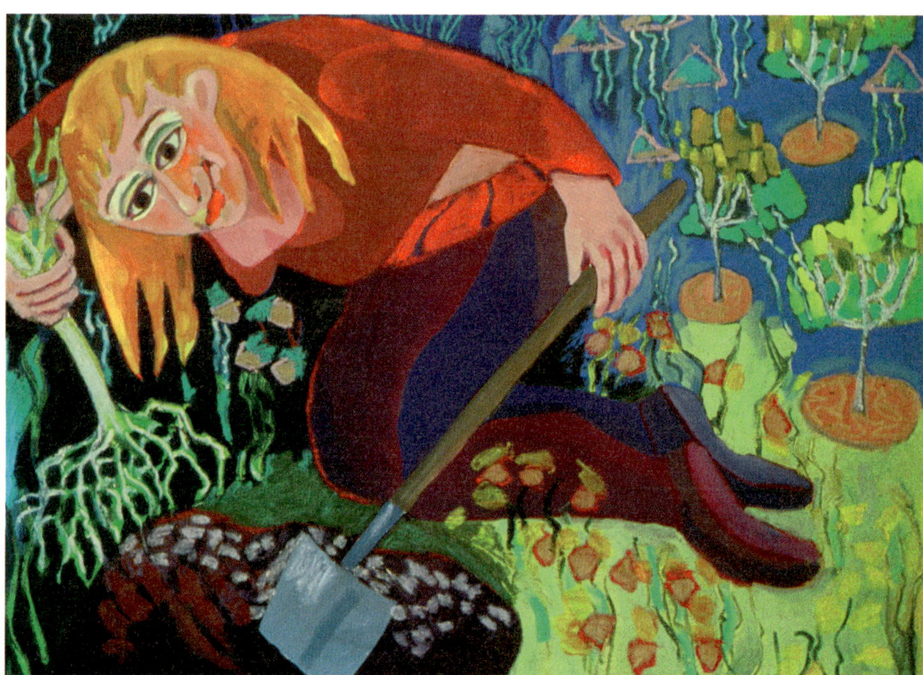

B. Tree Planter. Oil on paper, 38" x 50".

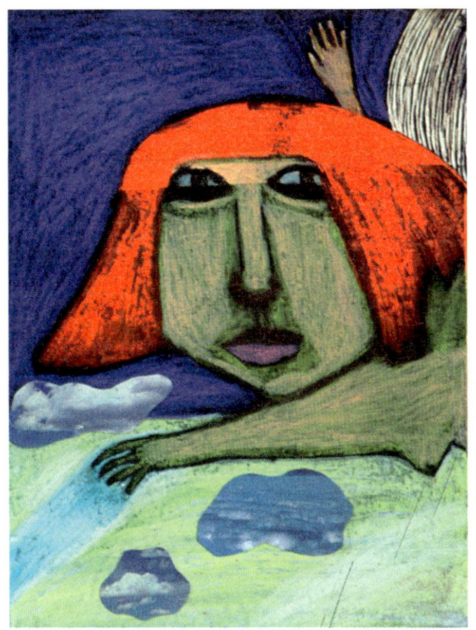

C. Angel with a Mission. Collage with Caran d'Ache, 9" x 7".

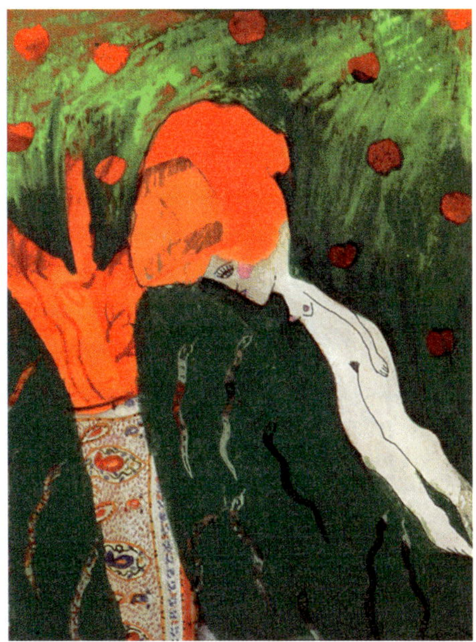

D. Eve's Dream. Collage with Caran d'Ache, 9" x 7".

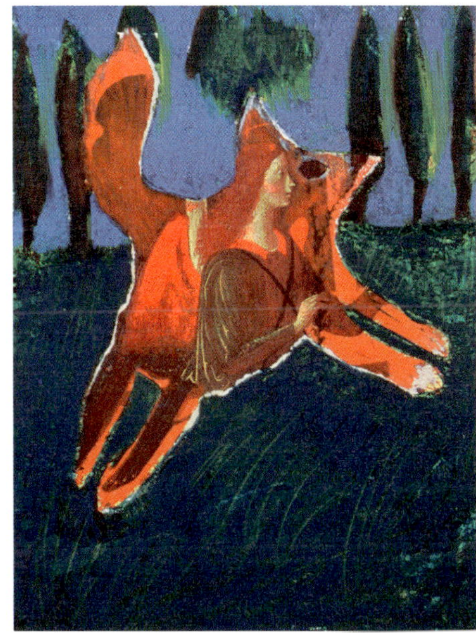

E. Fox Across Your Path. Collage with Caran d'Ache, 9" x 7".

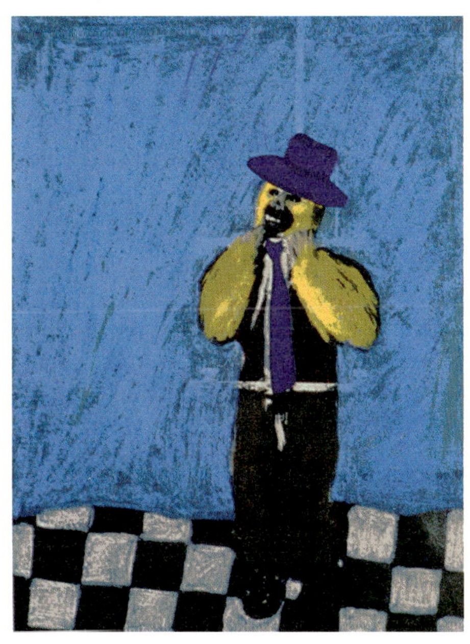

F. Monkey Suit. Collage with Caran d'Ache, 9" x 7".

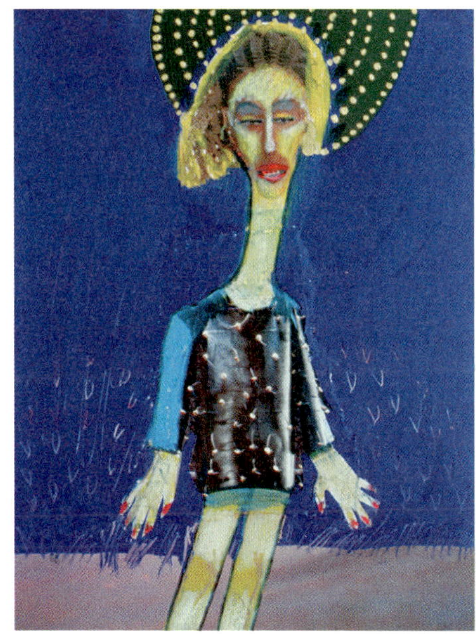

G. Royalty. Collage with Caran d'Ache, 9" x 7".

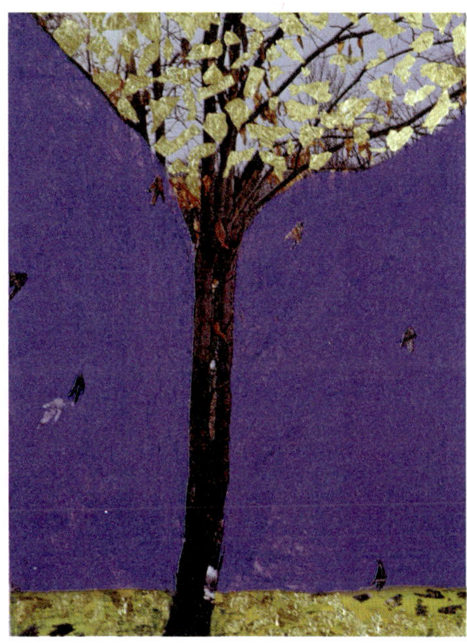

H. October Tree. Collage with Caran d'Ache, 9" x 7".

PRICE LIST

A..........................$675
B......................$1,000
C..........................$200
D..........................$200
E..........................$200
F..........................$200
G..........................$200
H..........................$200

Ellen **Pliskin**

Ellen Pliskin is a resident of Cheshire, CT, and New York City. She studied at Fordham University and then at Hunter College, where she earned a BA from the School of Visual Arts. Pliskin has since taught art classes and is currently a member of the graduate faculty of Fordham University.

Working primarily in watercolor and mixed media, Pliskin draws her subject matter from the landscape, devoting entire series of paintings to locations that inspire her. Her interest in color, texture and space make each painting an exploration of formal qualities as well as a study of a specific location. The results are works that blend representation and abstraction, with real objects and places being suggested by layers of color.

Pliskin has exhibited in museums and art galleries in Connecticut and New York City. She has had five solo shows, and has been represented in numerous group exhibitions, including Sotheby's 1990 show entitled "New York Artist Showcase." Pliskin's work is included in both public and corporate collections.

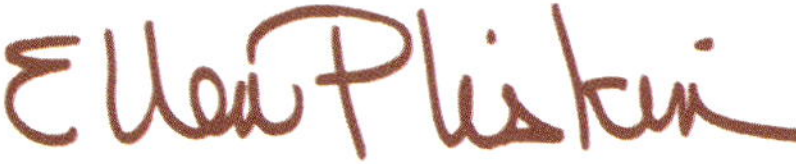

15 Promontory Drive
Cheshire, CT 06410
203-272-5987

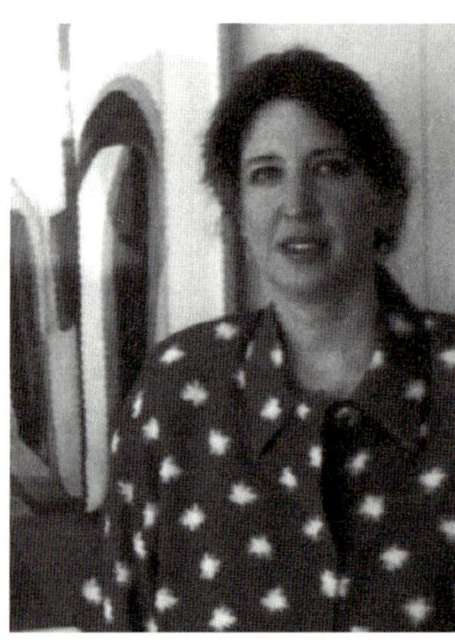

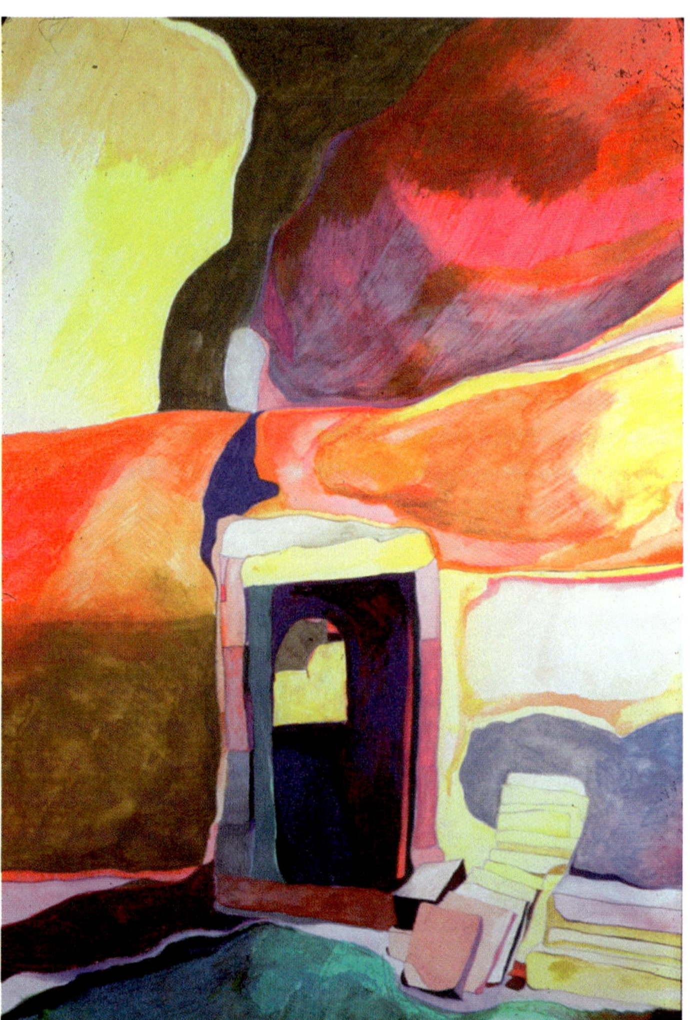

A. Toplou #1. Watercolor, gouache and pencil, 30" x 22½".

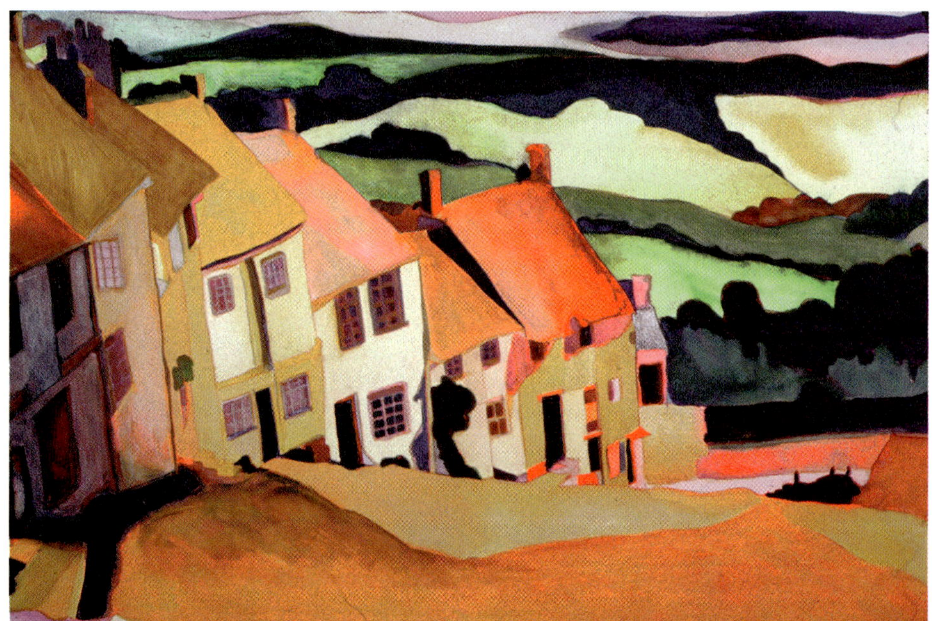

B. Golden Hill. Watercolor, gouache and pencil, 22" x 30".

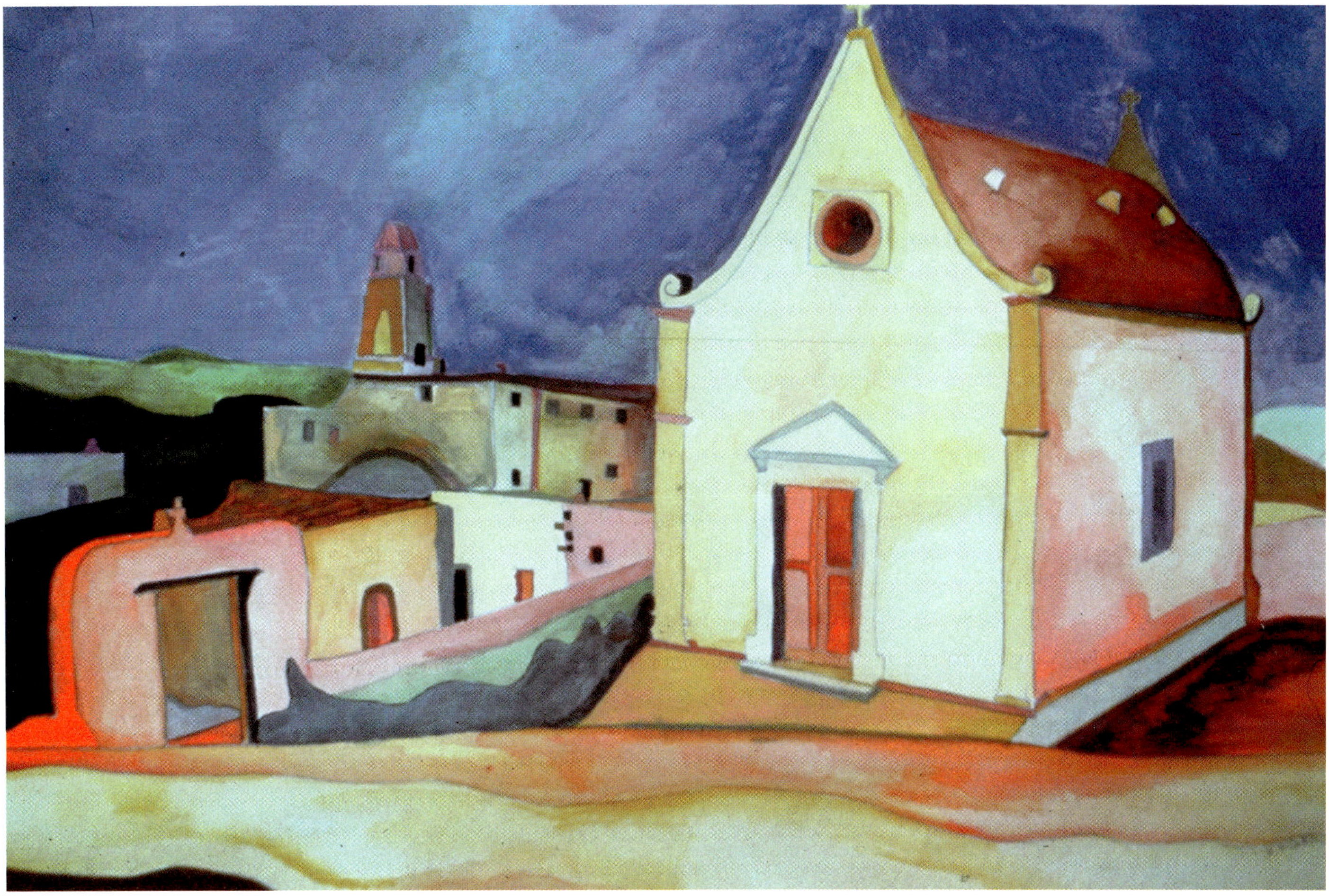

C. The Church of the Holy Cross. Watercolor, 22" x 30".

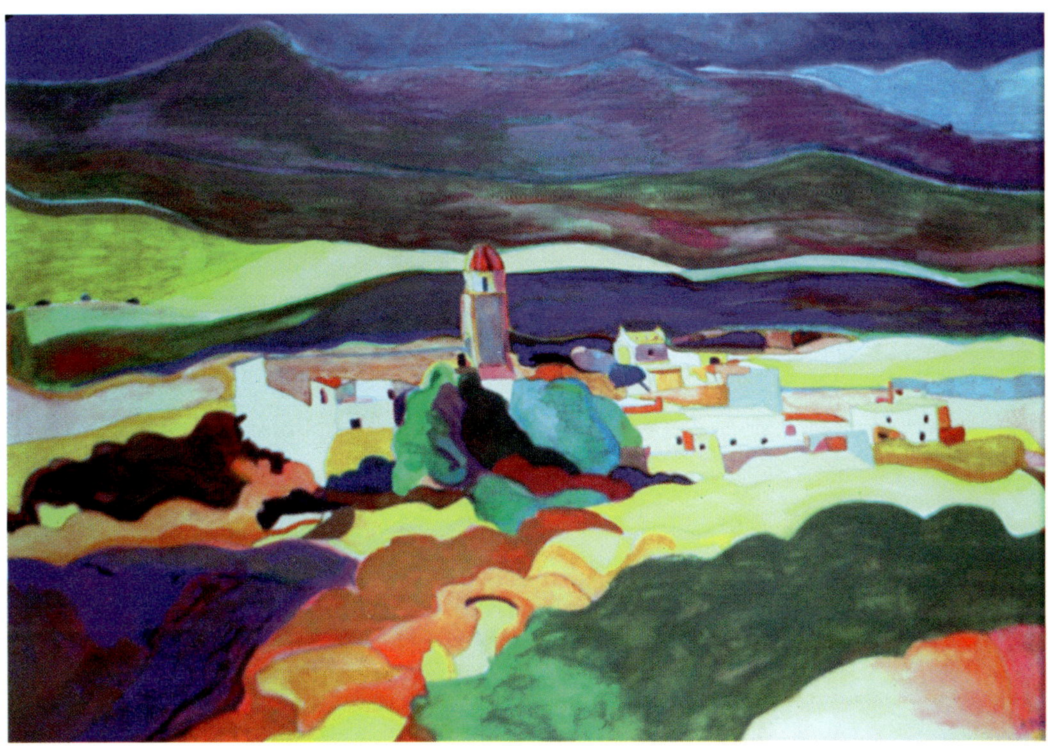

D. Monastery of Toplou: General View from the North. Watercolor, gouache and pencil, 22" x 30".

PRICE LIST

A.........................$900

B.......................$1,000

C.........................$900

D.........................$900

Elizabeth Kelner Pozen was born in Philadelphia, PA, and now lives in Newton Centre, MA. In 1968, she graduated from the University of Pennsylvania with a degree in cultural anthropology, and then studied social anthropology at Cambridge University and social work at Columbia University. Pozen's formal art training began in 1978. She studied art at schools in the Washington, DC, area through 1984. In 1988, she studied painting with James Aponovich at Bennington College.

Executed primarily in oil on canvas, Pozen's work takes its inspiration from her experience in social work and cultural anthropology. She is interested in internal reality – feelings and impressions that accompany life events – and in relationships among people. Her narrative and evocative images take a sometimes humorous, sometimes ambiguous look at tradition and its place in contemporary society.

Pozen has exhibited in numerous group shows since 1981. She had a solo show in Boston in 1990, and in 1992, her work was included in "Distinct Voices," a juried exhibition at the Federal Reserve Gallery in Boston.

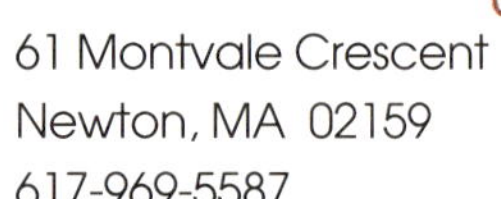

61 Montvale Crescent
Newton, MA 02159
617-969-5587

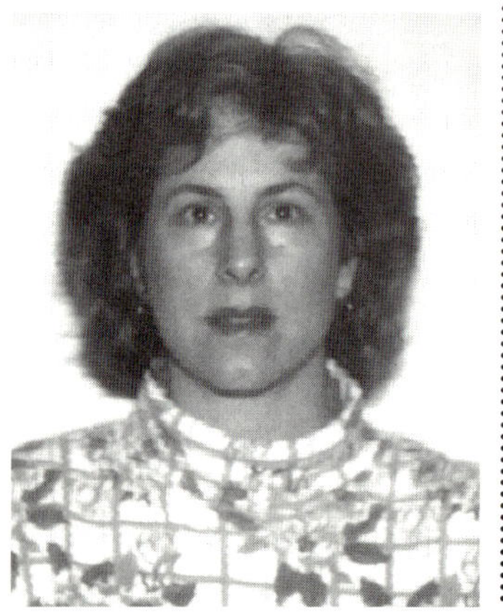

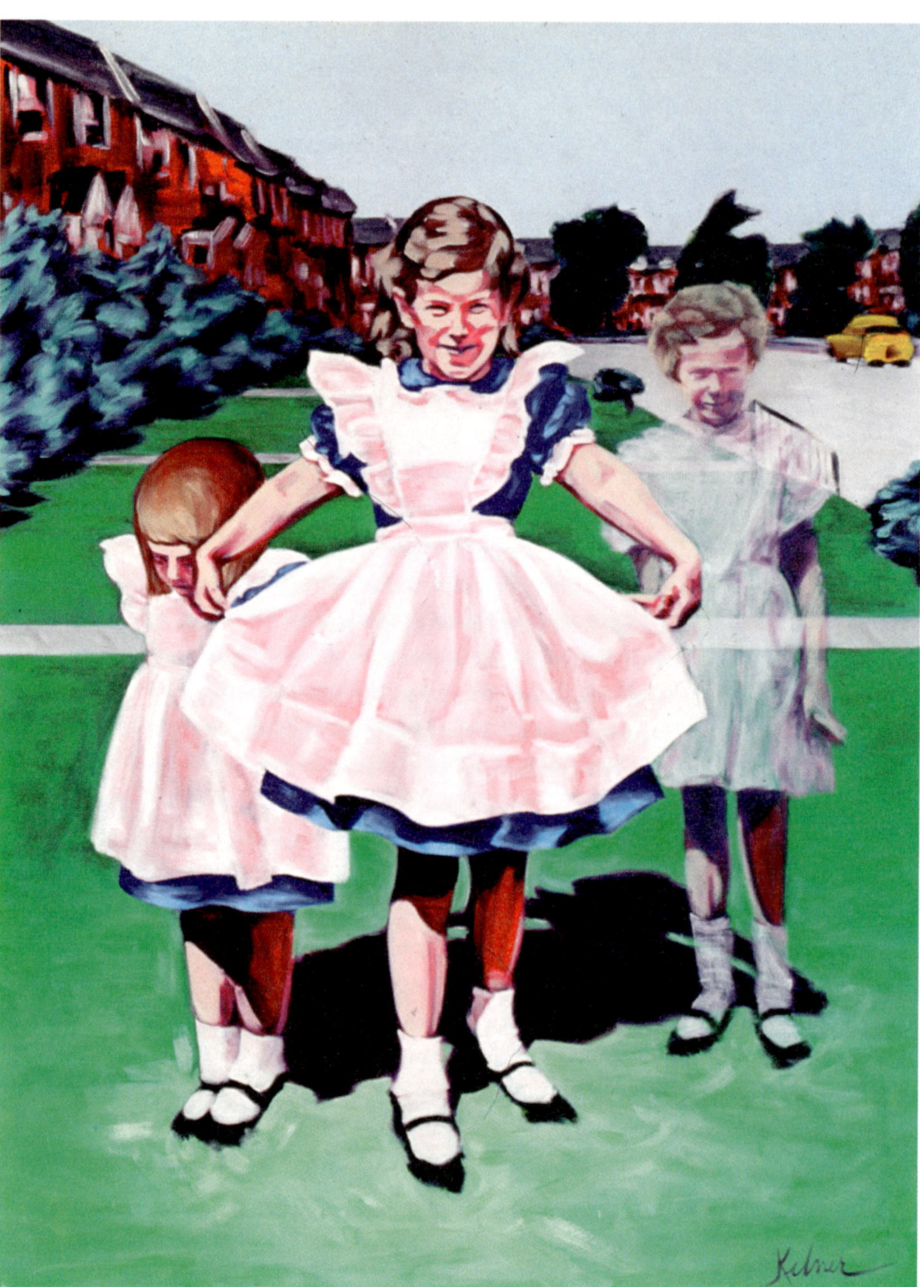

A. The Way It Really Was. Oil on canvas, 48" x 36".

PRICE LIST

A $2,200
B $2,200
C $2,200
D $1,200

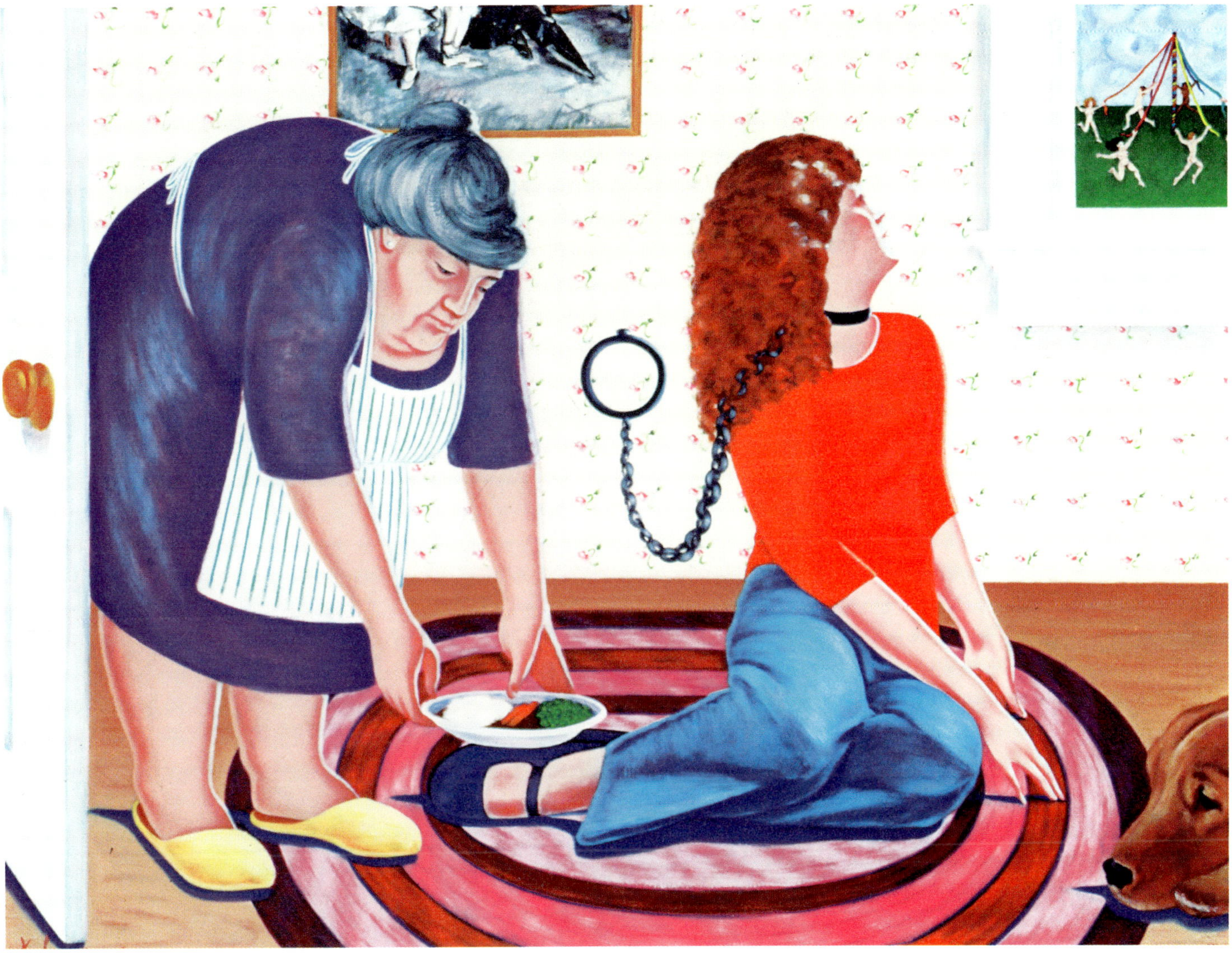

B. Conflict of Interest. Oil on canvas, 36" x 48".

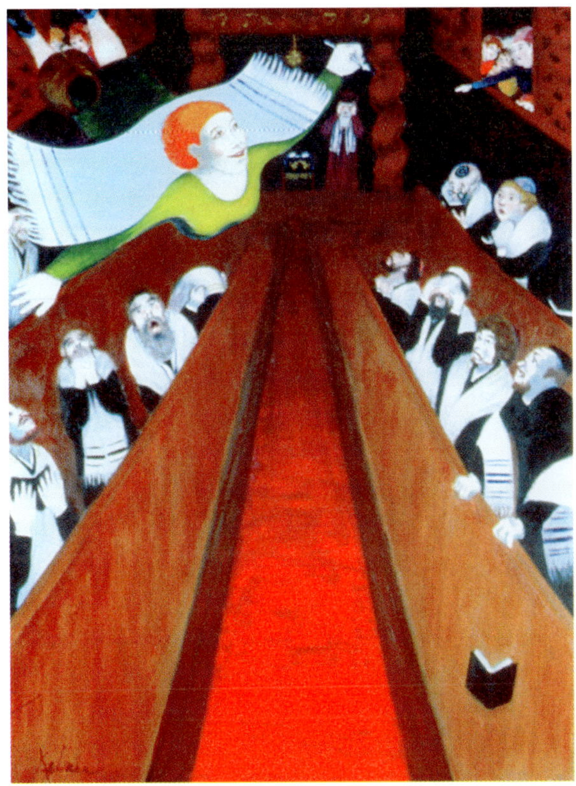

C. Dream of the Orthodox Woman. Oil on canvas, 48" x 36".

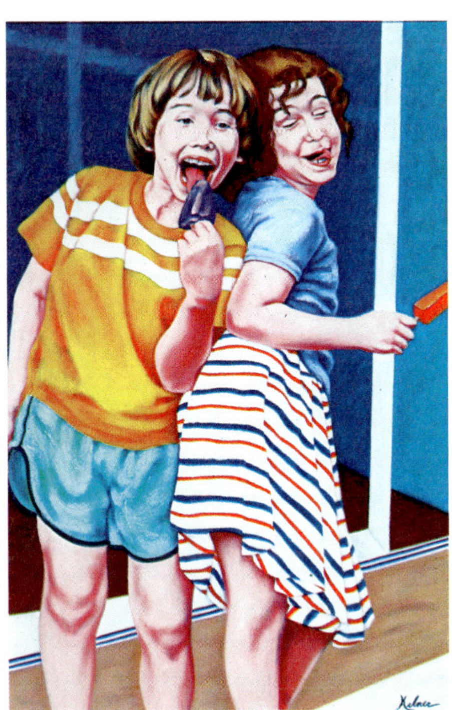

D. Popsicles II. Oil on canvas, 36" x 24".

Paul **Rahilly**

Paul Rahilly was born in Boston, graduated from Tufts University and studied painting at the Art Students League in New York City. He has been a full-time painter working in Boston since the mid-nineteen-sixties, and he has taught part-time at several area schools and colleges. Rahilly currently teaches life drawing at the Massachusetts College of Art.

Rahilly is known for his large, complex oil paintings of figures, still lifes and animals. The paintings are a profusion of rich color and dense pigment played out aginst a surface that is often cluttered with imagery. They are a celebration of paint itself, a working of contemporary visual ideas with subject matter that has always intrigued painters.

Rahilly has exhibited nationally for almost thirty years and he has received many awards. Among them are grants for painting from the National Endowment for the Arts, the Aldolph and Ester Gottlieb Foundation and the Massachusetts Artists Fellowship.

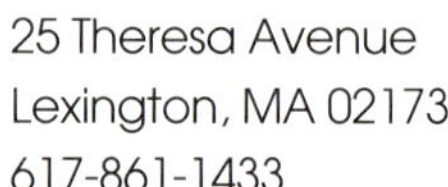

25 Theresa Avenue
Lexington, MA 02173
617-861-1433

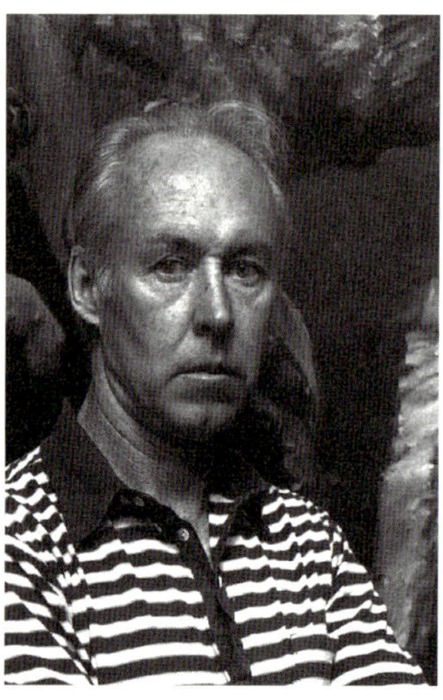

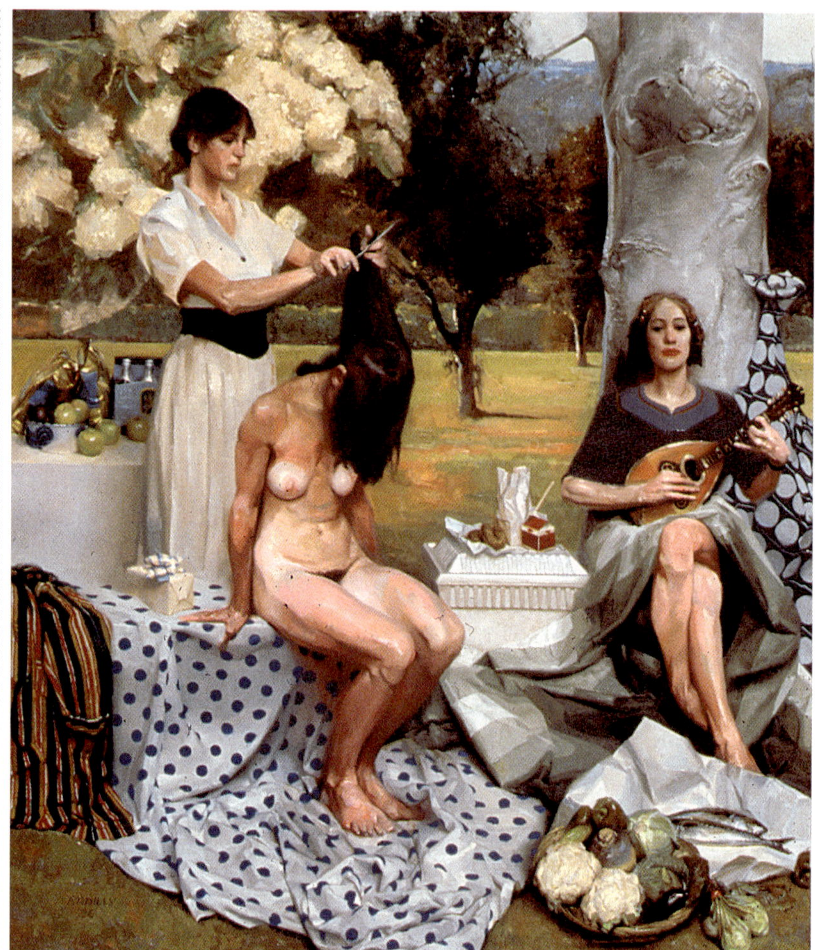

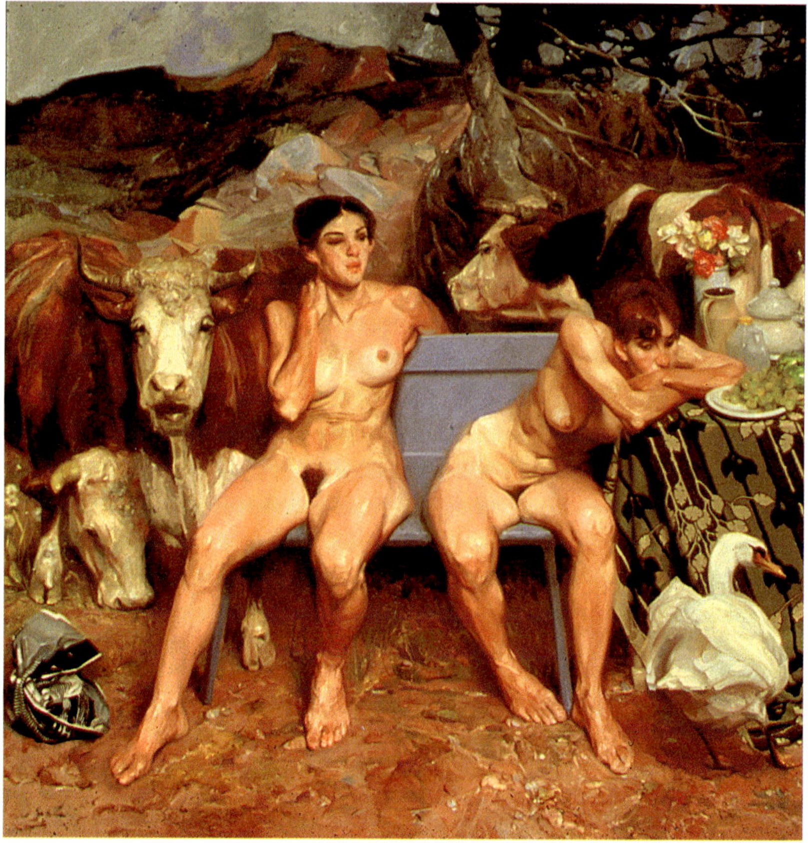

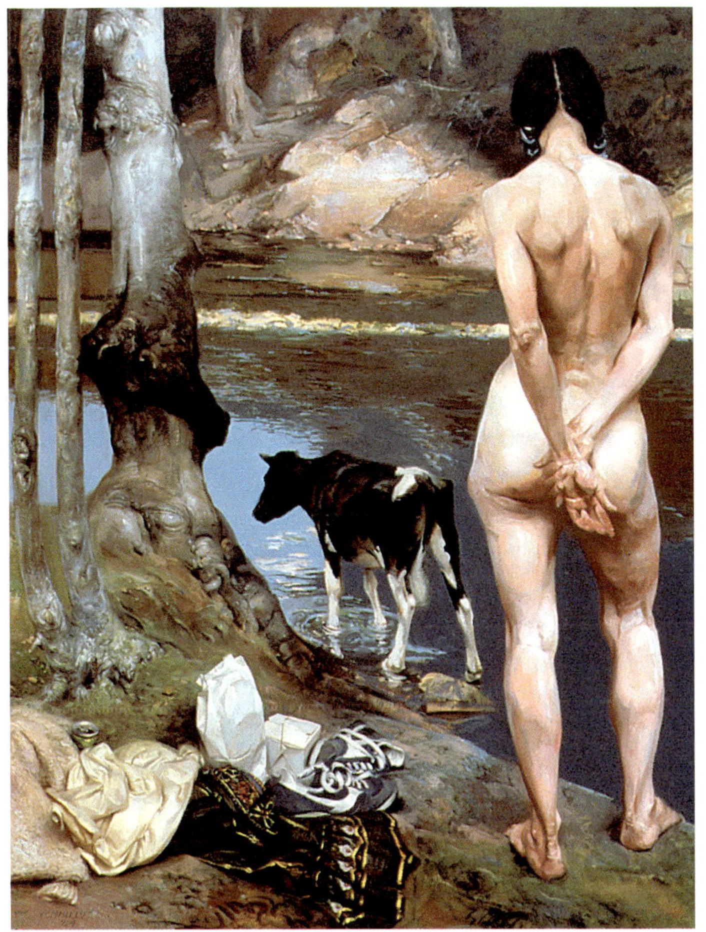

C. Figure with a Cow. Oil on canvas, 72" x 57". Private collection.

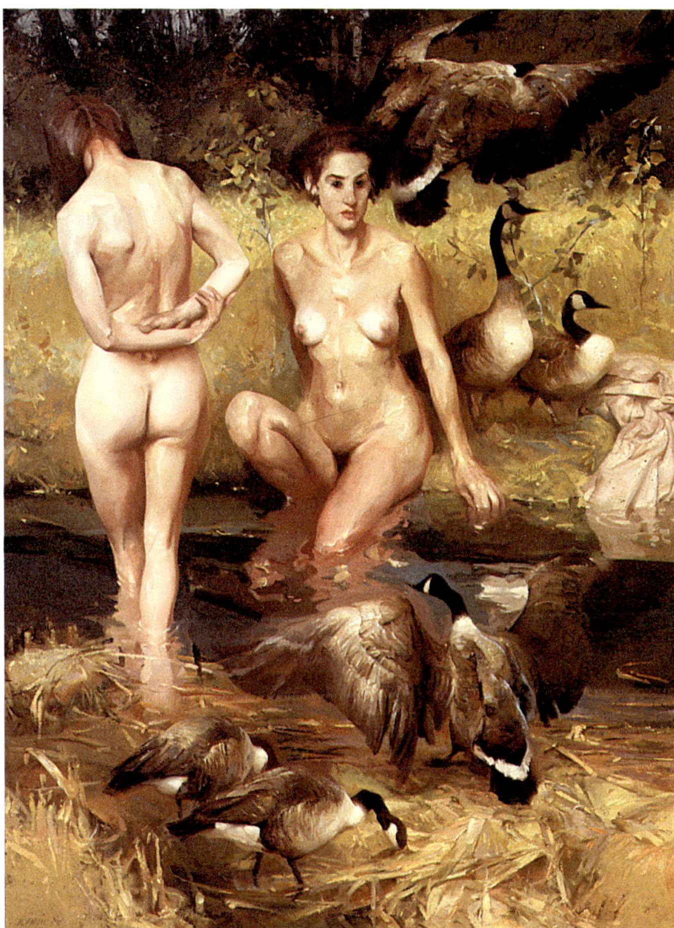

D. Figures in a Stream. Oil on canvas, 80" x 60".

A. (opposite above)
Figures on the Fenway.
Oil on canvas, 84" x 72".
Private collection.

B. (opposite below)
Figures on a Blue Bench.
Oil on canvas, 70" x 72".

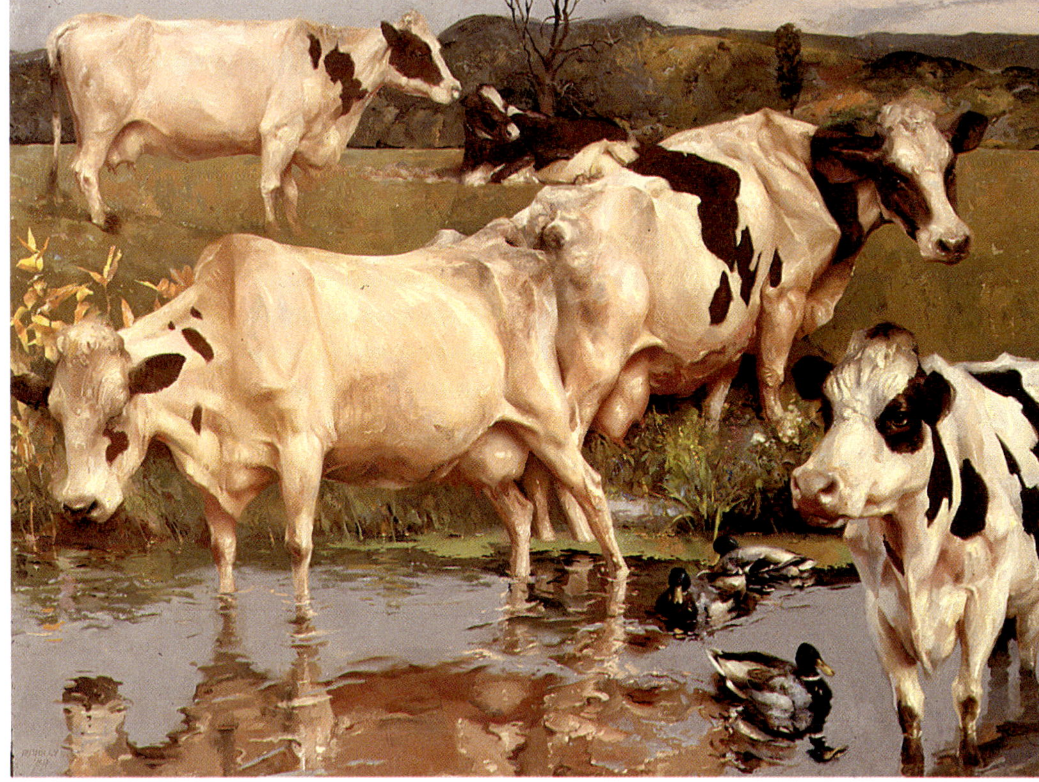

E. Cows at a Stream. Oil on canvas, 72" x 96" Private collection.

PRICE LIST

B.....................$35,000

D....................$32,000

Represented by
Gallery NAGA
Boston, MA

Shelley Reed first came to the Boston area to attended Brandeis University, where she earned a degree in psychology. A year later, she began painting at the School of the Museum of Fine Arts in Boston, and upon graduating in 1984 moved to London where she worked and exhibited for two years. Since returning to the United States, Reed has lived in Cambridge, MA.

Reed's large and well-crafted oil paintings contain images appropriated from the Netherlandish Mannerists – a group whose style deviated from visual realism and exaggerated figural proportions. By reinterpreting these originally small images on a life-size scale, Reed aims to enhance their inherent drama to create a one-on-one relationship with the viewer. Her paintings provoke feelings about the body, nudity, and beauty, and explore the connection between past art and contemporary works.

In the last four years, Reed's work has been exhibited throughout New England and New York in close to two dozen shows, including five solo shows – her most recent at Zoe Gallery in Boston.

Shelley Reed

82 Tremont Street
Cambridge, MA 02139
617-661-5861

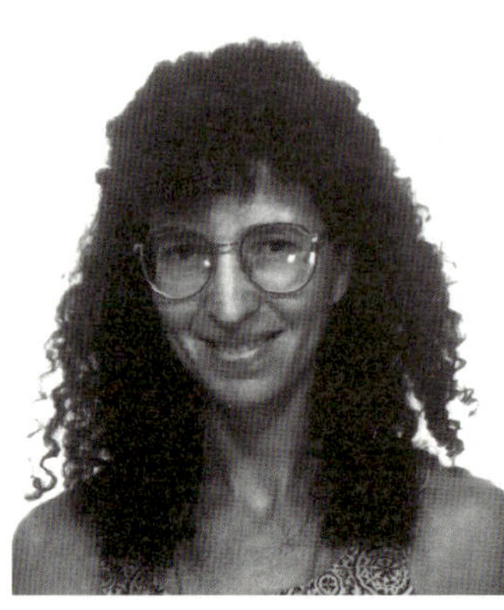

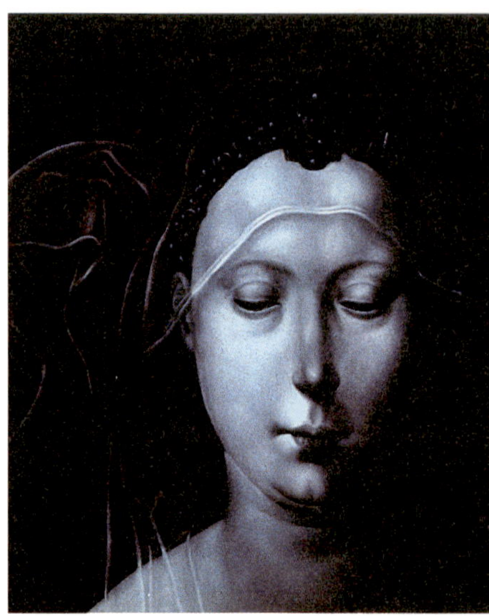

A. (left) **Salome.**
Oil on canvas,
24" x 18". Private collection.

B. (below)
Judith.
Oil on canvas, 79" x 55½".

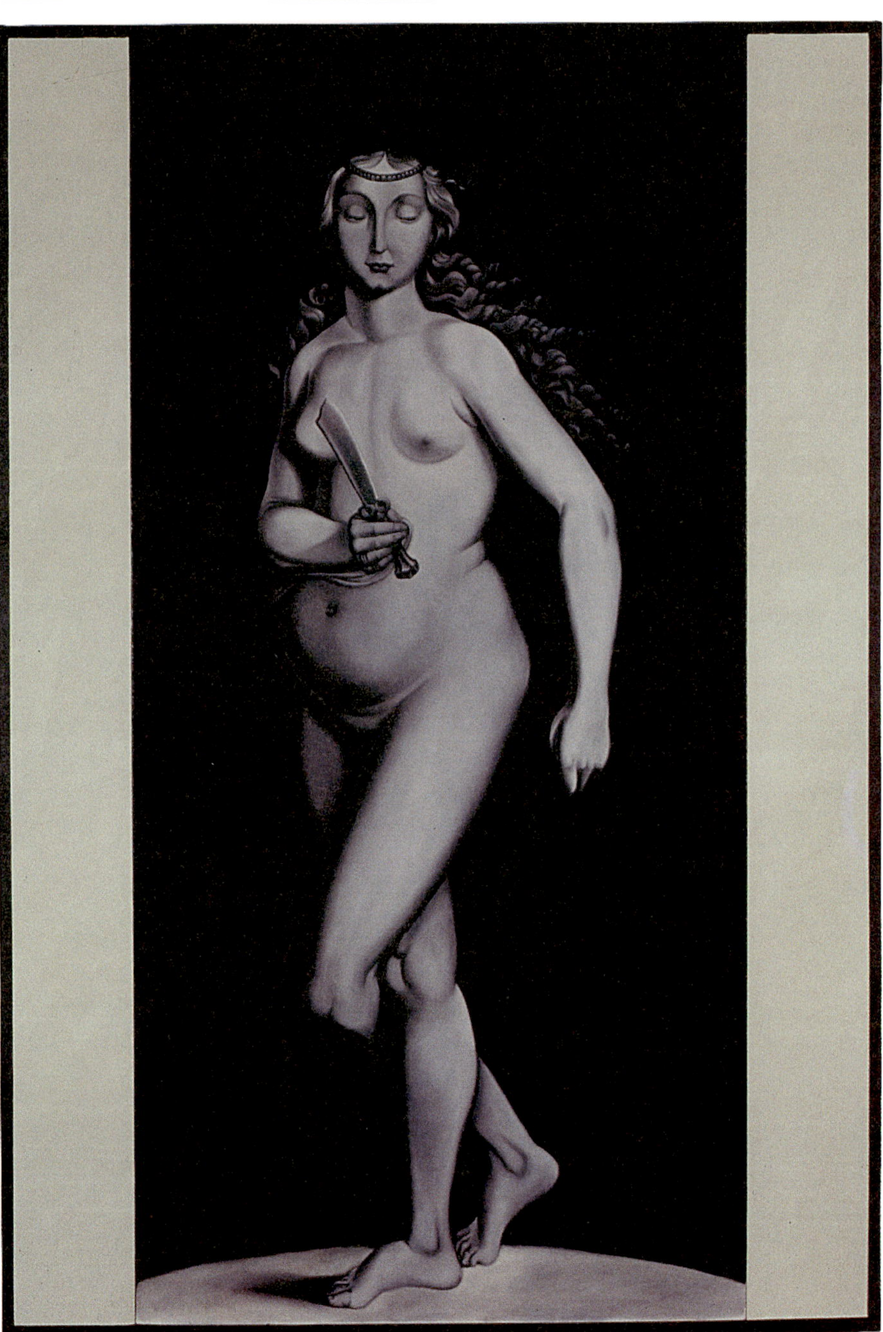

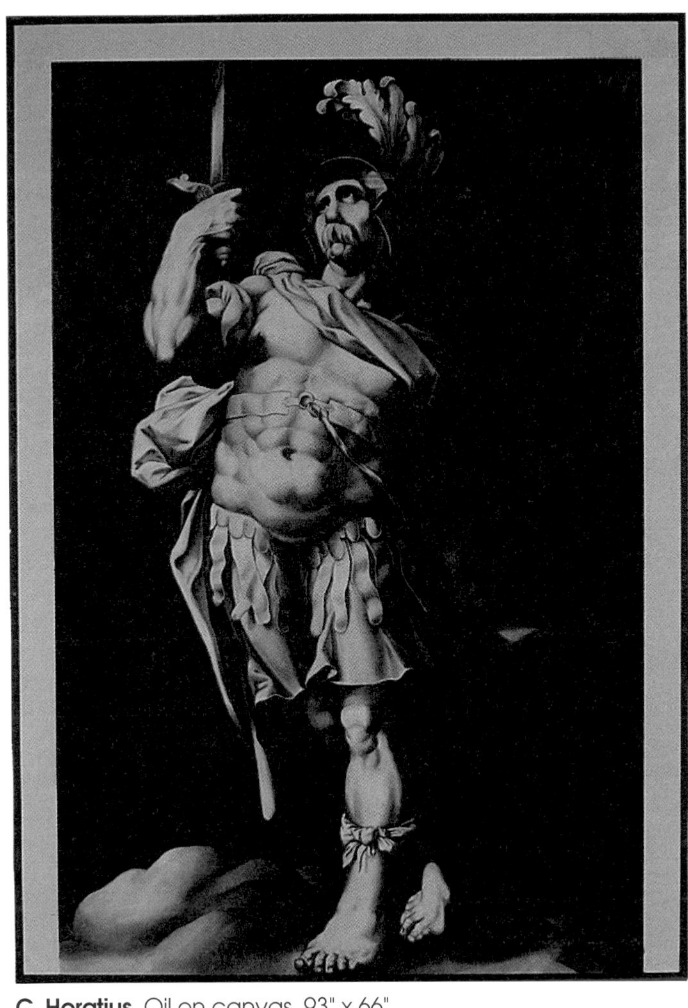

C. Horatius. Oil on canvas, 93" x 66".

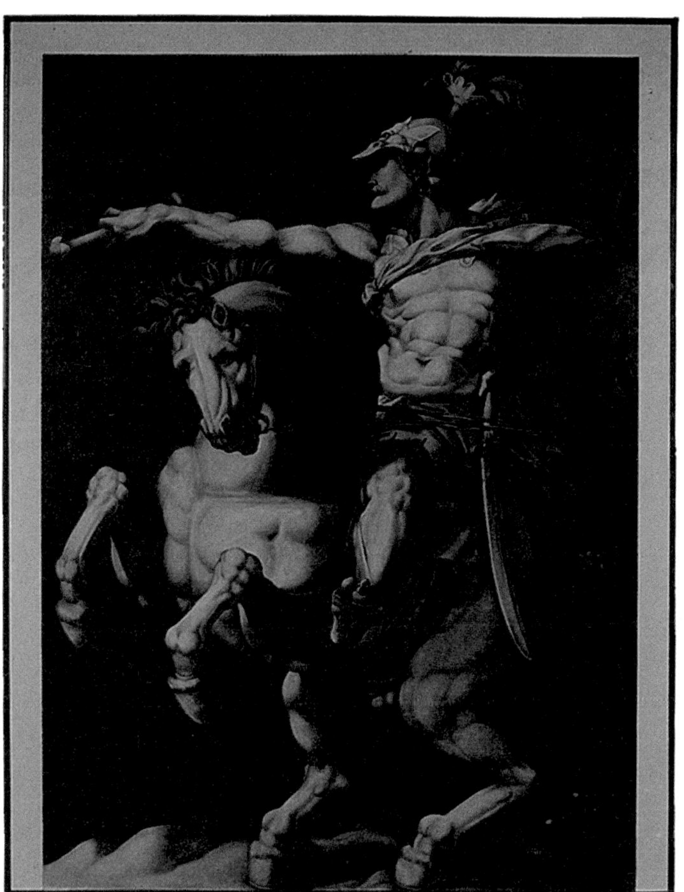

D. Marcus Curtius. Oil on canvas, 95½" x 75".

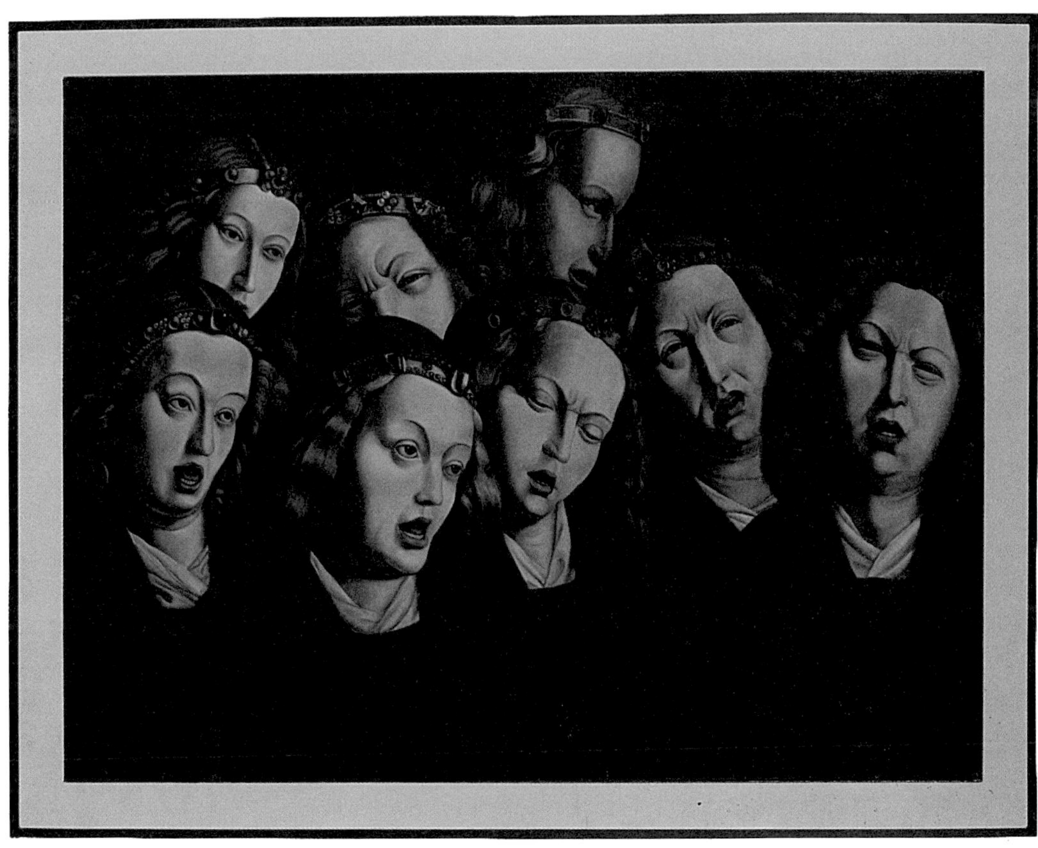

E. Choir. Oil on canvas, 63" x 81". Private collection.

PRICE LIST

A $2,200
B $6,000
C $6,500
D $7,000
E $6,000

Represented by
Bess Cutler Gallery
New York, NY
Gallery NAGA
Boston, MA

A resident of Boston, Paul Erik Richard is becoming an established figure in New England's art community. He received formal training at the University of Buffalo, the Massachusetts College of Art and at Harvard University, where he received a BA in European History. Richard is now a full-time artist, and he maintains a SOHO-esque studio in Boston's old factory district.

Richard's style and choice of motifs reflect an interest in pre-20th-century methods, although his paintings address contemporary issues. Process shares equal importance with imagery in the works. The materials Richard uses range from oil paint to screen printing to liquid emulsion printing, and his unique working process has evolved through continual experimentation with his media. Even Richard's hand milled frames are an integral part of each piece.

Richard's paintings have recevied increasing exposure over the last year. Most recently, his work was the focus of a one-man show at Brenda Taylor Gallery in Boston (sponsored by Mestat Works of Art). Earlier in 1992, a Richard work, which was among works of nationally known artists, received the highest bid at The Institute of Contemporary Art's annual silent auction.

Paul Richard

171 Newbury Street
Boston, MA 02116
617-421-1214

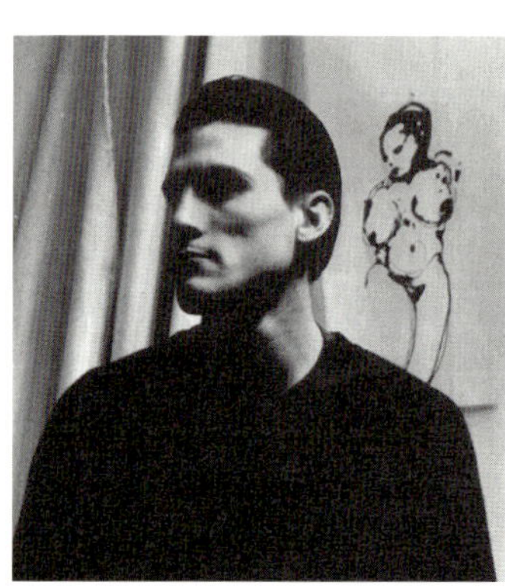

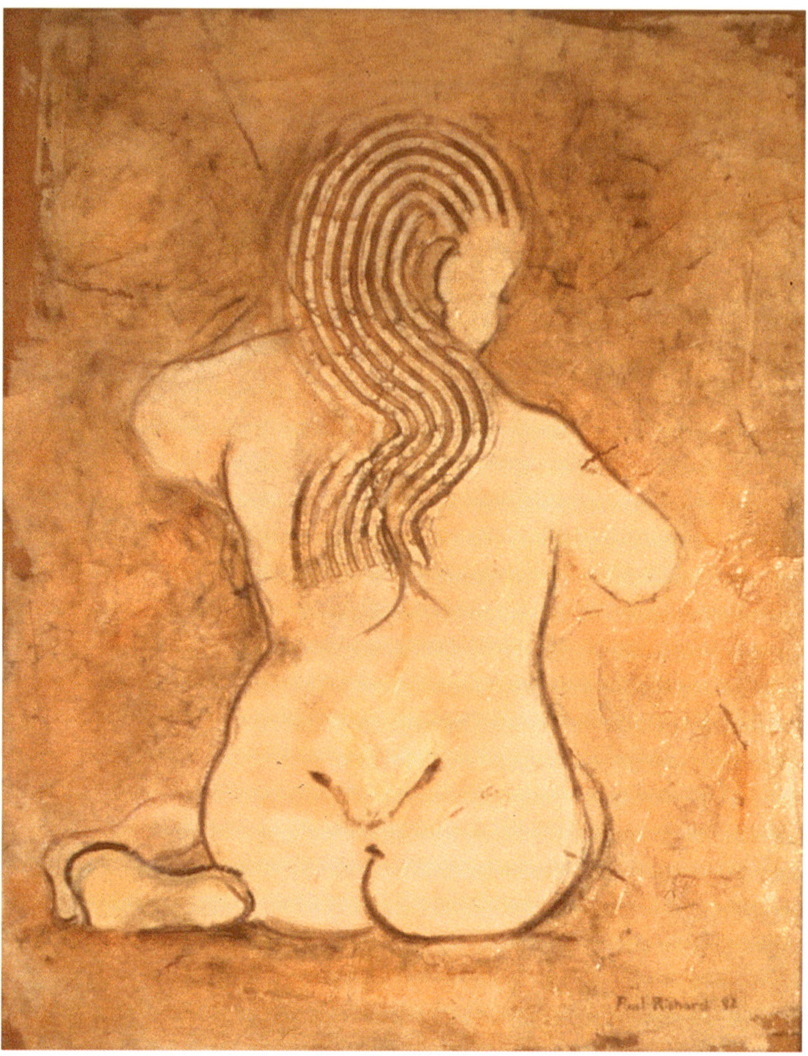

A. Female Torso, Sonia. Mixed media, canvas on panel. 24 ¼" x 20 ½".

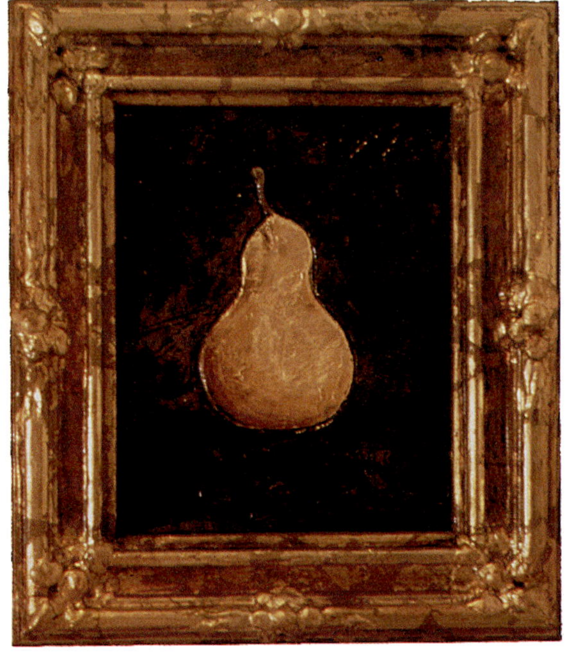

B. Gold Pear V. Mixed media, canvas on panel. 22 ¼" x 19 ¾".

PRICE LIST

A $2,900
B $3,000
C $4,000

Represented by
Mestat Works of Art
Boston, MA

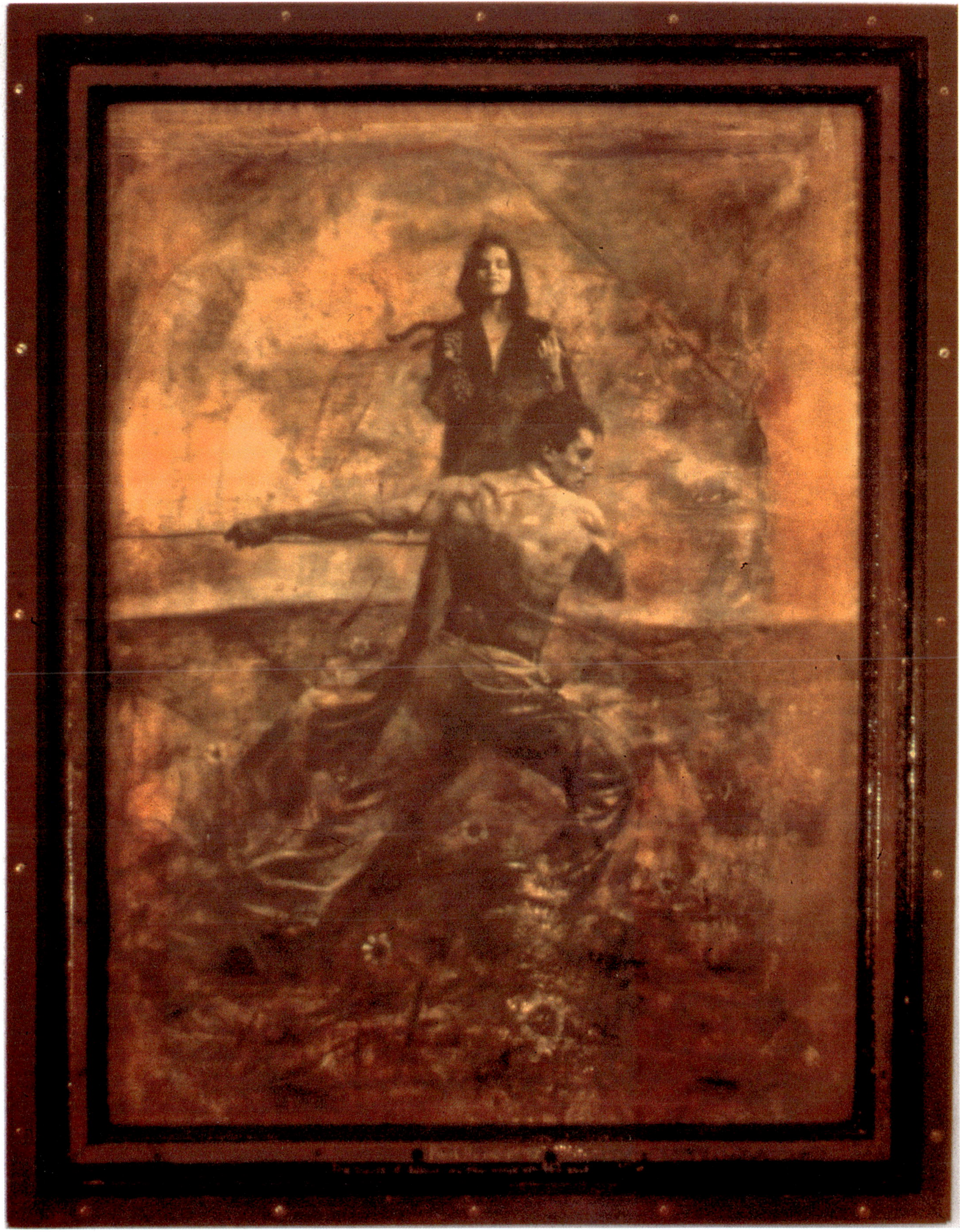

C. The Hands of Labor are the Wings of the Soul. Photo emulsion, mixed media, canvas on panel. 40 ½" x 32 ¼".

Ron Rizzi has been part of the Boston art community for over a decade. He currently maintains a studio in Jamaica Plain, MA. Rizzi has studied painting at Queens College in New York, Yale, and with Jean Liberte at the Art Students League in New York City. He has taught painting privately and now teaches at the School of the Museum of Fine Arts in Boston.

Rizzi works primarily with oils on linen. The relationship between light and dark – literally and metaphorically – has been a consistent theme in his paintings. The light portions of his works seem to emerge from the darkness surrounding them. Rizzi has applied this interest to subjects ranging from loss and destruction to homelessness.

Rizzi has had solo and group exhibitions in Boston and New York City. In 1991, he was chosen to exhibit in the Currier Gallery's biannual exhibition of emerging New England artists. Among numerous other awards, Rizzi received an Engelhard Foundation Fellowship, a Painting Fellowship from the Artists Foundation in Boston and a

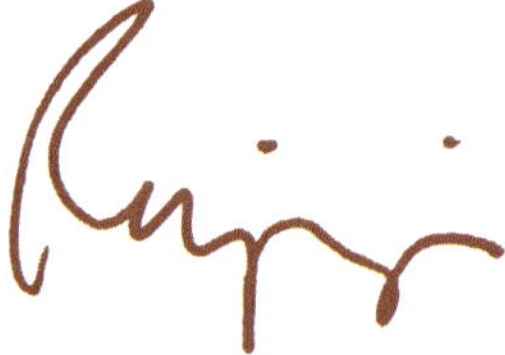

23 Parkton Road
Jamaica Plain, MA 02130
617-524-0121

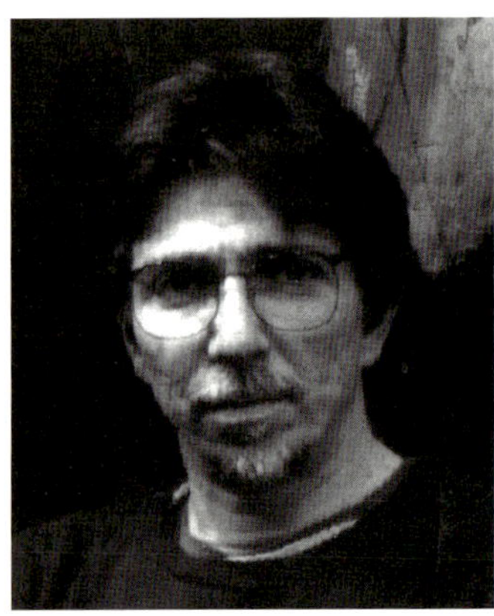

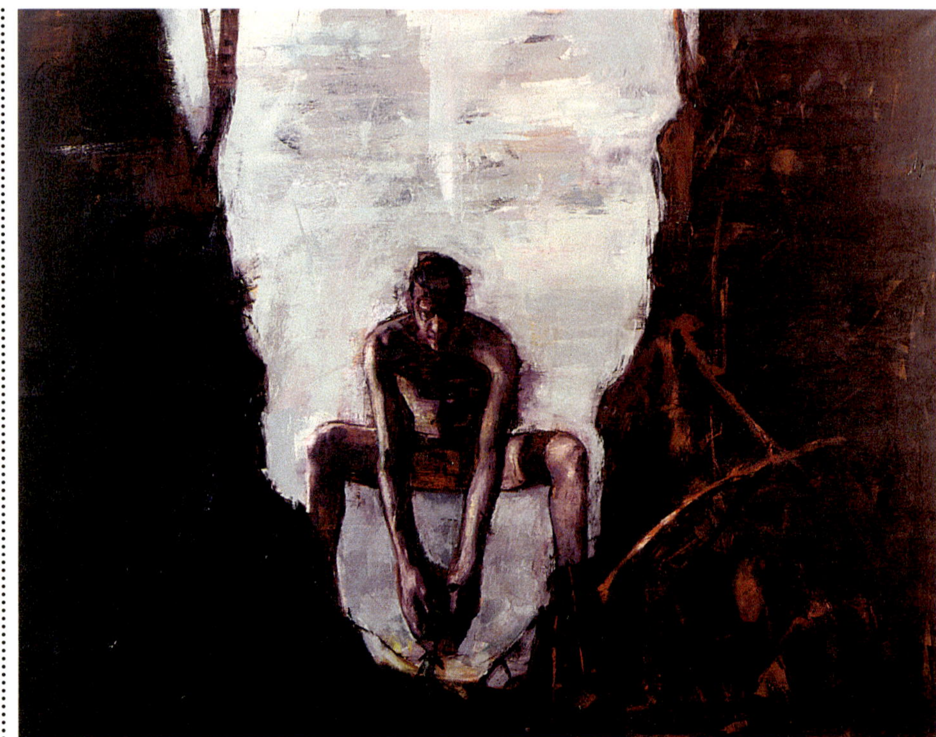

A. Torn Earth II. Oil on linen, 56" x 72". Private collection.

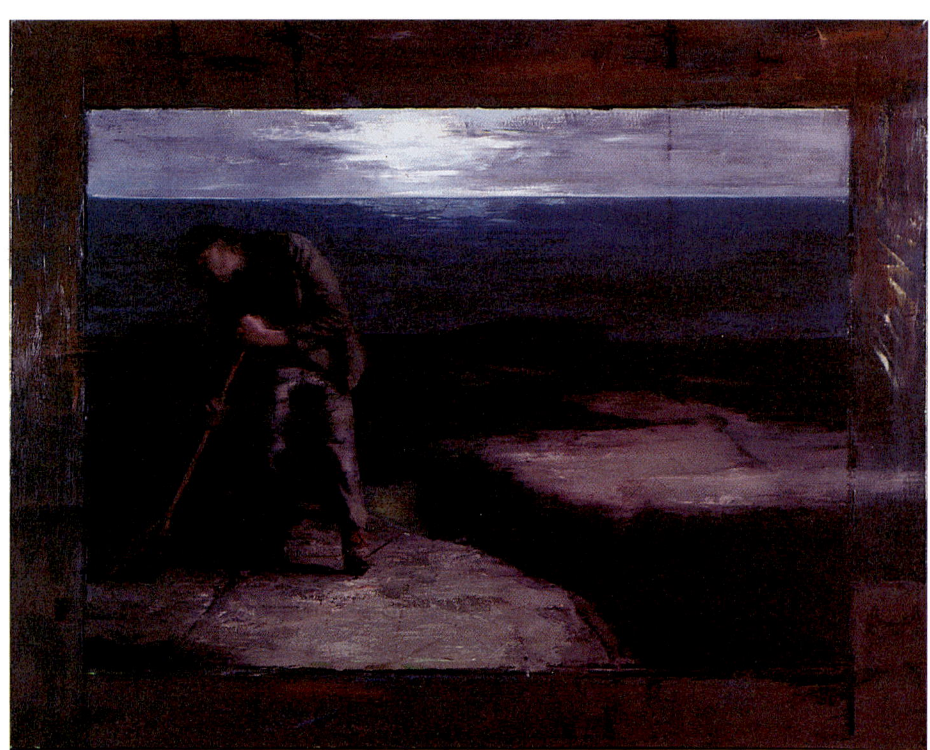

B. Sweeping the Stones. Oil on linen, 56" x 72". Collection of the Museum of Fine Arts, Boston, MA.

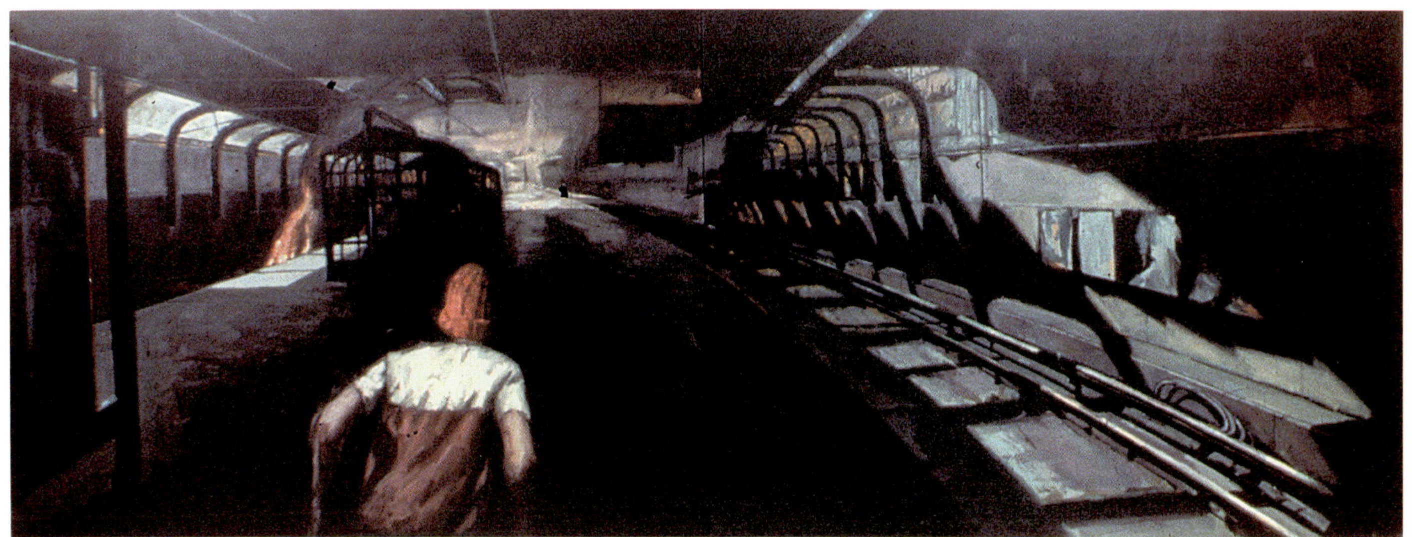

C. Tunnel Vision. Oil on linen, 56" x 144".

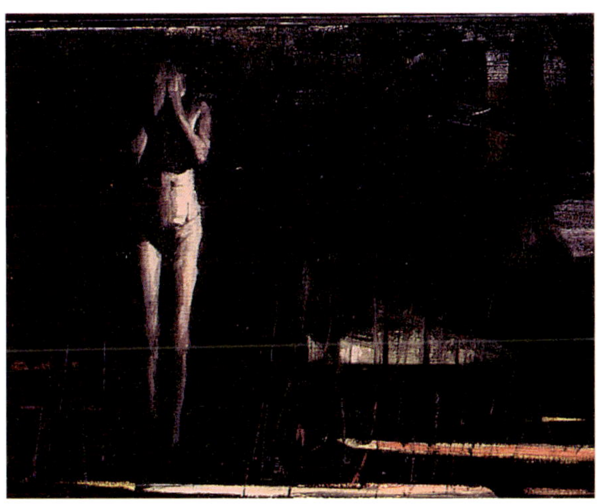

D. Night and Rain.
Oil on linen, 14" x 20".
Private collection.

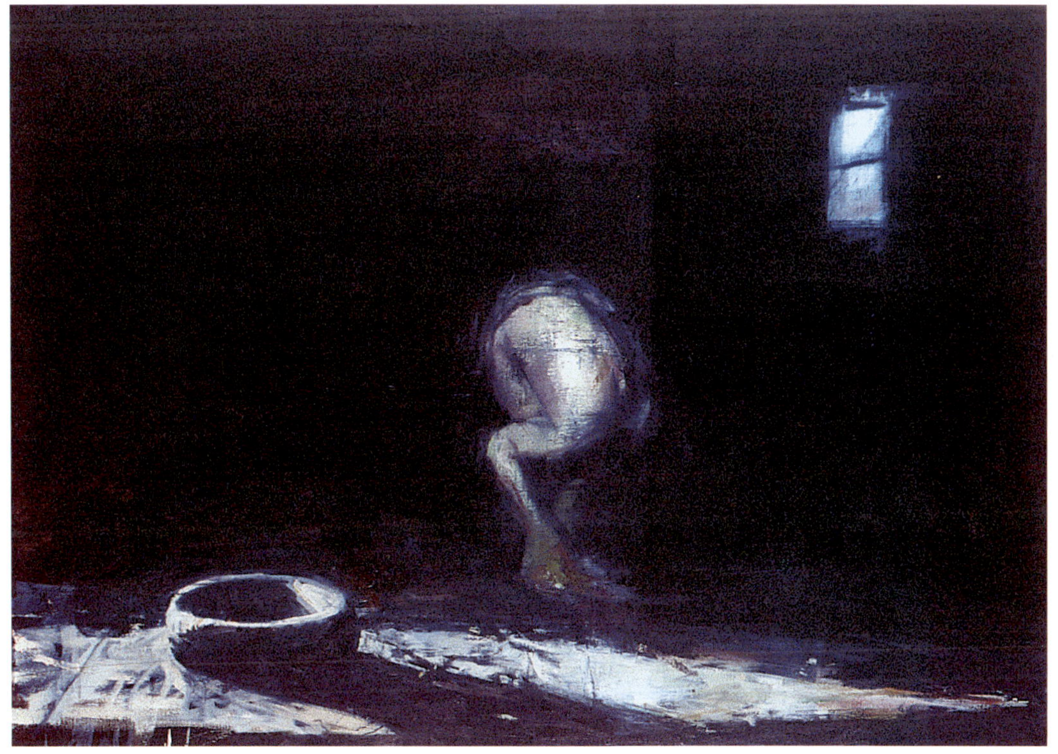

E. Garden. Oil on linen, 30" x 50". Private collection.

PRICE LIST

A $6,500

C $10,000

D $2,500

E $4,000

Represented by
Akin Gallery
Boston, MA

Ann C. Rosebrooks

Ann C. Rosebrooks was born and raised in Massachusetts and currently lives in North Grosvenordale, CT. She attended the Rhode Island School of Design, where she received a BFA in Painting.

Rosebrooks' paintings have a look that is somewhere between an ornate tapestry and illustrations in a children's book. She primarily works in acrylic on canvas using a bold, vibrant palette to create detailed images presented in flattened perspective. Some paintings may tell a story, others reflect on a thought or an emotion. Although based in reality, the paintings also include liberal doses of fantasy.

Rosebrooks' work was most recently exhibited at a two-person show at the Artworks Gallery in Hartford, CT. She has exhibited throughout New England and New York. Awards include First Prize in Painting from the juried exhibition "Arts Worcester." In 1985, she was chosen from among 600 artists for a two-person show at the Artists Showcase Gallery in Hartford, CT.

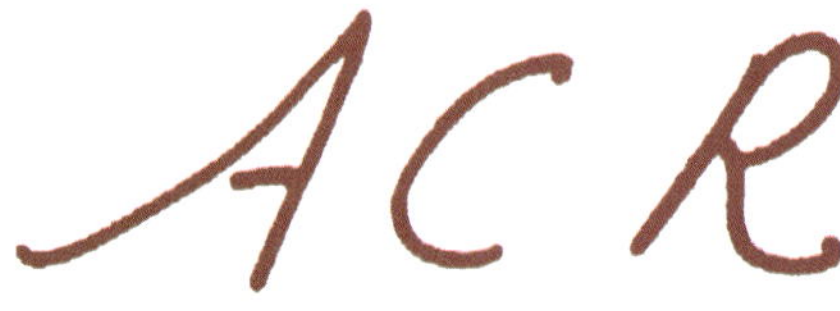

350 Ravenelle Road
N. Grosvenordale, CT 06255
203-923-2426

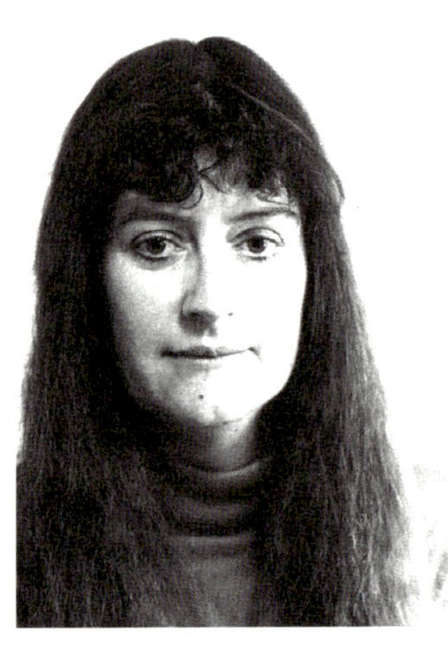

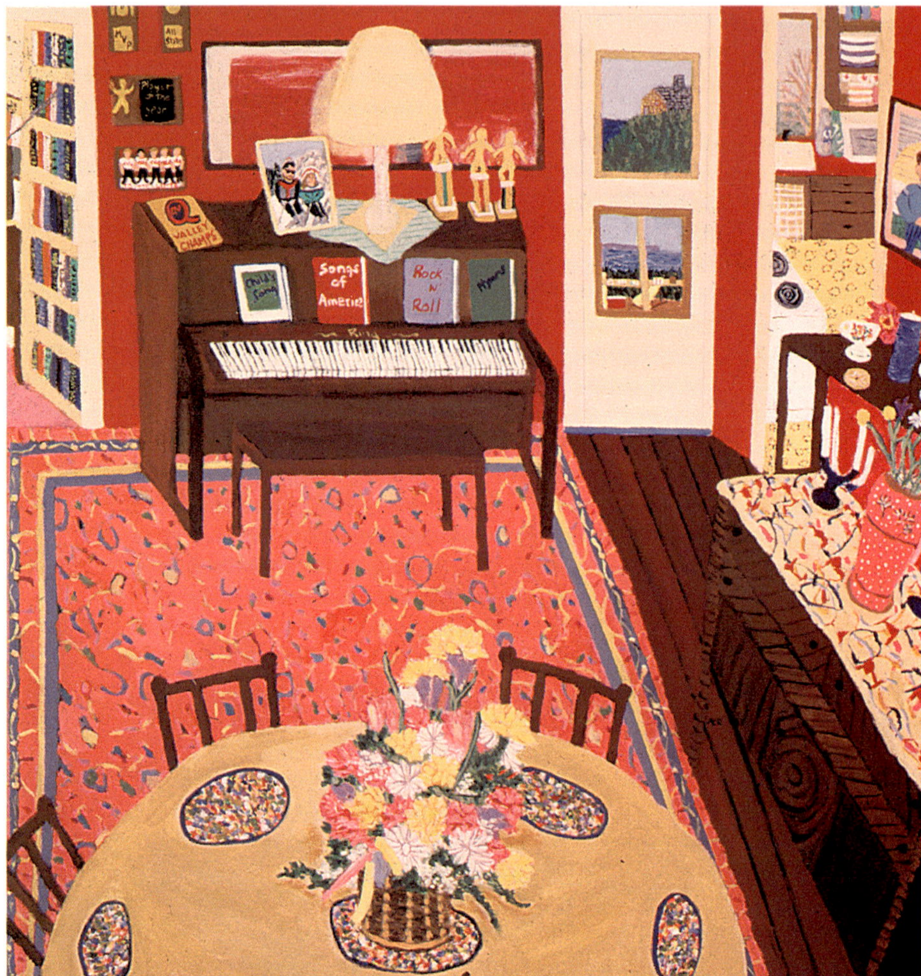

A. Sweet Harmony. Acrylic on canvas, 34" x 29" x 2". Courtesy of Uirge Lorentz and Richard Governale.

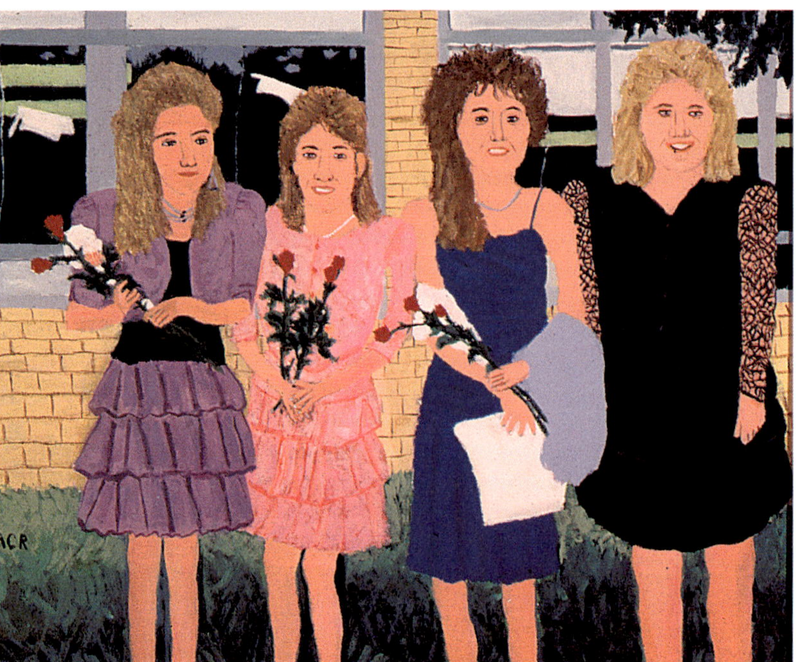

B. Rite of Passage. Acrylic on canvas, 18" x 22" x 2".

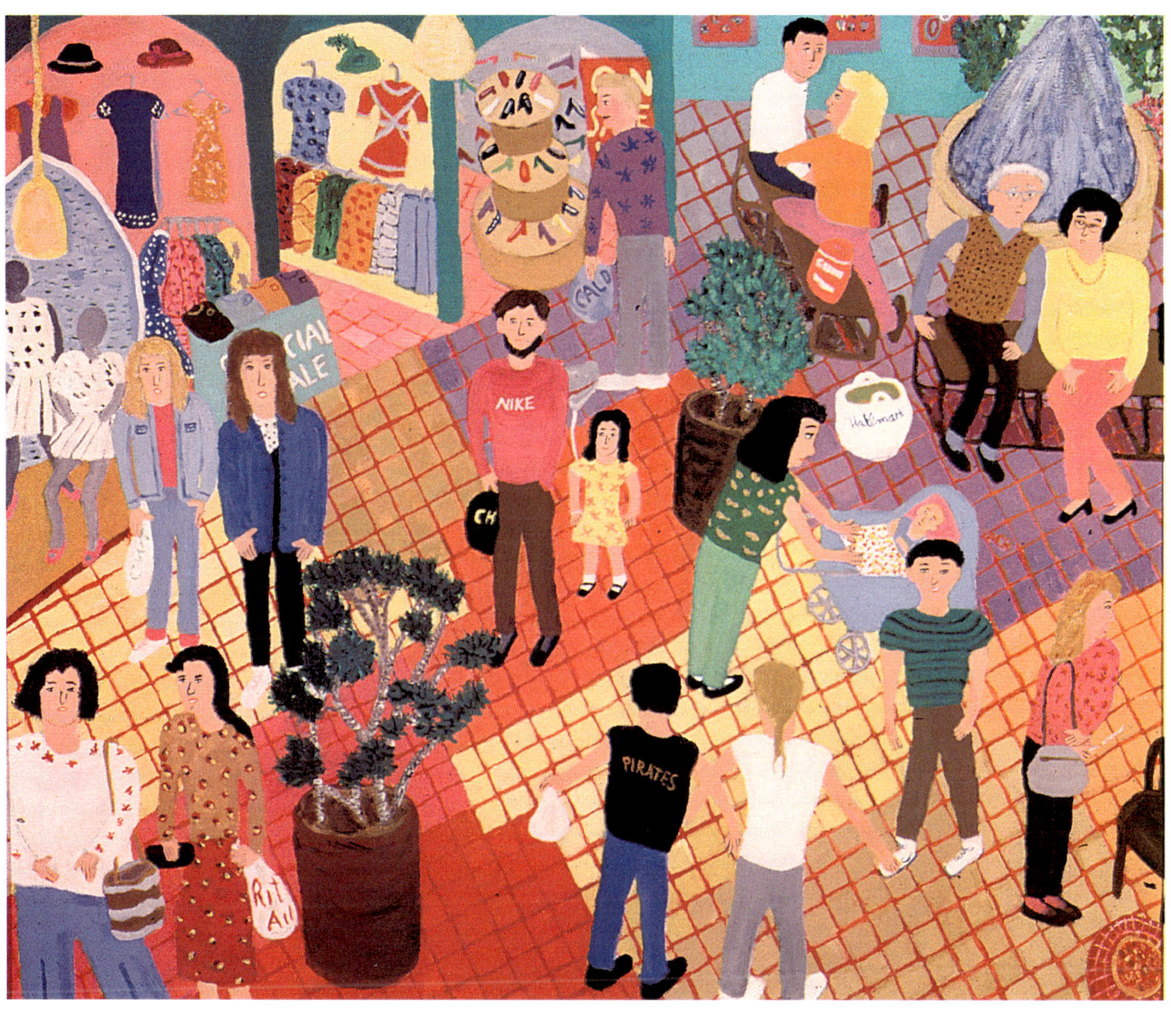

C. Sarah Shops. Acrylic on canvas, 31" x 37" x 2".

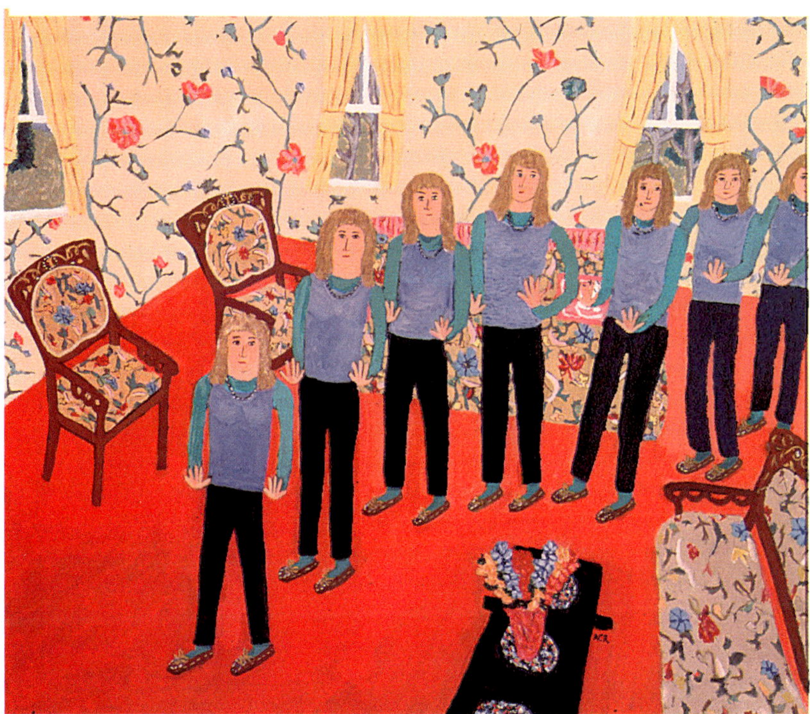

D. Pushing Myself. Acrylic on canvas, 36" x 37" x 2". Courtesy of Kathy and Donald Stevens.

PRICE LIST

A.......................... $400

B.......................... $300

C.......................... $450

D.......................... $400

Daniel Rosenbloom has an atypical background compared to many fine artists. He studied architecture at the University of Maryland at College Park, where he earned a Bachelor of Architecture in 1981. After working at architectural firms in the Washington, DC, area, Daniel became a licensed architect in the state of Maryland in 1984. His next move took him to Philadelphia to pursue an MBA at the Wharton School of Business. He received his degree in 1986 and moved to Boston, where he worked for a real estate investment firm. Since 1990, Daniel has devoted his time to painting, working at his studio in South Boston.

It is not surprising to find that Rosenbloom is drawn to the built environment for subject matter; images of industrialism particularly interest him. He works exclusively with acrylics on canvas, a medium that allows him to endow his simple images of structures with solidity and presence. His use of a flattened perspective and severe lighting occasionally remind one of the work of Giorgio de Chirico.

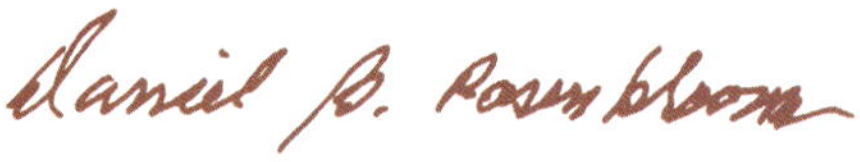

29 Bay State Road, #1
Boston, MA 02215
617-267-0978

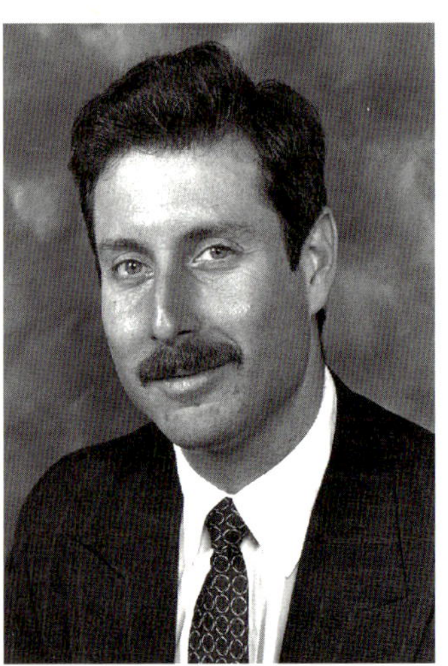

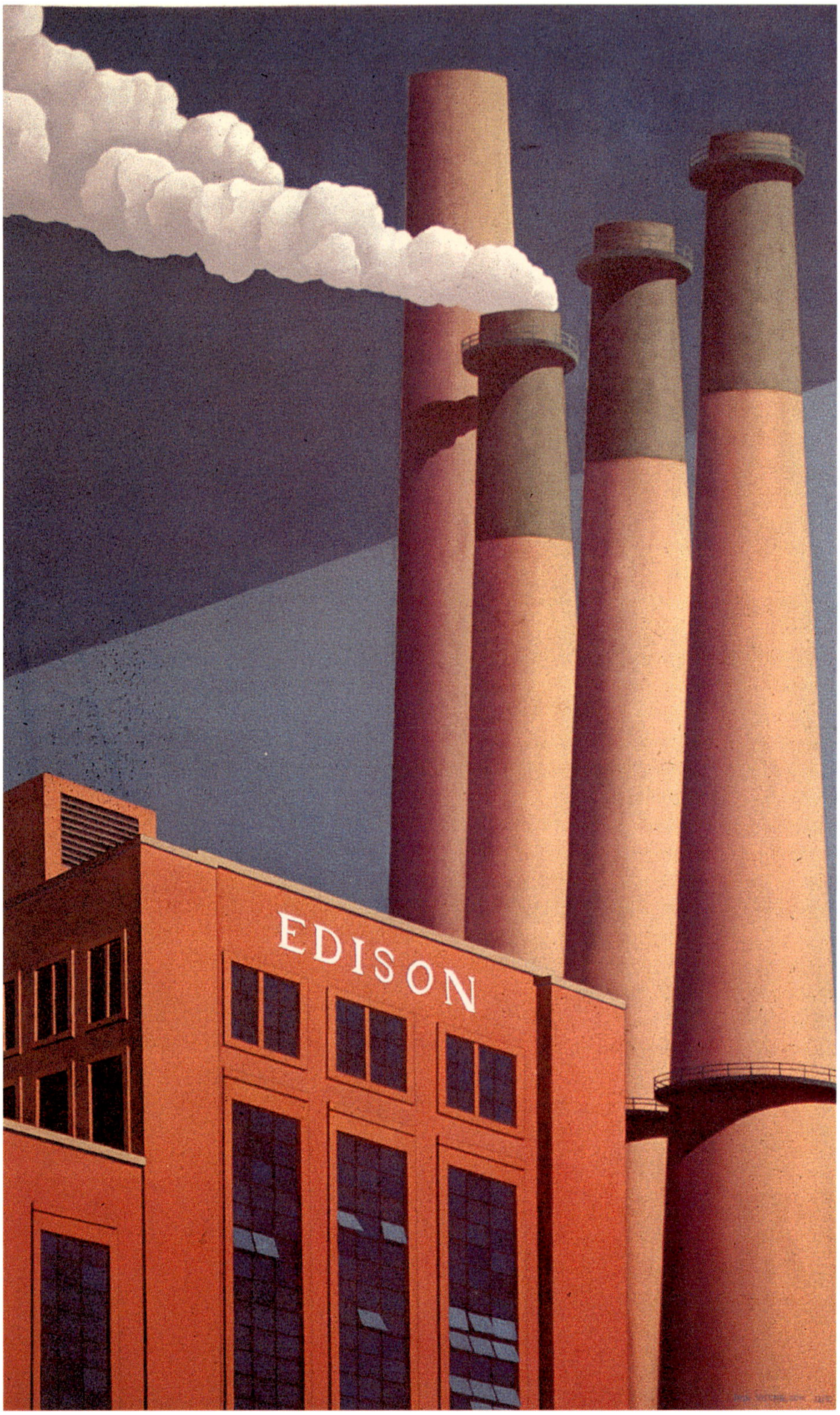

A. Boston Edison I. Acrylic on canvas, 48" x 30".

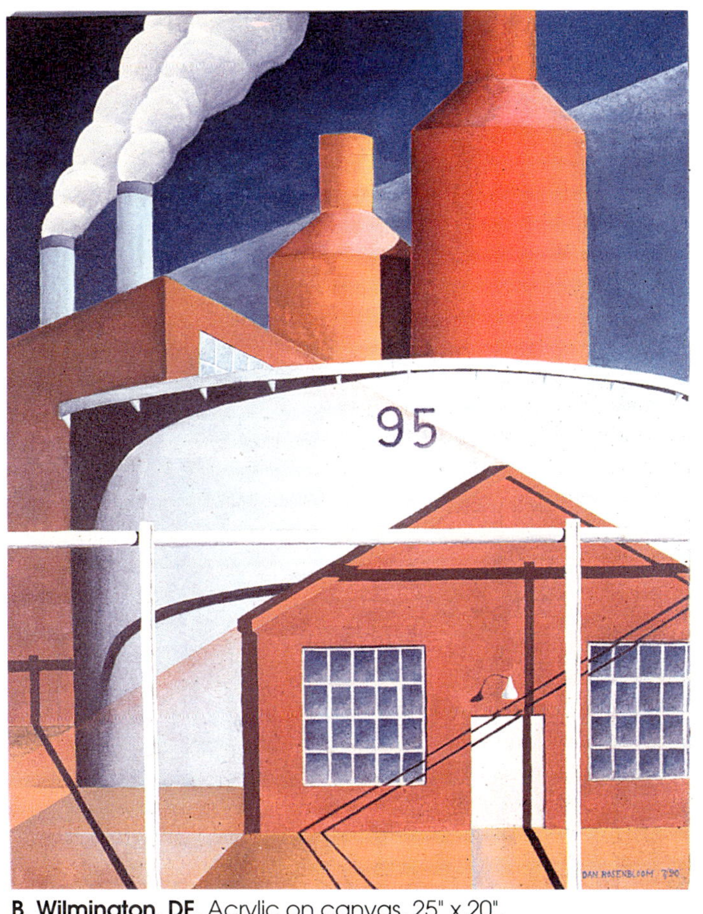

B. Wilmington, DE. Acrylic on canvas, 25" x 20".

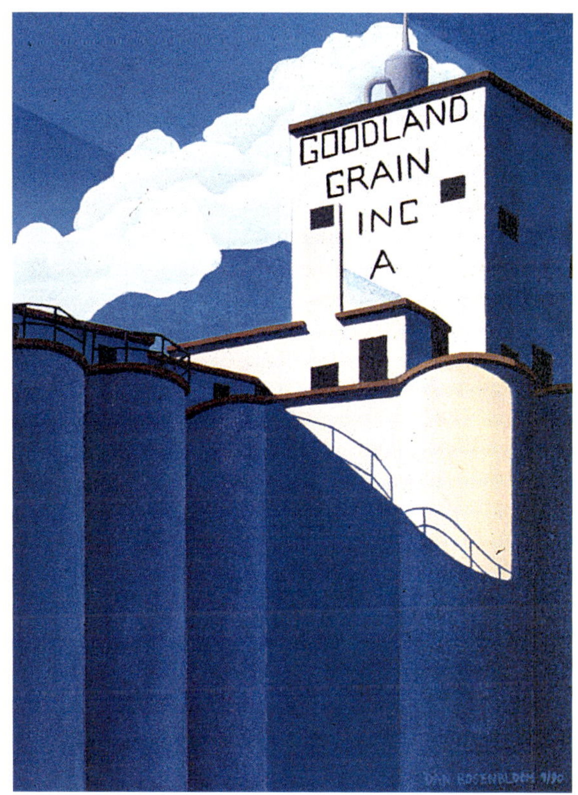

C. Goodland, KS. Acrylic on canvas, 17" x 13".

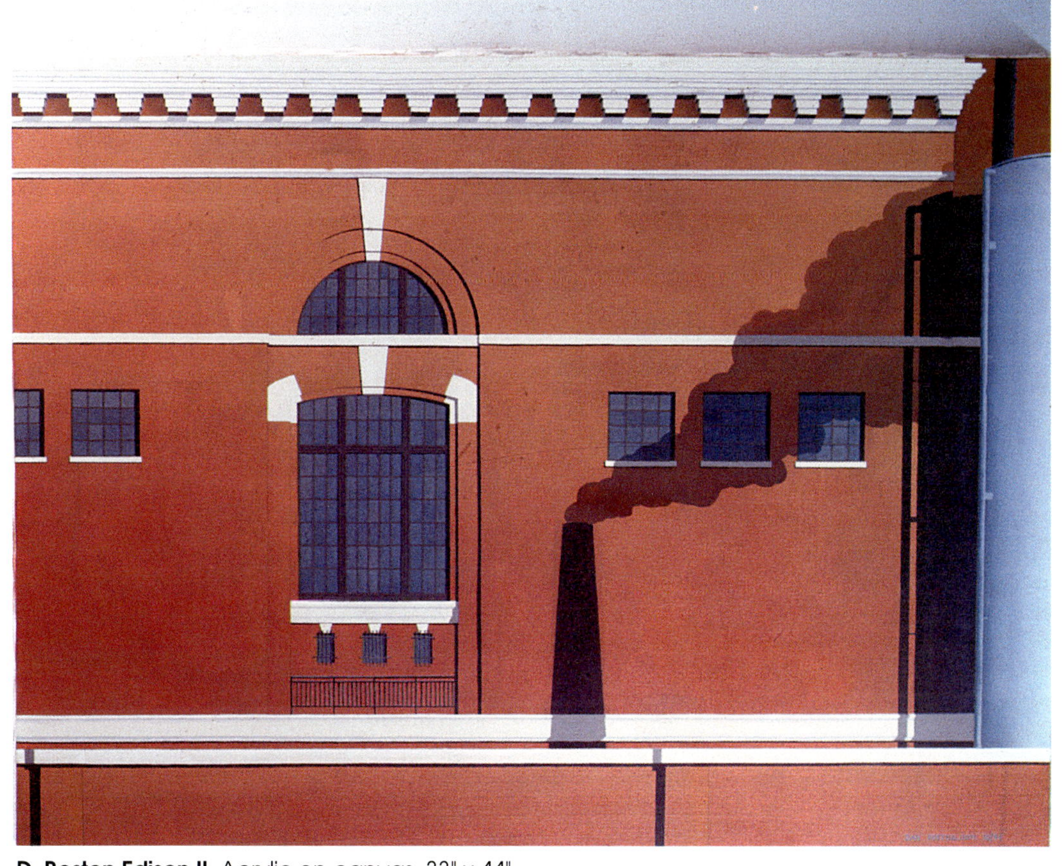

D. Boston Edison II. Acrylic on canvas, 33" x 44".

PRICE LIST

A $2,200

B $1,200

C $1,000

D $2,600

At age 27, Alexander Scott is one of the younger artists selected by our jury. Scott attended the Cleveland Institute of Art at the Lacoste School in France in 1984. His training continued in Boston, where he studied oil painting at the School of the Museum of Fine Arts and received a BA in art history from Boston University. Scott continues to live in Boston, and has gained increasing attention as an emerging talent.

Reflecting the influence of his studies in France, Scott's early work was executed with bravura technique in an impressionistic style. He now works in a reduced abstract style using mixed media. Through the use of low-key forms placed on dark textural fields, Scott suggests the opaque and the transparent; his work gives a glimpse of an immediate and energetic space.

Scott's work is included in private collections throughout the United States. He has had an annual show at the North Haven Art Association in Maine since 1987, and in 1990 he was invited to exhibit at Harvard University.

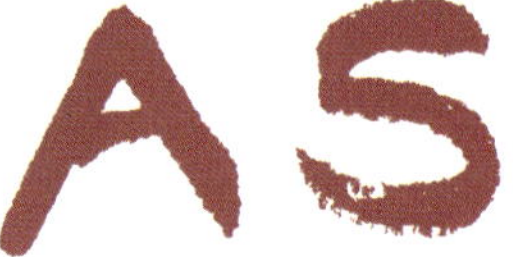

358 Marlborough Street
Boston, MA 02115
617-262-3869

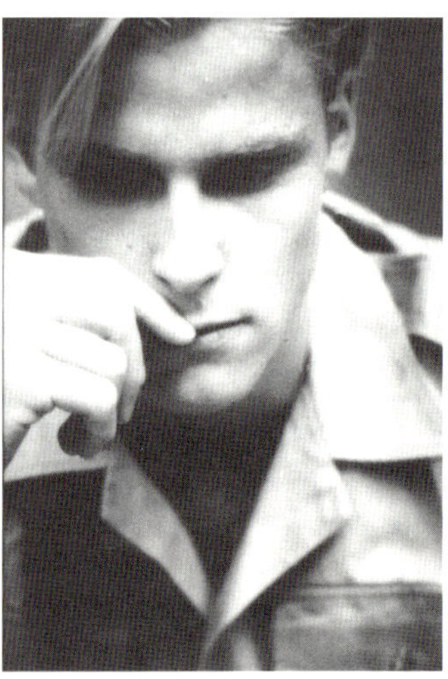

A. O. Mixed media on canvas, 24" x 20".

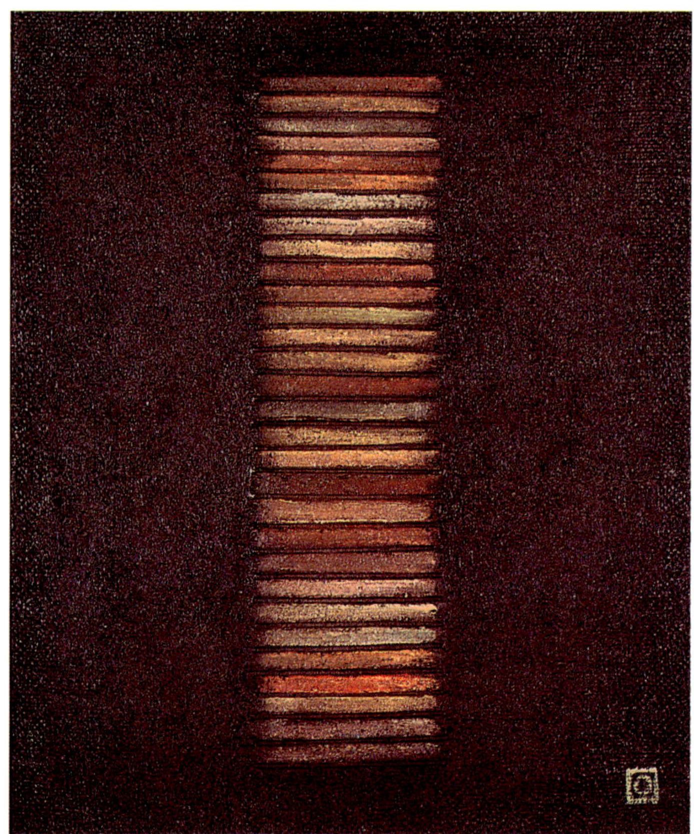

B. Discriminating Awareness I. Mixed media on canvas, 24" x 20".

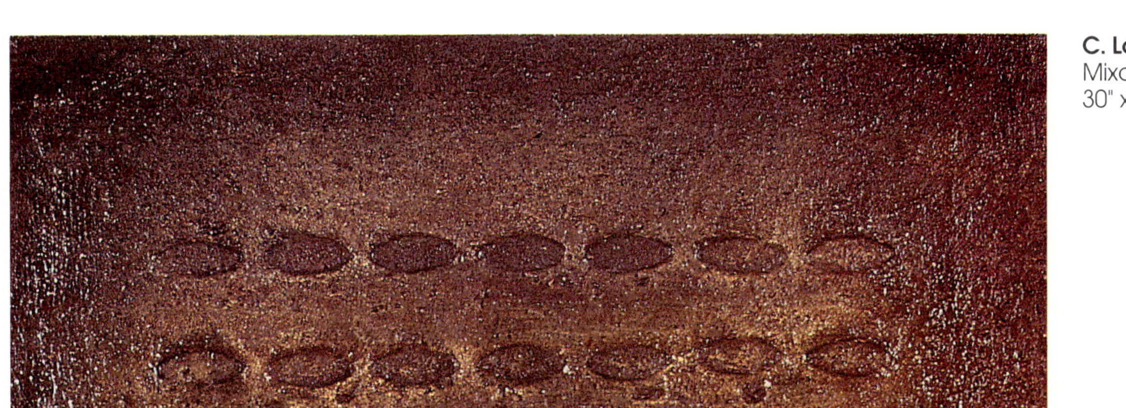

C. Lower Activity III.
Mixcd media on canvas,
30" x 30".

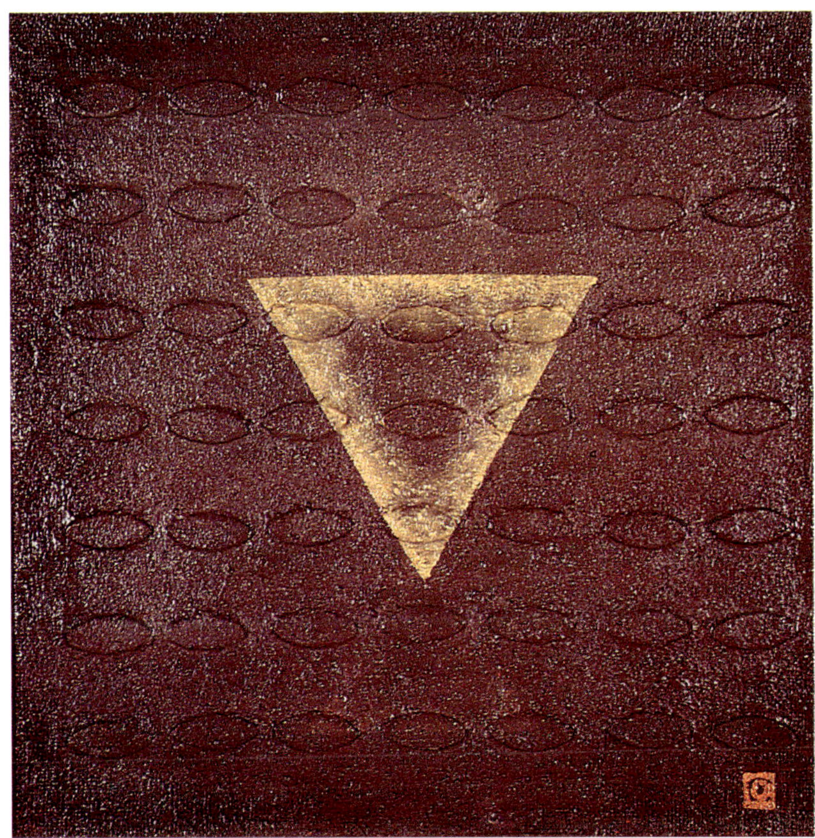

D. Lower Activity II.
Mixed media on
canvas, 24" x 24".

PRICE LIST

A $1,500
B......................$1,500
C $1,900
D $1,600

Wendy Seller

Wendy Seller lives at the Claflin School Studios – a grammar school that was renovated as an artist colony – in Newtonville, MA. She received a BFA from the Rhode Island School of Design and an MFA from the University of Illinois. During the 1980s, Seller produced ten large-scale works that involved the transformation of interior spaces into habitable works of art. She currently devotes her time to painting and teaches at the Rhode Island School of Design and Simmons College.

Seller is a narrative painter of the surrealist tradition. Her chosen images are used symbolically and invite multiple interpretations. Seller is interested in the relationship between fantasy and reality, and she explores different layers of life with her paintings.

In spring of 1993, Seller will have a solo show at the Penthouse Gallery in Santa Monica, CA. She has exhibited work at the Bannister Gallery in Providence, RI, the Addison Gallery of American Art in Andover, MA – both solo shows – and the "Boston 1990" triennial at the Fuller Museum of Art in Brockton, MA.

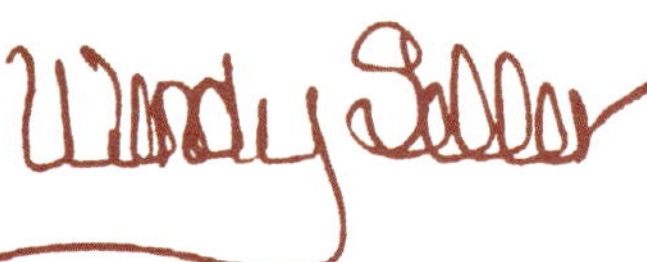

Claflin School Studios
449 Lowell Avenue, Unit 1
Newtonville, MA 02160
617-964-7912

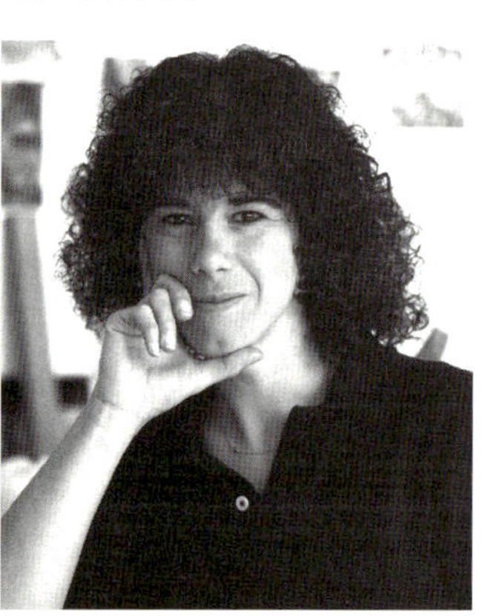

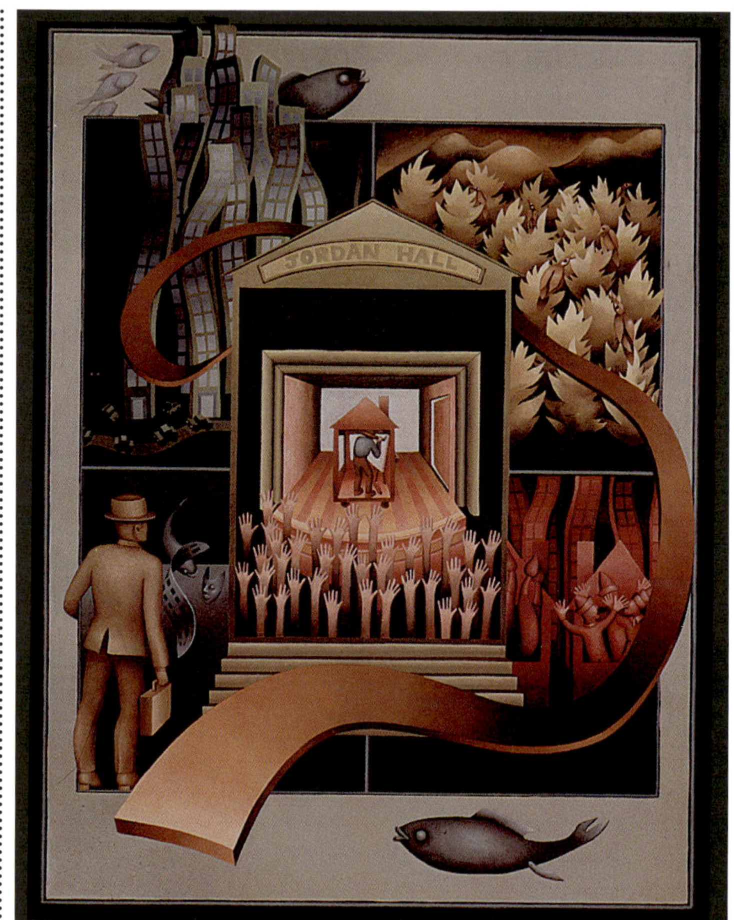

A. Portrait in Four Parts. Oil on canvas, 36" x 28".

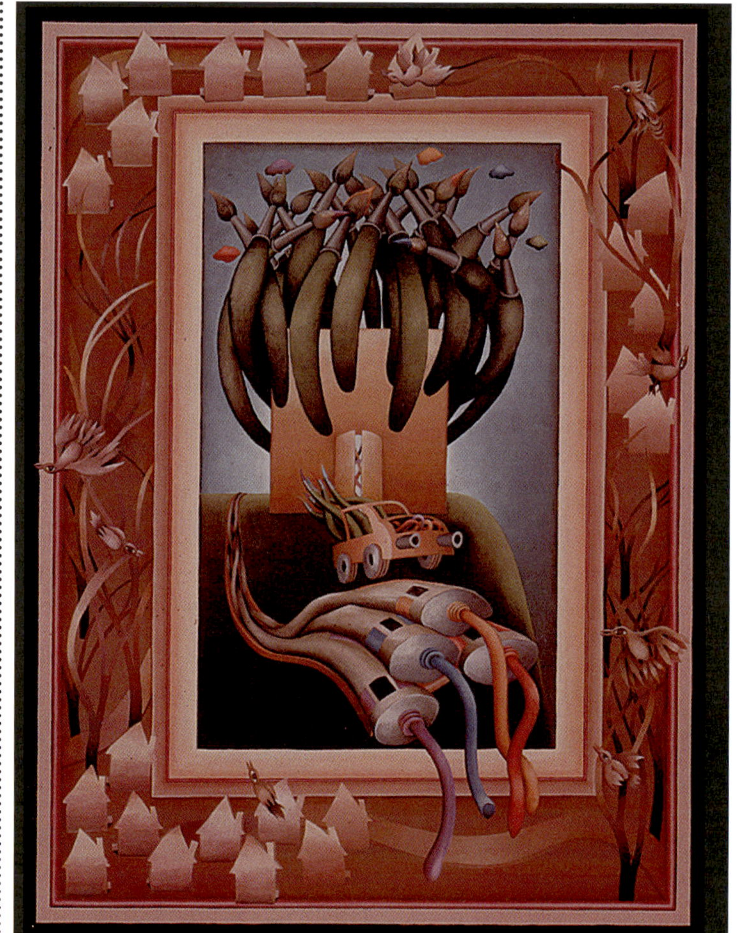

B. Artist's Condo in the Suburbs. Oil on canvas, 36" x 28".

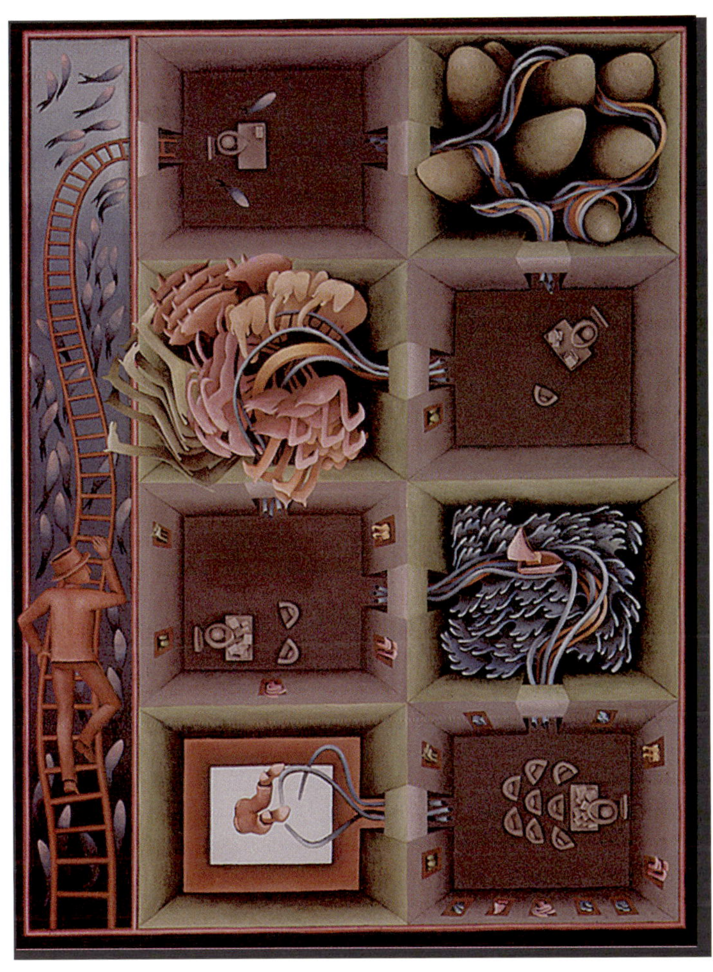

C. Lawyer's Ladder to Success. Oil on canvas, 36" x 28".

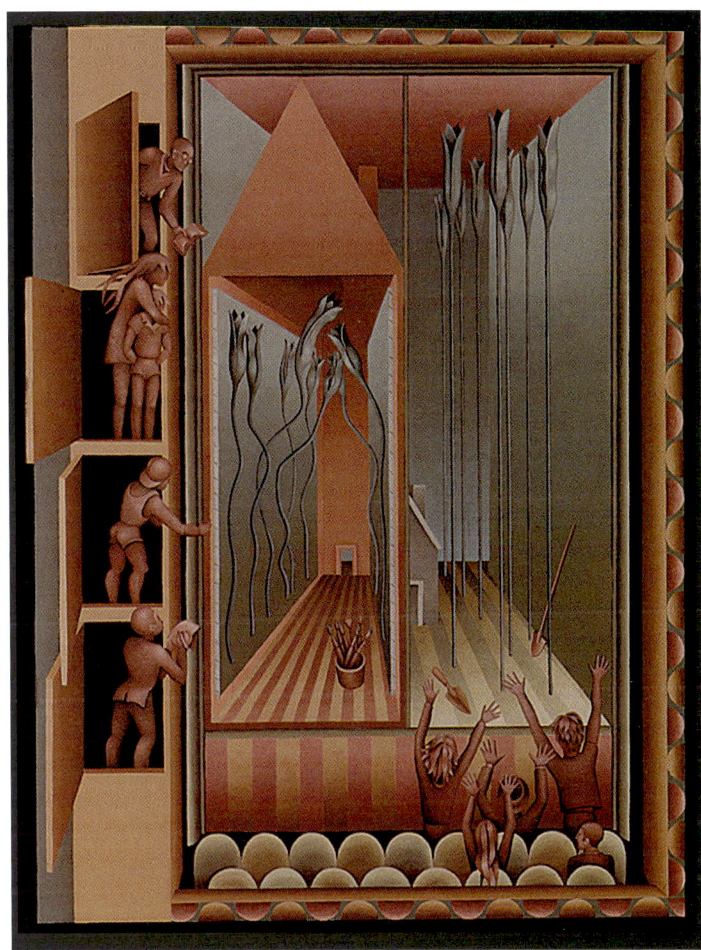

D. Two Realities. Oil on canvas, 36" x 28".

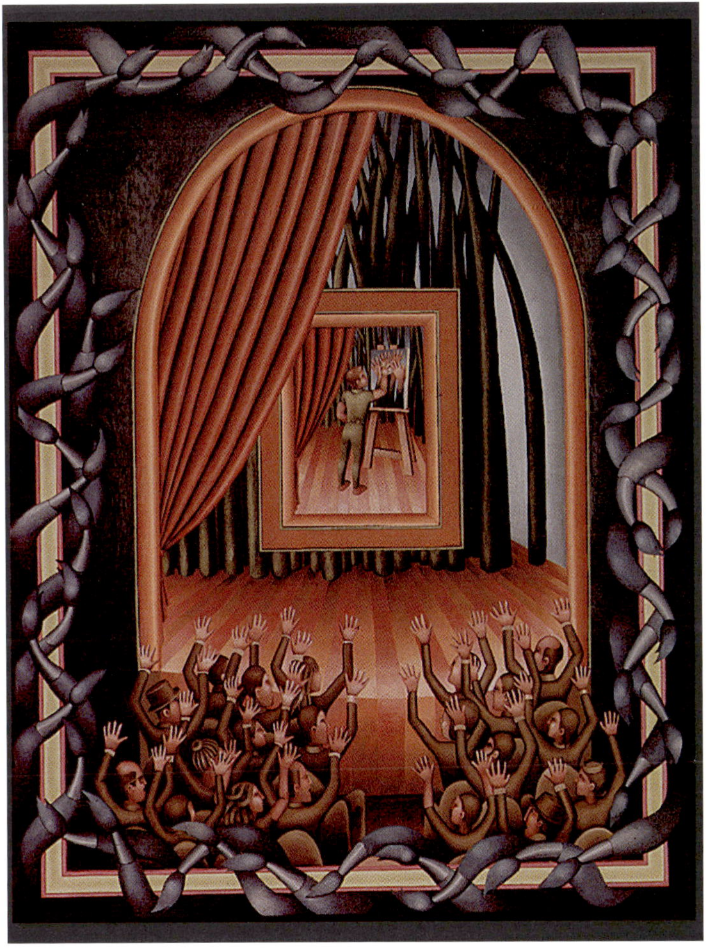

E. Painting for Applause.
Oil on canvas, 36" x 28".

PRICE LIST

A $4,000

B $4,000

C $4,000

D $4,000

E $4,000

Laura Shabott

Laura Shabott is a Boston and Provincetown, MA, based artist. She has studied at the Philadelphia College of Art in Pennsylvania and the Parsons School of Design in New York City. Although she has taught art classes at the New England School of Art and Design in the past, Shabott currently devotes her time and energies to painting.

Shabott works with oils on canvas and watercolors on paper. The figures in her paintings represent herself and simultaneously act as a metaphor for the female persona in contemporary culture. Influences that are evident in Shabott's work include ancient stylizations of the human form and the traditions of pre-Judeo-Christian culture.

Shabott's work has been exhibited in over fourteen shows in the last two years. Recently, her work was the focus of a favorably reviewed one-woman exhibition at the Stellwagen Gallery in Provincetown, MA. Shabott's paintings are included in private and corporate collections internationally.

General Delivery
Provincetown, MA 02657
617-482-6747

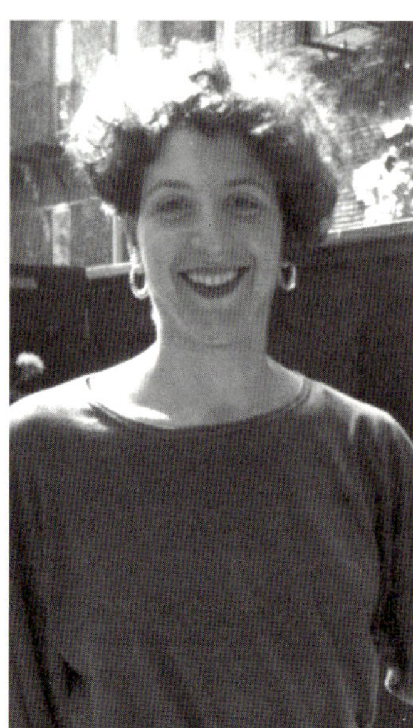

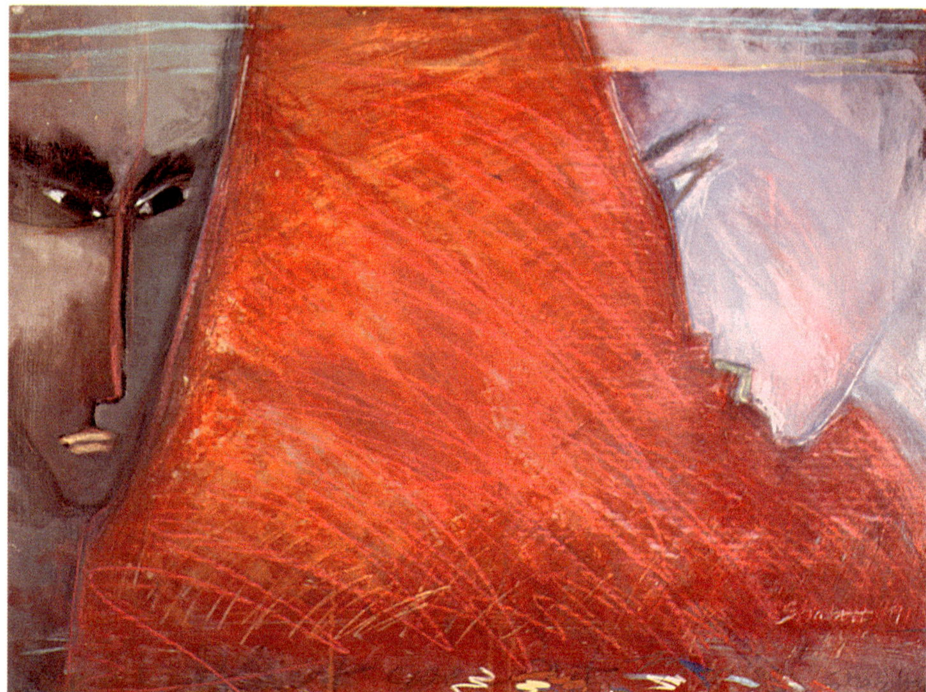

A. My Heart Goes Out. Gouache on paper, 22" x 30".

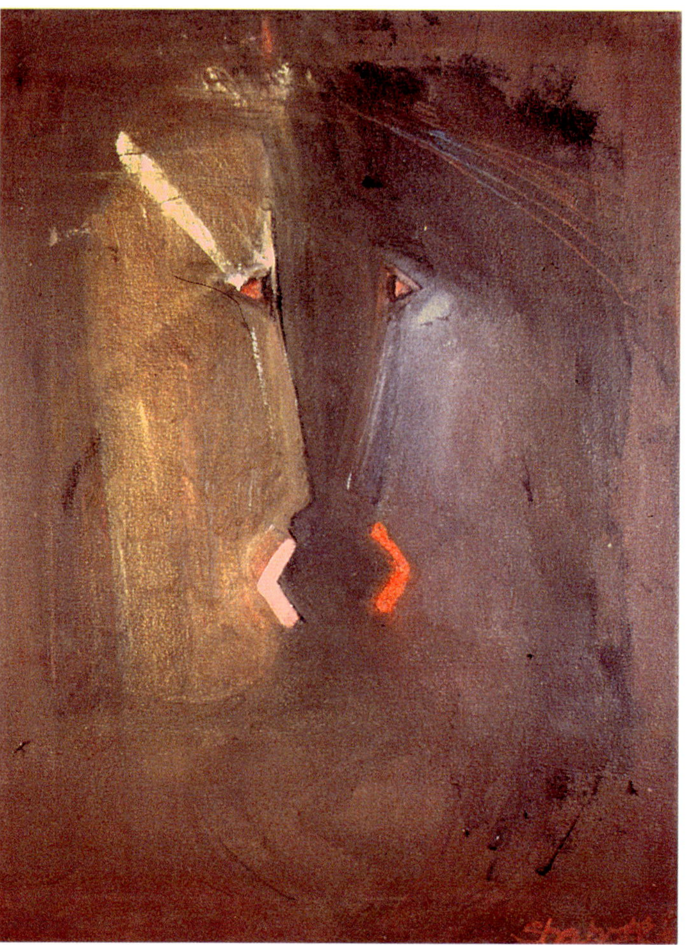

B. Strong Wills. Oil on canvas, 24" x 18".

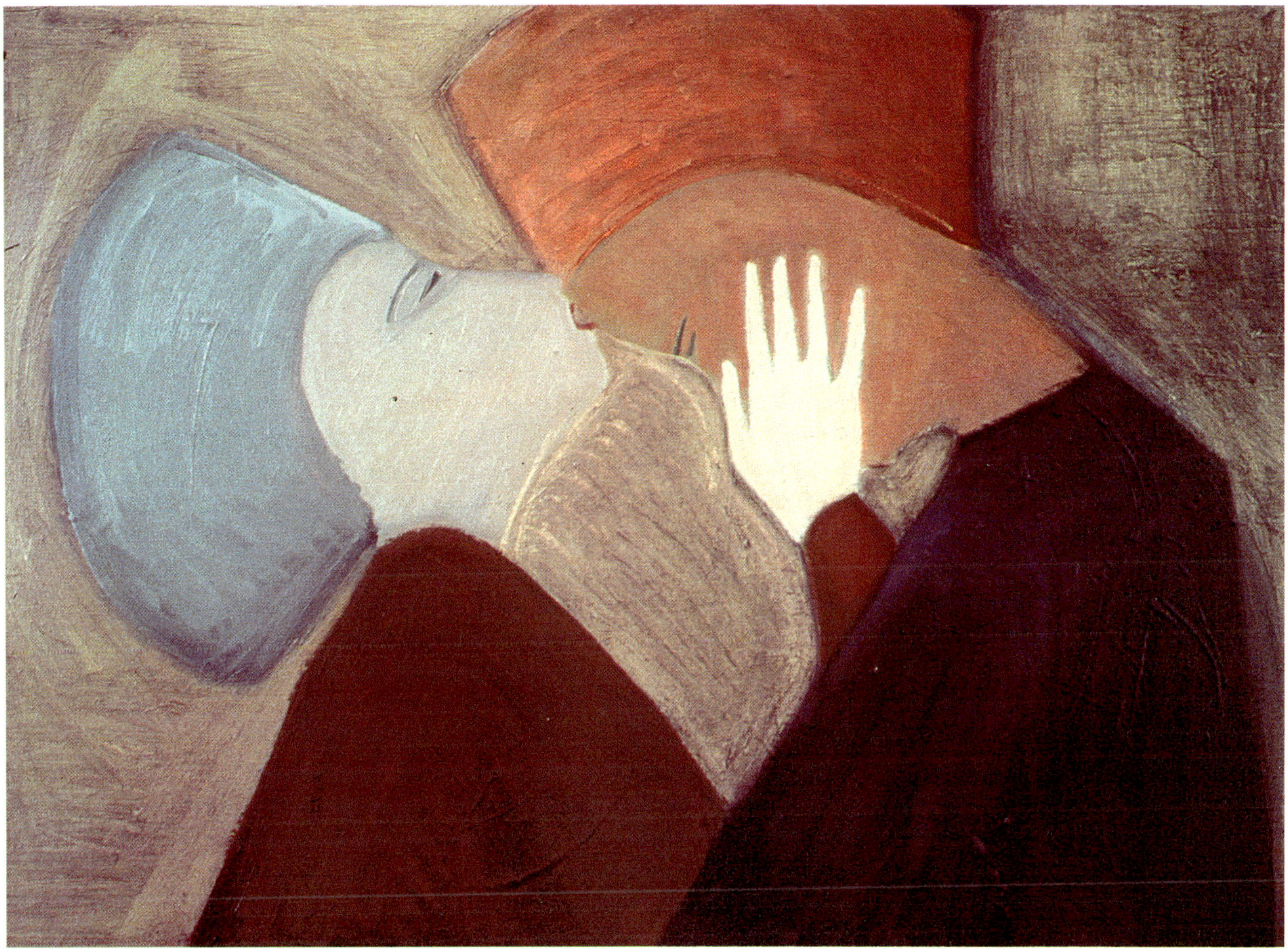

C. A Sacred Kiss. Oil on canvas, 32" x 40".

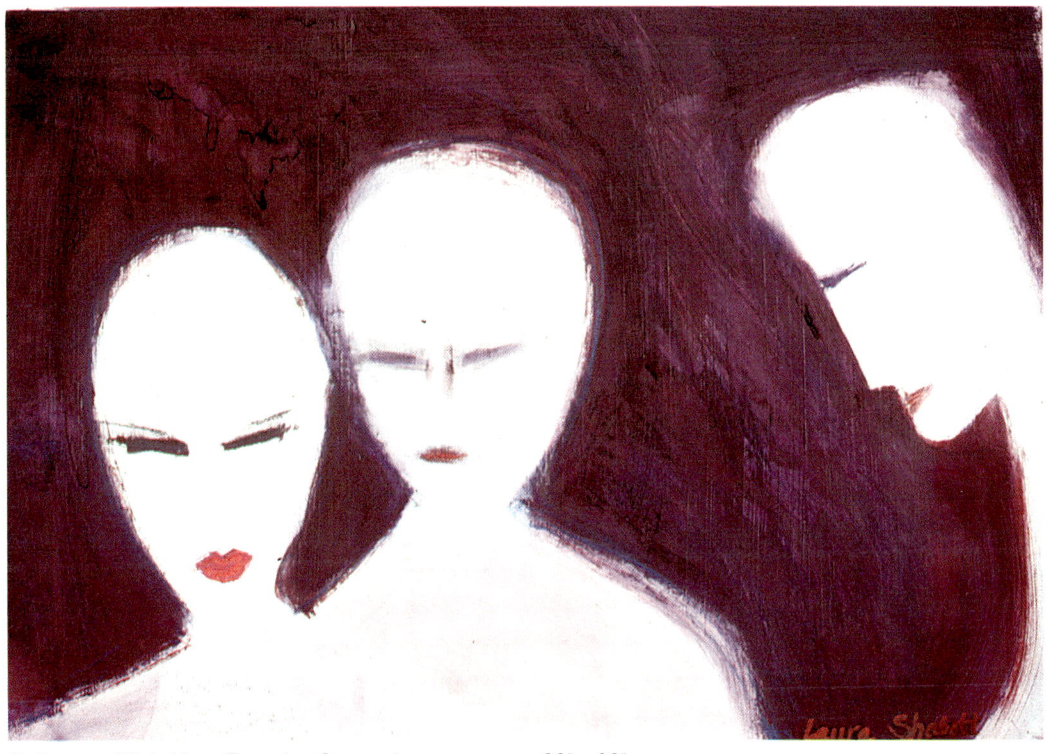

D. Person Watching Couple. Gouache on paper, 22" x 30".

PRICE LIST

A..........................$300

B..........................$400

C......................$1,600

D..........................$300

Represented by
Judith Wolou Design
Boston Design Center
Boston, MA
Stellwagen Gallery
Provincetown, MA

Elie Shamir

Elie Shamir was born and raised in Israel, where he actively painted and exhibited his work until 1989. He currently resides and maintains a studio in Brookline, MA.

Shamir works primarily with oils on canvas. His paintings are rich in symbolism, which the viewer is invited to decipher. Shamir is concerned with questions raised by mythology and how contemporary society answers and reformulates them. He explores dichotomies: man and woman, culture and nature, photography and painting. While he is ultimately concerned with the message his work conveys, Shamir is also conscious of the place of the fine arts in our culture.

During the 1980s, Shamir's work was exhibited frequently in Israel, and he has continued to show often since coming to the United States. Shamir will have his third solo show in Boston at the Ashuah-Irving Gallery in January of 1993. His work is contained in collections both in the United States and in Israel, where he is represented in the Israel Museum, the Haifa Museum and the Tel-Aviv Museum.

Elie Shamir

88 Columbia Street
Brookline, MA 02146
617-566-5371

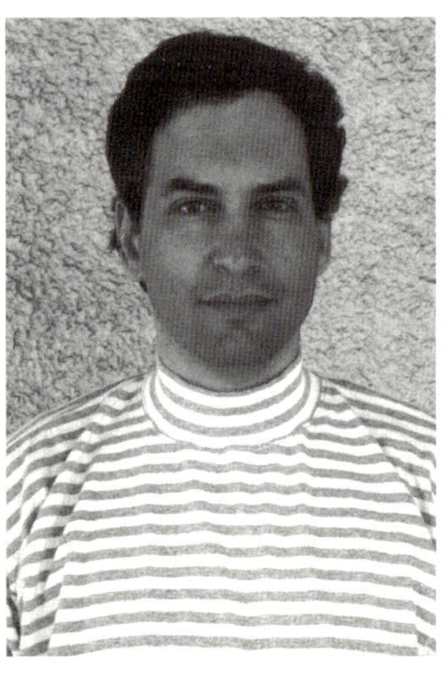

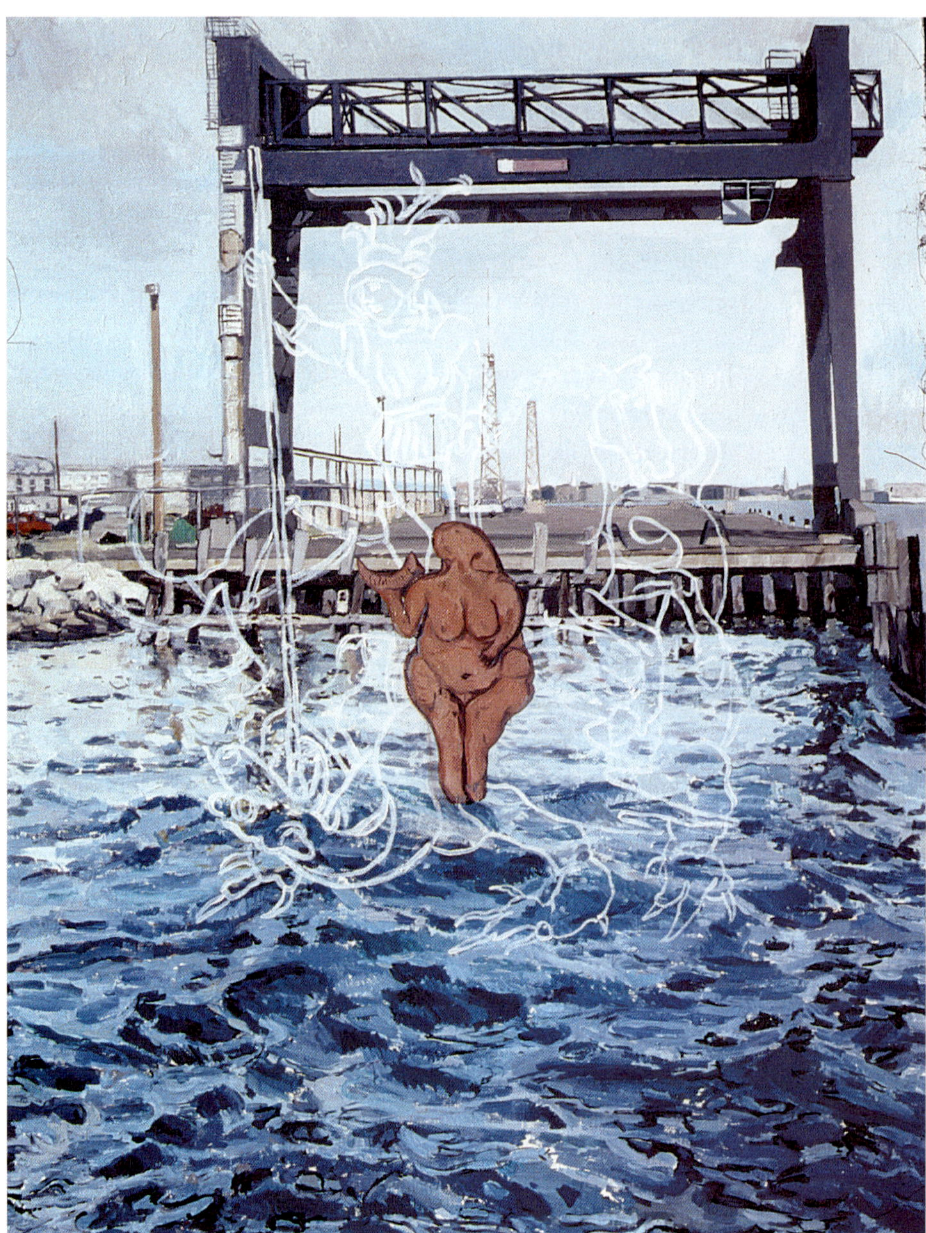

A. Land and Sea. Oil on canvas, 56" x 24".

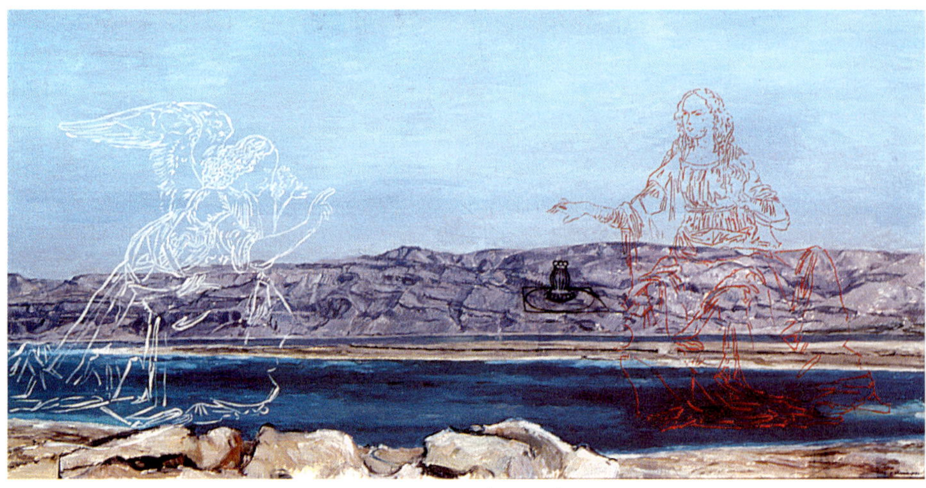

B. Dead Sea Annunciation. Oil on canvas, 30⅛" x 60⅛".

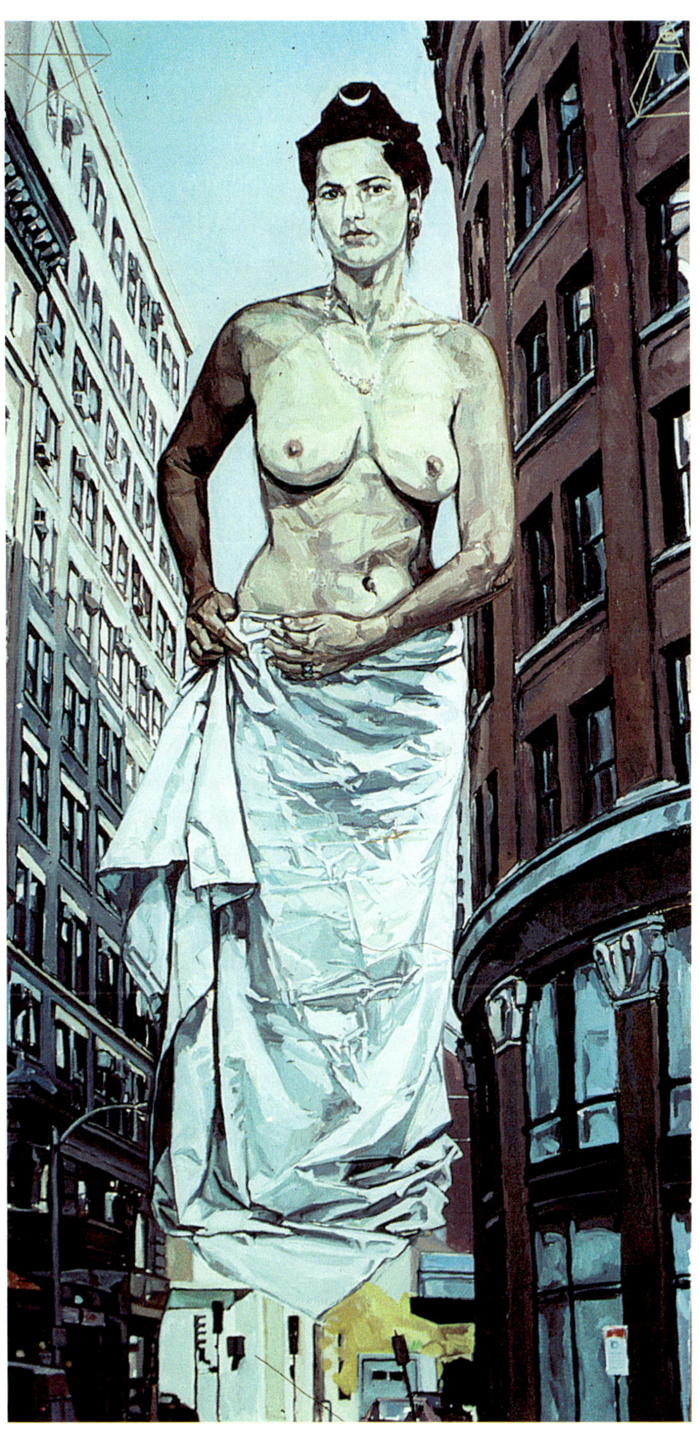

C. The Kidnap of Europa II. Oil on canvas, 72" x 36".
Private collection.

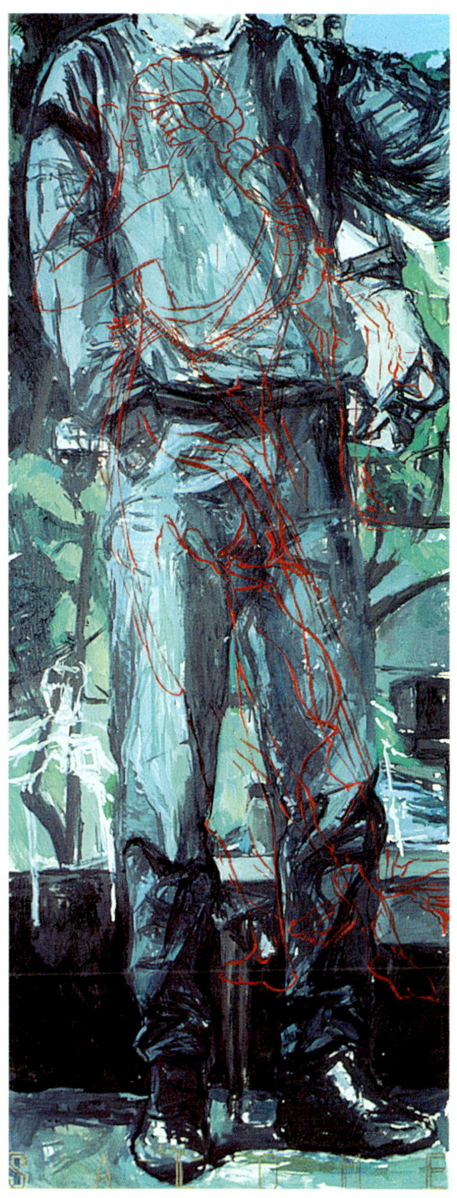

D. Salome. Oil on canvas, 60" x 22".

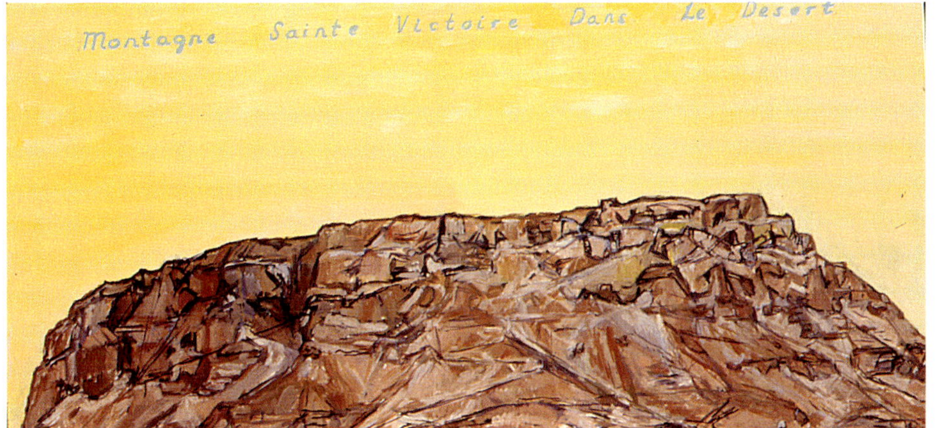

E. Mont Saint Victoire. Oil on canvas, 30⅛" x 60⅛".

PRICE LIST

A $4,500
B $4,200
C $5,500
D $4,200
E $4,200

Represented by
Ashuah-Irving Gallery
Boston, MA

Gaal Sheperd

Born in Gainesville, FL, Gaal Sheperd studied both theater and intaglio print making during the seventies. In the 1980s, she received art training at the Corcoran School of Art in Washington, DC. Since 1988, Sheperd and her husband have lived in Vermont, where she has studied with several prominent artists, including Wolf Kahn.

Sheperd concentrated primarily on figure and collage before she moved to New England, but all her work since has either openly or subtly reflected the Vermont landscape. She works in three different media: pastel, oil on canvas and painting on photographs.

Since 1974, Sheperd has exhibited her work often, winning numerous awards at shows throughout the country. In 1989 she had a one-woman show at the Pierre-Antoine Gallery in Washington, DC. Sheperd has had proposals accepted for shows to take place this January at Lyndon State College in Lyndonville, VT, and this spring at Beside Myself Gallery in Arlington, VT.

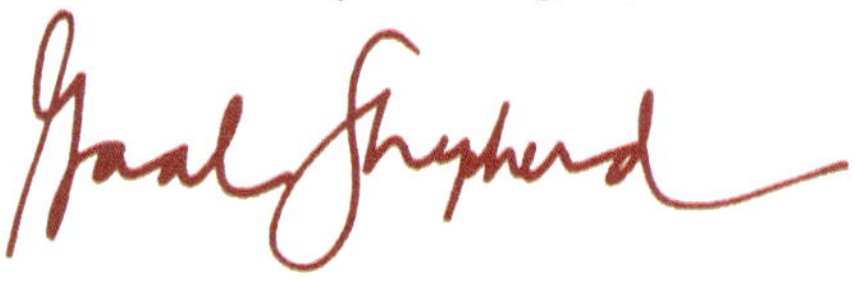

P.O. Box 289
Hyde Park, VT 05655
802-888-8589

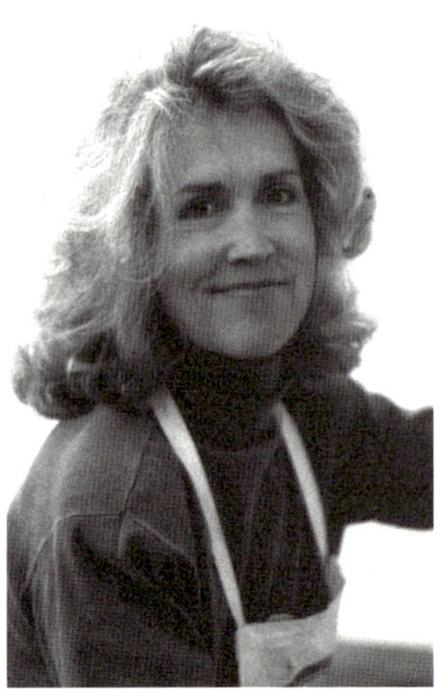

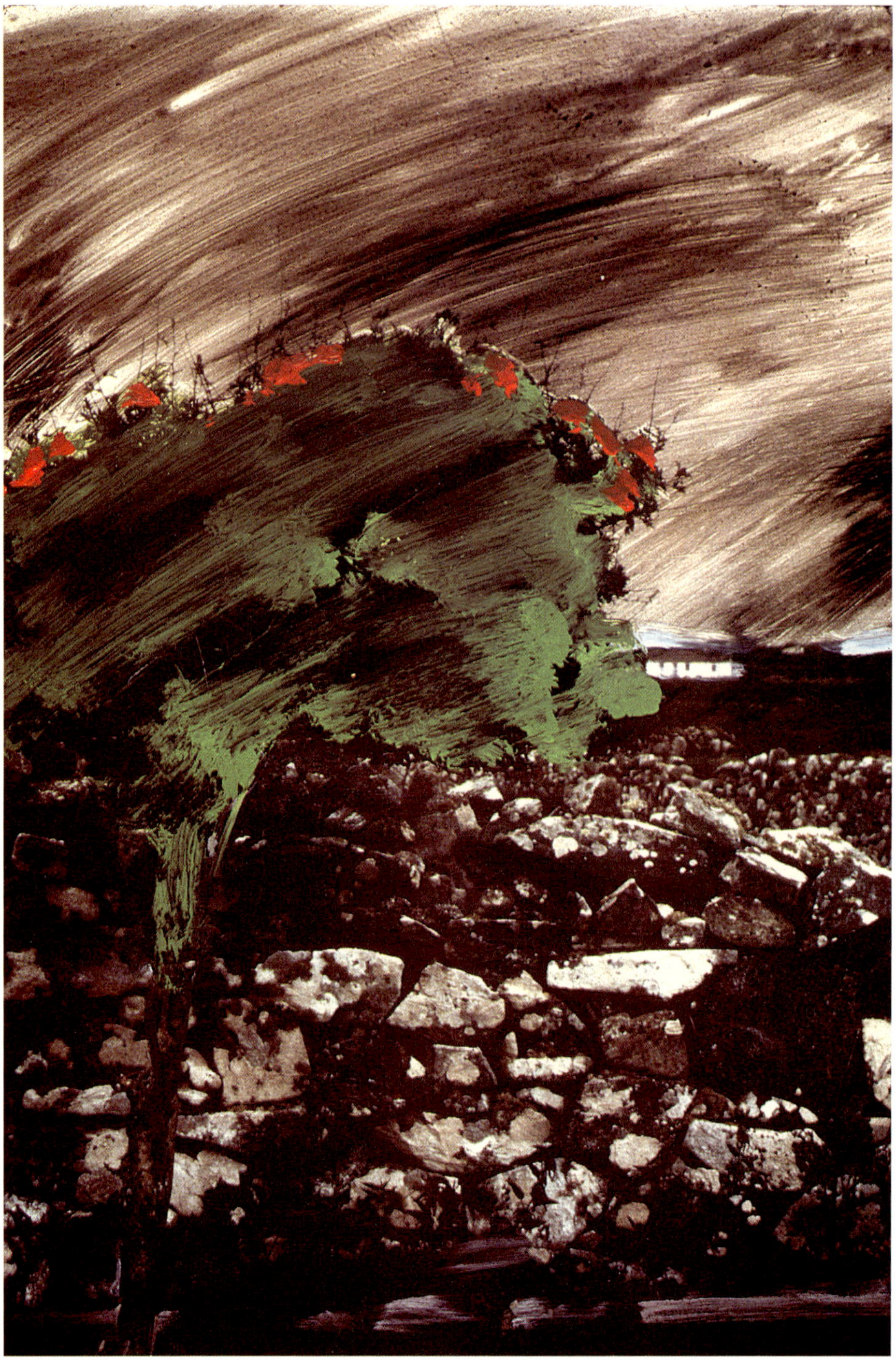

A. Black Wind in Connemara. Oil on liba, 20" x 18".

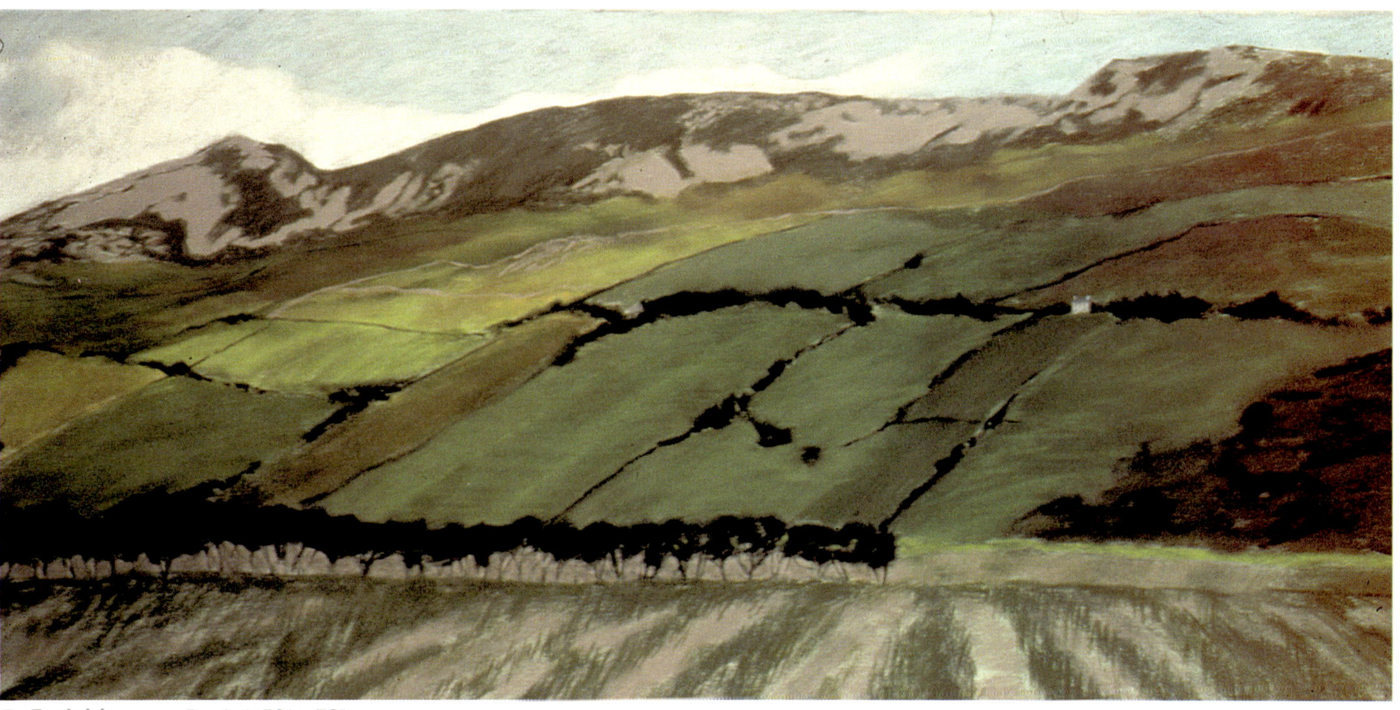

B. On Inishowen. Pastel, 50" x 70".

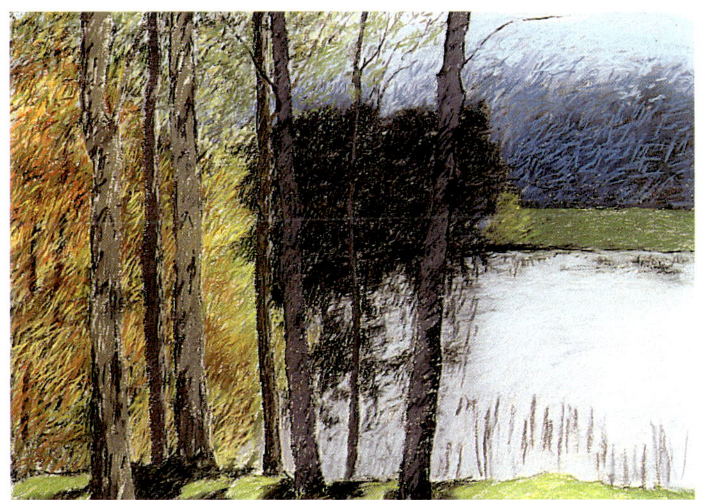

C. College Pond.
Pastel, 30" x 38".

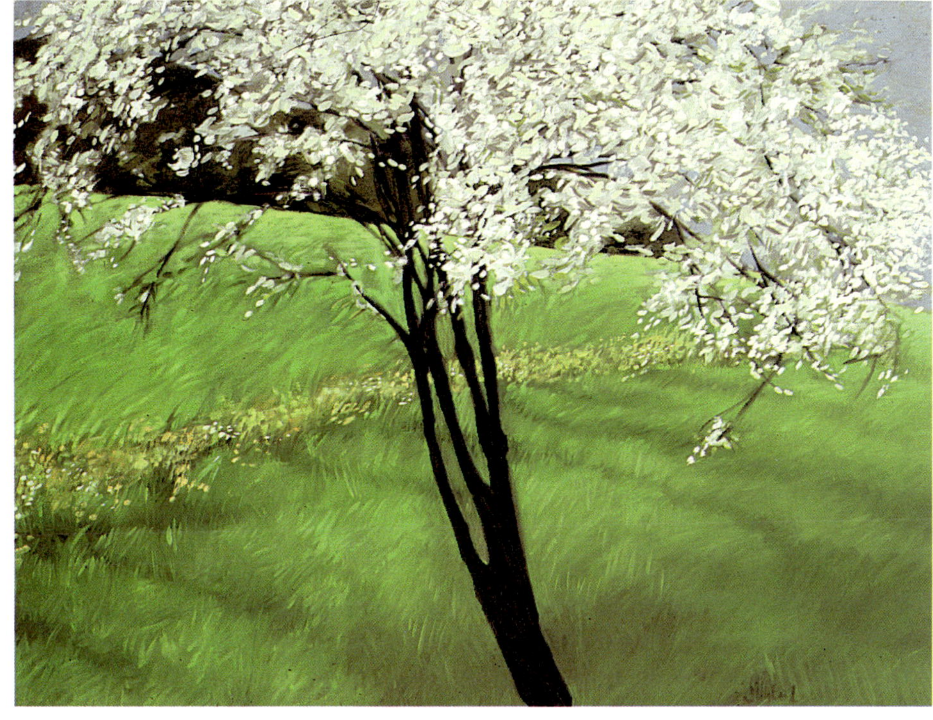

D. Tree at Reed's.
Oil, 36" x 48".

PRICE LIST

A..........................$250

B........................$3,000

C..........................$900

D........................$1,000

Represented by
Simon Pearce Showrooms
Quechee, VT and
North Wind
Artisans Gallery
Woodstock, VT
Boston Corporate Art
Woburn, MA

Mary **Sherman**

Born in Pensacola, FL, Mary Sherman studied painting at Boston College, where she received a BA in Studio Arts, and at Vienna's Akademie fur Angewandte Kunst. Sherman now lives in Boston, maintaining a studio at the Boston Center for the Arts.

Sherman's psychologically charged canvases are explorations of images that have made a strong impression on her. Through the medium of paint she attempts to express her initial attraction to her subject. Typically, the paintings depict isolated figures in undefined, claustrophobic environments. While content is important, formal issues remain Sherman's primary concern.

Sherman has exhibited extensively in Chicago and Boston, including a recent one-woman show at Judi Rotenburg Gallery in Boston. In 1991, she was one of eight artists selected to exhibit at the Currier Gallery's "Third Gloria Wilcher Memorial Exhibition," was included in Chicago's International Art Exposition and was awarded residency at the Ragdale Foundation in Lake Forest, IL.

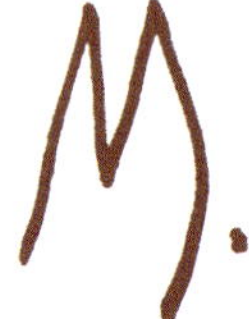

551 Tremont Street, #315
Boston, MA 02116
617-482-3827
Studio: 617-426-7807

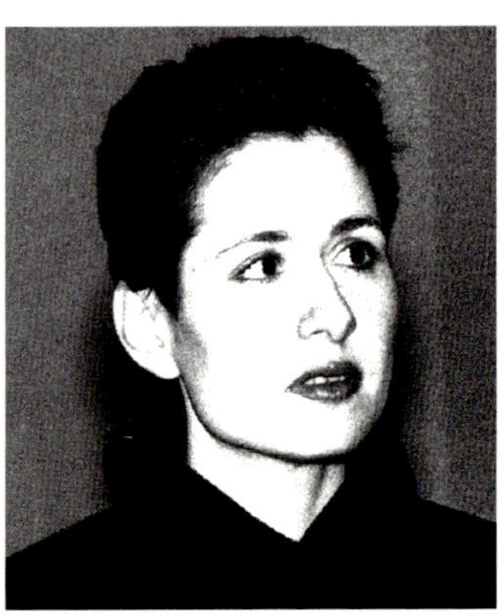

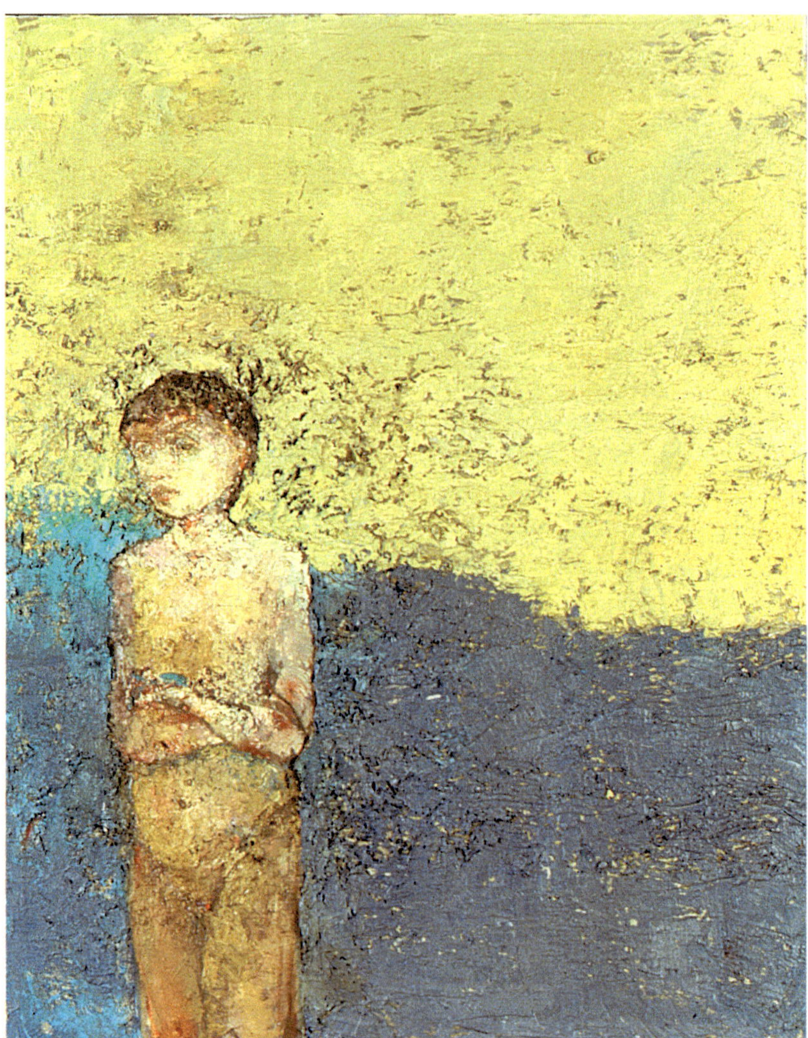

A. (above)
Nausicaa.
Oil on canvas,
45" x 36".
Courtesy of
Carol Van Zandt.

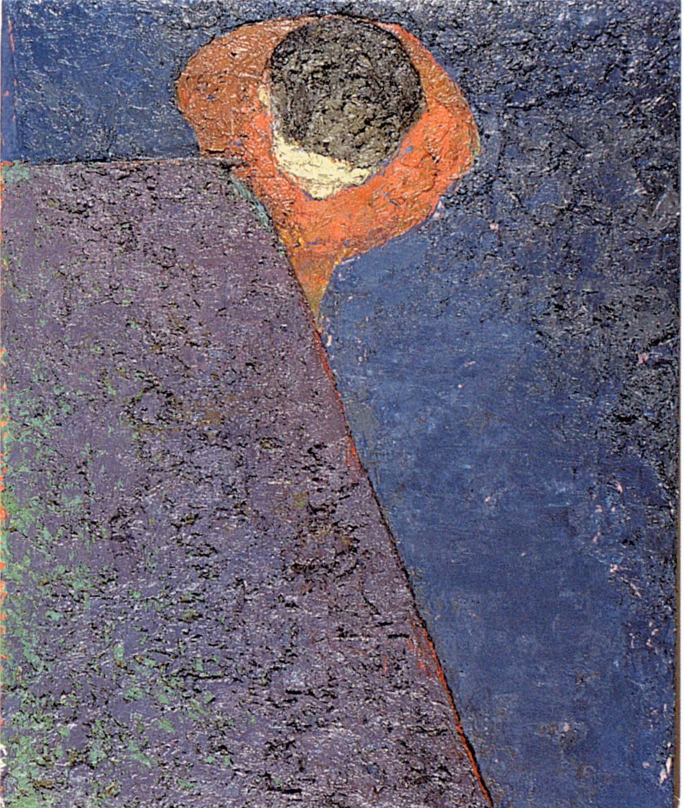

B. The Escape.
Oil on canvas,
36" x 24".
Courtesy of Oskar
Friedl Gallery.

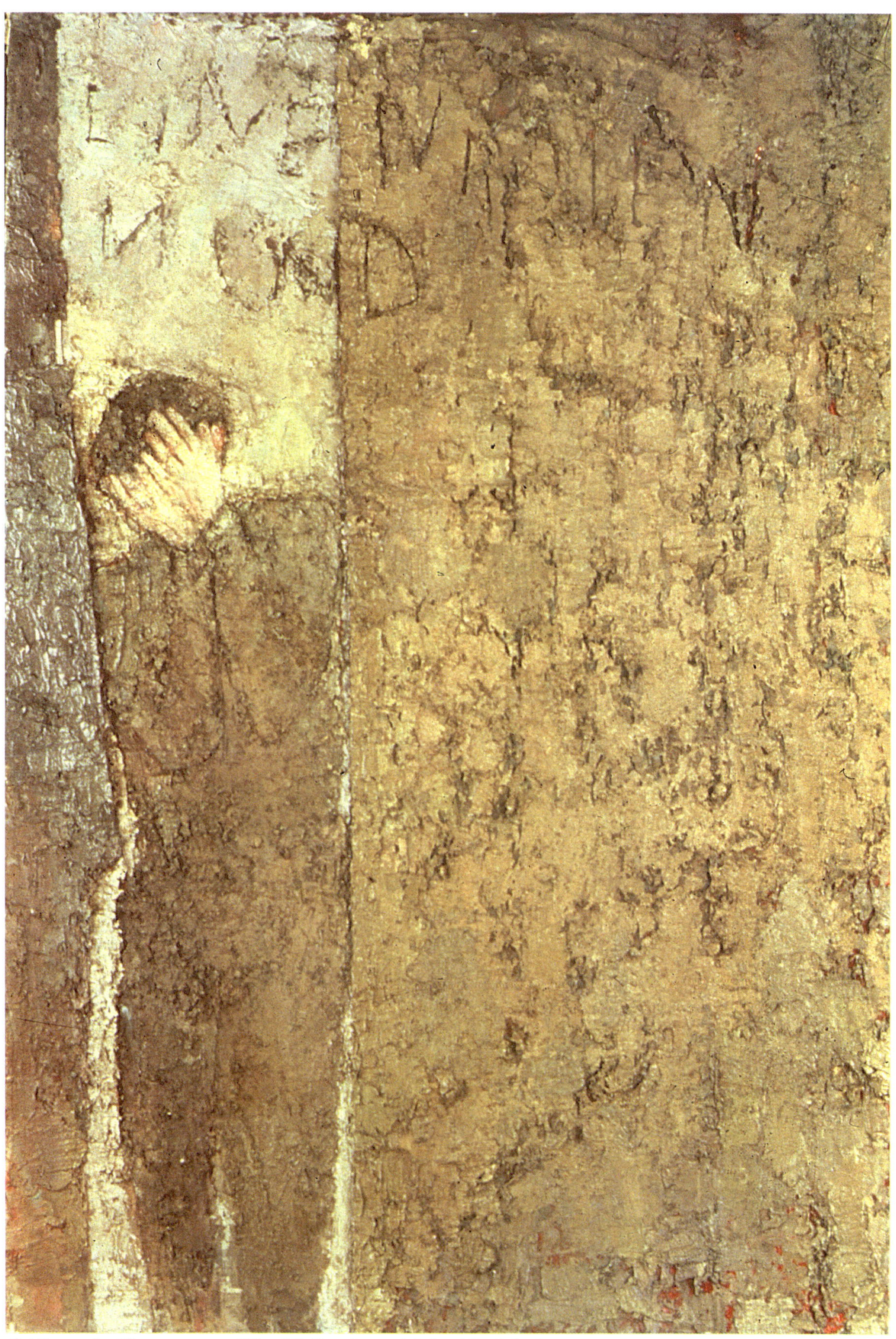

C. Wozzeck. Oil on canvas, 72" x 48". Courtesy of Oskar Friedl Gallery.

PRICE LIST

B $2,600

C $3,900

Represented by
Judi Rotenburg Gallery
Boston, MA
Oskar Friedl Gallery
Chicago, IL

Robert J. Smith was born and raised in Boston. Upon graduating from East Boston High School, where he first explored the fine arts, Smith opted to refine his talent with studies at the School of the Museum of Fine Arts, Boston. After a time, Smith left the Museum School and pursued musical training at Berklee College of Music in Boston. He currently devotes his time to painting.

Smith primarily works with oils on canvas. He uses surreal landscapes, executed in a baroque manner, to describe the world as he sees it: wonderful, violent and unpredictable. Smith's paintings are about daily news events and his reaction to them. Often, they develop with comical overtones.

Smith has won many awards and his work has been shown in Boston and New York City. He is currently represented by Randolph and Tate in New York City.

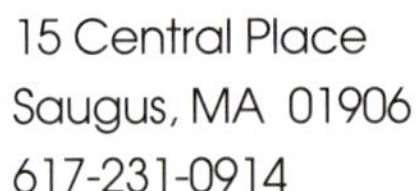

15 Central Place
Saugus, MA 01906
617-231-0914

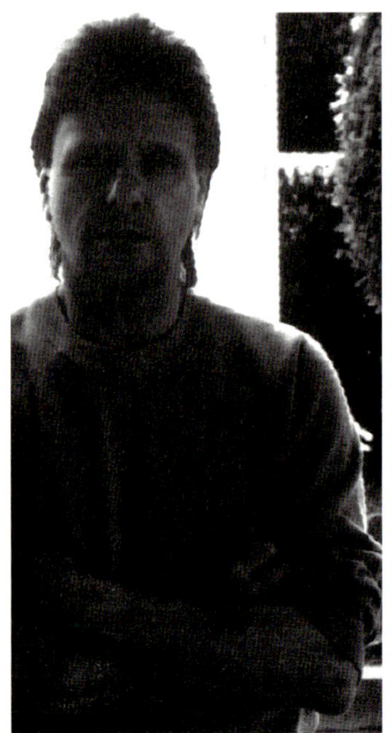

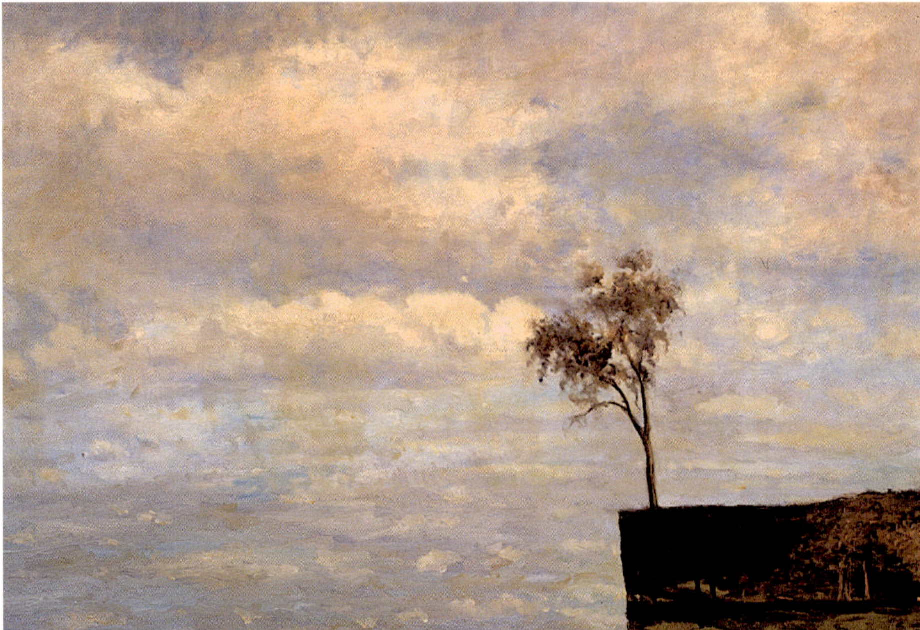

A. Virginia Place. Oil on canvas, 24" x 36".

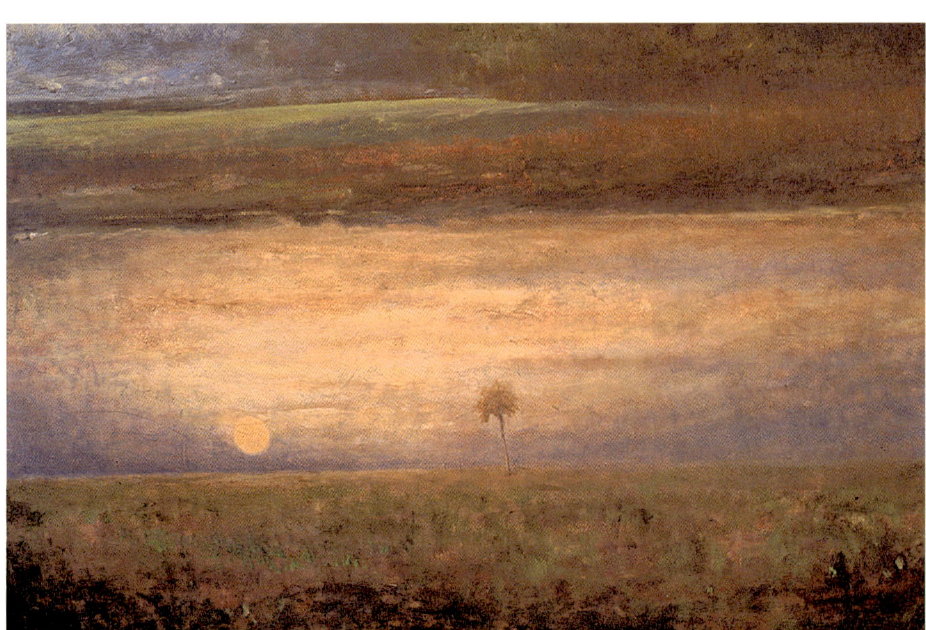

B. Your Next. Oil on canvas, 24" x 36".

PRICE LIST

A $1,600

B $1,600

C $1,600

D $1,600

Represented by
Randolph and Tate Gallery
New York City

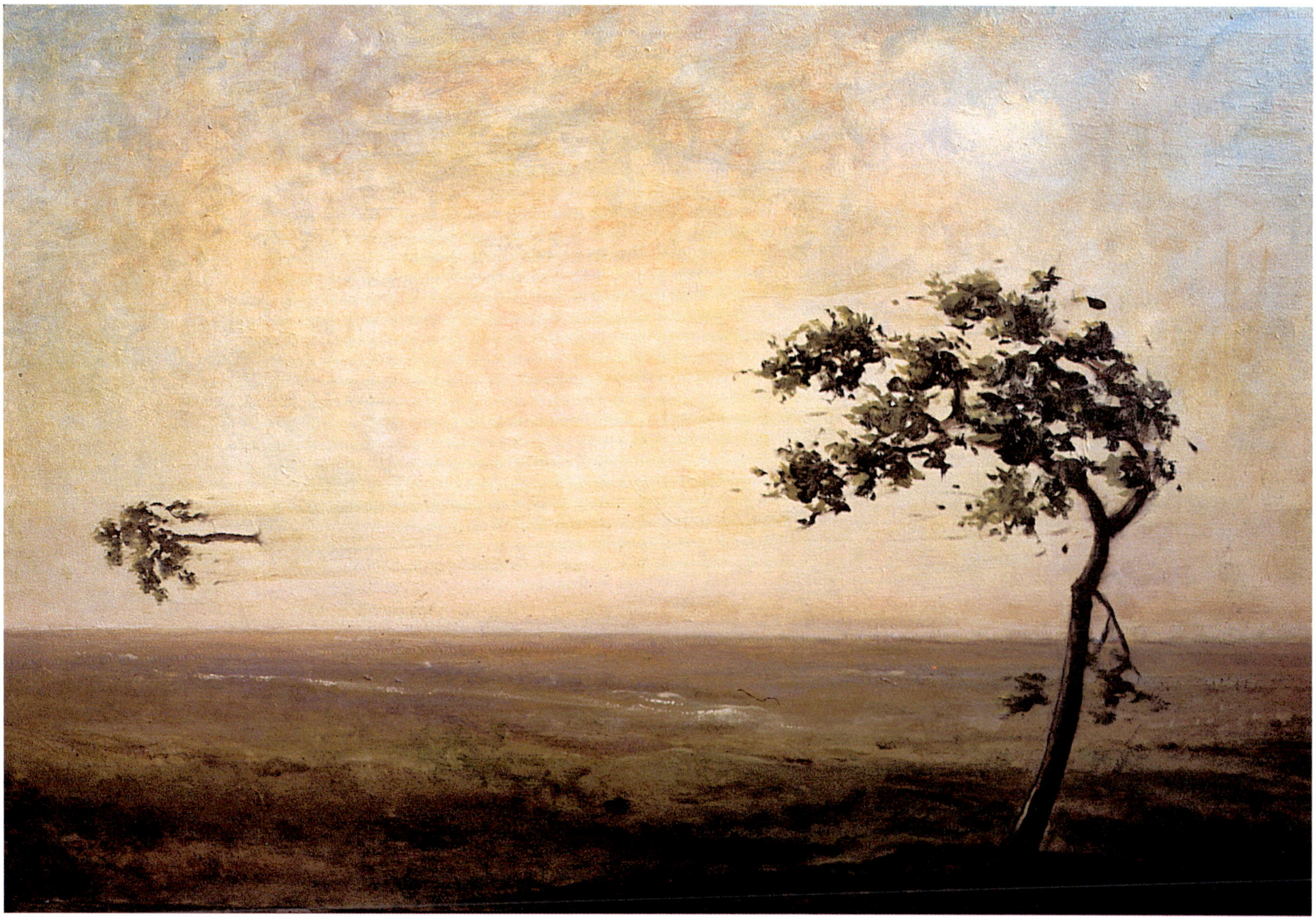

C. Communication Breakdown. Oil on canvas, 24" x 36".

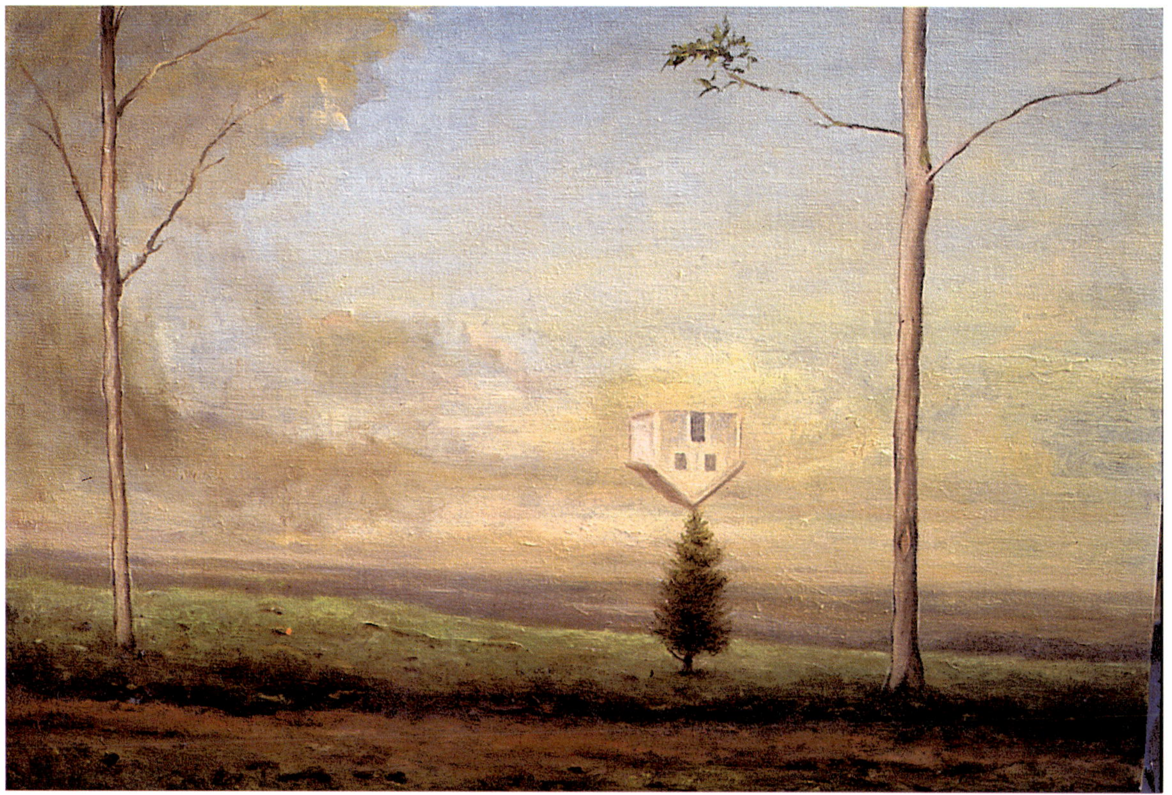

D. Martin's Dream. Oil on canvas, 20" x 24"

Mari Spirito

Mari Spirito is another representative of New England's twenty-something talent. Born in 1967, Spirito was raised in Hingham, MA, and now lives in the Jamaica Plain section of Boston. She attends the Massachusetts College of Art, from which she will receive a BFA in Painting. Active in Boston's art community, Spirito devotes her time to directing the M&M Gallery, which she founded, and to painting and graphic design.

Spirito's paintings are executed primarily in oil on canvas, but she also utilizes common household varnish and shellac to achieve the unusual layered effect that characterizes her work. Spirito's figurative, emotive images are created with a spontaneity which she admits often prevents her from knowing the true meaning of a work until it's completed. However, isolation is a recurrent theme.

Spirito's work has often been exhibited in the restaurants and clubs that form the backdrop of Boston's alternative art scene. A recent group show at Mu Gallery in Boston brought positive critical response to her work.

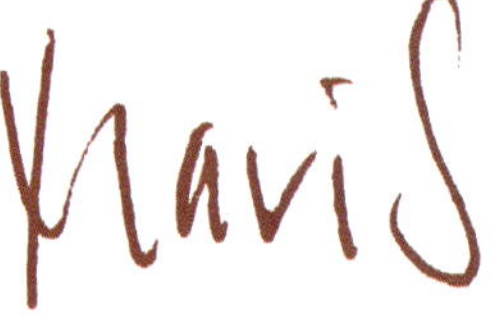

68 Green Street
Jamaica Plain, MA 02130
617-524-3242

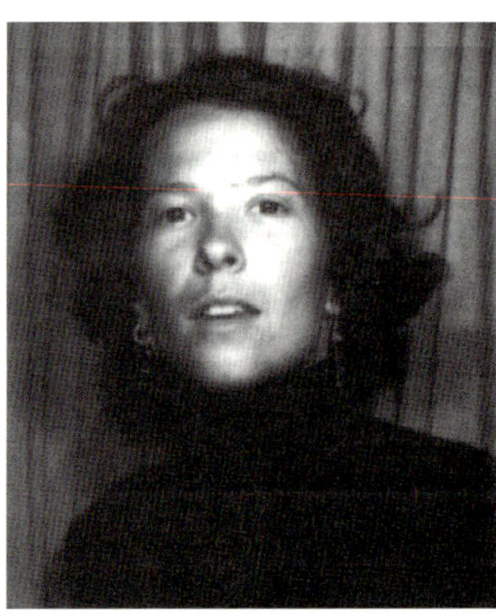

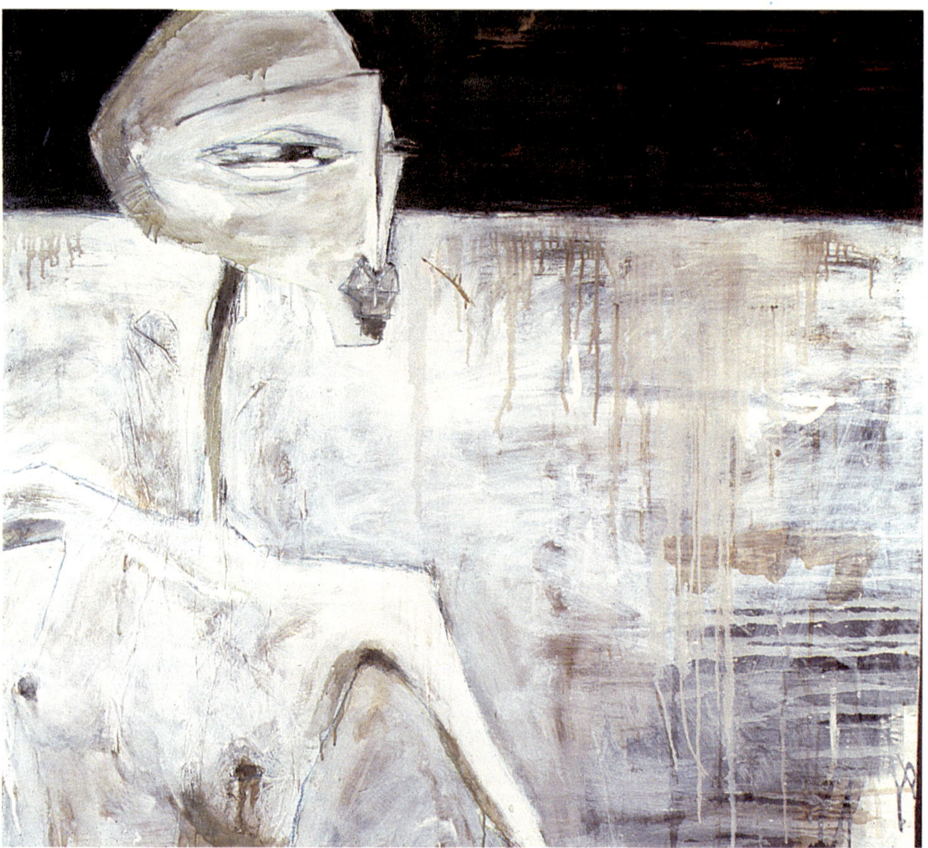

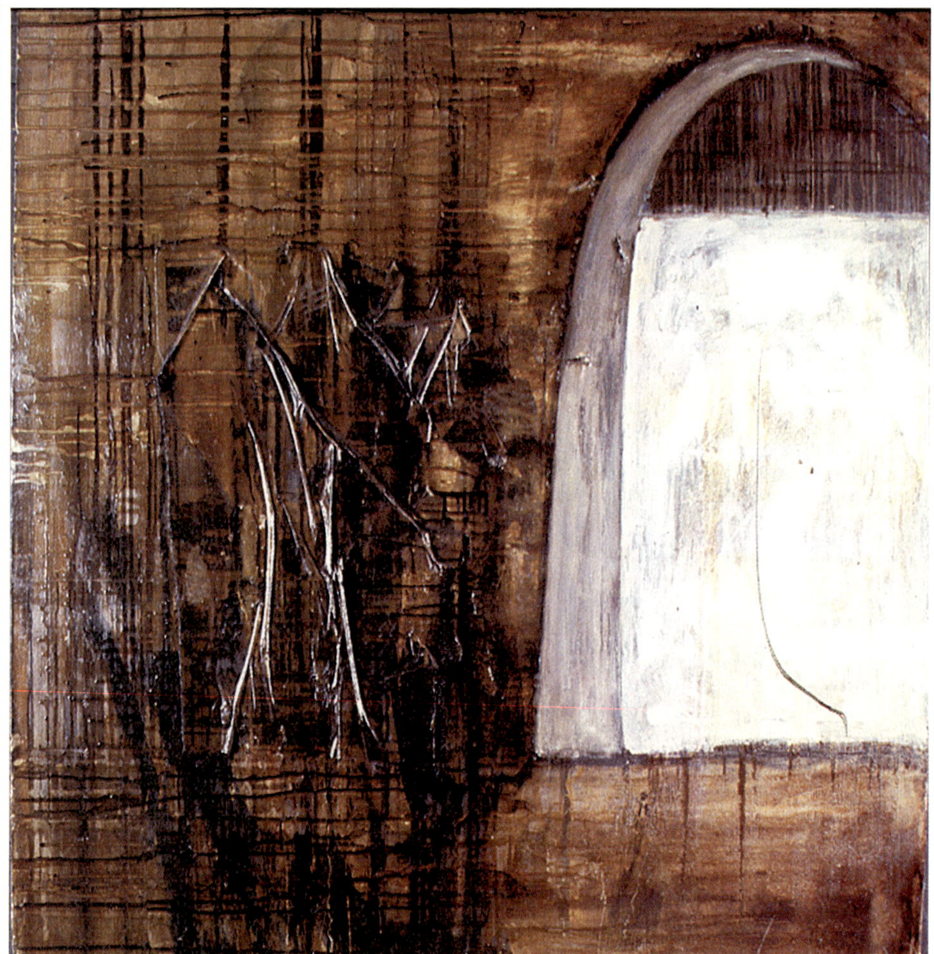

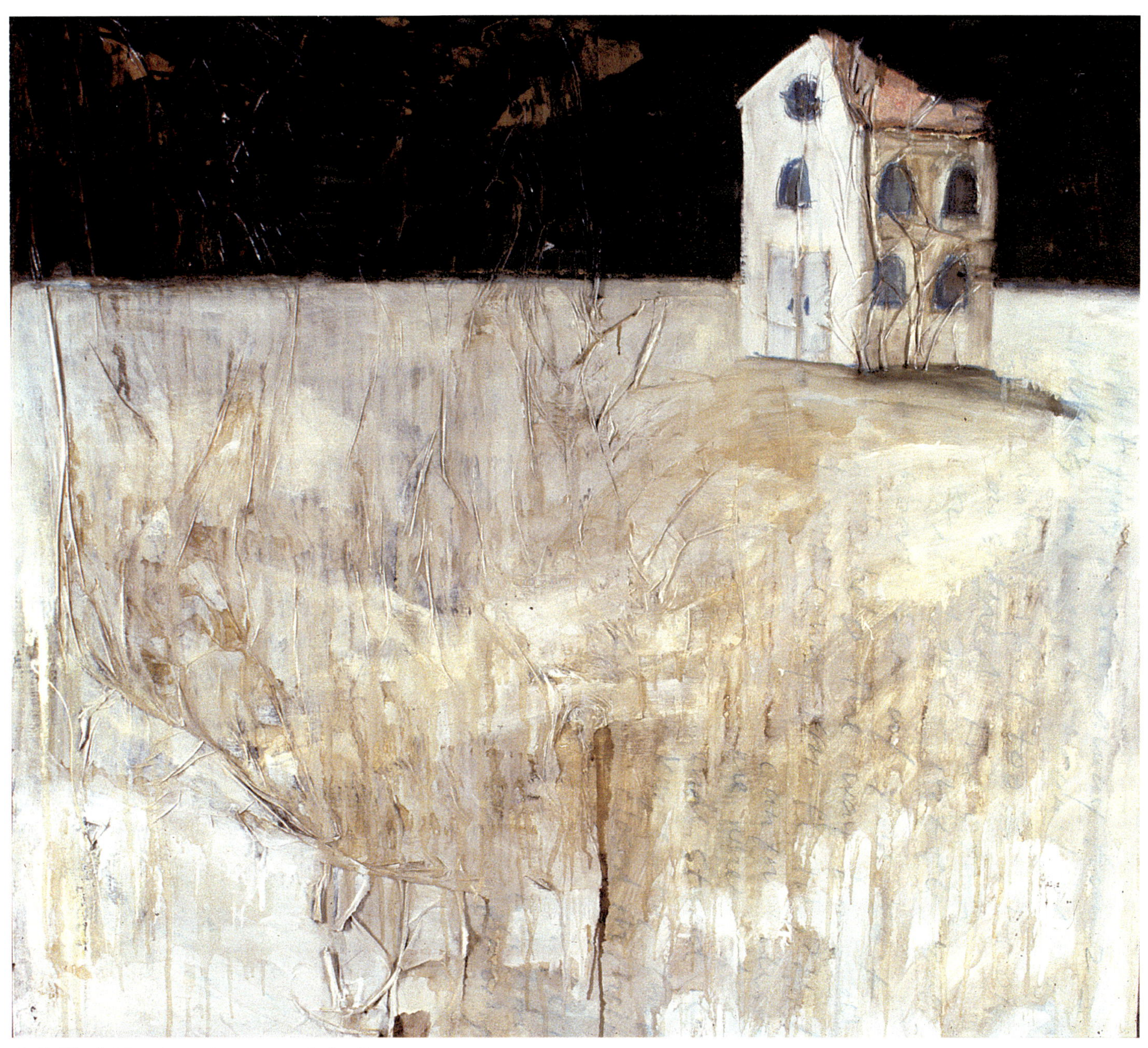

C. Untitled. Mixed media on wood, 4' x 4'.

A. (opposite above)
Untitled. Mixed media on wood, 4' x 4'.

B. (opposite below)
Untitled. Mixed media on wood, 4' x 4'.

PRICE LIST

A..........................$600

B..........................$600

C..........................$800

We are pleased to be showing the first collaborative work of husband and wife, sculptor and painter, Charles A. and Stephanie Mahan Stigliano. Both have received extensive art training; Charles earned his MFA from the University of North Carolina in 1984 and Stephanie earned hers from the Massachusetts College of Art in 1988. During the 1980s, Stephanie and Charles showed their individual works in group and solo shows throughout the Northeast and in North Carolina. Their first collaborative show was at the Ashuah-Irving Gallery in Boston in 1992.

Working together, they have produced a series of reliefs, which were sculpted by Charles and then painted by Stephanie. The works deal with a woman as an individual and as part of a relationship; each panel explores various levels of intimacy and isolation. Stephanie's coloring and the tendency of figure and ground to compete in a relief serve to either isolate or break down the boundaries between the depicted figure(s) and the environment. In this way, Charles and Stephanie explore the tension between the demands of individuality and partnership.

602 Highland Avenue
Malden, MA 02148
617-321-4087

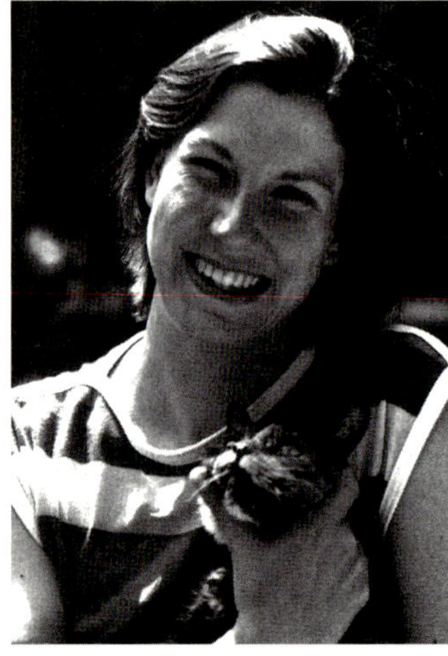

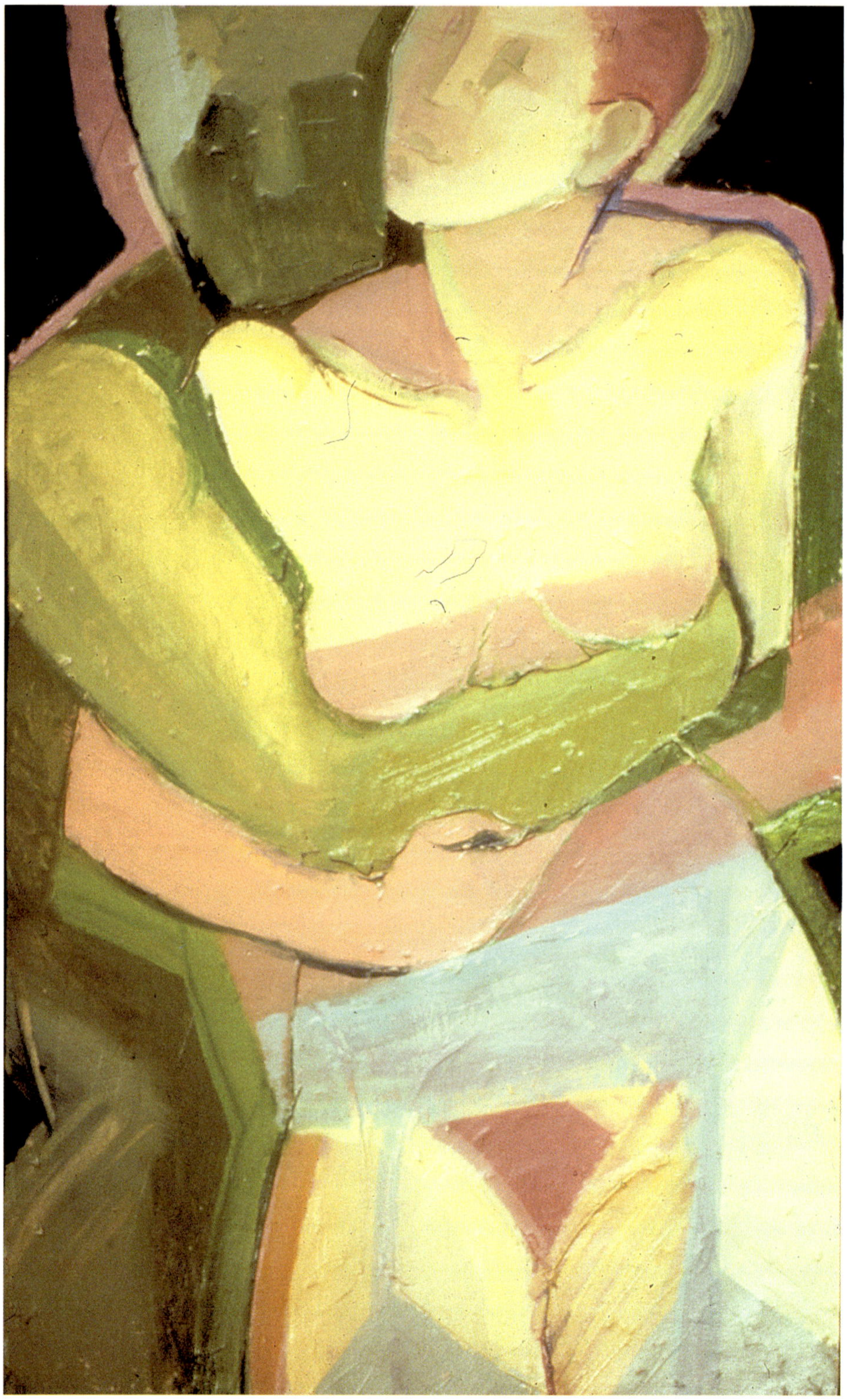

A. Couple II. Oil over prepared ultracal, 35" x 23" x 3".

PRICE LIST

A $1,600

B $1,600

C $1,600

D $1,600

E $1,600

Represented by
Ashuah-Irving Gallery

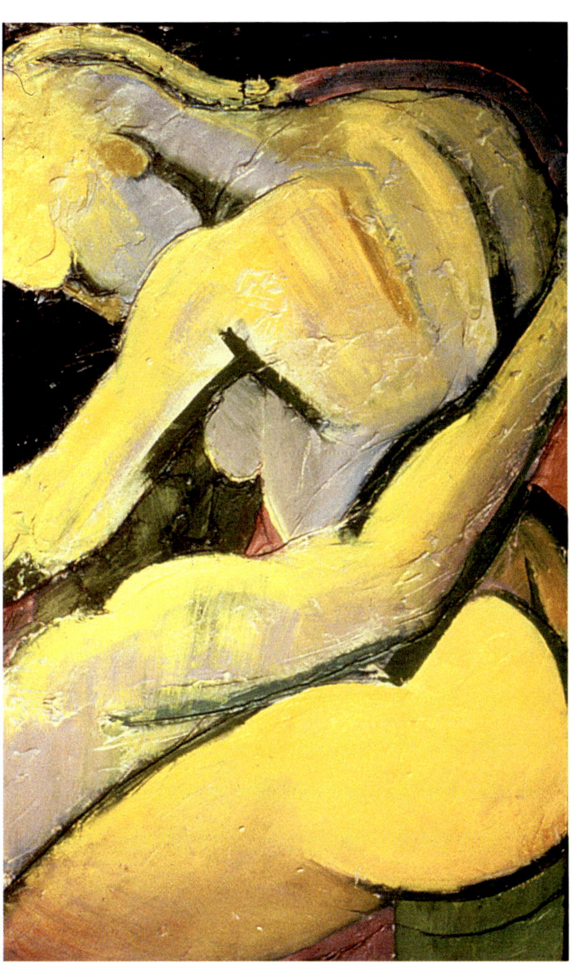

B. Embrace I. Oil over prepared ultracal, 35" x 23" x 3".

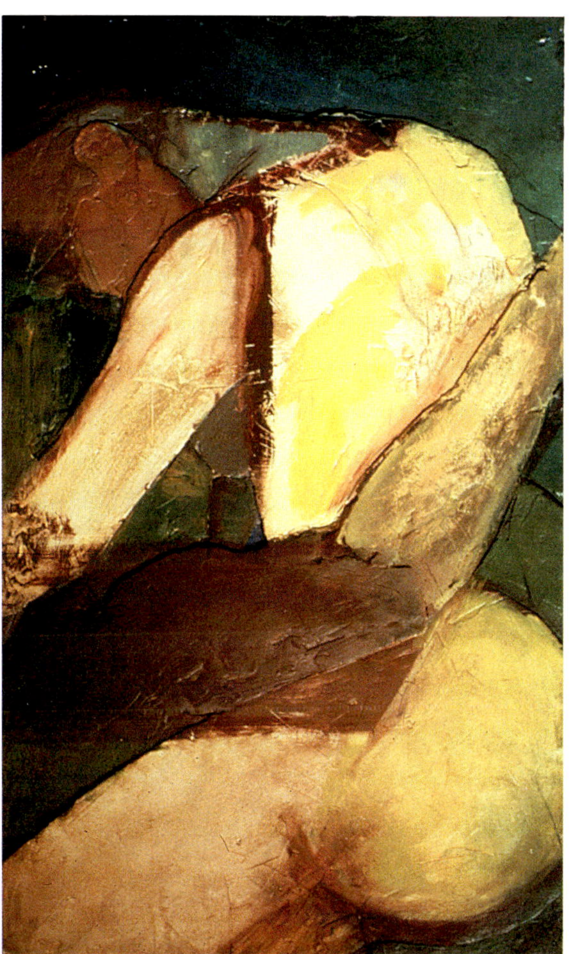

C. Embrace II. Oil over prepared ultracal, 35" x 23" x 3".

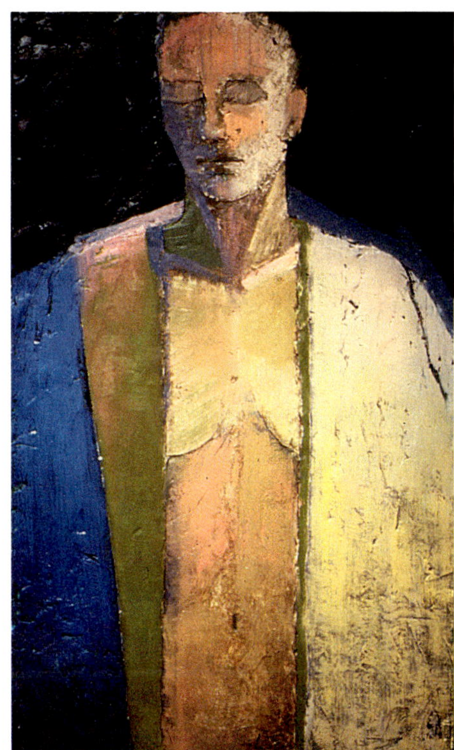

D. Woman in Robe I. Oil over prepared ultracal, 35" x 23" x 3".

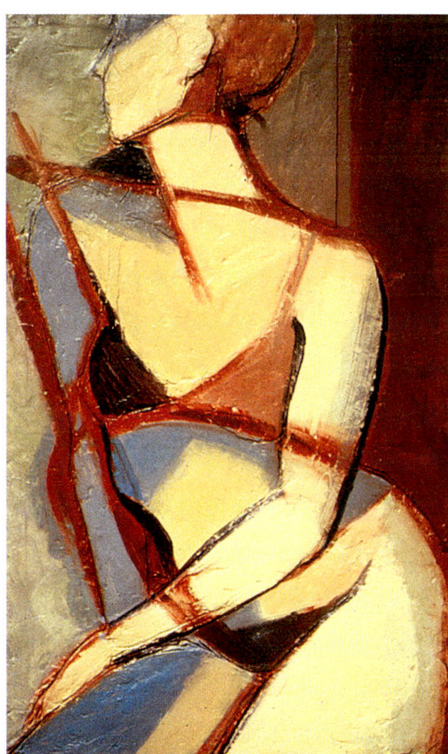

E. Seated I. Oil over prepasred ultracal, 35" x 23" x 3".

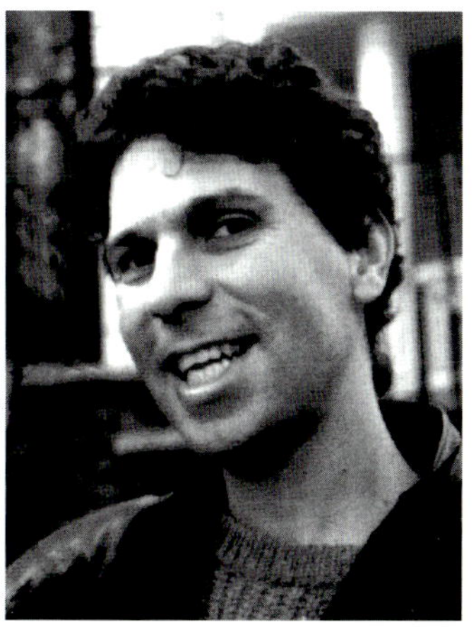

Patty Stone was born in Wisconsin in 1952 and now lives in Boston's South End. In 1977, Stone received an MFA from the Yale Graduate School of Art. She has taught at the School of the Worcester Art Museum, the Rhode Island School of Design, and currently teaches life drawing at the Museum of Fine Arts, Boston.

A recent one-year stay in Barcelona, Spain, launched Stone on an exploration of the themes of decay, deterioration and permanence, using simplified architectural forms as a motif. Through a combination of sand and acrylic paint on canvas, she aims to create a tactile presence and evoke the sense of crumbling walls or fragments of plaster.

Stone has participated in group shows throughout New England, including shows at the Newport Art Museum and the Rhode Island School of Design. She had solo exhibitions at the Mills Gallery in Boston in 1988 and 1985, and at the Currier House, Harvard University, in 1988.

Patty Stone

331 Shawmut Avenue, #3
Boston, MA 02118
617-262-3160

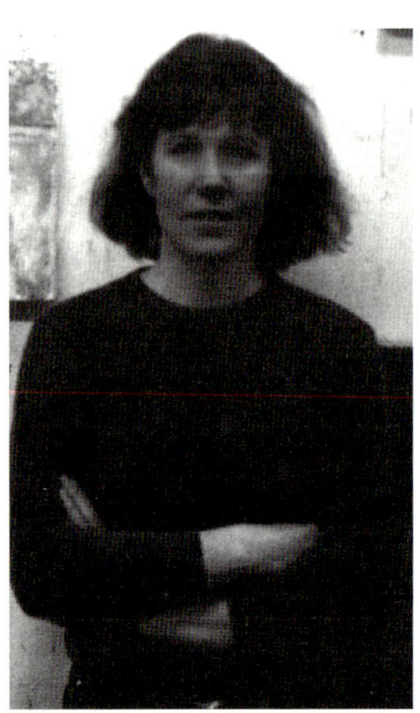

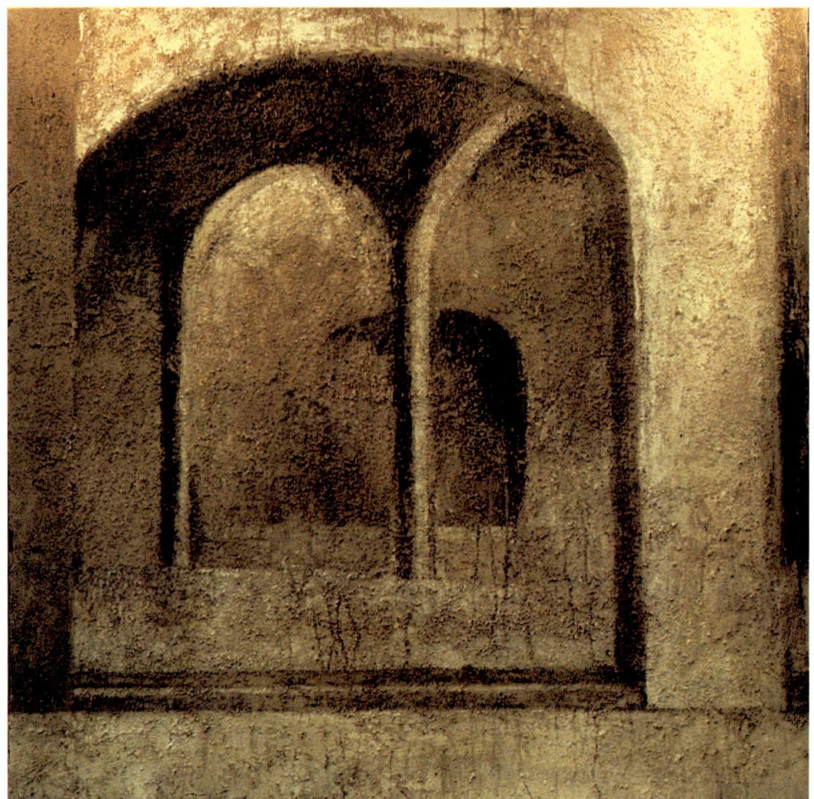

A. Hospital Santa Creu. Acrylic/sand on canvas, 51" x 51".

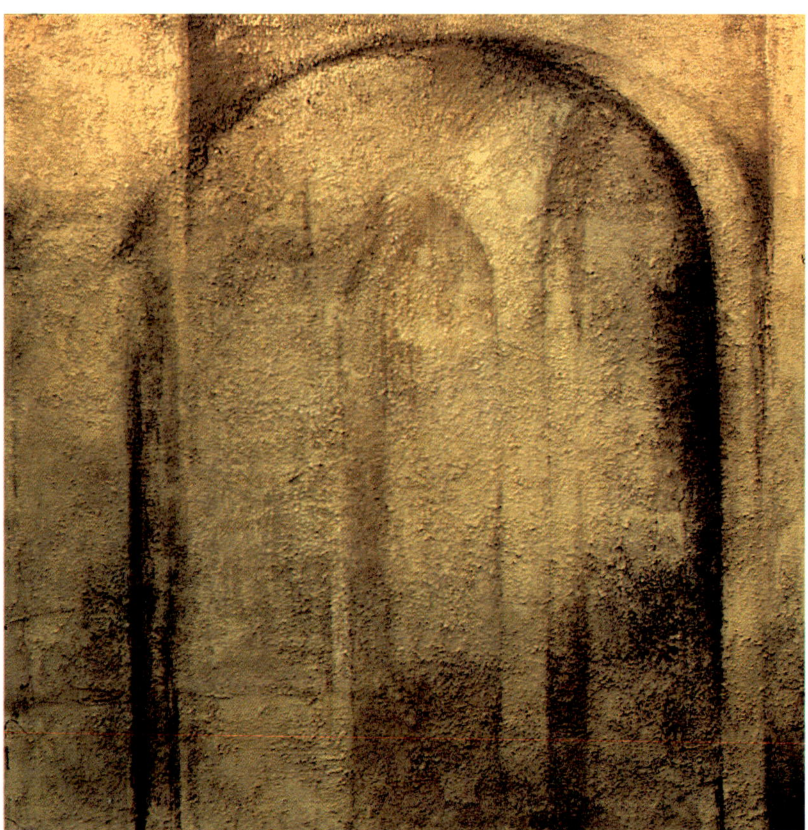

B. Hospital Santa Creu #2. Acrylic/sand on canvas, 51" x 51".

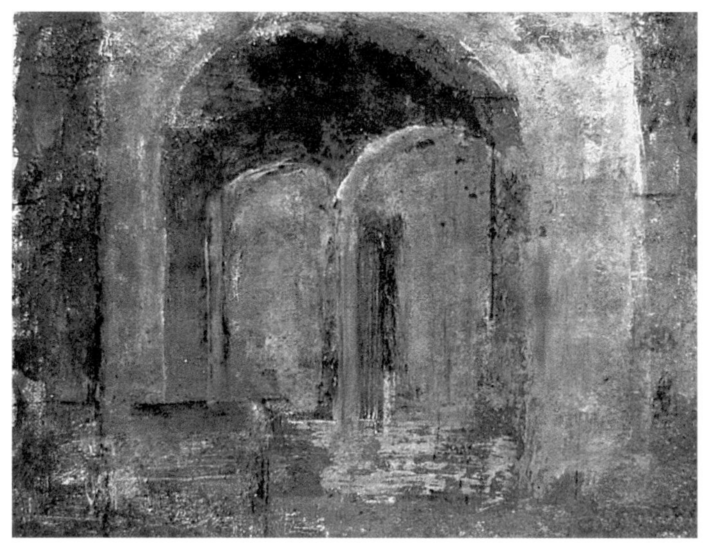

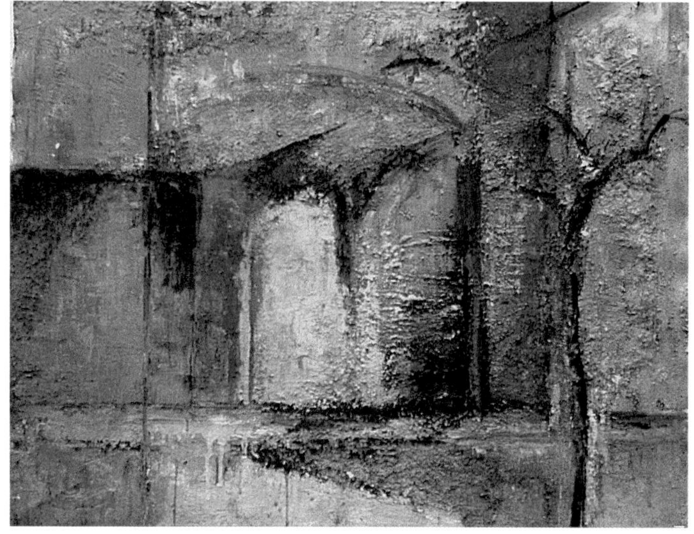

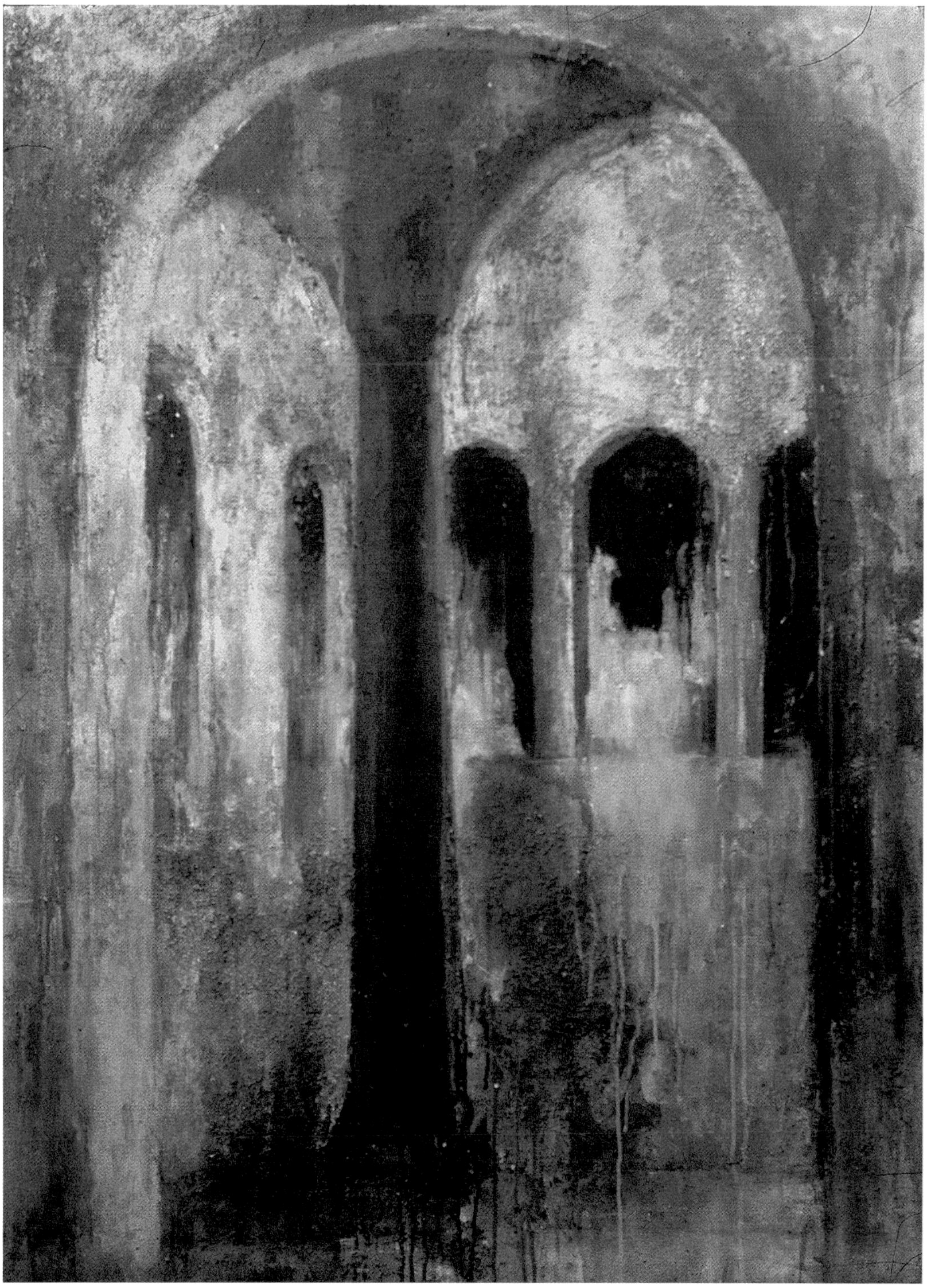

C. (above left)
Study for Hospital Santa Creu.
Acrylic/sand on paper
mounted on board,
19" x 25".

D. (above right)
Grey Tree.
Acrylic/sand on paper
mounted on board,
19" x 25".

E. (left)
Despues de Granada.
Acrylic/sand on canvas,
51" x 38".

PRICE LIST

A $2,000

B........................$2,000

C $600

D...........................$600

E $1,500

Christine Vaillancourt

Christine Vaillancourt moved to the Boston area in the late eighties and has since gained increasing notice as one of the up and comers in New England's art scene. Her education has included receiving an MFA from the Rhode Island School of Design in Providence, RI, as well as studies at Kent State University in Kent, Ohio, and the School of the Museum of Fine Arts, Boston.

Working largely in acrylics together with found materials on linen or wood panels, Vaillancourt's abstract paintings take a detailed look at the forces of time and man. The geometric symbols and variegated textures of her work represent man's attempt to create order. By presenting this flawed geometry on a stripped and weathered surface, Vaillancourt suggests the transient character of human creations and the power of time and nature.

Within the past three years, Vaillancourt has had three solo shows, most recently at the Bromfield Gallery in Boston, MA. Her work is represented in corporate collections throughout North America, including in the collections of MCI in Arlington, VA, and Xerox Corporation in Los Angeles.

Christine Vaillancourt

249 A Street, #36
Boston, MA 02210
617-345-9394

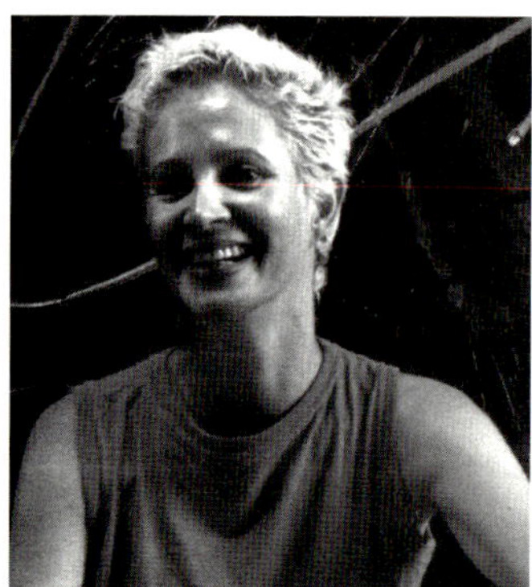

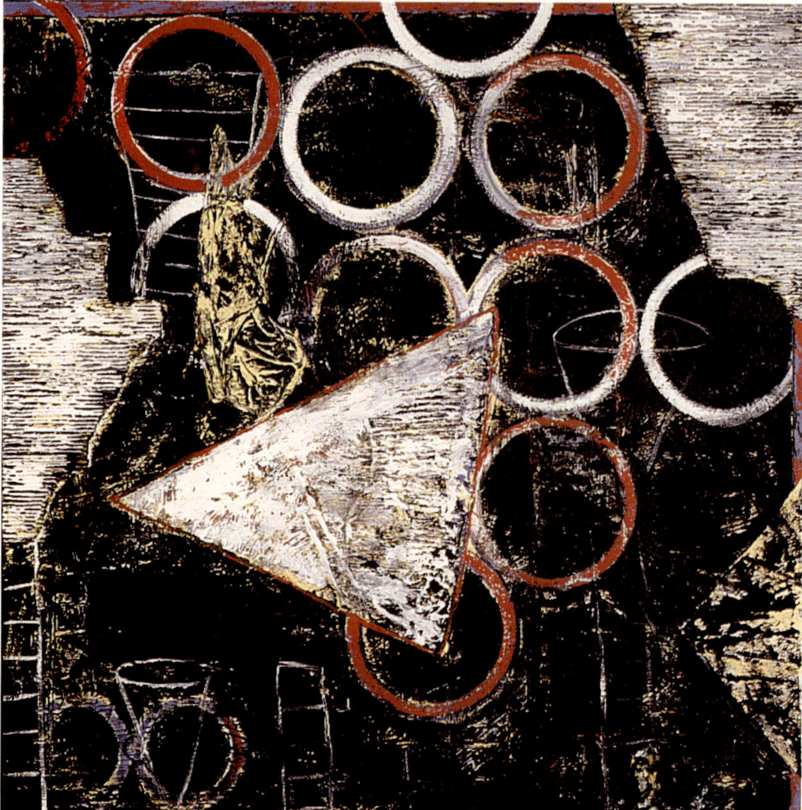

A. Palimpsest. Acrylic on linen, 66" x 66". Private collection.

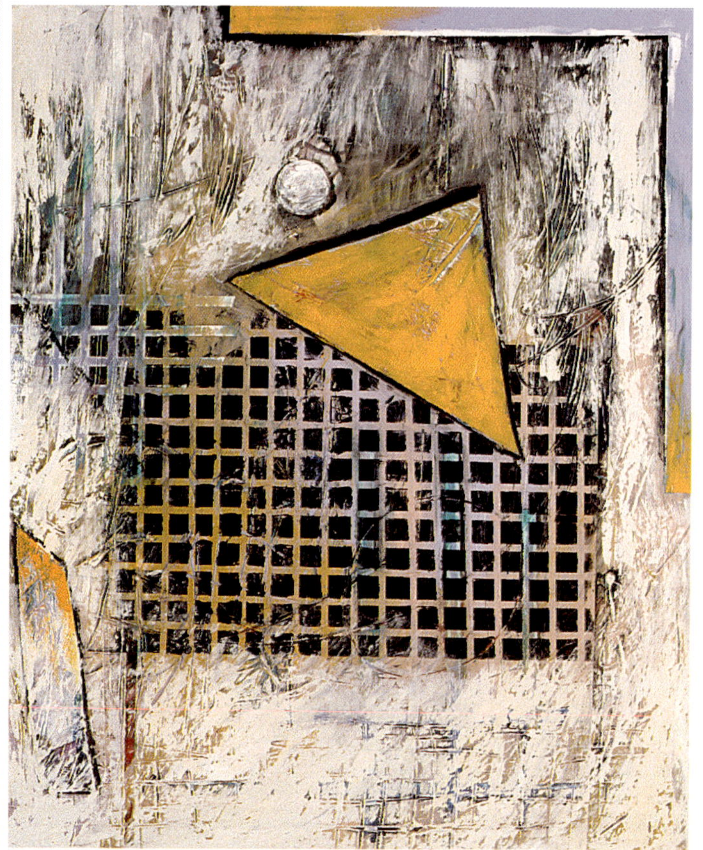

B. Flight. Acrylic on linen, 60" x 50".

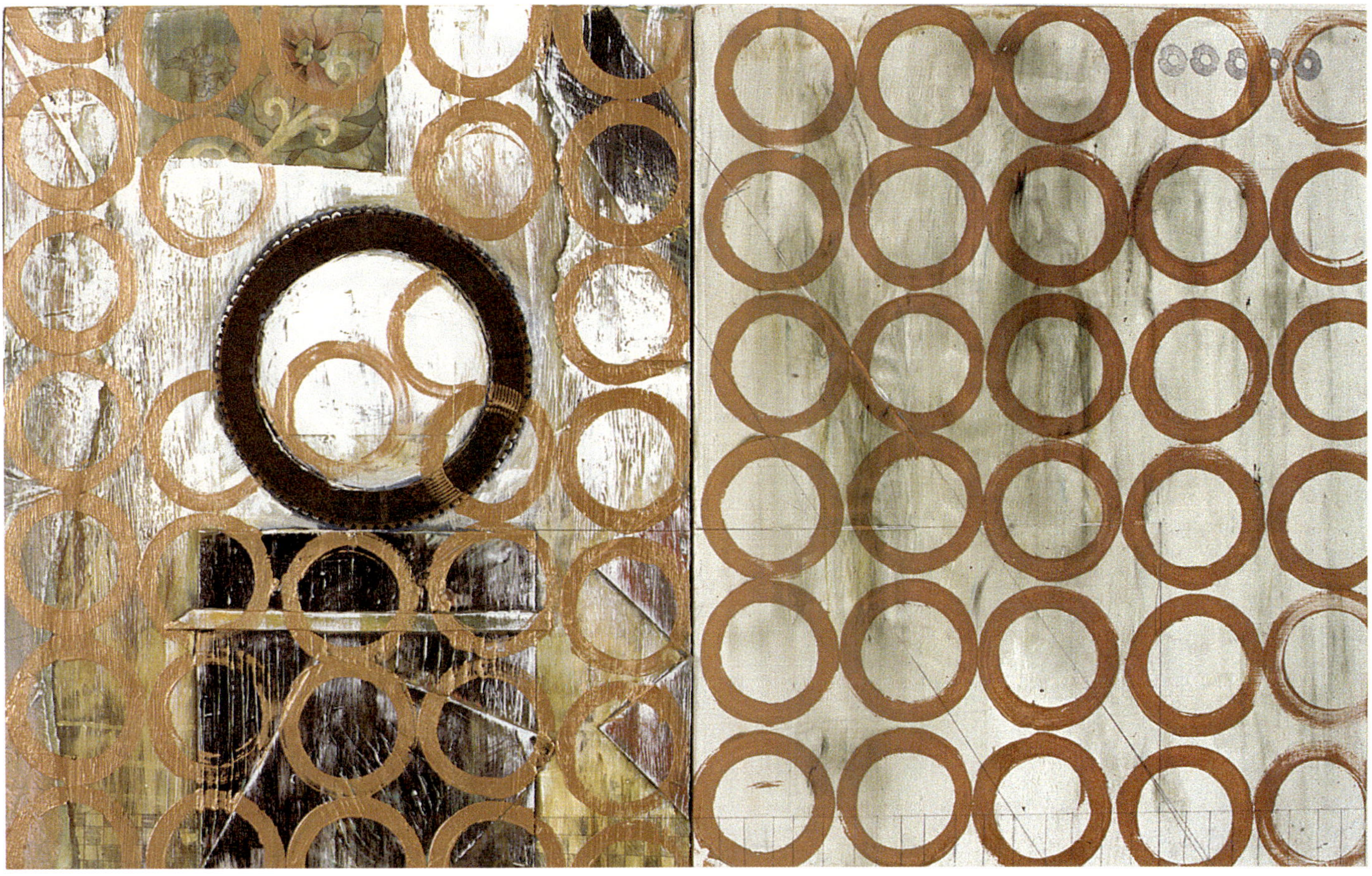

C. Calliope. Acrylic on wood, 30" x 48".

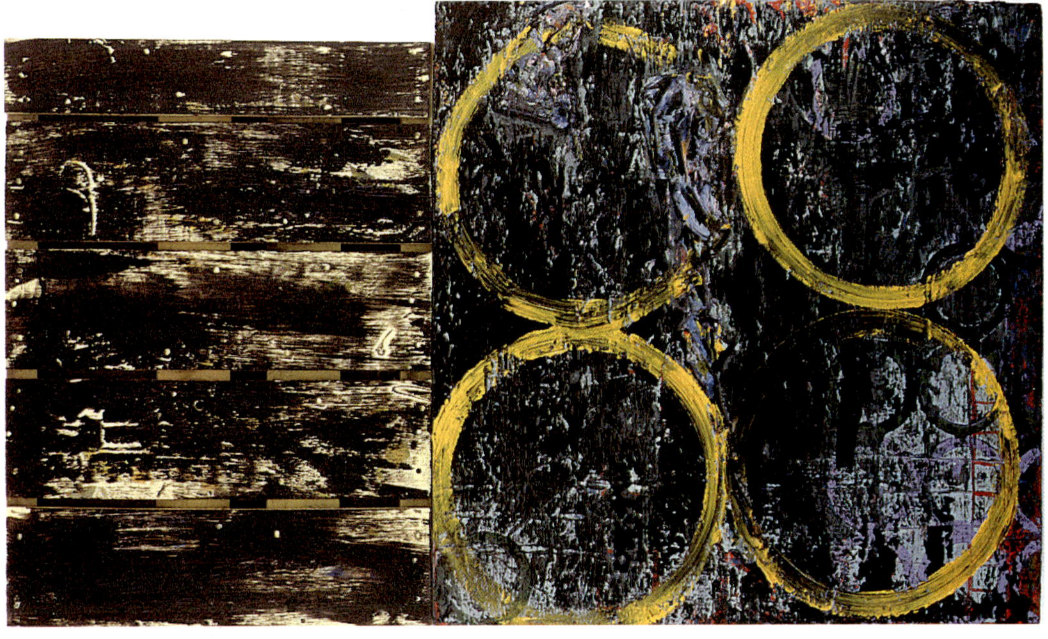

D. Façade. Acrylic on wood, 29" x 49".

PRICE LIST

A $5,000

B $3,500

C $2,000

D $2,000

After having been an art educator for over thirty years, Richard Warren Wolf retired in 1989 and now devotes his time to creating art. Wolf trained at the Art Institute of Buffalo as a scholarship student and then went on to receive his MFA from Cranbrook Academy in 1966. After leaving Cranbrook Academy, Wolf moved to Willimantic, CT, where he still resides, and taught at Eastern Connecticut State University until 1989.

Wolf's recent explorations in both painting and printmaking have drawn from cultural history for subject matter. His acrylic paintings of classical composers offer a light-hearted look at the revered masters. Wolf's palette leans towards pastel shades and his canvases, in effect, are made up of individual islands of color that come together like a collage.

Since 1963, Wolf has exhibited his work in various regional shows. Solo exhibitions have included a 1987 show at the Akus Gallery, ESCU, CT, a 1986 show at the Columbia Art Center, CT, and most recently, a 1991 show at the N.A.C. Gallery in Norwich, CT.

Richard W. Wolf

85 Lewiston Avenue
Willimantic, CT 06226
203-423-0873

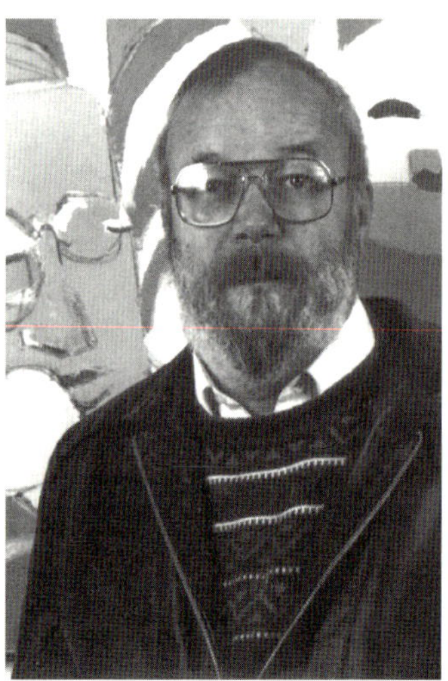

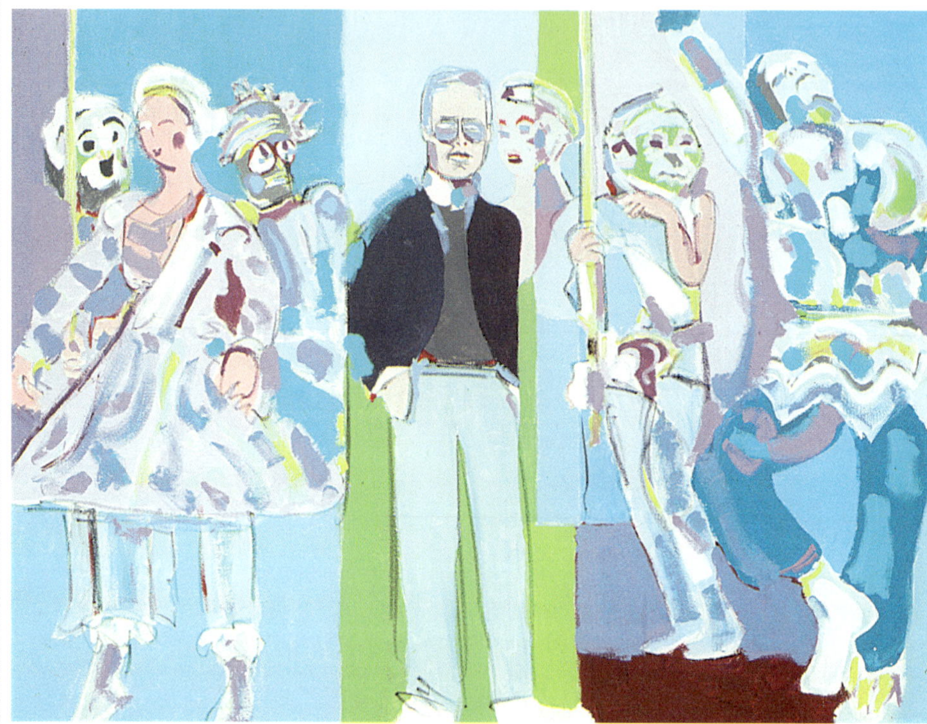

A. Stravinsky. Acrylic on canvas, 30" x 40".

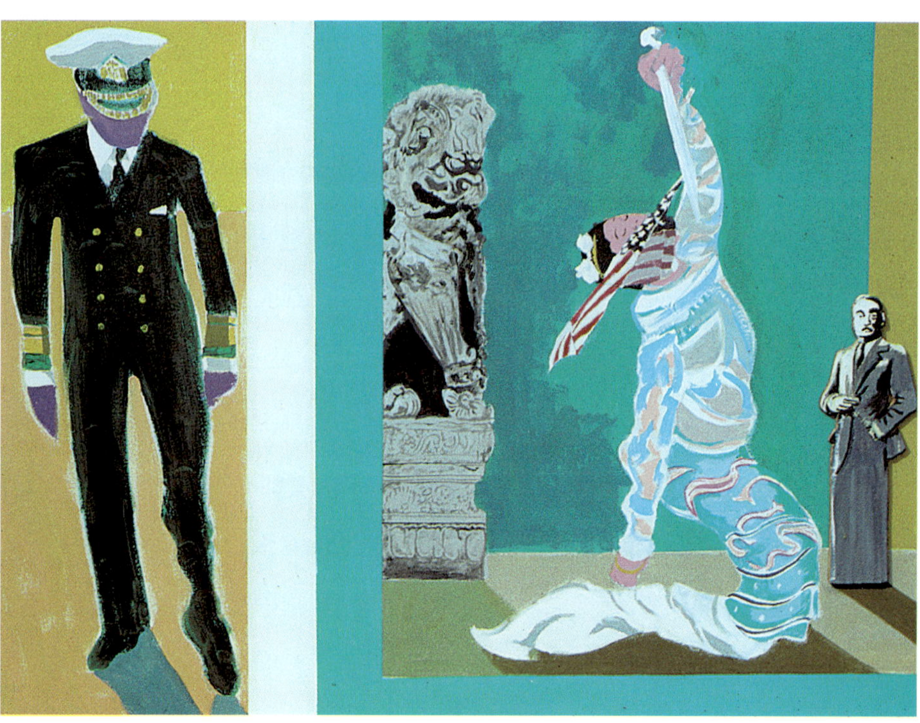

B. Madame Butterfly. Acrylic on canvas, 30" x 40".

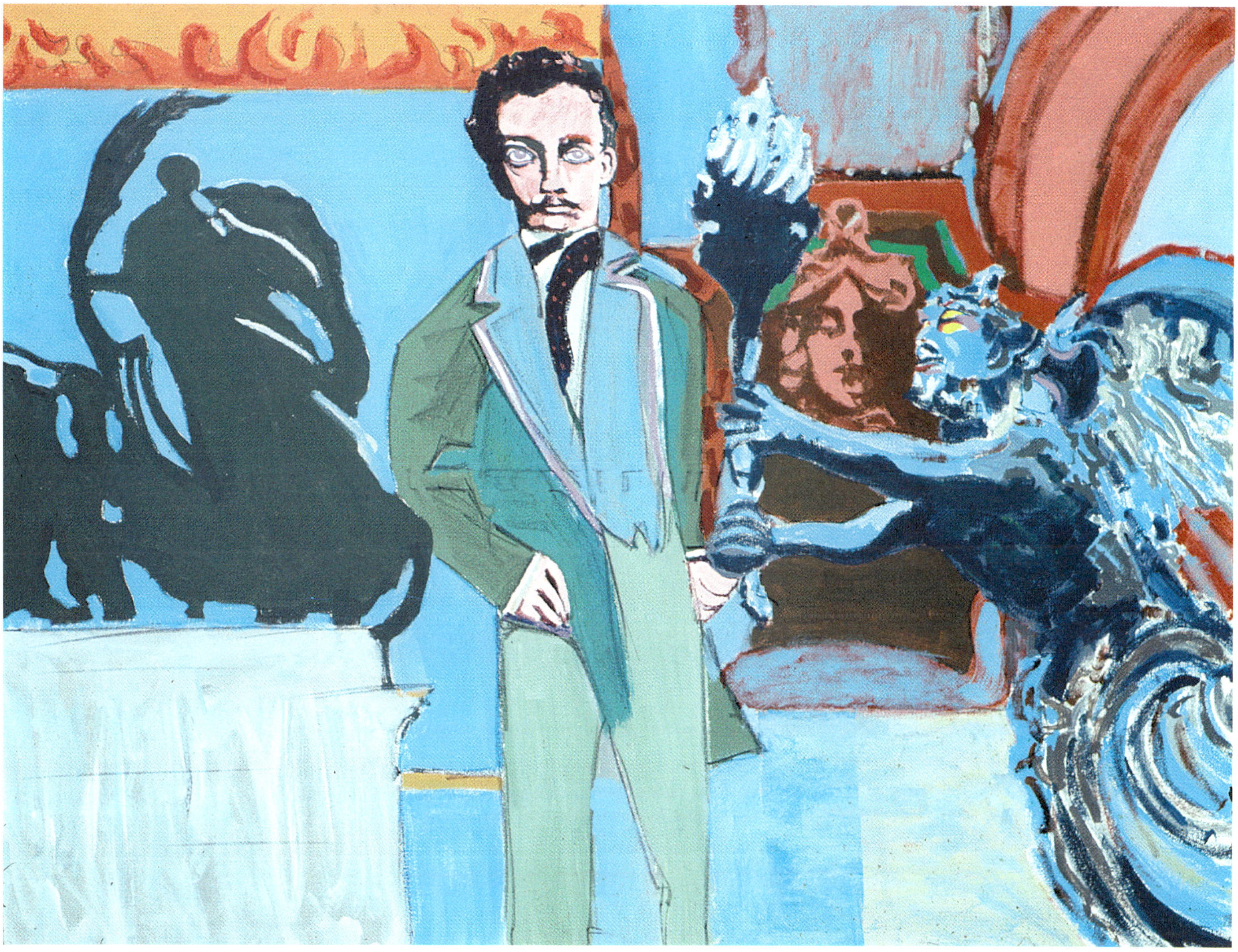

C. R. Strauss. Acrylic on canvas, 36" x 48".

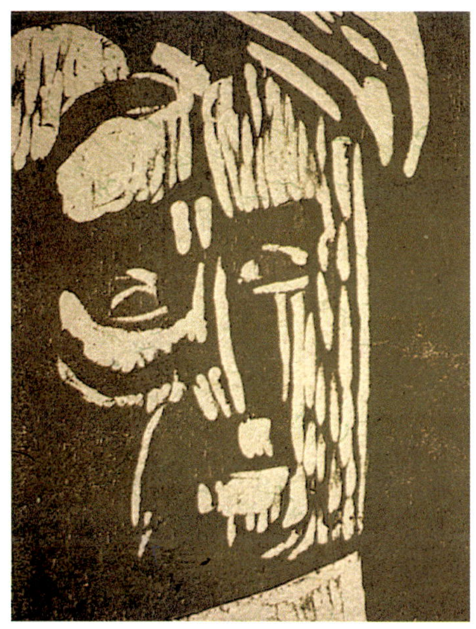

D. Vaughn-WMS. Wood block, 9" x 6".

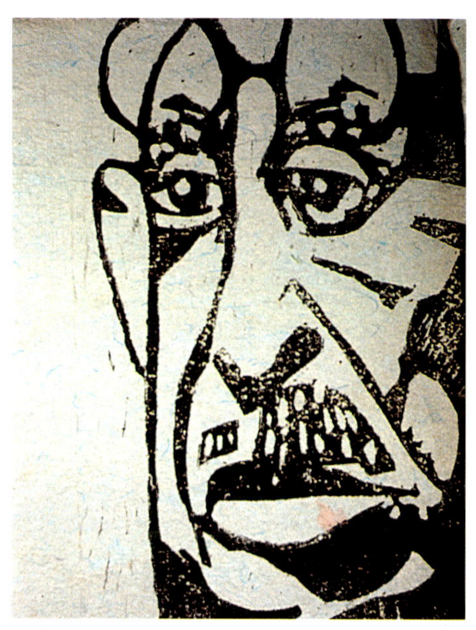

E. Stravinsky. Wood block, 9" x 6".

PRICE LIST

A $1,200
B $1,500
C $1,000
D $100
E $100

ISBN 1-883039-00-2
ISSN 1066-2235

CREDITS
Publisher: **Herbert Gliick**
Editor: **Steven Zevitas**
Production: **David Dauer**

Further information about The Open Studios Press and future regional editions of *New American Paintings* may be obtained by writing The Open Studios Press, 220-9 Reservoir Street, Needham Heights, MA, 02194. or by telephoning 617.449.6204 extension 23.